Criminal Appeal

2nd edition

Criminal Appeals Handbook

2nd edition

Joel Bennathan QC
Barrister, Doughty Street Chambers

Rebecca Trowler QC
Barrister, Doughty Street Chambers

Gregory Stewart
Solicitor and Higher Courts Advocate,
GT Stewart Solicitors & Advocates

Bloomsbury Professional

LONDON · DUBLIN · EDINBURGH · NEW YORK · NEW DELHI · SYDNEY

BLOOMSBURY PROFESSIONAL
Bloomsbury Publishing Plc

41–43 Boltro Road, Haywards Heath, RH16 1BJ, UK

BLOOMSBURY and the Diana logo are trademarks of
Bloomsbury Publishing Plc

British Library Cataloguing-in-Publication Data

A catalogue record for this book is available from the British Library

ISBN:	PB:	978-1-52650-885-0
	ePub:	978-1-52650-886-7
	ePDF:	978-1-52650-887-4

Typeset by Evolution Design and Digital (Kent)
Printed and bound by CPI Group (UK) Ltd, Croydon, CR0 4YY

To find out more about our authors and books visit
www.bloomsburyprofessional.com. Here you will find extracts, author
information, details of forthcoming events and the option to sign up for our
newsletters

Foreword

Apart from a few specialists, advocates practising in crime spend the vast majority of their time dealing with criminal cases in the Magistrates' and Crown Courts. Forays to the Court of Appeal Criminal Division can be few and far between and I suspect these infrequent appearances often engender feelings of uncertainty and apprehension. I vividly recall the challenge that is presented when all three members of the court are seemingly unimpressed by an argument, and proceed to fire difficult questions in rapid succession. The advocate can feel very lonely and ill equipped. Furthermore, appellate proceedings are in many ways a wholly different exercise to conducting first instance cases, and the procedure, the conventions and the jurisprudence are voluminous and can feel positively byzantine, especially to the uninitiated.

In order for the Court of Appeal Criminal Division to function efficiently and effectively, it is crucial that the advocates understand and apply the rules, and that the procedures of these courts are loyally followed. A relatively small number of judges deal with a high volume of work, and this is only possible if the applicants/appellants and the respondents prepare and present these cases in accordance with the established modus operandi. There are many elephant traps lying in wait for those who have not done their homework in advance. For the judiciary, it is a joy when cases are properly prepared, presented and economically argued and there is a risk that good points may be obscured if the court is forced to wrestle with a chaotically prepared case or when unfocussed submissions fail to distinguish between good and bad points.

This book is a wholly welcome addition to the relatively few guides that are available for advocates in this field. One of its great strengths is that it has been presented in a rigorously practical and intelligent way, and as a consequence it provides an impressive mix of purely practical assistance on basic procedure, along with detailed insight into some of the more legally challenging issues. The layout of the book means that it will be easy to use – the different stages are clearly delineated and it provides 'cradle to grave' assistance. It offers a clear route through the labyrinth and it is packed with excellent legal analysis. In the result, I suspect that many members of the judiciary will have it close at hand as a critical point of reference.

Lord Justice Fulford
Vice President of the Court of Appeal Criminal Division

Preface

Appealing against a conviction or a sentence that was imposed in the Crown Court can be a daunting business. There is a striking contrast to be found between the ease with which an appeal can be brought against a decision of the Magistrates' Court and the difficulties and uncertainties involved in appealing from the Crown Court.

A defendant who wishes to appeal against a conviction or a sentence that was imposed in the Magistrates' Court simply has to lodge a notice of appeal. He is then entitled to a complete re-hearing in the Crown Court. In contrast, appealing a conviction or sentence that was imposed in the Crown Court, which is always to the Court of Appeal, requires an application to be made for leave to the Court of Appeal. If leave is allowed, what is being granted is the right to a hearing at which the appellant has the opportunity to persuade the Court to allow the appeal. That opportunity is a narrow one. It often consists of a short hearing before a Court that has read the papers and may already have formed a clear preliminary view of the merits of the case.

This is a process that poses particular challenges for defendants and their lawyers. Defendants who have acclimatised themselves to the pace and formality of the Crown Court find themselves having to adjust to new and very different proceedings; there is a new set of legal terms to grapple with, further delays, a process from which they seem to be excluded, and that may culminate in a hearing at which trials that may have lasted for weeks are considered in minutes, and matters that seemed so crucial at trial are barely mentioned.

Their lawyers must seek to persuade a Court in which the swift, sometimes brutal dispatch of business and a ruthless focus on essentials replaces the comparatively relaxed pace of life in the Crown Court. It requires a different approach and even a different set of skills in order to achieve the best result for their clients.

The aim of this book is to assist those who seek to challenge a conviction or sentence or pre-trial order which was imposed in the Crown Court. It is intended for defence lawyers but also for defendants and their families who want a better understanding of the appeal process. For those who choose to represent themselves we hope to provide assistance, but it is not our intention to encourage anyone to do so. The need for effective legal representation is never more important than at the appeal stage. That effectiveness can only be increased when clients understand what they should expect of their lawyers and both lawyers and clients appreciate and can focus on the questions that will be of importance to the Court.

Because convictions and sentences that have been imposed on the Crown Court can only be appealed to the Court of Appeal, the focus of this book is largely on appealing to that Court. Chapter 1 provides a brief introduction to the Court, its judges, constitution, rules and administration. Chapter 2 considers the sources of law that it applies. Chapters 3 and 4 consider the tests for appeal, potential grounds and the powers of the Court in relation to conviction and sentence (including confiscation), respectively.

Chapters 5 to 8 then address the practicalities of appealing. Chapter 5 considers the important but often overlooked question of defence investigations, often the source of new material that provides the basis for an appeal. Chapter 6 deals with the practicalities of preparing the case; applying for leave, renewal of such applications and extensions of time, whilst Chapter 7 considers preparation for hearings. Chapter 8 deals with applying for legal aid to cover legal advice or representation whilst touching on the other ways of obtaining legal assistance, through private instruction, innocence projects and charities.

One of the most important features of the appeals process is the Criminal Cases Review Commission, which has the power to refer cases back to the Court of Appeal that have previously been considered and refused. Chapter 9 focuses on applying to the Commission whilst Chapter 10 sets out the procedure for appealing from the Court of Appeal to the Supreme Court.

Although a decision of the Court of Appeal or, very occasionally, the Supreme Court, will conclude the domestic appeal process, it need not always exhaust the search for justice. If a defendant's rights have been violated, he may apply for the case to be heard by the European Court of Human Rights. Chapter 11 addresses when and how such an application can be made and what can be achieved by doing so.

We have concluded with three chapters on subjects with which the defence practitioner will occasionally have to grapple. Chapter 12 deals with interlocutory appeals. Chapter 13 addresses the issue of responding to prosecution appeals against sentence (or 'Attorney General's references') and against acquittal. Chapter 14 deals with appeals against certain findings and orders made in the Crown Court against defendants who are found to be suffering from serious mental disorders.

In retaining the focus on appeals in relation to serious criminal offences we have deliberately omitted two topics. First, appeals from the Magistrates' Court. As already indicated, the process of appealing from the Magistrates' Court to the Crown is straightforward. Lawyers will find what they need to know in the general criminal practitioner's textbooks. Self-representing should also be able to comply with the procedural requirements for an appeal, perhaps with some assistance from the local Crown Court in relation to the completion of the relevant forms and time limits for doing so.

The second topic is that of judicial review of the decisions of the Magistrates' Court and judicial review of certain decisions of the Crown Court.[1] It is a topic of considerable scope and complexity. The law is covered briefly in the established practitioner's textbooks but more extensively in judicial review textbooks and now in a textbook devoted to judicial review in criminal proceedings.[2] We could not hope, in the limited space that might have been devoted to the topic in this book, to match the guidance that is to be found in such publications.

It should by now also be obvious that this book is not intended to be a comprehensive guide to the Court of Appeal and its wide array of powers. It is intended for those who act for those who have suffered a miscarriage of justice in the Crown Court and who seek redress. It was Parliament's purpose in creating the Court of Appeal to ensure that when such injustices occurred in the Crown Court there should be a remedy. We seek to assist defendants and their representatives to make best use of the rights of appeal that Parliament has provided.

Any practitioner in the criminal courts will have had the experience of getting a bad result, either the loss of a trial that should have been won or a sentence far harsher than predicted. Very soon, someone will ask, 'What next?' By combining our experience, knowledge and ideas in this book, we hope to assist in arriving at the right answer.

Joel Bennathan QC
Rebecca Trowler QC
Gregory Stewart
August 2019

---

1   Decisions in relation to trial on indictment may only be appealed to the Court of Appeal by virtue of the Senior Courts Act 1981, s. 29(3). However, decisions in relation to bail at an early stage in criminal proceedings (*R (M) v Isleworth Crown Court* [2005] EWHC 363 (Admin)), custody time limits, production orders and decisions in relation to appeals from the Magistrates' Court fall outside the scope of that section and may be challenged by way of judicial review.
2   Von Berg, P. (ed) (2014) *Criminal Judicial Review*, Oxford: Hart Publishing.

Acknowledgements

We are deeply grateful to Kiran Goss from Bloomsbury for her endless patience in guiding us from initial proposal to publication, and yet more patience in our work on this updated version. We would also like to thank our families for their support during the writing of this book.

Contents

Foreword   v
Preface   vi
Acknowledgements   ix
Table of Statutes   xv
Table of Statutory Instruments   xix
Table of Cases   xxi

Part 1: The Law   1

1   Introduction to the Court of Appeal   3
Introduction   3
The development of the Court of Appeal   3
The current statutory regime   6
Procedural rules and guidance   6
The judges of the Court of Appeal   7
The Registrar of Criminal Appeals and the Criminal Appeals
    Office   8
Where and when the Court sits   9
Communicating with the Court   9
Summary of key points   10

2   Applying the law: recent developments   11
Introduction   11
Stare decisis and the Court of Appeal   11
Judgments of the European Court of Human Rights   13
European Union law and international law   14
Summary of key points   15

3   Appeals against conviction   17
Introduction   17
The meaning of 'unsafe'   17
The Court's approach to common issues   23
The Court's powers   31
Summary of key points   36

4   Appeals against sentence   39
Introduction   39
Appeal against sentence on indictment and for cases sent from
    the Magistrates' Court   40
The principles: general   43
Rights of appeal: confiscation orders and other orders under the
    asset recovery legislation   48

Contents

Principles: confiscation   49
Powers of the Court: confiscation   50
Prosecution rights of appeal in confiscation cases   50
Summary of key points   51

Part 2: The Appeal Process   53

5   **Defence investigations   55**
Introduction   55
What are defence investigations? Who may carry them out?   57
The ethics of defence investigation   58
The techniques of investigation   59
Co-operating with other investigatory bodies   68
Summary of key points   69

6   **Applying for leave to appeal   71**
Introduction   71
Advice on appeal   72
Trial judge's certificate   78
The grounds of appeal   79
Particular issues   80
Citation of authorities   81
New arguments   82
Fresh evidence   83
Change in law appeals   84
Other applications which may be made along with the
      application for leave   86
Lodging the grounds – direct lodgement   88
Steps before the case is sent to the single judge   89
Decision of the single judge   91
Renewing an application for leave   91
Abandoning an application for leave   93
Summary of key points   96

7   **Preparing for hearings in the Court of Appeal   99**
Introduction   99
Preparing for the hearing   99
Listing the hearing   102
The hearing   102
Applications at the conclusion of the case   108
Summary of key points   110

8   **Public funding and pro bono assistance   113**
Introduction   113
Work under a Crown Court or Court of Appeal representation
      order   115
Claiming for work done in the Court of Appeal   119
Funding under the 2017 Standard Criminal Contract (SCC)   124

Pre-conditions – financial eligibility (means)   128
Practical issues   133
Specific applications and appeals against refusals   136
Alternative sources of advice and assistance   142
Summary of key points   144

Part 3: Applications from the Court of Appeal   147

9   The Criminal Cases Review Commission   149
Introduction   149
The establishment and role of the Criminal Cases Review
      Commission   150
The Commission's power to refer to the Court of Appeal   150
The test for referral   151
Applying to the Commission for a referral   152
Challenging a refusal to make a reference   156
The procedure following a reference being made to the Court of
      Appeal   156
An overview of the Commission's investigatory powers   157
Commission investigations at the direction of the Court of Appeal   159
Too high a test?   160
Summary of key points   160

10   Appealing to the Supreme Court   163
Introduction   163
The types of cases for which leave is given   164
Applying for leave   165
Preparing the case following leave   166
Hearings   167
Particular issues   168
Summary of key points   168

11   Applications to the European Court of Human Rights   171
Introduction   171
Whether to apply   171
Applying to the ECtHR   172
The consequences of a successful outcome   177
Summary of key points   178

Part 4: Other Rights of Appeal   181

12   Appeals against interlocutory rulings   183
Introduction   183
Appeals against rulings made at preparatory hearings in serious
      or complex fraud cases   184
Appeals under section 35 of the Criminal Procedure and
      Investigations Act 1996   186

Contents

Appeals against a ruling that a case should be tried by a judge
      and not a jury when there is a risk of jury tampering   187
Appeals against a decision to order a trial without a jury where
      jury tampering has taken place   188
Ruling that a judge should try certain counts alone following
      conviction by a jury on sample counts   189
Summary of key points   189

13   Responding to prosecution appeals   191
Introduction   191
The prosecution's rights of appeal   191
Prosecution appeals against rulings under section 58 of CJA 2003   192
Attorney-General's references   196
Summary of key points   200

**14   Appeals in relation to defendants suffering from a mental
disorder   203**
Introduction   203
Appeals against findings of unfitness to plead and findings that
      the accused made the act or omission charged   205
Appeals against a verdict of not guilty by reason of insanity   206
Appeals against an order made under section 5 of the Criminal
      Procedure (Insanity) Act 1964   207

Appendices
      A   Criminal Practice Directions, Division IX   209
      B   The Criminal Procedure Rules, Parts 36 to 44   221
      C   A Guide to Commencing Proceedings in the Court of
              Appeal (Criminal Division)   281
      D   Sample pleadings   313
      E   Court of Appeal costs   335
      F   New client appeal enquiry form   341

Index   349

Table of Statutes

All references are to paragraph numbers

Access to Justice Act 1999
  s 17.................................... 4.10
Administration of Estates Act 1925
  s 55(1)(xi)............................... 7.22
Administration of Justice Act 1960
  s 13..................................... 1.12
Children Act 1989
  s 17A.................................... 8.29
Children and Young Person's Act 1933
  s 37..................................... 7.26
  39....................................... 7.29
Constitutional Reform Act 2005 . 2.5;
                                10.1, 10.22
  s 40..................................... 10.1
  Sch 2
    Pt 1 (paras 4–9).................... 1.14
  Sch 9.................................... 10.1
Contempt of Court Act 1981
  s 8...................................... 3.40
  9.. 7.31
Coroners and Justice Act 2009
  s 52, 54, 55............................. 14.1
  116...................................... 3.21
  125...................................... 4.29
    (1).................................... 4.27
Courts Act 2003
  s 69, 74................................. 1.14
Crime and Courts Act 2013
  s 32..................................... 7.31
Crime and Disorder Act 1889
  s 8...................................... 4.16
  10(4)................................... 4.16
Crime and Disorder Act 1998
  Sch 3
    para 6................................ 4.6
Criminal Appeal Act 1907 .... 1.3, 1.4
  s 4(1)................................. 1.6, 1.10
Criminal Appeal Act 1964 .... 1.7
Criminal Appeal Act 1966 .... 1.7
Criminal Appeal Act 1967 .... 1.7
Criminal Appeal Act 1968 .... 1.8, 1.10;
                  3.63; 6.66; 9.5; 14.1, 14.5

Criminal Appeal Act 1968 – *contd*
  Pt I (ss 1–32)...................... 1.12, 1.13
  s 1(2)(b)............................. 6.15, 6.16
  2(1)................................. 1.10; 3.2
    (a)................................... 3.3
  3, 3A.................................. 3.64
  4...................................... 3.80
    (3).................................. 3.81
  7...................................... 3.82
    (1).................................. 3.67
    (2).................................. 3.68
  8(1B)(b).............................. 3.73
    (2)................................ 3.72, 3.75
  9...................................... 4.1
    (b).................................. 4.6
  10.................................. 4.1, 4.7
  11.................................... 4.2
    (1).................................. 4.2
    (1A).............................. 4.2; 6.15
    (3), (3A).......................... 4.51
  12................................. 14.1, 14.12
  13............................... 14.12, 14.13
  15.......... 14.1, 14.5, 14.7, 14.8, 14.9
    (2)(b).............................. 14.7
  16.................................... 14.9
    (3)(a), (b)........................ 14.8
  16A.............................. 14.1, 14.17
    (2)(b).............................. 6.16
  16B(1)............................... 14.18
    (2)–(5)............................ 14.19
  16C................................... 9.12
  18(2)................................. 6.8
    (3).................................. 6.9
  22.................................... 7.17
    (4).................................. 7.18
  23.......... 3.49, 3.83; 4.34, 4.46; 6.31
    (1)(a).............................. 6.76
    (b)................................. 6.31
    (2)................................. 6.31
    (a)................................. 3.47
    (b)............................. 3.47, 3.49
    (c), (d)........................... 3.47

Criminal Appeal Act 1968 – *contd*
s 23A 9.32
   (1)(aa) 9.32
   (1A) 9.32
   (4), (5) 9.32
29 .... 6.66
31 .... 6.14
31A(4) 6.76
Pt II (ss 33–44A) 1.12, 1.13
s 33 .... 7.42; 10.2, 10.3, 10.4;
                     12.10; 14.5
   (1) 12.25
34 .... 7.40; 10.9
36 .... 10.19
44A 7.22
   (2)(b) 10.22
46A 9.10
50 .... 4.8, 4.9, 4.11, 4.12, 4.13,
             4.14, 4.40, 4.41, 4.42
   (3) 4.10
Sch 2
   para 2(1) 3.77
      (3) 3.78
Criminal Appeal Act 1995 ..... 1.10, 1.11;
                   3.2; 9.3
s 8 .... 9.3
9 .... 9.4
   (2), (3) 9.5
   (5), (6) 9.4
12A 9.4
13 .... 9.7, 9.8, 9.9
   (a), (b) 9.11
14 .... 9.27
   (1) 9.5
   (2), (3) 9.21
   (4)(b) 9.27
   (4A), (4B) 9.27
15 .... 9.32
   (1) 9.30, 9.32
   (2)–(6) 9.32
16(1) 9.3
17 .... 9.28
   (2), (4) 9.28
18, 19 .... 9.28
20 .... 9.28
   (6) 9.32
21 .... 9.28
22 .... 9.28
   (1) 9.28
23–25 .... 9.28

Criminal Appeal Act 1995 – *contd*
  Sch 1
    para 6(3) 9.22
Criminal Justice Act 1925
  s 41 .... 7.31
Criminal Justice Act 1967
  s 9 .... 5.30
Criminal Justice Act 1972
  s 36(1) 13.2
Criminal Justice Act 1987 ..... 12.3, 12.19,
                       12.28
  s 7(1) 12.6
  9 .... 12.5
    (3) 12.7
     (b) 12.9
    (11) 12.8, 12.10
    (13), (14) 12.10
  11 .... 12.17
    (1), (5) 12.11
  12 .... 7.27
Criminal Justice Act 1988 .... 4.40, 4.42
  s 35 .... 13.2, 13.20
  36 .... 13.2, 13.20, 13.40
    (1), (2) 13.21
  36A 13.34, 13.35
  41 .... 4.6
  Pt VI (ss71–103) 4.8
  Sch 3 .... 13.23, 13.40
Criminal Justice Act 1993
  s 6 .... 12.7
Criminal Justice Act 2003
  s 43 .... 12.12
  44 .... 12.12, 12.18, 12.19
  45 .... 12.12, 12.19
  46 .... 12.24, 12.25
    (3) 12.18
  47 .... 12.20
    (2) 12.25
    (4) 12.21, 12.25
    (6) 12.25
  57(2)(a), (b) 13.5
    (4) 13.11
  58 .... 13.1, 13.2, 13.3, 13.5, 13.40
    (4) 13.5
    (8) 13.5, 13.7
    (13) 13.5
  61 .... 13.18
    (3) 13.7
  62 .... 13.2
  71 .... 7.27; 13.16

Criminal Justice Act 2003 – *contd*
s 74(1) 13.5
Pt 10 (ss 75–97) 13.2
s 172....................................... 4.26
240A 4.39
269(2) 13.34
313....................................... 9.32
Criminal Justice and Immigration
Act 2008
s 42.. 9.12
46... 13.35
Sch 8
para 10............................... 6.31
Criminal Procedure and Investigations Act 1996 .... 12.19, 12.28
s 3.. 5.17
13(3) 12.10
23.. 5.2
29.. 12.12
(1C), (6) 12.13
35............................. 12.12, 12.15,
12.16, 12.17
(1), (2)............................. 12.10
37... 7.27
(1) 12.17
54... 13.2
72... 5.17
Criminal Procedure (Insanity) Act 1964
s 4....................................... 14.6, 14.14
(5), (6).............................. 14.11
4A 14.6, 14.14
5 .... 14.11, 14.14,
14.16, 14.17
Crown Cases Reserved Act 1848   1.2
Data Protection Act 2018 .... 5.21, 5.25,
5.28, 5.36
s 7.. 5.26
45(1) 5.21
(3) 5.24
(4) 5.22
53.. 5.25
54.. 5.24
Sch 7...................................... 5.21
Domestic Violence, Crime and
Victims Act 2004.................. 12.28
s 17....................................... 12.28
(3)–(5).............................. 12.27
25.. 14.17
Drug Trafficking Act 4.8, 4.40
s 19.. 4.8

Football Spectators Act 1989
s 14A(5A)............................... 13.2
23.. 4.8
Freedom of Information Act
2000................................. 5.26, 5.36
s 1....................................... 5.26, 5.27
30.. 5.27
Health and Social Care Act 2001   8.29
Homicide Act 1957
s 2, 4..................................... 14.1
Human Rights Act 1998........ 2.2, 2.7, 2.8
s 2(1)(a)................................. 2.8
Immigration and Asylum Act 1999
s 31 .... 5.5; 9.20
Legal Aid, Sentencing and
Punishment of Offenders
Act 2012............................. 8.1, 8.7
s 13–15................................. 8.1
16.. 8.1, 8.7
17, 18................................... 8.1
19.. 8.1
(1) 8.7
42.. 8.7
Licensing Act 2003
s 129(2) 4.8
Mental Health Act 1983
Pt III (ss 35–55) 4.8
s 47, 49................................... 5.23
Modern Slavery Act 2015
s 45.. 5.5
Police and Criminal Evidence
Act 1984............................. 9.28
Powers of Criminal Courts
(Sentencing) Act 2000
s 14....................................... 4.8
137(1) 4.16
150....................................... 4.16
155....................................... 4.36, 4.45
(6) 4.40
Proceeds of Crime Act 2002 ....
4.40, 4.43, 4.52, 4.53; 13.2
Pt 1 (ss 1–5) 8.27
Pt 2 (ss 6–91) 4.8
s 10A 4.8, 4.52
19, 20.................................. 4.52
21, 22.................................. 4.8, 4.41
23 .... 4.41, 4.53
27, 28.................................. 4.52
29 .... 4.8, 4.41
31 .... 4.52

Proceeds of Crime Act 2002 – *contd*
s 31(3) 4.53
41 .... 8.29
65 .... 4.43
Prosecution of Offences Act
1985 .... 6.67
s 16A 8.14
18(2) 7.49
19(1) 7.50, 7.51
19A 7.52
19B 7.55
Protection from Harassment Act 1997
s 5A(5) 4.13
Regulation of Investigatory
Powers Act 2000 .... 9.28, 9.33
Senior Courts Act 1981 .... 1.9
s 2 .... 1.16
3 .... 1.15
9 .... 1.16
31A(2)(b) 1.23

Senior Courts Act 1981 – *contd*
s 53(2) 1.12
55(2) 1.18
(6) 1.19
Serious Organised Crime and
Police Act 2005
s 74(12) 7.26
75(2) 7.26
Sexual Offences (Amendment)
Act 1992 .... 7.27
s 2 .... 7.27
Terrorism Act 2000
s 17 .... 10.5
Trial of Lunatics Act 1883
s 2 .... 14.12
Welfare Reform Act 2012
Pt 4 (ss 77–95) 8.29
Youth Justice and Criminal
Evidence Act 1999
s 25 .... 7.26

Table of Statutory Instruments

All references are to paragraph numbers

Coroners and Justice Act 2009
(Commencement No 4,
Transitional and Saving
Provisions) Order 2010,
SI 2010/816...................... 4.26
Criminal Appeal Act 1995
(Commencement No 1 and
Transitional Provisions)
Order 1995, SI 1995/3061... 1.11
Criminal Legal Aid
(Determination by a
Court and Choice of
Representative) Regulations
2013, SI 2013/614.............. 8.4
Criminal Legal Aid (Financial
Resources) Regulations
2013, SI 2013/471.............. 8.1
 reg 2 .... 8.27, 8.29, 8.31
 Pt 2 (regs 5–15).................... 8.26
 reg 8 .... 8.29
  9 .... 8.28
  11 .... 8.29
  12 .... 8.29
  13 .... 8.30
  14 .... 8.27
Criminal Legal Aid (General)
Regulations 2013,
SI 2013/9........................... 8.1
 reg 2 .... 8.1
  6 .... 8.1
  33(c) 8.1
Criminal Legal Aid
(Remuneration) Regulations
2013, SI 2013/435...... 8.1, 8.7, 8.13,
         8.14, 8.39
 reg 6 .... 8.13
  26 .... 8.19
  31 .... 8.13
 Sch 1
  Pt 7 .... 8.15
 Sch 3..................................... 8.13
  para 1(2)............................. 8.13

Criminal Legal Aid
(Remuneration) Regulations
2013, SI 2013/435 – *contd*
 Sch 3 – *contd*
  para 2................................... 8.13
   (3)............................... 8.14
   3(1), (2) 8.14
   4................................... 8.16
   5............................... 8.13, 8.17
   8(2)............................... 8.15
   9(1)–(4) 8.17
   11................................... 8.18
 Sch 4....................................... 8.39
 Sch 5............................... 8.16, 8.40
Criminal Procedure Rules 2014,
SI 2014/1610.................... 6.4; 7.49;
         8.7; 13.23,
         13.24
 Pt 1 (rr 1.1–1.3)....................... 1.14
 r 1.1 .... 6.14
  4.3 .... 7.54
  4.7 .... 7.55
 Pt 6 (rr 6.1–6.36)..................... 7.28
 Pt 14 (rr 14.1, 14.2)................. 6.16
 Pt 16 (rr 16.1–16.10).............. 6.31
 Pt 18 (rr 18.1–18.7)................. 6.31
 Pt 20 (r 20.1) 6.31
 Pt 21 (r 21.1) 6.31
 Pt 22 (rr 22.1–22.9)................. 6.31
 Pt 34 (rr 34.1–34.5)................. 1.14
 Pt 35 (rr 35.1–35.6)................. 1.14
 Pt 36 (rr 36.1–36.7)........... 1.14; 13.9,
         13.40; 14.5
 r 36.2 .... 6.76
  36.6 .... 6.76
   (1)................................... 7.26
   (2)................................... 7.25
  36.7 .... 6.76
  36.8(5)............................... 6.16
  36.12(2)............................... 6.68
  36.13 .... 6.74
   (2)................................... 6.70

Table of Statutory Instruments

Criminal Procedure Rules 2014,
SI 2014/1610 – *contd*
Pt 37 (rr 37.1–37.18).......... 1.14; 12.3,
                                        12.28
r 37.1 .... 12.25
37.2 .... 12.10
37.3 .... 12.10
37.4 .... 12.10
37.5, 37.7 .... 12.10
37.8 .... 12.10
Pt 38 (rr 38.1–38.18).......... 1.14; 13.40
r 38.2(2)................................. 13.10
38.3 .... 13.10
38.5 .... 13.11
38.7 .... 13.13, 13.14
38.8 .... 13.10
38.11 .... 13.16
Pt 39 (rr 39.1–39.4).... 1.14; 6.51; 14.5
r 39.2 .... 9.27
39.3(2)(c) 6.43
     (g)........................... 6.54; 7.14
39.4 .... 6.16
39.6 .... 9.27
     (3)–(6)............................ 6.57
39.7(1)–(7)............................ 6.31
39.8 .... 6.38
39.9 .... 6.38
39.11 .... 6.76
Pt 40 (rr 40.1–40.8)................. 1.14
Pt 41 (rr 41.1–41.16)......... 1.14; 13.22,
                                        13.40

Criminal Procedure Rules 2014,
SI 2014/1610 – *contd*
r 41.2, 41.3 .... 13.23
41.4 .... 13.24
41.6 .... 13.27
Pt 42 (rr 42.1–42.11).............. 1.14
Pt 43 (r 43.1) 10.2
r 43.2 .... 10.9
45.6(8).................................. 7.49
45.8 .... 7.50
Pt 44 (rr 44.1–44.4)................ 1.14
Criminal Procedure Rules 2015,
SI 2015/490
Pt 26 (rr 26.1–26.5)................ 4.1
Pt 39 (rr 39.1–39.14).............. 4.1
Pt 42 (rr 42.1–42.20).............. 4.1
Regulation   of   Investigatory
    Powers   (Communications
    Data) (Additional Functions
    and   Amendment)   Order
    2006, SI 2006/1878............. 9.28
Supreme   Court   Rules   2009,
    SI 2009/1603
r 5 .... 10.17
11 .... 10.10
13 .... 10.12
14.2 .... 10.12
18(2)...................................... 10.17
19 .... 10.17
22(3)...................................... 10.17
46(1)...................................... 10.21

Table of Cases

All references are to paragraph numbers

A

A-G's Reference (No 2 of 2001) [2003] UKHL 68, [2004] 2 AC 72, [2004] 2 WLR 1 .... 3.17
A-G's Reference (Nos 3 & 5 of 1989) [1989] 10 WLUK 169, (1990) 90 Cr App R 358, (1989) 11 Cr App R (S) 489 .... 13.28
A-G's Reference (No 8 of 2007), Re [2007] EWCA Crim 922, [2008] 1 Cr App R (S) 1, [2007] Crim LR 642 .... 13.28
A-G's Reference (Nos 14 & 15 of 2006), Re [2006] EWCA Crim 1335, [2007] 1 All ER 718, [2007] 1 Cr App R (S) 40, [2006] Crim LR 943 .... 13.33
A-G's Reference (No 19 of 2005), Re [2006] EWCA Crim 785 .... 13.30
A-G's Reference (Nos 25 & 26 of 2008), Re [2008] EWCA Crim 2665, [2009] 1 Cr App R (S) 116 .... 13.31
A-G's Reference (No 45 of 2014) [2014] EWCA Crim 1566, [2014] 7 WLUK 21 .... 13.33
A-G's Reference (No 69 of 2013), Re; *sub nom* R v McLoughlin [2014] EWCA Crim 188, [2014] 3 All ER 73, [2014] 2 Cr App R (S) 40, [2014] HRLR 7, [2014] Crim LR 471, (2014) 158 (8) SJLB 37 .... 2.10
A-G's Reference (No 74 of 2010), Re [2011] EWCA Crim 873 .... 13.30
A-G's Reference (No 79 of 2015), Re [2016] EWCA Crim 448, [2016] 4 WLR 99, [2016] 3 WLUK 670 .... 13.30
A-G's Reference (Nos 86 & 87 of 1999), Re [2000] 10 WLUK 779, [2001] 1 Cr App R (S) 141, [2001] Crim LR 58 .... 13.31
Associated Provincial Picture Houses Ltd v Wednesbury Corpn [1948] 1 KB 223, [1947] 2 All ER 680, (1947) 63 TLR 623 .... 3.30, 3.31

B

Bestel (Jean Pierre) v R [2013] EWCA Crim 1305, [2014] 1 WLR 457, [2013] 2 Cr App R 30 .... 4.50
Boodram v The State [2002] 1 Cr App R 103 .... 3.58

D

Dowsett v Criminal Cases Review Commission [2007] EWHC 1923 (Admin) 11.3
DPP v Majewski [1975] 3 WLR 401; [1975] 3 All ER 296; (1976) 62 Cr App R 5 .... 1.11
DPP v Patterson [2017] EWHC 2820 (Admin), [2017] 11 WLUK 46, [2018] 1 Cr App R 28 .... 2.6
Duppin v Croatia (Application No 363868/03) (7 July 2009) 11.9

E

Evans v Bartlam [1937] AC 473, [1937] 2 All ER 646 .... 3.30

I

Ivey v Genting Casinos UK Ltd (t/a Crockfords Club) [2017] UKSC 67,
[2018] AC 391, [2017] 3 WLR 1212 .... 2.6

L

LSA [2008] EWCA Crim 1034 .... 13.7

M

Manoussos v Czech Republic (Applicaion No 46488/99) (7 September 2002). 11.28
Morelle Ltd v Wakeling [1955] 2 QB 379, [1955] 2 WLR 672, [1955] 1 All
ER 708, (1955) 99 SJ 218 .... 2.5

P

P (Barrister) (Wasted Costs Order), Re [2001] EWCA Crim 1728, [2002] 1 Cr
App R 19, [2001] Crim LR 920 .... 7.53
Porter v Magill; Weeks v Magill [2001] UKHL 67, [2002] 2 AC 357, [2002]
2 WLR 37 .... 3.45

R

R v Abu Hamza [2006] EWCA Crim 2918, [2007] QB 659, [2007]
2 WLR 226 .... 3.46
R v Achogbuo [2014] EWCA Crim 567, [2014] 2 Cr App R 7 .... 6.13
R v Ahmed (Shabir) [2014] EWCA Crim 619 .... 9.31
R v Aldridge (Trevor); R v Eaton (Thomas) [2012] EWCA Crim 1456 .... 4.12
R v Antoine (Pierre Harrison) [1999] 3 WLR 1204, [1999] 2 Cr App R 225,
(1999) 96 (21) LSG 37, (1999) 143 SJLB 142 ....
14.3, 14.4
R v Arnold (Louise Sarah) [2008] EWCA Crim 1034, [2008] 1 WLR 2881,
[2009] 1 All ER 1103, [2008] 2 Cr App R 37, [2008] RTR 25 .... 13.3, 13.6, 13.7
R v B [2008] EWCA Crim 1144 .... 13.17
R v B [2014] EWCA Crim 2078, [2014] 10 WLUK 647 .... 13.7
R v Ball (Kenneth John) (1951) 35 Cr App R 164, (1951) 95 SJ 790 .... 4.19
R v Baybasin (Mehmet Sirin) [2013] EWCA Crim 2357, [2014] 1 WLR 2112,
[2014] 1 Cr App R 19 .... 3.42
R v Bennett (David Joseph) [1968] 1 WLR 988, [1968] 2 All ER 753, (1968)
52 Cr App R 514 .... 4.3
R v Bentley (Derek William) (dec'sd) [2001] 1 Cr App R 21, [1999] Crim
LR 330 .... 3.32
R v Blackwood (Romaine) [2012] EWCA Crim 390, [2012] 2 Cr App R 1,
[2012] Cim LR 786 .... 3.71
R v Bolivar (Luyisa de Marillac); R v Lee (Matthew John) [2003] EWCA Crim
1167, (2003) 148 SJLB 538 .... 3.58
R v Booker (Edward Martin) [2011] EWCA Crim 7, [2011] 3 All ER 905,
[2011] 1 Cr App R 26 .... 3.76
R v Bryant (Patrick) [2005] EWCA Crim 2079 .... 3.33
R v Bukhari (Daniyal) [2008] EWCA Crim 2915, [2009] 2 Cr App R (S) 18,
[2009] Lloyd's Rep FC 198 .... 4.45

R v Burley (unreported) 6.11
R v Chalkley (Tony Michael); R v Jeffries (Tony Brisbane) [1998] QB 848,
 [1998] 3 WLR 146, [1998] 2 Cr App R 79 .... 3.29
R v Clarke (Ronald Augustus); R v McDaid (James Andrew) [2008] UKHL 8,
 [2008] 1 WLR 338, [2008] 2 All ER 665 .... 3.21
R v Clinton (Dean) [1993] 1 WLR 1181, [1993] 2 All ER 998, (1993) 97 Cr
 App R 320 .... 3.55
R v Cooper (Sean) [1969] 1 QB 267, [1968] 3 WLR 1225, [1969] 1 All ER 32
 3.3, 3.24
R v Cottrell (Steven) *sub nom* R v Fletcher (Joseph) [2007] EWCA Crim 2016,
 [2007] 1 WLR 3262, [2008] 1 Cr App R 7, [2008] Crim LR 50 .... 9.12
R v Coutts (Graham James) [2006] UKHL 39, [2006] 1 WLR 2154, [2006]
 4 All ER 353 .... 3.35
R v Criminal Cases Review Commission, ex p Pearson [1999] 3 All ER 498,
 [2000] 1 Cr App R 141, [1999] Crim LR 732, [1999] COD 202 .... 3.3, 3.5,
 3.24; 9.26
R v D (David Michael) [2001] EWCA Crim 911 .... 14.10
R v Davies (David William) [1983] 76 Cr App R 120 .... 3.29
R v Davis (Michael George) (No 3); R v Rowe (Raphael George) (No 3); R v
 Johnson (Randolph Egbert) (No 3) [2001] 1 Cr App R 8, [2000] HRLR 527,
 [2000] UKHRR 683 .... 3.6, 3.13, 3.27
R v Davis (Zantoe); R v Thabangu (Mercedes) [2013] EWCA Crim 2424 .... 6.13
R v Day (Mark Darren) [2003] EWCA Crim 1060 .... 3.56, 3.57
R v Dolan (Joseph Daniel Philip) (1976) 62 Cr App R 36, [1976] Crim
 LR 145 .... 3.80
R v Doski (Niwar) [2011] EWCA Crim 987, [2011] Crim LR 712 .... 6.46
R v Dunn (James Lee) [2010] EWCA Crim 1823, [2011] 1 WLR 958, [2010] 2
 Cr App R 30, [2011] Crim LR 229 .... 7.42
R v Dyer (Richard) [2013] EWCA Crim 2114, [20143] 11 WLUK 47, [2014]
 2 Cr App R (S) 11 .... 4.30
R v Edwards (Regina) [2018] EWCA Crim 595, [2018] 4 WLR 64, [2018]
 3 WLUK 660 .... 14.1
R v Erskine (Kenneth) [2009] EWCA Crim 1425, [2010] 1 WLR 183, [2010]
 1 All ER 1196, [2009] 2 Cr App R 29, [2009] MHLR 215, [2010] Crim
 LR 48, (2009) 153 (28) SJLB 30 .... 3.48, 3.49; 4.31; 6.24,
 6.25, 6.26, 6.27;
 7.15, 7.58
R v Falconer-Atlee (Joan Olive) (1974) 58 Cr App R 348 .... 3.34
R v Fawcett (Keneth John) (1983) 5 Cr App R (S) 158 .... 4.35
R v Ferizi (Orhan) [2016] EWCA Crim 2022, [2016] 11 WLUK 509, [2017] 1
 Cr App R (S) 26 .... 13.33
R v Fletcher (Joseph) *see* R v Cottrell (Steven)
R v Forbes (Anthony Leroy) [2001] 1 AC 473, [2001] 2 WLR 1, [2001] 1 Cr
 App R 31 .... 3.15
R v Foster (Mark) [2007] EWCA Crim 2869, [2008] 1 WLR 1615, [2008] 2 All
 ER 597 .... 3.35
R v Geraghty [2016] EWCA Crim 1523, [2017] 1 Cr App R (S) 10 .... 4.14, 4.17
R v Gerald [1999] Crim LR 315 .... 9.15
R v Ghosh (Deb Baran) [1982] QB 1053, [1982] 3 WLR 110, [1982] 2 All
 ER 689 .... 2.6

R v Gibson (Ivano) [1983] 1 WLR 1038, [1983] 3 All ER 263, (1983) 77 Cr
App R 151, (1983) 147 JP 683, [1983] Crim LR 679, (1983) 80 LG 2133,
(1983) 127 SJ 509 .... 8.12

R v Gilbert (Jean) [2006] EWCA Crim 3276, [2006] 12 WLUK 182 .... 13.12

R v Gilbey (Raymond Giles) (1990-91) 12 Cr App R (S) 49 .... 3.32

R v Gogana (Sanjeev) (The Times, 12 July 1999) 6.31

R v Gooch (Malcolm George) (No 1) [1998] 1 WLR 1100, [1998] 4 All ER 402,
[1998] 2 Cr App R 130, (1998) 95 (7) LSG 32, (1998) 142 SJLB 61 .... 7.21

R v Goodyear (Karl) [2005] EWCA Crim 888, [2005] 1 WLR 2532, [2005]
3 All ER 117, [2005] 2 Cr App R 20, [2006] 1 Cr App R (S) 6, [2005]
Crim LR 659 .... 13.31

R v Gordon (Gavin Stephen) [2007] EWCA Crim 165, [2007] 1 WLR 2117,
[2007] 2 All ER 768 .... 4.39

R v Gould (John Arthur) [1968] 2 QB 65, [1968] 2 WLR 643, 52 Cr App
R 152 .... 2.6

R v Graham [1997] 1 Cr App R 302; [1997] Crim LR 340 .... 3.65

R v Grant-Murray (Janhelle) [2017] EWCA Crim 1228, [2017] 8 WLUK 160,
[2018] Crim LR 71 .... 3.53

R v Gray (Dean Andrew) [2014] EWCA Crim 2372, [2014] 10 WLUK 169,
[2015] 1 Cr App R (S) 27 .... 6.14, 6.67

R v H [2003] UKHL 1 .... 14.1

R v H [2008] EWCA Crim 483, [2008] 2 WLUK 321 .... 13.10

R v H (Interlocutory Application: Disclosure) [2007] UKHL 7, [2007]
2 AC 270, [2007] 2 WLR 364, [2007] 3 All ER 269, [2007] 2 Cr App R 6,
[2007] Crim LR 731, (2007) 151 SJLB 332 .... 12.9, 12.15

R v H (Peter) [2002] EWCA Crim 730, [2002] Crim LR 578 .... 3.50

R v Hallam (Sam) [2012] EWCA Crim 1158 .... 9.27, 9.28

R v Hanson (Nicky) [2005] EWCA Crim 824, [2005] 1 WLR 3169, [2005] 2
Cr App R 21 .... 3.31

R v Hart (Clifford) [2006] EWCA Crim 3239, [2007] 1 Cr App R 31, 2007] 2
Cr App R (S) 34, [2007] Crim LR 313 .... 6.67

R v Hayden (Joseph Anthony) [1975] 1 WLR 852, [1975] 2 All ER 558,
(1974) 60 Cr App R 304 .... 4.10

R v Hedworth (Peter John) [1997] 1 Cr App R 421 .... 12.4

R v Height (John); R v Anderson (Malcolm) [2008] EWCA Crim 2500, [2009]
1 Cr App R (S) 117, [2009] Crim LR 122 .... 4.28

R v Hirani (Amin Mohammed) [2008] EWCA Crim 1463 .... 4.47

R v Hoath (Terence); R v Standage (Terence Edward) [2011] EWCA Crim 274,
[2011] 1 WLR 1656, [2011] 4 All ER 306 .... 4.12

R v Horncastle (Michael Christopher) [2009] EWCA Crim 964, [2009]
4 All ER 183, [2009] 2 Cr App R 15, (2009) 153 (21) SJLB 28; *aff'd*
[2009] UKSC 14, [2010] 2 AC 373, [2010] 2 WLR 47 .... 2.9, 2.10

R v Horseferry Road Magistrates' Court, ex p Bennett (No 1) [1994] 1 AC 42,
[1993] 3 WLR 90, [1993] 3 All ER 138 (HL) 3.16

R v I (C) [2009] EWCA Crim 1793, [2010] 1 WLR 1125, [2010] 1 Cr App
R 10, [2010] Crim LR 312 .... 12.15

R v JH [2014] EWCA Crim 2618 .... 6.13

R v James [2018] EWCA Crim 285 .... 6.14; 7.13

R v Jogee (Ameen Hassan) [2016] UKSC 8, [2017] AC 387, [2016]
2 WLR 681 .... 3.59

R v Johnson (Lewis) [2016] EWCA Crim 1613, [2017] 4 WLR 104, [2017]
    4 All ER 769... 3.59; 6.32
R v Joof (Adam) [2012] EWCA Crim 1475... 9.31
R v Kalia (Daya) (1974) 60 Cr App R 200, [1975] Crim LR 181 .... 6.40
R v Kalis (Christopher) [2003] EWCA Crim 1080 .... 6.16
R v Keene (Daniel) [2010] EWCA Crim 2514, [2011] Crim LR 393................ 3.38
R v Kirk (Phillip John) [2015] EWCA Crim 1764, [2015] 10 WLUK 112........ 6.14
R v L [2013] EWCA Crim 1913.. 6.73
R v L; R v HVN; R v THNl R v T [2013] EWCA Crim 991, [2014] 1 All
    ER 113, [2013] 2 Cr App R 23, [2014] Crim LR 150 .... 2.14
R v Lane (Sally) & Letts (John) (AB & CD) [2018] UKSC 36, [2018]
    1 WLR 3647, [2019] 1 All ER 299.. 10.5
R v Lashley (Angela) [2005] EWCA Crim 2016, [2006] Crim LR 83 .... 3.33
R v Lee (James) [2014] EWCA Crim 2928, [2014] 7 WLUK 828 .... 6.13
R v Legal Aid Board, ex p RM Broudie & Co [1994] 3 WLUK 252,
    [1994] COD 435, (1994) 138 SJLB 94... 8.15
R v Lewis (Ian) [2013] EWCA Crim 776... 3.43; 9.31
R v McCann (John Paul) (1991) 92 Cr App R 239, [1991] Crim LR 136, (1990)
    140 NLJ 629... 3.30, 3.46
R v McCook [2014] EWCA Crim 734 .... 5.12; 6.11,
                                                                                                                6.13, 6.14
R v McDonald (Michael Christopher) [2004] EWCA Crim 2614, (2004)
    SJLB 1218.. 7.30
R v McGill [2018] EWCA Crim 1228, [2018] 5 WLUK 157 .... 6.11, 6.13
R v Mackinlay (Craig) [2018] UKSC 42, [2019] AC 387, [2018] 3 WLR 556.. 10.5
R v McLoughlin (Ian) *see* A-G's Reference (No 69 of 2013), Re
R v Mackle (Plunkett Jude) [2014] UKSC 5, [2014] AC 678, [2014]
    2 WLR 267 .... 4.47, 4.48
R v Magro (Anthony) [2010] EWCA Crim 1575, [2011] QB 398, [2010]
    3 WLR 1694, [2011] 2 All ER 935, [2010] 2 Cr App R 25, [2011] 1 cr
    App R (S) 73, [2010] Crim LR 787 .... 2.6
R v Mahendran (Kajanthan) [2011] EWCA Crim 608...................................... 4.28
R v Mateta (Koshi Pitshou) [2013] EWCA Crim 1372, [2014] 1 WLR 1516,
    [2014] 1 All ER 152, [2013] 2 Cr App R 35, [2014] Crim LR 227 .... 9.20
R v Medway (Andrew George) [1976] QB 779, [1976] 2 WLR 528, [1976]
    1 All ER 527, (1976) 62 Cr App R 85, [1976] Crim LR 118.................. 6.72, 6.74
R v Millard (Gary Michael) [2003] EWCA Crim 3629 .... 3.37
R v Mitchell (Emma) [2013] EWCA Crim 1072.. 9.31
R v Mohamed (Noor Bana) [2010] EWCA Crim 2464...................................... 6.72
R v NT [2010] EWCA Crim 711, [2010] 1 WLR 2655, [2010] 4 All ER 545... 13.7
R v Nealon (Victor) [2014] EWCA Crim 574.. 9.13
R v Nolan (Terence) [2017] EWCA Crim 2449, [2017] 11 WLUK 766........... 6.67
R v Noye (Kenneth) [2011] EWCA Crim 650, (2011) 119 BMLR 151 .... 3.11
R v Oates (Emma Louise) [2002] EWCA Crim 1071, [2002] 1 WLR 2833,
    [2002] 4 WLR 496 .... 8.11
R v O'Connor [1997] Crim LR 516... 3.19
R v Okedare (Charles) [2014] EWCA Crim 228, [2014] 1 WLR 4071, [2014]
    3 All ER 109..6.6; 7.21
R v Ordu (Mehmet) [2017] EWCA Crim 4, [2017] 1 WLUK 340, [2017] 1 Cr
    App R 21 .... 6.34

R v Pendleton (Donald) [2001] UKHL 66, [2002] 1 WLR 72, [2002] 1 All
ER 524 .... 3.10, 3.12
R v Phelps (David Robert) [2017] EWCA Crim 2403, [2017] 9 WLUK 23 ......   13.33
R v Pinfold (Terence Joseph) [1988] QB 462, [1988] 2 WLR 635, (1988) 87 Cr
App R 15 ....   4.17
R v Pope [2013] EWCA Crim 2241, [2013] 1 Cr App R 14; [2013] Crim
LR 421 ....   3.24
R v Quinn (Phillip Craig) [1996] Crim LR 516 ....   3.31
R v R (Amer) [2006] EWCA Crim 1974, [2007] 1 Cr App R 10, [2007] Crim
LR 79 ....   3.59
R v Razaq (Salim) [2011] EWCA Crim 1518 ....   4.25
R v Randall (Barry Victor) [2002] UKPC 19, [2002] 1 WLR 2237, [2002] 2 Cr
App R 17 ....   3.15
R v Reynolds (Michael Edwin) [2007] EWCA Crim 538, [2008] 1 WLR 1075,
[2007] 4 All ER 369 ....   4.3
R v Roberts (Mark) [2016] EWCA Crim 71, [2016] 1 WLR 3249, [2016]
3 WLUK 564 ....   6.11
R v Rogers (Georgina) [2016] EWCA Crim 801, [2017] 1 WLR 481, [2016] 2
Cr App R (S) 36 ....   4.34
R v Rowe [2007] EWCA Crim 635, [2007] QB 975, [2007] 3 WLR 177, [2007]
3 All ER 36, [2007] 2 Cr App R 14, [2007] 2 Cr App R (S) 92, [2007]
Crim LR 744, [2008] Crim LR 72 ....   2.6
R v Salik (Abdulrahman) [2004] EWCA Crim 2936 ....   3.29
R v Salloum [2010] EWCA Crim 312 ....   7.21
R v Secretary of State for the Home Department, ex p Hickey (No 2) [1995]
1 WLR 734, [1995] 1 All ER 490, (1995) 7 Admin LR 549, (1994)
144 NLJ 1732 .... 9.24, 9.28
R v Siddall (John Stephen) [2006] EWCA Crim 1353, (2006) 150 SJLB 809 ..   9.27
R v Simpson (Ian McDonald) [2003] EWCA Crim 1499, [2004] QB 118,
[20013] 3 WLR 337, [2003] 3 All ER 531, [2003] 2 Cr App R 36, [2004]
1 Cr App R (S) 24, [2003] Crim LR 652, (2003) 100 (27) LSG 34, (2003)
147 SJLB 694 ....   2.6
R v Simpson (John Lee) [2001] EWCA Crim 468, [2001] 2 WLUK 504 ....   3.60
R v Singh (Kunwar Ajit) [2017] EWCA Crim 466, [2018] 1 WLR 1425, [2017]
3 WLUK 705 .... 6.13, 6.31
R v Skanes (Tony Alan) [2006] EWCA Crim 2309 ....   3.77
R v Smith (Brian Peter) [1997] QB 836, [1997] 2 WLR 588, [1997] 1 Cr App
R 390 ....   3.22
R v Smith (Paul James) [2013] EWCA Crim 2388, [2014] 2 Cr App R 1, [2014]
Crim LR 612 ....   6.73
R v Smith (Wallace Duncan) (No 4) [2004] EWCA Crim 631, [2004] QB 1418,
[2004] 3 WLR 229, [2004] 2 Cr App R 17 ....   9.9
R v Spruce (Ronald Arthur) [2005] EWCA Crim 1090, [2006] 1 Cr App R (S)
11 ....   7.19
R v Stroud (John Richard) (No 1) [2004] EWCA Crim 1048 ....   4.46
R v Suggett (Philip) (1985) 81 Cr App R 243, (1985) 7 Cr App R (S) 123,
[1985] Crim LR 607, (1985) 82 LSG 2008 ....   6.37
R v Tarrant [1998] Crim LR 342 ....   3.39
R v Taylor (John William) [1950] 2 KB 368, [1950] 2 All ER 170, 34 Cr App
R 138 ....   2.6

R v Taylor (Michelle Ann) (1994) 98 Cr App R 361 .... 3.46
R v Thelwall (Kenneth) [2016] EWCA Crim 1755, [2016] 10 WLUK 549,
  [2016] CTLC 180... 4.31
R v Thompson (Glyn) [2006] EWCA Crim 2849, [2007] 1 WLR 1123, [2007]
  2 All ER 205, [2007] 1 Cr App R 15, [2007] Crim LR 387......................... 13.8
R v Thompson (Benjamin) [2010] EWCA Crim 1623, [2011] 1 WLR 200,
  [2011] 2 All ER 83... 3.40
R v Thornley (James William) [2011] EWCA Crim 153, [2011] 2 Cr App R (S)
  62, [2011] Crim LR 415.. 4.29
R v Thorsby (Adrian Kenneth) [2015] EWCA Crim 1, [2015] 1 WLR 2901,
  [2015] 1 WLUK 345 .... 6.9
R v Togher(Kenneth) (Appeal against Conviction) [2001] 3 All ER 463 , [2001]
  1 Cr App R 33, [2001] Crim LR 124 .... 3.14, 3.17, 3.29
R v Ul Hamid (Ibbtsam) [2016] EWCA Crim 449, [2016] 3 WLUK 506, [2016]
  2 Cr App R 29 .... 3.43
R v Vowles (Lucinda) [2015] EWCA Crim 45, [2015] 1 WLR 5131, [2015]
  2 WLUK 161... 14.1
R v Warren (Davis Lewis) [2017] EWCA Crim 226, [2017] 4 WLR 71, [2017]
  3 WLUK 76... 6.1
R v Watton (Joseph) (1979) 68 Cr App R 293, [1979] Crim LR 246 .... 6.36
R v Waya (Terry) [2012] UKSC 51, [2013] 1 AC 294, [2012] 3 WLR 1188 ..... 4.49
R v Whittaker [1967] Crim LR 431 .... 4.3
R v Williams [2010] EWCA Crim 3289.. 6.11
R v Wilson (David Steve) [2016] EWCA Crim 65, [2016] 2 WLUK 236 .... 6.10
R v X [2010] EWCA Crim 2367 .... 3.75
R v Zabotka [2016] EWCA Crim 1771 .... 6.74
RM Broudie & Co (a firm) v Lord Chancellor [2000] 5 WLUK 442, [2000] 2
  Costs LR 285.. 8.15
R (on the application of Cleeland) v Criminal Cases Review Commission
  [2009] EWHC 474 (Admin) 9.26
R (on the application of Langley) v Preston Crown Court [2008] EWHC 2623
  (Admin), [2009] 1 WLR 1612, [2009] 3 All ER 1026................................... 4.11
R (on the application of Nunn) v Chief Constable of Suffolk Constabulary
  [2014] UKSC 37, [2014] 3 WLR 77, [2014] 4 All ER 21, [2014] 2 Cr App
  R 22... 5.18
R (on the application of TB) v Combined Courts at Stafford [2006] EWHC 1645
  (Admin), [2007] 1 WLR 1524, [2007] 1 All ER 102, [2006] 2 Cr App
  R 34... 6.48
Reilly v UK (Application No 53731/00) (26 June 2003)................................... 11.7

S

Scozzai v Italy (13 July 2000, ECHR).. 11.9
Selvanayagam v UK (Application No 57981/00) (12 December 2002)............ 11.7
Stafford v DPP [1974] AC 878, [1973] 3 WLR 719, [1973] 3 All ER 762 .... 3.9

T

Tucka v UK (No 1) (Application No 34566/10) (18 January 2011)................... 11.7

Table of Cases

V

Van Duyn v Home Office (Case C-226/07) [1974] ECR 1337 .... 2.12

Y

Young v Bristol Airplane Co Ltd [1944] KB 718, [1944] 2 All ER 293, (1945)
   78 Ll L Rep 6 .... 2.5, 2.6

Part 1
The Law

Chapter 1

Introduction to the Court of Appeal

INTRODUCTION

1.1   The Court of Appeal (Criminal Division) ('the Court') sits in the gothic setting of the Royal Courts of Justice, London, in courtrooms of dark and intimidating antiquity. This should not mislead us into thinking that the Court is itself one of our ancient institutions. It was created in the 20th century, following years of campaigning by legal reformers and fierce opposition from successive governments and members of the judiciary.[1] Its core function then, as now, is to hear appeals from the Crown Court against conviction and sentence (including appeals against confiscation orders). However, Parliament has since loaded the Court with powers to hear appeals from a variety of other decisions of the Crown Court and Courts Martial. Although the focus of this book is on appeals against conviction and sentence, the additional powers that are most significant for general criminal litigation are also considered.[2]

THE DEVELOPMENT OF THE COURT OF APPEAL

1.2   The roots of the jury trial can be traced back to the middle ages. But if the jury system was one of the historic strengths of the English system of justice, the absence of a system of appeal against decisions of the jury was one of its great weaknesses. Before 1907 those who wished to challenge a conviction or a sentence imposed in the Assize and Sessions Courts (the predecessors of today's Crown Court) had two potential avenues of redress,

---

1   See Cornish, W. and Clarke, G. (1989) *Law and Society in England 1750–1950*, London: Sweet & Maxwell, pp. 619–623.
2   The prosecution's own rights of appeal, which are considered in Chapter 13; appeals against interlocutory rulings, which are considered in Chapter 12; appeals against restraint, receivership and foreign confiscation requests, which are considered in Chapter 4.

neither of them satisfactory.[3] The principal argument against the creation of a criminal court of appeal that was made in the 19th century (in which some 50 bills for the creation of a Court of Appeal were introduced to Parliament but failed to become law[4]) was that the role of the jury would be undermined if judges could, on appeal, overturn, the jury's decisions.[5] However, opposition was also driven by the perceived need for finality in criminal litigation[6] and a refusal, among some, to accept that the existing system was the cause of significant injustices.[7]

1.3   When Parliament finally bowed to public pressure and passed the Criminal Appeal Act 1907, these concerns found expression in the requirements for leave (or 'permission' as it is referred to in civil cases) to appeal in certain cases and also in the limited grounds upon which the Court could quash a conviction. Although the 1907 Act was repealed, it set the mould in which subsequent legislation was cast.

1.4   The 1907 Act created the 'Criminal Court of Appeal', which had the power to determine appeals against conviction and sentence from cases that had been heard on indictment in the Assize and Sessions Courts. An appeal against conviction could be brought without the need for leave of the Court when it was based upon a question of law. However, the leave of the Court or the certificate of the trial judge was required when an appeal was brought on a question of fact alone.

1.5   The Court had the power to set aside a conviction if it was:

(a)   unreasonable;

(b)   did not accord with the evidence;

(c)   was wrong in law.

---

3   From 1848 onwards a convicted person could ask the trial judge to refer the case to the Court for Crown Cases Reserved, which was established by the Crown Cases Reserved Act 1848, but only if the correctness of the conviction rested on a point of law. If the trial judge declined to refer the case, the only alternative was to fall back on the ancient practice of petitioning the government to grant a royal pardon. In contrast all but one US state had a criminal appeals court by 1840 (Grossberg, M. and Tomlins, C. (eds) (2008) *The Cambridge History of Law in America*, Vol. 2, New York: Cambridge University Press).
4   Radzinowicz, L. and Hood, R. (1986) *A History of English Law and it Administration from 1750*, Vol. V, London: Stevens & Sons, p 758.
5   Cornish and Clarke (1989), pp 619–623.
6   As R. Spencer noted in Delmas-Marty, M. and Spencer, J. R. (eds) (2002) *European Criminal Procedures*, Cambridge: Cambridge University Press, at p 28: 'In England the Jury was introduced as a substitute for the Judgment of God pronounced through the ordeal, and like the Judgment of God it was not open to challenge on the ground that it has given an answer that was wrong'.
7   Radzinowicz and Hood (1986), p 763.

1.6   Even if the Court found that any of these criteria were satisfied, it did not have to set aside the conviction if 'no substantial miscarriage of justice had occurred'.[8]

1.7   A number of reforms were introduced by the Criminal Appeal Acts 1964, 1966 and 1967. Most notably, the 1966 Act re-constituted the Court as a branch of the existing civil Court of Appeal, enabling all High Court judges and Lord Justices of Appeal to sit in both Courts. Thereafter the Court was known as the Court of Appeal (Criminal Division).

1.8   These changes were consolidated by the Criminal Appeal Act 1968 (CAA 1968) which (much amended by later legislation) contains the powers of today's Court of Appeal in relation to appeals against conviction and sentence.

1.9   The Senior Courts Act 1981 contains the overarching framework that now governs the Court of Appeal (Criminal Division) in all its activities. The need for such a framework is a testament to the many other appeals from the decisions of the Crown Court with which, since 1968, Parliament has empowered the Court to determine.

1.10   The last major reforms of the Court's powers are contained in the Criminal Appeal Act 1995, which made a number of amendments to the 1968 Act, the most important of which were:

(a)   The introduction of a new test for appeal against conviction. Whilst the original criteria from section 4(1) of the 1907 Act (see 1.5) had been preserved in section 2(1) of the Criminal Appeal Act 1968, the Criminal Appeal Act 1995 amended section 2(1) by replacing that criteria with a single test: the Court has to ask whether the conviction is 'safe'.

(b)   The removal of the automatic right of appeal against conviction in those cases where appeal is based on a point of law. Thereafter, either leave to appeal from the Court of Appeal or a certification from the trial judge would be required for all criminal appeals.

(c)   The creation of the Criminal Cases Review Commission ('the Commission') (the role of which is considered in Chapter 9).

Appeals from cases which pre-date the coming into force of CAA 1995

1.11   The test of unsafety applies to appeals against all convictions, whether they took place before or after the commencement of CAA 1995.[9] However, the

8   Criminal Appeal Act 1907, s 4(1).
9   By virtue of the Criminal Appeal Act 1995 (Commencement No. 1 and Transitional Provisions) Order 1995 (SI 1995/3061).

pre-1995 rules in relation to leave remain in force in respect of appeals against convictions that took place before 1 January 1996. If one appeals against such a historic conviction there will be no requirement for leave where the appeal involves a question of law only.[10]

THE CURRENT STATUTORY REGIME

1.12   The jurisdiction of the Court is set out in section 53(2) of the Senior Courts Act 1981. It provides that the Criminal Division of the Court of Appeal shall exercise:

(a)   all jurisdiction of the Court of Appeal under Parts I and II of the Criminal Appeal Act 1968;

(b)   the jurisdiction of the Court of Appeal under section 13 of the Administration of Justice Act 1960 (appeals in cases of contempt of court) in relation to appeals from orders and decisions of the Crown Court;

(c)   all other jurisdiction expressly conferred on that division by this or any other Act; and

(d)   the jurisdiction to order the issue of writs of *venire de novo* (a rarely used remedy that can be used to remit a case to the Crown Court where the Court is satisfied that the proceedings were so irregular that they did not constitute a proper trial).

1.13   Part 1 sets out the Court's powers when determining appeals against conviction or sentence from the Crown Court. Part II sets out its powers when determining applications for leave to appeal from that Court to the Supreme Court.

PROCEDURAL RULES AND GUIDANCE

1.14   Although the Court is a creature of statute and its powers are limited to those which Parliament has provided it, it does have the power to regulate its own procedures. Therefore, the statutory provisions relating to the conduct of appeals are supplemented by detailed procedural rules and guidelines from the following sources:

(a)   The Criminal Procedure Rules (Crim PR)[11] – Part 1 contains the rules that apply to all criminal proceedings. Parts 34 to 44 contain the rules which apply to appeals to the Court of Appeal.

---

10   See *DPP v Majewski* [1975] 3 All ER 296 for the meaning of 'a question of law'.
11   The Criminal Procedure Rules are set out in statutory instruments that are promulgated under the Courts Act 2003, s 69. The Criminal Procedure Rules Committee, which is chaired by the Lord Chief Justice, is responsible for drawing them up. Unless otherwise stated, references to 'CPR' are to the 2015 Rules. See Appendix B.

(b)   The Criminal Practice Directions ('the Practice Directions')[12] – Section IX of the Practice Directions is specifically concerned with Appeals to the Court of Appeal Against Conviction and Sentence. The Practice Directions are updated periodically.

(c)   The 'Guide to Commencing Proceedings in the Court of Appeal (Criminal Division)' ('the Guide') was published in August 2018. It was prepared by Court of Appeal lawyers under the direction of the Registrar. Guidance notes are produced by the Court for appellants, lawyers and others with an interest in the appeal process.[13]

(d)   The case law of the Court – The Lord Chief Justice or Vice President of the Criminal Division occasionally use particular cases to provide guidance on what the Court expects from the parties. These individual decisions are often incorporated into the Practice Direction when it is updated.

THE JUDGES OF THE COURT OF APPEAL

1.15   The Court of Appeal is presided over by the Lord Chief Justice who is appointed by the Lord Chancellor. He may in turn appoint another judge as Vice President of the Criminal Division to assist him.[14]

1.16   The other permanent judges of the Court are a small number of holders or former holders of certain high judicial offices, and a larger number of 'ordinary' judges who on appointment to the Court of Appeal are known as Lord or Lady Justices of Appeal.[15] In addition, the Lord Chief Justice may ask High Court judges (referred to in the legislation as 'puisne judges') or judges who sit in the Crown Court ('circuit judges') to sit in the Court of Appeal.[16]

1.17   When a judge is sitting in the Court of Appeal, he or she should be addressed as my Lord or my Lady.

---

12   The Lord Chief Justice has the power, under the Courts Act 2003, s 74 and the Constitutional Reform Act 2005, Sch 2, Pt 1 to make directions as to the practice and procedure of the criminal courts.

13   They can be found at: www.justice.gov.uk/courts/rcj-rolls-building/court-of-appeal/criminal-division.

14   Senior Courts Act 1981, s 3.

15   Senior Courts Act 1981, s 2.

16   Senior Courts Act 1981, s 9.

The composition of the Court

1.18   The Court is constituted, for the purposes of exercising any of its powers, when it sits as an uneven number of judges, not less than three.[17] In practice it usually sits as a Court of three judges, presided over by a Lord or Lady Justice of Appeal. A court of five judges will occasionally sit on important cases when the Lord Chief Justice deems it appropriate. There may never be more than one circuit judge sitting in any one court.

1.19   A Court of two judges may be constituted by two High Court judges or a High Court judge and a Circuit judge.[18] It may only hear the following appeals:

(a)   an appeal against sentence;

(b)   a renewed application for leave to appeal against conviction or sentence where the single judge has already refused leave.

The 'single judge'

1.20   An application for leave to appeal against conviction or sentence is generally considered by a single judge, in practice this will be a High Court judge. The single judge may determine other applications (for example, an application for bail) that are made along with or following the application for leave. Alternatively, he may refer applications on to the full Court for its determination. Although her decisions are usually made on paper she may choose to hold oral hearings.

THE REGISTRAR OF CRIMINAL APPEALS AND THE CRIMINAL APPEALS OFFICE

1.21   The role of the Registrar of Criminal Appeals ('the Registrar') is to assist the Court in the effective management of cases. It is an administrative but also a judicial role in that she (as the current occupier of the office is) has a number of case management powers, some of which are considered in Chapters 6 and 7 of this book.

1.22   The Registrar herself is assisted by the lawyers and administrative staff at the 'Criminal Appeals Office'. Cases will be assigned to a lawyer and caseworker who will then take responsibility for preparing the case and communicating with the parties.

---

17   Senior Courts Act 1981, s 55(2).
18   Senior Courts Act 1981, s 55(6).

1.23 Their work is undertaken in the name of 'the Registrar', and it is the 'the Registrar' to whom correspondence with the Court should generally be addressed. However, it should be assumed that routine casework is undertaken without the Registrar's personal involvement.[19]

WHERE AND WHEN THE COURT SITS

1.24 The Court may sit anywhere in England and Wales but it is based in the Royal Courts of Justice in the Strand (sitting usually in Courts 4 to 9) along with the Registrar and the Criminal Appeal Office.

1.25 It sits at the following times of year:[20]

(a) the Michaelmas sittings, which begin on 1 October and end on 21 December;

(b) the Hilary sittings, which begin on 11 January and end on the Wednesday before Easter Sunday;

(c) the Easter sittings, which begin on the second Tuesday after Easter Sunday and end on the Friday before the spring holiday; and

(d) the Trinity sittings, which begin on the second Tuesday after the spring holiday and end on 31 July.

COMMUNICATING WITH THE COURT

1.26 Correspondence to the Court should be addressed to:

The Registrar of Criminal Appeals
The Royal Courts of Justice
Strand
London
WC2A 2LL
DX 44451 Strand
Email: criminalappealoffice.applications@hmcts.x.gsi.gov.uk

1.27 All correspondence to the Court should contain the case reference number which is to be found on all correspondence from the Court.

1.28 In practice, most correspondence will be considered and replied to by the lawyer or the caseworker who has been assigned to the case. The lawyer may pass on correspondence to the Registrar herself if the nature of the issues

---

19 Senior Courts Act 1981, s 31A(2)(b).
20 Civil Procedure Direction 2F.

requires her consideration. If the case is being prepared for hearing and a presiding judge has already been assigned, the lawyer may pass correspondence on to the judge's clerk.

SUMMARY OF KEY POINTS

- The Court of Appeal (Criminal Division) hears all appeals against conviction and sentence from the Crown Court. It also has power to hear a number of other appeals from decisions of the Crown Court and the Courts Martial.

- The Court was created by statute. Its powers and jurisdiction are therefore defined by statute. Its overarching framework is contained in the Senior Courts Act 1981.

- Its powers in relation to appeals against conviction or sentence are to be found in the Criminal Appeal Act 1968 as amended by subsequent legislation, most notably the Criminal Appeal Act 1995. However, appeals against decisions that were made before 1 January 1995 take place under the provisions that were then in force.

- It has the power to regulate its own procedures. The legislation is supplemented by a number of procedural rules and guidelines that are to be found in the relevant Criminal Procedural Rules, the relevant parts of the Criminal Practice Direction, decisions of the Court itself and the Court's written guidance for advocates.

- It is based in the Royal Courts of Justice (sitting usually in Courts 4 to 9) where the Registrar of Criminal Appeals and the Criminal Appeal Office are also based.

- Communication with the Court should be through written correspondence addressed to the Registrar and should contain the Court's own case reference number.

Chapter 2

Applying the law: recent developments

INTRODUCTION

2.1   The Court interprets and applies law from the following sources:

(a)   Acts of Parliament;

(b)   Statutory Instruments;

(c)   decisions of the Superior Courts;

(d)   the European Convention on Human Rights and decisions of the European Court of Human Rights;

(e)   European Union law and international law.

2.2   The overriding requirement to apply statutes remains a constant feature of our criminal law. However, in the last 25 years a once crystal clear hierarchy of norms has become clouded as the Human Rights Act and the growing impact of European Union law and international law has added complexity to the business of interpreting the domestic criminal law. It has also been a period in which the Court of Appeal has returned on several occasions to the question of when it is entitled to depart from its own previous decisions. The focus of this chapter is upon these developments.

STARE DECISIS[1] AND THE COURT OF APPEAL

2.3   The Court of Appeal must follow the decisions of the Supreme Court and those of its predecessor, the Judicial Committee of the House of Lords.[2] The judges who sit in the Supreme Court also sit in the Judicial Committee of the Privy Council which hears appeals from a number of Commonwealth countries. Its decisions are not strictly binding on the Court of Appeal but

---

1   The doctrine of *stare decisis* is an abbreviation of the maxim '*stare decisis at non quieta movere*', which translates as 'to stand by things decided and not disturb settled points'.

2   The Supreme Court was created by the Constitutional Reform Act 2005. It came into existence on 1 October 2009.

will carry great weight and are likely to be followed unless there is very good reason to depart from them.

2.4   As a general rule the Court of Appeal is bound to follow its own decisions. However, there are exceptions to that rule. It is the scope of those exceptions that needs to be considered.

2.5   In *Young v Bristol Airplane Co Ltd*[3] the Court of Appeal (Civil Division) held that the Court of Appeal was bound to follow a previous decision of the Court unless one of the following exceptions applied:

(a)   There is a conflict between two Court of Appeal authorities and the Court must decide which to follow.

(b)   The decision of the Court of Appeal cannot stand with a decision of the Supreme Court.

(c)   The decision was *per incuriam* (taken without consideration of relevant statutory provision or binding case law (*Morelle Ltd v Wakeling*[4])).

2.6   The rule of *stare decisis* is less strictly applied in the Criminal Division of the Court of Appeal, dealing as it must with questions involving the liberty of the subject.[5] It has been established that the Criminal Division of the Court of Appeal has a residual discretion to decline to follow a previous decision for reasons that lie outside the categories identified in *Young v Bristol Airplane*. The scope of that discretion has been considered in three cases in which the Court was presided over by successive Lord Chief Justices (*R v Simpson*,[6] *R v Rowe*[7] and *R v Magro*[8]). These cases indicate differing approaches to the scope of the discretion. However, the following principles emerge:

(a)   It is only in very rare cases that the Court will decline to follow a previous decision of the Court of Appeal.

(b)   If it is considering doing so it will usually sit as a Court of five judges rather than the usual two or three. Such a Court will usually be presided over by the Lord Chief Justice.

---

3   [1944] KB 718.
4   [1955] 2 QB 379.
5   *R v Taylor* [1950] 2 KB 368, 34 Cr App R138; *R v Gould* [1968] 2 QB 65, 52 Cr App R 152. In *DPP v Patterson* [2017] EWHC 2820, the Admin Court held that the test as to dishonesty set out in *R v Ghosh* [1982] QB 1053 no longer represented the law in light of the decision in *Ivey v Genting Casinos (UK) Ltd* [2017] UKSC 67 and that it was clear from *Gould* that the Court of Appeal might depart from *Ghosh* without the matter returning to the Supreme Court.
6   [2003] EWCA Crim 1499.
7   [2007] EWCA Crim 635.
8   [2010] EWCA Crim 1575.

(c) If the effect of refusing to follow a previous decision would be to render the appellant guilty of a crime of which he or she would not otherwise be guilty, the Court will be bound to follow the decision in question.

(d) If failing to follow the previous decision has the effect of exposing the appellant to some lesser disadvantage, that may be a powerful factor against departing from the decision.

(e) If the previous decision can be said to be *per incuriam*, very broadly understood (for example, if the matter in issue was not properly argued or if all the relevant authorities were not drawn to the Court's attention), the Court may in those circumstances decide not to follow that decision.

(f) However, if the previous decision was reached following full argument on the point and careful consideration of all the relevant authorities and statutory provisions, the Court may regard itself as being bound to follow that decision.

JUDGMENTS OF THE EUROPEAN COURT OF HUMAN RIGHTS

2.7 The European Convention on Human Rights ('the Convention') is a Convention between European states which was incorporated by the Human Rights Act 1998 (HRA 1998) into domestic law. The effect of HRA 1998 is to require the Courts to:

(a) Interpret legislation in so far as possible to give effect to the Convention. However, Parliament remains the ultimate source of law. Therefore if the Court is unable to interpret a statute so as to render it compatible with the Convention, it must make a declaration of incompatibility that will require Parliament to consider amending the legislation.

(b) Interpret statutory instruments in accordance with the requirements of the Convention or refuse to apply them if they cannot be interpreted in a way that is compatible with the Convention.

(c) Develop the common law so as to give effect to the Convention.

2.8 The European Court of Human Rights (ECtHR) determines cases brought against a state that is a signatory to the Convention. HRA 1998 requires that in determining the scope of Convention rights the domestic courts must 'take account' of any relevant judgment of the ECtHR.[9]

2.9 This requirement is interpreted by the domestic courts as meaning that they should give great weight to the judgments of the ECtHR and strive to

---

9   Human Rights Act 1998, s 2(1)(a).

follow them. However, they do not regard themselves as bound to follow the ECtHR. If, after careful consideration, the domestic courts reach a different conclusion as to what the Convention requires, the courts should not follow the jurisprudence of the ECtHR.[10]

2.10   The case law[11] suggests that when the Court of Appeal is contemplating disagreeing with the ECtHR it will sit as a Court of five judges presided over by the Lord Chief Justice or the Vice President. Faced with a conflict of approach between the Supreme Court and the ECtHR the Court of Appeal is bound by the doctrine of precedent to follow the Supreme Court.

2.11   Whether the ECtHR provides a useful avenue of redress, when an appeal against conviction or sentence is refused is considered in Chapter 11, below.

EUROPEAN UNION LAW AND INTERNATIONAL LAW

2.12   The European Union has explicit but limited powers to legislate in matters of substantive criminal law[12] and criminal procedure.[13] It may only do so through directives. They must usually be incorporated into domestic law by legislation in order to have effect. Clearly, EU law will be an important aid to the interpretation of legislation that seeks to bring it into domestic effect. However, EU law may also shape our domestic criminal law even in the absence of such domestic legislation, if and when it confers rights on individuals that may be relied on in court.[14] If and when the United Kingdom leaves the European Union following the 2016 referendum, EU law will cease to apply to the UK save to the extent that it has already been incorporated into domestic law or its application is preserved by the exit Treaty.

2.13   International law consists of customary international law (general international practice which is accepted as law) and international treaties. Like European Union law, it too may shape the common law even when it has not been incorporated into domestic law, when the effect of a rule or principle of international law is to create individual rights.

2.14   An important example of the role that both EU and international law can play in the criminal law lies in the protection of victims of human

---

10   *R v Horncastle* [2009] UKSC 14.
11   *R v Horncastle* [2009] EWCA Crim 964; *R v McLoughlin* [2014] EWCA Crim 188.
12   Treaty of the European Union, Art. 83.
13   Treaty of the European Union, Art 82(2).
14   *Van Duyn v Home Office* (Case C-226/07) [1974] ECR 1337.

trafficking. International conventions[15] and an EU Directive on human trafficking[16] require the UK to take steps to ensure that victims of trafficking who have been compelled to commit an offence as a direct consequence of having been trafficked are not prosecuted for those offences. In *R v L, HVN, THN & T*[17] the Court found that, in order to comply with its international and EU obligations, the domestic courts should stay, as an abuse of process, the prosecution of a victim of trafficking whose offending was carried out as a direct result of having been trafficked.

2.15   Although international and EU law may be sources of rights, it is a well-recognised principle that criminal offences may now only be created by Parliament. Whilst there are several old common law offences which the courts still recognise, the courts will not recognise new offences unless they are created by domestic legislation. Therefore, neither EU law nor international law can be used to establish or extend the bounds of criminal liability without being incorporated into domestic law by Parliament.

SUMMARY OF KEY POINTS

- The Court of Appeal (Criminal Division) is bound to follow the decisions of the Supreme Court and its predecessor, the Judicial Committee of the House of Lords.

- It is generally bound to follow previous decisions of the Court of Appeal. However, there are certain exceptions that would allow it to depart from such a decision.

- The Court is bound to interpret the law in accordance with the requirements of the European Convention on Human Rights. If it cannot interpret a statute in accordance with the requirements of the Convention it must make a declaration of incompatibility.

- In interpreting the requirements of the Convention, it must have regard to the decisions of the European Court of Human Rights. However, it is not bound by them.

- As things stand, the Court may take into account important principles of EU as well as international law when interpreting the requirements of our criminal law, even when it has not been incorporated into domestic law by statute.

---

15 Council of Europe Convention on Action against Trafficking in Human Beings 2005 (CETS No 197) and the Protocol to Prevent, Suppress and Punish Trafficking in Persons, especially Women and Children ('the Palermo Protocol'), supplementing the United Nations Convention against Transnational Organised Crime 2000.

16 EU Directive 2011/36/EU on Preventing and Combating Trafficking in Human Beings and Protecting its Victims.

17 [2013] EWCA Crim 991.

2.15   *Applying the law: recent developments*

- However, although there are several old common law offences that are recognised by the courts, statute is now the only source of new criminal liability.

- Upon exit from the EU, EU law will cease to apply to the UK save to the extent that it has been incorporated into domestic law or its application is preserved by the exit Treaty.

Chapter 3

Appeals against conviction

INTRODUCTION

3.1   To succeed in an appeal against conviction, the applicant has to meet a single test: whether the conviction is unsafe.

THE MEANING OF 'UNSAFE'

3.2   Section 2(1) of CAA 1968, as amended by CAA 1995, provides that:

'Subject to the provisions of this Act, the Court of Appeal –

(a)   shall allow an appeal against conviction if they think that the conviction is unsafe; and

(b)   shall dismiss such an appeal in any other case.'

3.3   The meaning of the term 'unsafe' was considered by Lord Bingham CJ, as he then was, in the judgment of the Court in *R v Criminal Cases Review Commission, ex p Pearson*[1] at para 10:

'The expression "unsafe" in section 2(1)(a) of the 1968 Act does not lend itself to precise definition. In some cases unsafety will be obvious, as (for example) where it appears that someone other than the appellant committed the crime and the appellant did not, or where the appellant has been convicted of an act that was not in law a crime, or where a conviction is shown to be vitiated by serious unfairness in the conduct of the trial or significant legal misdirection, or where the jury verdict, in the context of other verdicts, defies any rational explanation. Cases however arise in which unsafety is much less obvious: cases in which the court, although by no means persuaded of an appellant's innocence, is subject to some lurking doubt or uneasiness whether an injustice has been done (*R v Cooper [1969] 1 QB 267 at 271*). If, on consideration of all the facts and circumstances of the case before it, the court entertains real doubts whether the appellant was

---

1   [2000] 1 Cr App R 141.

guilty of the offence of which he has been convicted, the court will consider the conviction unsafe. In these less obvious cases the ultimate decision of the Court of Appeal will very much depend on its assessment of all the facts and circumstances.'

3.4   An unsafe conviction, then, can be considered a wrongful conviction. Although Lord Bingham was careful not to seek to provide a comprehensive definition of the factors that might lead the Court to regard a conviction as unsafe, the passage outlines some of the key features of the test.

Error or new evidence giving rise to doubt as to guilt

3.5   Is a conviction unsafe only when there are grounds to doubt the guilt of the convicted person or does it involve wider questions of fairness and procedural regularity in the trial process? As Lord Bingham's speech from *Pearson* indicates, the Courts have come to embrace the broad understanding of the test; a conviction may be unsafe even where there is no doubt as to guilt, where the conviction has been obtained following a trial that was unfair.

3.6   However, it is only in rare cases that the Court will be prepared to find a conviction unsafe in the absence of any real doubt as to guilt. In most appeals, the Court's approach is to consider whether, had the error or irregularity not occurred, 'the only proper and reasonable verdict be one of guilty.' (*R v Davis, Rowe and Johnson*[2]). If the Court concludes that the verdict would still have been one of guilty, it is likely to find that the conviction is safe.

3.7   This approach has at times involved the Court placing itself in the position of the jury and asking how the matter that is the subject of the appeal may have led to its returning a different verdict. In another series of cases, however, the Court has made clear that it is they who decide which convictions are, or are not, safe.

3.8   In relation to grounds of appeal concerning a failure of disclosure, the Court should ask whether 'there was a real possibility of a different outcome – if the jury might reasonably have come to a different view on the issue to which it directed its verdict if the withheld material had been disclosed to the defence.'[3]

---

2   [2001] 1 Cr App R 8 at 132.
3   Lord Kerr, speaking in an extra-judicial capacity, at the Justice Scotland International Human Rights Day Lecture 2013, Miscarriage of Justice – When Should an Appellate Court Quash Conviction? 10 December 2013.

The jury impact test

3.9   The correctness of this 'jury impact' approach was considered in appeals that turned on the admission of fresh evidence. In *Stafford v DPP*,[4] the House of Lords held that when fresh evidence was received by the Court, the Court itself had to assess the impact of that evidence on the safety of the conviction and not what effect it might have had upon the jury.

3.10   In *R v Pendleton*,[5] the majority of the House of Lords found that whilst the fundamental question of whether the conviction was safe was for the Court itself, the Court might be at a disadvantage in relating that evidence to the evidence that the jury had heard. Therefore, in all but the clearest cases, it would be wise for the Court to consider whether the evidence might reasonably have affected the verdict of the jury.

3.11   In the subsequent case law differently constituted Courts emphasised either the potential jury impact of fresh evidence or the Court's own task of assessing for itself the potential impact of the evidence (see *R v Noye*[6]).

3.12   Although the two approaches will generally produce the same result there may be some benefit to the defence to frame arguments in terms of the potential jury impact of the error or new evidence that is the subject of the grounds of appeal. It may be cited so long as it is couched in the terms that were recognised as correct in *Pendleton* and the latter case law. However it is done, it remains crucial to address the strength of the prosecution evidence untouched by any legal flaw, failure in disclosure or whatever other ground is advanced. By whichever intellectual route the Court assesses what is 'unsafe', an appeal in which they form the impression that a convicted applicant was manifestly guilty is almost certain to fail.

'Unsafe' and 'unfair'

3.13   Article 6(1) of the European Convention of Human Rights, provides the right to a fair trial, with Article 6(3) providing a number of specific fair criminal trial guarantees. After the Human Rights Act brought the Convention into domestic force, an unfair trial was an unlawful trial and a conviction following such a trial is unsafe. This logic was not immediately recognised by the Court of Appeal in *R v Davis, Rowe and Johnson*[7] which, at para 135 stressed that an unfair trial and an unsafe conviction were two distinct concepts.

---

4   [1974] AC 878.
5   [2001] UKHL 66.
6   [2011] EWCA Crim 650.
7   See fn 2, above

However, without eliding the two tests, the Court has since made it clear that a trial that is unfair will almost certainly also be unsafe.

3.14   In *R v Togher*,[8] Lord Woolf CJ said: 'we consider that if a defendant has been denied a fair trial it will almost be inevitable that the conviction will be regarded as unsafe.'

3.15   This principle was confirmed in subsequent cases such as *R v Forbes*[9] and the Privy Council case of *R v Randall*,[10] in which Lord Bingham made clear that in the absence of a fair trial a conviction was likely to be unsafe even in the face of strong evidence of guilt:

> 'There will come a point where the departure from good practice is so gross, or persistent, or prejudicial, or irremediable that an appellate Court will have no choice but to condemn the trial as unfair and quash the conviction as unsafe, however strong the grounds for believing the defendant to be guilty.'

3.16   This jurisprudence is consistent with the law in relation to abuse of process, which recognises that a prosecution may give rise to abuse of process if either a fair trial was not possible or it would not be fair to try the defendant (*R v Horseferry Road Magistrates' Court, ex p Bennett*[11]). The refusal of the trial judge to stay a case as an abuse of process may itself be the subject of appeal.

3.17   However, it is not every breach of the right to a fair trial that will render a conviction unsafe. It will only be if the trial itself could be said to be unfair that the conviction would be considered unsafe *(R v Togher*[12]). To take an obvious example, a trial that was so delayed as to lead to a violation of the Article 6 right to a trial 'within a reasonable time' will very rarely be the basis of a successful appeal if it was fair in all other regards, see *AG's Ref (No 2 of 2001)*.[13]

3.18   This is not to say that individual breaches of Article 6, particularly Article 6(3), cannot form the basis of successful grounds as long as the appellant has been able to show that had these breaches not taken place there was a real chance that he or she would not have been convicted or that the unfairness was so profound as to amount to an abuse of process.

---

8   [2001] 1 Cr App R 33, para 30.
9   [2001] 1 Cr App R 31.
10   [2002] UKPC 19.
11   [1993] 3 All ER 138 (HL).
12   See fn 8, above.
13   [2004] 2 AC 72.

Procedural irregularity

3.19   When the Court can be satisfied that a procedural irregularity in the trial process materially disadvantaged a defendant such that in the absence of the defect the jury may have had a doubt as to their guilt, then the usual approach of considering whether there are real grounds to doubt the appellant's guilt can be applied without difficulty. An example of this approach in action can be found in relation to the judge's decision to allow an amendment to the indictment in *R v O'Connor*,[14] where the applicant would be expected to explain how the amendment was unfair and how it disadvantaged him or her in the conduct of the case.

3.20   In such cases, it will be important to be able to explain whether the procedural flaw was raised at trial and if so, why not. The Court will wish to know that the defence did not make a deliberate tactical decision not to raise the point, in the belief that this would give the defendant some advantage at trial, only to switch tactics on appeal; if the Court does form such a view, it will be much harder for any appeal to succeed.

3.21   If the defendant has suffered no clear disadvantage, will procedural irregularity lead to the conviction being quashed? The approach of the Courts is to ask whether it was the intention of Parliament that the failure to follow the procedure in question should render the proceedings a nullity. If so, then it is likely that the conviction will be unsafe. An example of this principle at work can be found in *R v Clarke and McDaid*[15] in which the House of Lords held that the failure to sign an indictment rendered the trial process a nullity because Parliament had provided in sections 1 and 2 of the Administration of Justice (Miscellaneous Provisions) Act 1993 that an indictment must be signed to be valid and a trial could only take place on the basis of a valid indictment.[16]

3.22   A further example is to be found in relation to misjoinder. When charges wrongly joined are therefore in breach of rule 9 of the Indictment Rules (*R v Smith (Brian Peter)*[17]), the misjoined charge will be quashed. However, this misjoinder will not render the proceedings a nullity and the remaining charges will be unaffected, unless prejudice is caused to the defence.

---

14   [1997] Crim LR 516 (CA).

15   [2008] UKHL 8.

16   However, following the Coroners and Justice Act 2009, s 116, it is no longer the case that an indictment must be signed in order for it to be valid.

17   [1997] 1 Cr App R 390 (CA).

'Lurking doubt'

3.23   Despite all that has been said above about the need to advance particular grounds, the Court may in rare circumstances be prepared to conclude that a conviction is unsafe, in the absence of either irregularity at trial or new evidence, if it nonetheless has some doubt or uneasiness about the verdict which makes the Court wonder if an injustice had been done.

3.24   This was recognised as a proper basis to quash a conviction in *R v Cooper*.[18] That this ground has survived the introduction of the new test of unsafety was indicated by Lord Bingham in *Pearson* although in *R v Pope*[19] the Court indicated that it would only be in the most exceptional circumstances that a conviction would be found to be unsafe on this ground alone.

Conclusion: 'unsafe' as a flexible test

3.25   The above comments are illustrations of how the Court has approached the question of unsafety in particular circumstances. They should not be regarded as immutable doctrines. The Court has repeatedly emphasised that there is a single statutory test of unsafety and has shown considerable flexibility in its application.

3.26   The Court does not always elaborate on the basis upon which it has concluded that the conviction is unsafe. This is often so when the Court finds that the conviction is unsafe because of the cumulative effect of a number of errors that are detailed in a number of distinct grounds.

3.27   When the Court's basis for finding a conviction to be unsafe is set out, the Court may approach the issue of fairness and jury impact in a number of different ways. For example, the closer that the error complained of goes to a core feature of a fair trial, the more likely it is that the Court will be prepared to find that the conviction was unsafe without extensive enquiry as to what the verdict might have been if the error had not been made. So, when the judge fails to direct the jury on the balance and burden of proof, it has been held only when the case was overwhelming that the conviction would be regarded as safe (*Davis, Rowe and Johnson*[20]).

3.28   This does not make it easy for lawyers who are asked to advise on appeal against conviction. Given that an unsafe conviction is a wrongful conviction, it may be helpful to consider, in each case, why is it that the

---

18   [1969] 1 QB 267 (CA) at 271.
19   [2013] EWCA Crim 2241.
20   See fn 2, above.

conviction must be regarded as wrongful. This is likely to provide the best guide to the way in which the Court will approach the case.

THE COURT'S APPROACH TO COMMON ISSUES

Appeal following a guilty plea

3.29   The fact that a defendant has pleaded guilty does not act as a bar to any appeal against conviction. However, the guilty plea is likely to be regarded by the Courts as a very significant factor in favour of the safety of the conviction. The Court has been prepared to allow appeals against conviction following a guilty plea, in the following circumstances:

(a)   Guilty pleas will be treated as a nullity and quashed where they were equivocal. However, in those circumstances an application should first have been made to the Crown Court to re-open. Any appeal must be against the judge's ruling.

(b)   Guilty plea following flawed legal advice: the advice must go to the heart of the guilty plea. The elements of the offence may do so, advice on the likely length of sentence will not (*R v Saik*[21]).

(c)   Guilty plea following erroneous ruling by the judge may be regarded as giving rise to an unsafe conviction but only where the ruling has the effect of depriving the defendant of a real choice as to whether to plead guilty (*R v Chalkley and Jeffries*[22]).

(d)   In *R v Togher*,[23] other defendants had secured a stay as a result of non-disclosure. At the time when he pleaded guilty, the appellant was not aware of the material upon which the abuse of process application was based. The Court found that it would be iniquitous for the conviction to stand.

(e)   Lack of jurisdiction or procedural irregularity that rendered the proceedings a nullity (*R v Davies*[24]).

Trial rulings

3.30   There is a high threshold to cross when challenging the decision of a judge in relation to a ruling made at trial. How high is less clear. It is not sufficient that the Court may not have reached the same decision. What is less certain is whether the ruling must be so manifestly wrong as to be regarded as

---

21   [2004] EWCA Crim 2936.
22   [1998] 2 Cr App R 79.
23   See fn 8, above.
24   [1983] 76 Cr App R 120.

Wednesbury unreasonable or whether it was sufficient for the Court to form its own view that the decision was wrong. The better view seems to be that when the Court reaches the view that it is 'clearly wrong' it should go on to consider the safety of the conviction. This was the approach adopted in *R vMcCann*[25] in which it was said that:

> 'To reverse the judge's ruling it is not enough that the members of this Court would have exercised their discretion differently. We must be clearly satisfied that the judge was wrong; but our powers to review the exercise of his discretion is not limited to cases in which he has erred in principle or there is shown to have been no material on which he could properly have arrived at his decision. The Court must, if necessary, examine anew the relevant facts and circumstances to exercise a discretion by way of review if it thinks that the judge's ruling may have resulted in injustice to the appellants. See *Evans v. Bartlam [1937] AC 473.*'

3.31   In the subsequent case of *R v Quinn*,[26] it was held that the Court of Appeal would not interfere with a ruling of the trial judge unless and until the judge failed to take into account relevant factors or took account of irrelevant factors. However, in *R v Hanson*[27] in relation to rulings on bad character, the Court held:

> 'If a judge has directed himself or herself correctly, this Court will be very slow to interfere with a ruling either as to admissibility or as to the consequences of noncompliance with the regulations for the giving of notice of intention to rely on bad character evidence. It will not interfere unless the judge's judgment as to the capacity of prior events to establish propensity is plainly wrong, or discretion has been exercised unreasonably in the *Wednesbury* sense.'

Defective summing up

Judge commenting on the evidence

3.32   The judge is entitled to comment on the facts. It is the role of the judge to provide guidance on factual as well as legal issues. However, these comments should not jeopardise the jury's own consideration of the evidence by being clearly partisan. The judge should direct the members of the jury that they were the judges of fact and should only take into account views expressed by the judge to the extent that it agreed with their own. If this direction is provided, it will be regarded by the Court as an important factor in considering whether any comments made by the judge might have improperly influenced

---

25   (1991) 92 Cr App R 239.
26   [1996] Crim LR 516.
27   [2005] EWCA Crim 824, para 15.

the jury. However, in a case in which the judge's comments were particularly extreme or damaging, the conviction will not be made safe by the parrot-like recitation that 'it is matter for you, the jury'; see Lord Bingham in *R v Bentley*,[28] citing with approval the judgment of Lloyd LJ in *Gilbey*.[29]

3.33   As always, the key test is whether the judge's conduct is such as to render the conviction unsafe. Appeals may succeed if the judge has made clear his or her preference for the prosecution case (see *R v Bryant*[30]), has undermined the advocate in the eyes of the jury, or has interrupted so much as to prevent the defence from being able to properly advance its case (see *R v Lashley*,[31] another successful appeal from the same trial judge as in *Bryant*).

Summing up on a different basis to that advanced at trial

3.34   There is no bar to the judge summing up the prosecution case on a different basis to that which it was put by the prosecution at trial. However, the judge must proceed with caution. There is an obvious danger that the fairness of the trial will be prejudiced where the judge introduces lines of argument to which the defence have had no opportunity to respond to (*R v Falconer-Atlee*[32]).

Leaving alternative verdicts to the jury

3.35   Whether to leave alternative, lesser counts to the jury is a matter that the judge should raise with counsel but is ultimately a matter for the judge. It should generally be done where it obviously arises on the evidence. A failure to do so is highly likely to lead to a verdict being quashed (*R v Coutts*[33] and *R v Foster*[34]) though the Court of Appeal will often defer to the view of the trial judge, who has had the advantage of hearing and seeing the evidence.

Getting the law wrong

3.36   As discussed above at **3.27**, a failure to properly direct the jury on the balance and burden of proof will be regarded as highly likely to render a conviction unsafe. Other failures in directing the jury on the law, such as to correctly identify the elements of the offence or the defence relied upon may

---

28   [2001] 1 Cr App R 21.
29   (unreported) 26 January 1990.
30   [2005] EWCA Crim 2079.
31   [2005] EWCA Crim 2016.
32   (1974) 58 Cr App R 348.
33   [2006] UKHL 39.
34   [2007] EWCA Crim 2869.

provide powerful grounds of appeal. However, it should never be assumed that such errors will automatically lead the Court to conclude that the conviction is unsafe. If the judge has not provided the correct wording in a particular passage, the Court will look to the summing up as a whole to see whether it provided the jury with the appropriate guidance. Even in those cases where it failed to do so, the Court is likely to consider whether, in the circumstances of the case, there is a real risk that it leads the jury to adopt the wrong approach.

The significance of 'specimen directions'

3.37　The Court of Appeal has made it clear that the specimen directions are not blueprints that must be slavishly followed (*R v Millard*[35]). In the forward to the *Judicial Studies Board Crown Court Bench Book* (2010), the Lord Chief Justice placed increased emphasis on the importance of the judge crafting his or her own directions:

> 'We are all familiar with the so-called "specimen directions" for juries. We read of them in the news. We hear much about them in the Court of Appeal. And, of course, we use them in the Crown Court. But the great value of the specimen direction has also the potential to be a weakness. What was intended to provide guidance and assistance to judges has, on many occasions, to all intents and purposes, operated as if judges were bound by them when they were preparing their summing up and sometimes the specimen directions have been incanted mechanistically and without any sufficient link with the case being tried.
>
> In this Benchbook, the objective has been to move away from the perceived rigidity of specimen directions towards a fresh emphasis on the responsibility of the individual judge, in an individual case, to craft directions appropriate to that case.'

3.38　It is clear from this that a failure to follow the specimen directions that are contained in the Bench Book will not itself render a direction defective. A direction will be defective only to the extent that it fails to clearly and accurately set out the relevant law as the jury should apply it (*R v Keene*[36]).

Grounds in relation to the jury

Jury selection

3.39　Irregularities in the selection of the jury may give rise to an appeal. In certain circumstances the failure to follow the correct procedure for jury

---

35　[2003] EWCA Crim 3629.
36　[2010] EWCA Crim 2514, para 20.

selection may render the trial a nullity, leading to the issue of the writ of *venire de novo* (*R v Tarrant*[37]). See 3.82–3.83 below, on retrials and *venire de novo*.

Allegations of jury misconduct

3.40   It has been known for a convicted person, their family or lawyers to be contacted by former jurors who express disquiet at what took place in the jury room. If this occurs, those taking a statement from the former juror are in danger of committing an offence if they pose questions whose answers would breach section 8 of the Contempt of Court Act 1981, which prohibits the disclosure of a jury's deliberations. The Courts are not subject to that section and can authorise enquiries; see *R v Thompson*.[38] However, evidence in relation to jury deliberations is inadmissible unless the juror's approach involves a complete repudiation of his or her oath to try the case on the evidence or involves extraneous material being introduced into jury deliberations. It is therefore only in one of these two circumstances that jury deliberations can form a ground of appeal.

3.41   The sensible course for any lawyer coming into possession of complaints about the jury's deliberations from former jurors is to swiftly contact the Registrar to seek guidance and to draft grounds of appeal in reliance on what they have already, then allow the Court to control any further investigations.

3.42   If grounds are drafted based on a former juror's account, the Court may ask the Criminal Cases Review Commission to undertake enquires by tracing the whole jury and taking statements from them. It should not be assumed that these enquiries will be made as a matter of course; in *R v Baybasin*[39] the Lord Chief Justice stated that where a complaint is first raised after verdict, the Court will assume that any genuine problem would have been raised before, and will therefore not order enquiries to be made in the absence of any other 'strong and compelling evidence'.

3.43   Even after an investigation, the Court may be wary of relying on the allegations made by former jurors when those matters were not raised at trial. Usually, the Court will proceed on the basis that a complaint made by a juror after a trial is simply a protest against a verdict with which he disagreed (see *R v Lewis*[40]). Similarly, a juror who assented to a verdict but then swiftly said he or she harboured doubts was found to have no basis to allow an appeal; second thoughts after conviction were not, said the Court, relevant, see *R v Ul*

---

37   [1998] Crim LR 342.
38   [2010] EWCA Crim 1623.
39   [2013] EWCA Crim 2357.
40   [2013] EWCA Crim 776.

Hamid and Khan.[41] All this said, the reservations expressed by the Court are never in absolute terms. If a former juror is able to produce a powerful account such as casts doubt on the safety of the verdict, and if he or she has a credible explanation for not raising the matter during the trial, such later complaints can be the foundation for an appeal.

Possible jury bias

3.44   Allegations of jury bias will often not require investigation into what occurred in the jury room. That is because the Court's starting point is to consider the appearance of potential bias.

3.45   The Court will consider whether 'the fair minded and informed observer having considered the facts would conclude that there was a real possibility that the jury were biased' (*Porter v Magill; Weeks v Magill*[42]).

Adverse publicity

3.46   The Court takes the view that jurors know their duty and will be robust in disregarding what they have read or viewed in the media; see the trial direction of Hughes J, as he then was, later cited with approval by the Court in *R v Abu Hamza*.[43] The cases where appeals founded on adverse publicity have met with any success have almost all been where the publicity was during the trial and was focused on the facts of the case itself or had a direct and obvious link, such as *R v McCann*[44] and *R v Taylor*.[45]

Fresh evidence

3.47   The Court has the power to receive fresh evidence after a conviction where it is in the interests of justice to do so. The considerations that the Court must have regard to are set out in section 23(2)(a)–(d) of CAA 1968 and are:

(a)   whether the evidence is capable of belief;

(b)   whether the evidence may afford any ground for allowing the appeal;

(c)   whether the evidence would have been admissible at trial; and

(d)   whether there is a reasonable explanation for the failure to adduce that evidence at trial.

---

41   [2016] 2 Cr App R 29.
42   [2001] UKHL 67.
43   [2006] EWCA Crim 2918.
44   (1991) 92 Cr App R 239.
45   (1994) 98 Cr App R 361.

3.48   The Court has emphasised that the application of these considerations is highly fact sensitive but that all four need to be addressed in any application (see *R v Erskine*[46]). In the same case, Lord Judge CJ said at para 39: 'the considerations … are neither exhaustive nor conclusive'.

3.49   The most usual occasions in which one might seek to adduce fresh evidence that does not meet all the section 23 criteria, however, is where there is no sound reason why the evidence was not called at trial (usually an application to adduce such evidence will also be accompanied by criticism of trial lawyers for failing to adduce, see below). This is not to say that the Court encourages such applications, but the comment by Lord Judge in *Erskine* confirms that the considerations are not prerequisites and so fresh evidence can be received if it is in the interests of justice to do so even where they are not met [though it is hard to think of a case wherein the Court would admit evidence that failed to meet the section 23(2)(b) consideration, as there could be no point in doing so].

3.50   The Court has also made clear that it will normally not allow an appellant to run a different case on appeal from the one advanced at trial. For example in *R v H*,[47] Lord Justice Judge, as he then was, said at para 82: 'It follows that this court will only permit an appellant to present a factual case inconsistent with his instructions and sworn testimony at the trial at which he was convicted in the most exceptional circumstances'.

3.51   It is obvious from all the above that the Court is eager not to encourage convicted defendants from trying to appeal by acquiring and deploying further evidence. All that said, when a convicted person or their legal advisors have compelling evidence that suggests he may be innocent of the offence, this type of application for leave to appeal should be pursued. The test that the Court has to apply in determining whether a conviction is unsafe in the light of fresh evidence is considered above at 3.9–3.12. The procedures for doing so are considered in at 6.31.

Errors of defence lawyers

3.52   Allegations that the defendant's trial lawyers committed serious errors in the conduct of the defence case can provide a perfectly sound basis for an appeal, but there are three important things to bear in mind. First, the trial lawyers have to be given the chance to explain how they conducted the case. Secondly, the Court will require clear evidence of fault before this ground succeeds, and thirdly (as always), the Court must determine whether the errors make the conviction unsafe.

---

46   [2009] EWCA Crim 1425.
47   [2002] EWCA Crim 730.

3.53   There is no one method for seeking the views of trial lawyers, as long as it is done fully and fairly, but when an appeal relies on any criticism of trial lawyers, it is crucial to ask focused questions that fully explore the issue that is being advanced on appeal, see *R v Grant-Murray*[48]. The applicant will have to waive privilege and the trial lawyers need to be given a clear indication of what questions are being asked of them and what criticisms are being made. The practicalities of obtaining a waiver and communicating with previous representatives are considered at 6.13–6.14.

3.54   If the reply by the trial team conflicts with the applicant's account of what took place, the Court is likely to prefer the lawyers' recollections unless there are contemporaneous records that contradict them. So obtaining as many of the trial notes and papers as possible is always a good idea.

3.55   Historically, the Court made clear that the decisions of trial lawyers made in good faith after proper consideration of the competing arguments and, where appropriate, after consultation with the defendant, would not make a verdict unsafe even though the Court disagreed with that decision. On the other hand, if a decision was taken in defiance of, or without, proper instruction, or when 'all promptings of reason and common sense pointed the other way', that may render a conviction unsafe (see *R v Clinton*[49]).

3.56   In more recent cases based on the failings of trial lawyers, the Court has moved away from any test of incompetence and instead focused on the single statutory test of safety (see *R v Day*[50]).

3.57   However, *Day* has not altered the Court's traditionally cautious approach to criticism of former representatives. It tends to be robust in finding that trial lawyers who take decisions in the heat of a trial are not to be criticised unless those decisions were very clearly flawed. It is wary of applying the benefit of hindsight to difficult forensic decisions.

3.58   The final requirement is that the failings of the trial lawyers have the effect of making the conviction unsafe. These would have to be major and significant events in the case, for example not calling powerful alibi evidence or not advising the defendant properly about the advantages of giving evidence. Without such a connection, there can be very serious problems with the trial lawyers but no successful appeal will result. In a spectacular example of this principle in action, the Court found that two murder convictions were safe even though trial counsel was under investigation for serious sexual offences and the supply of class A drugs, and was also made bankrupt whilst simultaneously conducting two trials in different parts of the country. In rejecting the appeal,

---

48   [2017] EWCA Crim 1228.
49   (1993) 97 Cr App R 320.
50   [2003] EWCA Crim 1060.

the Court reviewed not only the manner in which the advocate conducted the trials but also the strength of the evidence (which in the case of both appellants was overwhelming) (*R v Bolivar; R v Lee*[51]). While this may be very unlikely to occur, the appellate courts have suggested the possibility of representation being so disastrous that the subsequent conviction should be overturned regardless of safety, as the effect had been to deprive the convicted person of any sort of due process, see *Boodram v The State*.[52]

Changes in the law

3.59   Changes in the law since conviction may provide grounds of appeal but only if this change has given rise to substantial injustice (*R v R (Amer)*[53]). This has been applied very robustly indeed; when the Supreme Court changed the *mens rea* for a joint enterprise in *R v Jogee*,[54] the Court of Appeal 'applie'" the 'substantial injustice' test in such robust terms in *R v Johnson and others*[55] as to lead to minuscule number of subsequent successful appeals.

Categories not closed

3.60   As made clear at the start of this chapter, there is but one test: whether the conviction under appeal is 'unsafe'. If an event occurs at trial that proffers a basis for arguing it rendered the conviction unsafe, no lawyer should be put off initiating an appeal just because there seems to be little precedent. A striking example occurred in *R v Simpson*[56]: In a finely balanced case where, on one view, the complainant may have made allegation of rape as she was so upset by the defendant's callous behaviour on the occasion of her first sexual encounter. The jury were visibly repelled by defence counsel's closing speech which included 'Life was not a Mills and Boon novel and many women would rather forget the occasion when they lost their virginity up against a wall in a back alley'. Prosecution counsel noted: 'I could feel the antagonism of the jury to the way this point was expressed'. Faced with a weak case with troubling features and an extraordinarily ill-judged speech, the Court allowed the appeal.

THE COURT'S POWERS

3.61   The Court may either allow or dismiss an appeal. If it allows the appeal it must quash the conviction. Unless it orders a re-trial the effect of the

---

51   [2003] EWCA Crim 1167.
52   [2002] 1 Cr App R 103.
53   [2006] EWCA Crim 1974.
54   [2016] UKSC 8.
55   [2016] EWCA Crim 1613.
56   [2001] EWCA Crim 468.

conviction being quashed is to require the Crown Court to record a judgment and verdict of acquittal.

3.62   If the Court quashes a conviction it is not required to make any further order. However, it may:

(a)   substitute the conviction with a conviction for an alternative offence upon which he could have been convicted in the Crown Court; or

(b)   order that a re-trial take place; or

(c)   re-sentence the appellant in respect of related convictions for which the sentence was not quashed.

3.63   Although CAA 1968 does not expressly frame these as alternatives, it would be difficult to see how they could be fairly combined.

Substituting a conviction

3.64   Where a defendant was convicted of a particular count but might, on the same evidence, have been convicted on an alternative count, the Court of Appeal has the power to substitute the conviction of one offence for a conviction for another.[57]

3.65   In *R v Graham*[58] the Court held that the power could only be exercised when the following criteria were met:

(a)   The jury could, on the indictment, have found the appellant guilty of some other offence, because the allegation in the count of which the appellant was convicted expressly or impliedly included this other count.

(b)   By their verdict of guilty on the count that is subject to appeal, the jury must also have been satisfied of the facts that rendered the appellant guilty of this other offence.

3.66   The Court must impose a sentence for the new count but that sentence cannot be so long as to increase the overall length of sentence above that which was imposed in the Crown Court.

---

57   CAA 1968, s 3 in respect of offences for which he was convicted by a jury, s 3A in respect of offences to which the appellant had originally pleaded guilty.
58   (1997) 1 Cr App R 302.

Re-trials

The circumstances in which a re-trial can be ordered

3.67   The test for whether to order a re-trial is whether it is in the interests of justice to do so.[59] This may involve consideration of a number of factors. The following are commonly considered by the Court:

(a)   how much of the original sentence the appellant has already served;

(b)   the seriousness of the offence;

(c)   the time that elapsed since the commission of the offence and any particular difficulties that the passage of time may cause the parties in now conducting the case;

(d)   whether the appeal was allowed as a result of errors in the original trial which can be easily remedied at a re-trial (for example, errors in the legal directions that were provided to the jury) or whether difficulties in the original trial are likely to be present in any future trial (for example, abuse of process caused by delay, inherent weakness in the prosecution's case); and

(e)   personal circumstances of the appellant (for example, age or poor health).

3.68   The type of convictions that may be subject to a retrial are set out in s 7(2):

'(2)   A person shall not under this section be ordered to be retried for any offence other than –

(a)   the offence of which he was convicted at the original trial and in respect of which his appeal is allowed as mentioned in subsection (1) above;

(b)   an offence of which he could have been convicted at the original trial on an indictment for the first-mentioned offence; or

(c)   an offence charged in an alternative count of the indictment in respect of which the jury were discharged from giving a verdict in consequence of convicting him of the first-mentioned offence.'

The procedure for making an order for re-trial

3.69   Whether to order a re-trial is a matter for the Court. There is no statutory requirement for an application for a re-trial to have been made before the Court

---

59   CAA 1968, s 7(1).

makes an order. However, it will usually only make it upon application of the prosecution. Therefore, the Court will expect the advocate who is appearing on behalf of the prosecution to have been provided instructions on this point prior to the appeal hearing. The defence advocate should be prepared to make submissions on the matter at the conclusion of the hearing.

3.70   If prosecuting counsel does not have instructions, the Court may put the matter back in order for him to do so. If it puts the case back to a future date for a final hearing to formally pronounce judgment and determine whether to allow a re-trial, it may consider whether to grant bail in the interim.

3.71   Once the decision of the Court to quash the conviction is formally recorded in the Crown Court as an acquittal, the Court of Appeal has no power to order a re-trial. Even if the application for a re-trial is made before this takes place, if by the time that the Court comes to consider the application the verdict of acquittal has been entered, the Court has no power to grant the application prosecution (*R v Blackwood*[60]).

The procedure once an order for re-trial is made

3.72   Once a re-trial is ordered the defendant must be arraigned on a new indictment that has been preferred by direction of the Court of Appeal, in the Crown Court. Arraignment must take place within two months of the order having been made.[61]

3.73   If it is does not take place within two months, it may only take place if the prosecution applies to the Court of Appeal for leave for arrangement to take place and the Court is satisfied both that:

(a)   'The prosecution has acted with all due expedition'; and

(b)   'That there is good and sufficient cause for a retrial' in spite of the lapse of time since the order for a retrial was made.[62]

3.74   The Court may list the matter for legal argument. If it is not satisfied that both conditions are made out, the Court will direct that an order for acquittal be recorded by the Crown Court.

3.75   When it makes an order for a re-trial, the Court has power to grant bail or order that the defendant be remanded in custody.[63] In practice, the Court of Appeal will often direct that any bail application should be made to the

---

60   [2012] EWCA Crim 390.
61   CAA 1968, s 8(2).
62   CAA 1968, s 8(1B)(b).
63   Section 8(2).

relevant Crown Court. Once an indictment is preferred in the Crown Court, any applications in relation to bail must be made to the Crown Court itself. The position during the period between an order being made and an indictment being preferred is unclear. However, there is dicta in *R v X*[64] to suggest that the Crown Court does have the power to deal with bail after an order for re-trial was made.

3.76   Once the Crown Court is seized of the matter it has the power to amend the indictment. However, when considering the fairness of any application to amend, the Crown Court must take into account that the purpose of the order made by the Court of Appeal is to allow the defendant to be retried for the offences that they originally faced, not tried for new matters (*R v Booker*[65]).

3.77   The key limitation upon the power of the Crown Court is that a sentence that is passed in respect of a conviction that was secured following a re-trial may not be more severe than the sentence that was originally imposed by the Crown Court.[66] There is dicta to suggest that when a defendant originally pleaded guilty, successfully appealed their conviction, but then was convicted by a jury, a sentence that was longer than that which was originally imposed (to take account of the fact a discount was originally made to reflect the guilty plea) may not necessarily be regarded as 'more severe' (*R v Skanes*[67]).

3.78   A sentence of imprisonment that is imposed following a re-trial takes effect as if it was imposed on the date of the original sentence. However, time spent on bail following an order for re-trial and time in custody before trial that would not have been counted towards the original sentence is to be deducted from this period.[68]

3.79   Legal aid to cover the re-trial is not granted by the Court of Appeal. Instead, an application must be made to the Legal Aid Agency.

Re-sentencing

3.80   If the appellant was convicted of two or more offences on an indictment, the Court may re-sentence him in respect of those remaining sentences.[69] The power is often exercised to reduce the remaining sentences to take account in the reduction in the total level of criminality following the quashing of a conviction. But the Court may impose harsher sentences for the

---

64   [2010] EWCA Crim 2367.
65   [2011] EWCA Crim 7.
66   By virtue of CAA 1968, Sch 2, para 2(1).
67   [2006] EWCA Crim 2309.
68   CAA 1968, Sch 2, para 2(3).
69   CAA 1968, s 4.

remaining offences than were originally imposed, including for an offence for which no separate penalty was originally imposed *(R v Dolan*[70]*)*.

3.81 However, the Court may not impose a sentence that would have the effect of rendering the overall length of sentence longer than the overall length of sentence which was originally imposed in the Crown Court.[71]

Retrial and venire de novo

3.82 In a case in which the Court finds that there was never a valid conviction, because the proceedings were so irregular so as not to constitute a proper trial, it may make an order for *venire do novo*. The effect of this is to require proceedings to start again in the Crown Court, with the original 'conviction' set aside. If the Court makes such a finding, any re-trial is free of the procedural constraints in respect of re-trials under section 7 of CAA 1968.

3.83 A writ of *venire* may be issued where the proceedings were not properly commenced or the verdict was not returned by a properly constituted jury. It may also be available in respect of other fundamental procedural errors that render the trial a nullity.

SUMMARY OF KEY POINTS

- In determining appeals against conviction the Court applies the single statutory test of whether the conviction is 'unsafe'.

- A conviction that was obtained following a trial that was fundamentally unfair will usually be considered unsafe regardless of the strength of the evidence. However, not every unfairness that occurs during trial will render a conviction unsafe. In most instances the Court will consider the impact that the error or other unfairness may have had on the verdict of the jury.

- In relation to appeals that turn on fresh evidence the Court has emphasised that the jury impact test may assist the Court but it was ultimately for the Court itself to assess the potential impact of the evidence in question.

- The Court may be prepared to allow an appeal on the basis of its 'lurking doubt', in the absence of other grounds, in the most exceptional of circumstances.

- There are a limited number of circumstances in which a conviction may be appealed following a guilty plea. They include when the plea was

---

70   (1976) 62 Cr App R 36.
71   CAA 1968, s 4(3).

entered following incorrect legal advice that went to the heart of the decision to plead guilty.

- A procedural error may form the basis for grounds of appeal. However, unless the error was of such a serious nature that it rendered the proceedings a nullity, it will usually be necessary to show that it caused serious prejudice to the defence in the conduct of the trial.

- A wrongful trial ruling may provide grounds of appeal. However, the ruling must have been clearly wrong or unreasonable, not merely a ruling that the Court would not itself have made.

- The failure of the defence representative may give rise to grounds of appeal. But they must be given the opportunity to answer any criticism and the Court will distinguish between genuine error and criticism of tactical decisions made with the benefit of hindsight. Any proven or admitted failure must have had the effect of rendering the conviction unsafe.

- If fresh evidence is relied on, the considerations of section 23 of CAA 1968 must be addressed though not all need be met.

- If the Court allows the appeal and quashes the conviction it may, in certain circumstances, substitute a conviction for another offence or re-sentence the defendant for any offences that remain on the indictment or order a re-trial.

- If a re-trial is ordered, arraignment must take place within two months. Any application to extend this time must be made to the Court of Appeal.

- If the defendant is convicted following a re-trial, any sentence imposed may not be more severe than the sentence that was originally imposed.

Chapter 4

Appeals against sentence

INTRODUCTION

4.1   Under sections 9 and 10 of the Criminal Appeal Act 1968, a defendant may appeal to the Court of Appeal against any sentence that was imposed by the Crown Court on indictment and, in certain circumstances, against sentences imposed by the Crown Court, following a conviction in the Magistrates' Court. The rules regulating the bringing of an appeal against sentence are to be found in the Criminal Procedure Rules 2015, Parts 36 and 39 (and Part 42 in relation to confiscation orders) and in the Criminal Practice Direction 2015, Division X. Regard should also be had to the 'Guide to commencing proceedings in the Court of Appeal Criminal Division'[1] published by HM Courts & Tribunals Service.

4.2   The right of appeal against sentence is subject to leave being granted by the Court of Appeal[2] or otherwise a certificate being issued by the sentencing judge stating that the case is fit for appeal.[3]

By section 11 of the Criminal Appeal Act 1968 the Court of Appeal has the following powers when determining appeals against sentence:

'(3) On an appeal against sentence the Court of Appeal, if they consider that the appellant should be sentenced differently for an offence for which he was dealt with by the court below may –

(a)   quash any sentence or order which is the subject of the appeal; and

(b)   in place of it pass such sentence or make such order as they think appropriate for the case and as the court below had power to pass or make when dealing with him for the offence;

but the Court shall so exercise their powers under this subsection that, taking the case as a whole, the appellant is not more severely dealt with on appeal than he was dealt with by the court below.'

---

1   August 2018.
2   Section 11(1) Criminal Appeal Act 1968.
3   Section 11(1A) Criminal Appeal Act 1968.

4.3   The injunction upon the Court not to impose a more severe sentence than that which was originally imposed is clear and unequivocal. The Court cannot even impose a sentence that would be mandatory for a sentencing Court to impose (*R v Reynolds*[4]). However, whether a sentence is 'more severe' than the sentence that was the subject of appeal is not always clear. A life sentence cannot be imposed in place of a determinate sentence (*R v Whittaker*[5]). However, in *R v Bennett*,[6] the Court held that a hospital order with a restriction with an indefinite period in place of a determinate sentence, was not more severe than a determinate sentence.

4.4   In order to understand how the Court employs its powers it is necessary to turn from the statute to the body of principles that it has developed. The grounds upon which the Court may be prepared to allow an appeal against sentence overlap and the terms are not always used consistently. The precise classification of grounds is less important than ensuring that the grounds clearly and succinctly identify why the sentence is wrong, by applying the underlying principles to the facts of the case.

4.5   This chapter therefore considers the types of orders that can be appealed as sentences and then sets out the principles to be applied to such appeals. There are distinct principles and powers in relation to appeals against confiscation orders. Therefore, confiscation orders are considered separately in the latter part of the chapter. However, because of the wide range of orders which may be appealed as appeals against sentence, the principles that the Court has developed in relation to appeals against confiscation orders may well also be applicable to other sentence appeals.

APPEAL AGAINST SENTENCE ON INDICTMENT AND FOR CASES SENT FROM THE MAGISTRATES' COURT

4.6   The Court may hear appeals against sentences imposed in the Crown Court following a conviction on indictment. It may also hear appeals against sentence for summary offences that had been sent to the Crown Court for trial under section 41 of the Criminal Justice Act 1988 (power of Crown Court to deal with summary offence where person committed for either way offence) or under paragraph 6 of Schedule 3 to the Crime and Disorder Act 1998 (power of Crown Court to deal with summary offence where person sent for trial for indictable-only offence).[7]

---

4   [2007] EWCA Crim 538.
5   [1967] Crim LR 431.
6   (1968) 52 Cr App R 514.
7   CAA 1968, s 9(b).

4.7   In addition, pursuant to section 10 CAA 1968 the Court may also hear appeals against sentence for other offences sent from the Magistrates' Court in various circumstances.

What counts as a sentence?

4.8   Section 50 of CAA 1968 provides:

'(1) In this Act "sentence", in relation to an offence, includes any order made by a court when dealing with an offender including, in particular –

(a)   a hospital order under Part III of the Mental Health Act 1983, with or without a restriction order;

(b)   an interim hospital order under that Part;

(bb)   a hospital direction and a limitation direction under that Part;

(c)   a recommendation for deportation;

(ca)   a confiscation order under Part 2 of the Proceeds of Crime Act 2002 (but not a determination under section 10A of that Act);

(cb)   an order which varies a confiscation order made under Part 2 of the Proceeds of Crime Act 2002 if the varying order is made under section 21, 22 or 29 of that Act (but not otherwise);

(d)   a confiscation order under the Drug Trafficking Act 1994 other than one made by the High Court;

(e)   a confiscation order under Part VI of the Criminal Justice Act 1988;

(f)   an order varying a confiscation order of a kind which is included by virtue of paragraph (d) or (e) above;

(g)   an order made by the Crown Court varying a confiscation order which was made by the High Court by virtue of section 19 of the Act of 1994; and

(h)   a declaration of relevance within the meaning of section 23 of the Football Spectators Act 1989; and

(i)   an order under section 129(2) of the Licensing Act 2003 (forfeiture or suspension of personal licence).

(1A) Section 14 of the Powers of Criminal Courts (Sentencing) Act 2000 (under which a conviction of an offence for which ... an order for conditional or absolute discharge is made is deemed not to be a conviction except for certain purposes) shall not prevent an appeal under this Act, whether against conviction or otherwise.'

4.9   Since the list at section 50 is not exhaustive, the Court has had to consider whether a number of other orders are sentences.

Costs

4.10   Section 50(3) specifically provides that an order for recovery of defence costs under section 17 of the Access to Justice Act 1999 is not a sentence within the meaning of section 9. However, an order that the defendant pay towards the costs of the prosecution is a sentence within the meaning of the section and may therefore be appealed (*R v Hayden*[8]).

Criminal behaviour orders

4.11   The making of a criminal behaviour order following conviction is a sentence within the meaning of section 50 as is a subsequent decision of the Crown Court to vary or refuse an application to vary the order (*R v Preston Crown Court, ex p Langley*[9]).

Making and varying of sexual offences prevention orders

4.12   The making of a sexual offences prevention order and also a subsequent decision of the Crown Court in relation to varying such an order is a sentence within the meaning of section 50 (*R v Hoath; R v Standage,*[10] approved in *R v Aldridge; R v Eaton*[11]).

Restraining orders

4.13   A restraining order that is made following conviction is clearly within the scope of section 50. However, by virtue of section 5A(5) of the Protection from Harassment Act 1997, so too is a restraining order that is made following an acquittal.

Financial reporting orders

4.14   Financial reporting orders are sentences for the purposes of section 50 (*R v Geraghty*[12]).

Appeals in relation to sentences fixed by law

4.15   A defendant who is the subject of a mandatory life sentence may appeal against the minimum term that he must serve.

---

8   (1974) 60 Cr App R 304.
9   [2008] EWHC 2623 (Admin).
10   [2011] EWCA Crim 274.
11   [2012] EWCA Crim 1456.
12   [2017] 1 Cr App R (S) 10.

Appeals by parents and guardians

4.16 Parents and guardians may appeal against:

(a) an order that they pay a fine, costs or compensation that has been imposed on a child or young person (Powers of Criminal Courts (Sentencing) Act 2000, s 137 (1));

(b) an order, under section 150 of the Powers of Criminal Courts (Sentencing) Act 2000 that they enter into a recognisance to take proper care of a child or to pay a fine in lieu;

(c) a parenting order made pursuant to section 8 of the Crime and Disorder Act 1889 (s 10(4)).

A single right of appeal – more than one sentence

4.17 There is a single right of appeal against sentence (*R v Pinfold*[13]). A defendant cannot appeal against a particular aspect of their sentence and then separately appeal against another[14], unless the case is referred back to the Court by the Criminal Cases Review Commission.

4.18 The significant exception to this relates to orders that are made on different dates as separate sentencing exercises. This occurs mainly in relation to confiscation orders, which may be made weeks or months after the original sentence was imposed. It will also apply to appeals against refusals to vary orders that were made on an earlier occasion. The 28-day time limit will run from the date when the order that is subject to appeal is made.

THE PRINCIPLES: GENERAL

What are the grounds of appeal?

4.19 The grounds upon which the Court has been prepared to allow appeals against sentence are numerous and overlapping. The terminology with which the Court describes sentencing grounds is not always consistently used. The most well-known terms are 'manifestly excessive or wrong in principle'. Although it may be said that the two terms themselves overlap (see *R v Ball*[15]), their meaning is sufficiently clear and broad to capture the variety of grounds that may be advanced. The Court will regard a sentence as manifestly excessive if it is improperly severe as a result, for example, of the judge having failed to

---

13 (1988) 87 Cr App R 15.

14 *R v Geraghty* [2016] EWCA Crim 1523.

15 (1951) 35 Cr App R 164.

apply the relevant guidelines, given too much weight to an aggravating feature or too little weight to a guilty plea or some piece of mitigation. A sentence may be wrong in principle if it was wrong for some other reason: if, for example, it was unlawful, or passed following a procedural failure, breach of legitimate expectation or some other important sentencing principle.

4.20 It may be helpful, therefore, for the grounds of appeal to state whether the sentence is challenged on the basis that it is manifestly excessive or wrong in principle. However, it is far more important that the grounds should go on to state clearly and succinctly exactly why it is said that the sentence is wrong. An appeal against sentence will not fail because the grounds have been misclassified. However, leave to appeal is often refused because the nature of the challenge is simply unclear.

Manifestly excessive

4.21 The term 'manifestly excessive' tends to induce a high degree of caution in the minds of many advocates. If this caution is based on a correct understanding of the term then it is justified. It is intended to exclude those sentences in which different judges might disagree. The Court often states that the test is not whether they would have passed the same sentence but whether it is outside the range that could properly be imposed for the offence.

4.22 However, it is sometimes understood that the term 'manifestly excessive' means very or significantly excessive. It does not. If a sentence can be shown to be clearly outside that range, whether by a substantial or limited period, it is manifestly excessive.

4.23 It is right that the Court does not 'tinker' with sentences, but if a custodial sentence is manifestly excessive by months or even, in the case of shorter sentences, by weeks, then a reduction in sentence by months or weeks will hardly be considered 'tinkering' by the person who has to serve it or by a fair-minded tribunal.

4.24 Whether a sentence is manifestly excessive will depend on the facts of each case. However, the following general principles apply:

The Court will consider whether the total sentence is wrong

4.25 When a defendant is sentenced for a number of offences, the Court of Appeal is generally concerned with the correctness of the overarching sentence (the total length of the sentences imposed in a single sentencing exercise) that was imposed (*R v Razaq*[16]). So, if it can be shown that an individual sentence

---

16   [2011] EWCA Crim 1518.

was excessive but the overarching sentence was correct, an application for leave is likely to be refused.

Failure to follow the guidelines

4.26 When it passes sentence for an offence that was committed before 6 April 2010, the Crown Court must have regard to any sentencing guideline that was promulgated by the Sentencing Guidelines Council.[17]

4.27 However, when the offence in question was committed after that date, the Court is bound by the stronger injunction of section 125(1) of the Coroners and Justice Act 2009 which provides:

'Every court –

(a) must, in sentencing an offender, follow any sentencing guidelines which are relevant to the offender's case, and

(b) must, in exercising any other function relating to the sentencing of offenders, follow any sentencing guidelines which are relevant to the function,

unless the court is satisfied that it would be contrary to the interests of justice to do so.'

4.28 The effect of this is that if the Crown Court fails to follow the applicable guideline without giving good reason for doing so or if it applies them incorrectly, this may provide a ground for appeal (*R v Mahendran*[18]). However, the sentencing judge is free to apply the guidelines in a flexible manner in order to achieve a just result:

'we have lost count of the number of times when this court has emphasised that these provisions are not intended to be applied inflexibly. Indeed, in our judgment, an inflexible approach would be inconsistent with the terms of the statutory framework ... even when the approach to the sentencing decision is laid down in an apparently detailed and on the face of it intentionally comprehensive scheme, the sentencing judge must achieve a just result.' (*R v Height and Anderson*[19])

4.29 The existence of a specific guideline will supersede previous Court of Appeal case law. However, section 125 has not diminished the weight to be attached to decisions of the Court of Appeal. Therefore the sentencing Court

---

17 CJA 2003, s 172, as preserved by the Coroners and Justice Act 2009 (Commencement No 4, Transitional and Saving Provisions) Order 2010 (SI 2010/816).
18 [2011] EWCA Crim 608.
19 [2008] EWCA Crim 2500 at para 29.

should take into account any significant sentencing guidance that is contained in authorities of the Court of Appeal that post-date the relevant guideline.

> 'The "interests of justice" consideration which now, and we assume always has and always will underpin the work of the Sentencing Guidelines Council (now the Sentencing Council), undoubtedly involves consideration of the subsequent thinking of this court and of the legislature on sentencing issues which may impact on every original definitive guidance. Just as the guidelines are not tramlines – an observation made time and time again – nor are they ring-fenced.' (*R v Thornley*[20])

4.30   The role of the Court of Appeal is to interpret the guidelines and provide practical illustrations of their operation, including examples where departure from them might be appropriate (*Dyer*[21]).

4.31   A distinction should be drawn between authorities that have an impact upon the guidelines and those cases which merely apply the guidelines to the facts of the case. Advocates should recall the injunction of the Court in *Erskine*[22] about the citation of cases which are merely fact specific. In *Thelwall*[23] the Court of Appeal made it plain that the sentencing system now proceeds on the basis of guidelines, not case law, and so the citation before the Court of Appeal of appellate decisions which were simply illustrations of the operation of a sentencing guideline on particular facts was unlikely to be of assistance. The only exception to that principle was where the Court had said something to clarify the terms of the guideline.

Procedural unfairness

4.32   A failure to follow the proper procedures may provide grounds of appeal. However, the general approach of the Court is to decline to interfere with a sentence where, had the correct procedures been followed, the sentence that would have been imposed would have been essentially the same.

Post-sentence developments

4.33   The Court is not confined to considering only the material to which the sentencing judge had access. It may, in its discretion, consider material that was not before the Court or events that have occurred since the sentence took place. The appellant's conduct following sentence will often play an important part in the sentencing process. If leave is granted, the Court may ask for a

---

20 [2011] EWCA Crim 153.
21 [2014] 2 Cr App R (S) 11 (61).
22 [2010] EWCA Crim 1425.
23 [2016] EWCA Crim 1755.

report from the prison on the appellant's progress on their sentence. The Court can order its own probation report in cases where it is of the view that it may be assisted by one, even if there was no probation report in the lower court.

4.34   In *Rogers*[24] the Court of Appeal emphasised the limitations on the use of new material in appeals against sentence. The material the Court will hear without an application under the Criminal Appeal Act 1968, s 23 for the court to admit 'fresh evidence' will include updated pre-sentence and prison reports on conduct in prison after sentence. However, it will not include fresh psychiatric or psychological evidence in support of an argument that a finding of dangerousness ought not to have been made or a hospital order should have been made. If an appellant seeks to introduce material of that type, the Court will apply the provisions of s 23.

Disparity in sentence

4.35   An unjustified disparity in sentence between co-defendants may give rise to grounds of appeal but only if 'right thinking members of the public with knowledge of the relevant facts and circumstances, learning of this sentence would consider that something had gone wrong with the administration of justice' (*R v Fawcett*[25]).

Unlawful sentences and the slip rule

4.36   When the Crown Court passes a sentence that is unlawful, in the sense that the Court does not have the power to impose it, the sentence may be appealed. However, consideration should first be given to returning to the Crown Court under the slip rule and asking the sentencing judge to correct the error. Section 155 of the Powers of the Criminal Courts (Sentencing) Act 2000 provides that a sentence that was imposed by the Crown Court can be 'varied or rescinded' up to 56 days from the date when the sentence was passed.

4.37   It is only if the judge refuses, wrongly, to correct the error or the matter is not listed within the time limit for correction that an appeal to the Court of Appeal should be lodged.

4.38   In a case where there are other grounds of appeal, it may be tempting to bypass the Crown Court entirely and have all matters dealt with on appeal. However, the time limit for appeal runs from the date of any variation[26] so nothing is lost by resolving such matters that can be resolved in the Crown Court.

---

24   [2016] 2 Cr App R (S) 36 (370).
25   (1983) 5 Cr App R (S) 158.
26   Powers of the Criminal Courts (Sentencing) Act 2000, s 155(6).

Failure to credit time spent on a qualifying curfew

4.39   Although the sentencing judge is no longer required to specify the number of days spent on remand that should count towards sentence, he must still state the amount of time spent on a qualifying curfew.[27] If the judge fails, without good reason, to state the period on curfew that should be counted to towards the sentence or if the period was miscalculated, the approach outlined by the Court in *R v Gordon*[28] should be followed.

RIGHTS OF APPEAL: CONFISCATION ORDERS AND OTHER ORDERS UNDER THE ASSET RECOVERY LEGISLATION

4.40   Section 50 of CAA 1968 provides that an appeal against a confiscation order, whether under the Proceeds of Crime Act 2002 (POCA 2002) or the Drug Trafficking Act 1994 (except when the order has been made by a High Court judge) or the Criminal Justice Act 1988 is an appeal against sentence. However, there are a number of other orders that a Crown Court can make under this legislation, only some of which attract a right of appeal against sentence.

4.41   A refusal to vary a confiscation order under section 23 of POCA 2002 is not a sentence and there is no appeal to the Court of Appeal. Therefore, the only way such an order can be challenged is by way of judicial review. However, as section 50 provides, decisions in relation to a reconsideration of benefit and available amount (POCA 2002, ss. 21 and 22) and variations of orders made whilst the defendant was considered an absconder (s 29) under POCA 2002 are considered sentences.

4.42   In contrast, any variation or refusal to vary a confiscation order under the Drug Trafficking Act 1994 (except when the confiscation order has been made by a High Court judge) or the Criminal Justice Act 1988 is a sentence within the meaning of section 50.

4.43   Appeals against restraint or receivership orders under POCA are not appeals against sentence. However, they attract their own rights of appeal.[29]

---

27   Criminal Justice Act 2003, s 240A.
28   [2007] EWCA Crim 165.
29   The rights of Appeal in relation to receivership orders are to be found at POCA 2002, s 65.

PRINCIPLES: CONFISCATION

Grounds of appeal

4.44   There are no prescribed grounds of appeal against confiscation orders. Common grounds of appeal are that the judge erred in fact or law. The Court is often cautious about interfering with errors of fact, unless they are clear and significant. It normally accords considerable respect to factual findings of the Crown Court judge who heard the case, particularly if their judgment depends to a significant extent on assessment of live evidence that the judge heard in either the course of the confiscation hearing or the preceding trial.

The slip rule

4.45   Section 155 of the Powers of Criminal Courts (Sentencing) Act 2000 applies to confiscations orders (*R v Bukhari*[30]).

Fresh evidence

4.46   The statutory rules in relation to fresh evidence apply to confiscation proceedings (*R v Stroud*[31]). A party seeking to adduce fresh evidence must therefore meet the requirements of section 23 of CAA 1968. Much of the case law on fresh evidence in appeals against conviction is applicable to appeals against confiscation order.

Appeals against confiscation orders made by consent

4.47   In *R v Mackle*,[32] the Supreme Court held that a confiscation order that had been made with the consent of the defendant but following clearly erroneous legal advice may be appealed. This overturned the decision of the Court of Appeal in *R v Hirani*[33] in which the Court found that in the absence of exceptional circumstances a defendant was bound by an order to which he consented, even if that consent was based on an entirely incorrect understanding of what he was consenting to, following bad legal advice.

4.48   *Mackle* did not provide any guidance as to how the Court of Appeal should now approach appeals based upon allegations of consent being given as a result of flawed legal advice. However, it is likely that the Court will approach

---

30   [2008] EWCA Crim 2915.
31   [2004] EWCA Crim 1048.
32   [2014] UKSC 5.
33   [2008] EWCA Crim 1463.

in a similar manner to appeals against conviction in which it is argued that a guilty plea was tendered following bad legal advice.

Extension of time to appeal against a confiscation order following a change in the law

4.49   Following the judgment of the Supreme Court in *R v Waya*,[34] in which the Court held that the First Protocol of the Convention required the Crown Court to ensure that any confiscation order represents a proportionate interference with the defendant's property, a number of applications for extension of time within which to appeal against sentence were made by applicants whose confiscation order had been made some time ago and had not appealed because the law, prior to *Waya*, provided no grounds upon which to do so.

4.50   In *Bestel v R*,[35] the Court held that the principle of finality that decisions made under the law as it was then understood should not be disturbed unless this would cause substantial injustice, should be followed in confiscation cases.

POWERS OF THE COURT: CONFISCATION

4.51   The Court has the power under section 11(3) Criminal Appeal Act 1968 to impose an alternative sentence to that which was subject to appeal. However, it also has the power, under section 11(3A) to quash a confiscation order and then to remit the case to the Crown Court with a direction that a new confiscation hearing take place. When it does so, the Court of Appeal must give directions to the Crown Court as to the conduct of the new hearing. The Crown Court must not impose a confiscation order that is more severe than that which was subject to appeal.

PROSECUTION RIGHTS OF APPEAL IN CONFISCATION CASES

4.52   The prosecution enjoy rights of appeal against the terms of a confiscation order or the refusal to make a confiscation order under POCA 2002 only. Section 31 of POCA 2002 provides:

'(1)   If the Crown Court makes a confiscation order the prosecutor may appeal to the Court of Appeal in respect of the order.

---

34   [2012] UKSC 51.
35   [2013] EWCA Crim 1305.

(2)   If the Crown Court decides not to make a confiscation order the prosecutor may appeal to the Court of Appeal against the decision.

(3)   Subsections (1) and (2) do not apply to an order or decision made by virtue of section 10A, 19, 20, 27 or 28.'

4.53   As subsection (3) provides, the prosecution enjoy none of the rights of appeal against variations of a confiscation order that are enjoyed by the defence.

SUMMARY OF KEY POINTS

- The only statutory test on an appeal against sentence is whether 'the appellant should be sentenced differently for an offence'.

- The Court had recognised a number of grounds of appeal against sentence, the most well-established of which are that a sentence is 'manifestly excessive' or 'wrong in principle'. Between them these terms cover most of the types of arguments that can be advanced. However, for the applicant, the classification of grounds is less important than ensuring that the grounds clearly identify the way in which it is said that the sentence in question is flawed.

- In determining whether a sentence is manifestly excessive, the Court will consider whether the sentence as a whole is excessive.

- The Court may be prepared to find that a failure to follow the sentencing guidelines renders a sentence manifestly excessive. However, it has reiterated that guidelines are not a straightjacket and may in any event be interpreted in a flexible manner.

- The unjustified disparity in sentence between co-defendants may give rise to grounds of appeal but only if 'right thinking members of the public with knowledge of the relevant facts and circumstances, learning of this sentence would consider that something had gone wrong with the administration of justice'.

- A failure to follow the proper procedures may provide grounds of appeal. However, the general approach of the Court is to decline to interfere with a sentence where, had the correct procedures been followed the sentence that would have been imposed would have been essentially the same.

- An unlawful sentence may be corrected on appeal. However, consideration should first be given to whether the unlawful element of the sentence can be corrected by returning to the Crown Court under the slip rule.

- If the Court allows an appeal it may quash the sentence and replace it with any sentence that the Crown Court had the power to impose. However, this new sentence must not be more severe than the sentence that was appealed.

- Confiscation orders may be appealed as well as decisions in relation to the variations of confiscation orders but not variations under section 23 of POCA 2002.

- When appeal is based on alleged errors of fact, the Court may be reluctant to interfere with the findings of the Crown Court judge save in the clearest circumstances.

- A confiscation order that has been made with the consent of the defendant may be appealed if it can be shown that, as a result of bad legal advice or some other reason, the defendant did not understand the order he was agreeing to.

- If the Court allows an appeal against a order it may simply quash the order, impose a new order or remit the case to the Crown Court for a new confiscation hearing to take place.

- The prosecution may also appeal against a confiscation order or a refusal to make a confiscation order but only when proceedings are under POCA 2002.

Part 2
The Appeal Process

Chapter 5

Defence investigations

INTRODUCTION

5.1   Defence investigations can play a vital role in correcting miscarriages of justice. However, they are often undervalued and can be regarded with suspicion by the prosecution, the courts and even some defence lawyers. That is because the adversarial defence lawyer can be typecast as merely responding to the prosecution case, rather than actively investigating the crime scene or engaging with actual witnesses. The general principle that 'there is no property in a witness' is subject to many practical difficulties as police will guard the crime scene and their witnesses against any contact from defence lawyers, who are viewed as a potential source of interference or even intimidation. Appellants often complain that inadequate effort was made by police, and sometimes the original defence team, to fully investigate what happened by failing to speak to all the potential witnesses or seizing all the relevant material. Given the lack of resources on both sides, they may be right.

5.2   When investigating a crime the police have a duty to pursue all reasonable lines of enquiry and to obtain evidence which points away from, as well as towards, the suspect.[1] This includes material the investigator believes may be in the hands of third parties. If that is the case then the investigator should inform the disclosure officer who, in turn, should ask the party to retain it and this should be recorded and notified to the prosecutor.[2] As recent history has highlighted, especially when budgets are cut, it should not be assumed that has been done.[3] The failure of disclosure and the collapse of several high-profile trials in recent years has brought about a public outcry and led to the House of Commons' Justice Committee looking into serious

---

1   Criminal Procedure and Investigations Act 1996 (CPIA), s 23; Para 3.5 CPIA Code of Conduct; Para 17 Attorney General's Guidelines on Disclosure.
2   Para 3.6 CPIA Code of Conduct.
3   A critical report by HM Inspectorate of Constabulary led the police and prosecution to issue joint guidance in July 2017 in an effort to improve the process: 'Making it Fair – A Joint Inspection of the Disclosure of Unused Material in Volume Crown Court Cases' (www. justiceinspectorates.gov.uk/hmicfrs/publications/making-it-fair-disclosure-of-unused-material-in-crown-court-cases).

failings in disclosure by police and prosecutors. They published their findings in the summer of 2018.[4]

It is often the case that by the time a defendant is charged the police will be firmly committed to a particular view of the case and it is inevitable that resources will be focused on obtaining evidence that will help secure a conviction. Every day we all generate huge amounts of electronic data on our phones and social media. Police usually seize any electronic devices found on the suspect, as well as from their home and sometimes their workplace. Often that is used to bolster the prosecution case by adducing potentially harmful messages, pictures and social contacts, which are then used to build associations with co-defendants and cell siting of where the defendant was. Less often is that material considered for prosecution witnesses who may not be telling the truth or who may have misremembered events. In cases where the parties are known to each other or the prosecution witnesses have an ulterior motive in making the accusations, this material may be either highly relevant to the defence or help to undermine the prosecution case. The potential problems with seizure and disclosure has been recognised by the Attorney-General, who published an important review of how disclosure should operate in practice to take account of these concerns.[5]

5.3   In an age of austerity when police do not have the budget to do everything they should it is all the more important that defence lawyers appreciate that they are not solely dependent on the efforts of the police investigators. They can actively pursue other avenues themselves to obtain potentially relevant information. Indeed, some of these avenues may not be open to the police as witnesses may be reluctant to speak to them or the police may be unaware of information that the defendant has.

If this was not considered properly pre-trial then it becomes indispensable after conviction because, at that point, most prosecution investigations will cease entirely. It will only be those who act on behalf of the potential appellant who have an interest in continuing to work on the case. Such defence investigations may uncover evidence to start an appeal or they may reveal material that triggers further prosecution disclosure or persuades the Criminal Cases Review Commission to commence their own investigation using their extensive powers (see Chapter 9).

---

4   Including the widely publicised case of Liam Allen, who was acquitted in December 2017 (https://publications.parliament.uk/pa/cm201719/cmselect/cmjust/859/859.pdf).
5   Review of the efficiency and effectiveness of disclosure in the criminal justice system, November 2018 (https://assets.publishing.service.gov.uk/government/uploads/system/uploads/attachment_data/file/756436/Attorney_General_s_Disclosure_Review.pdf).

WHAT ARE DEFENCE INVESTIGATIONS AND WHO MAY CARRY THEM OUT?

5.4 Defence investigations are attempts to obtain relevant material in a way that maximises the chances of it being admitted as fresh evidence by the Court of Appeal.

5.5 Although the term 'defence investigations' conjures up complex enquiries in relation to convictions for grave crimes, in reality most appeal cases will benefit from new material that supports the appellant's case. A primary example is good background proofing and checking. For example, in the most straightforward appeal against sentence it may be possible to obtain medical evidence that was never before the Crown Court or a compelling character witness who was never asked to give a statement. Fresh material can be especially relevant for young appellants. The Sentencing Council guidelines require the sentencing judge to actively consider relevant material about the defendant's background and take that information into account when considering mitigating factors and take specific account of welfare considerations. These include any difficulties the defendant faced as a child and any issues that might impact upon culpability due to their lack of maturity.[6] Often educational assessments, psychological reports or social services records will not have been obtained prior to the original sentence. These should have been considered by the original defence team in order to provide the sentencing judge with a full picture of the young person's circumstances and the difficulties they may have faced and contributed to their offending. These investigations can throw up mental health issues or show that the defendant had been subject to coercive and controlling behaviour. It may show that the defendant was a victim of forced labour or trafficking;[7] it may reveal that they were a refugee who had a defence to a false document offence.[8] Sometimes insufficient efforts will have been made given the increasing rush to plead guilty and maximise credit, to identify these underlying issues which can go to sentence and, in some cases, the question of whether they should have pleaded guilty in the first place. However, whether the Court will be prepared to admit this material as fresh evidence is a different matter (see Chapter 3).

5.6 As to who may carry out the investigation, the short answer is 'anyone'. The longer answer is that investigations should be carried out under the direction of the defence lawyers. Investigation carried out by a solicitor is much more likely to result in evidence that will be admitted by the Court of Appeal. As officers of the Senior Courts they are subject to the discipline of

---

6 Overarching Principles of Sentencing Children and Young People: www.sentencingcouncil. org.uk/overarching-guides/crown-court/item/sentencing-children-and-young-people.
7 Modern Slavery Act, s.45.
8 Immigration and Asylum Act 1999, s.31.

their professional body should they mislead the Court or attempt to conceal the true picture, which may make the Court more likely to attach weight to the material that they uncover. However, there is no reason why evidence obtained by non-lawyers should not be admitted as long as it was obtained in a proper manner. Many private investigators are former police officers who are experienced in producing relevant witness statements that can be independently corroborated. The Legal Aid Agency will be more likely to agree to fund their work as it saves public money given it is billed at a lower hourly rate and paid as a disbursement rather than the slightly higher hourly rate that can be claimed by the solicitor.[9] This is an important factor in investigative work that can be time-consuming and open-ended. Of course, you will need to agree the scope of the work in advance and obtain prior approval from the Legal Aid Agency (or your private client) for the anticipated work (see Chapter 8).

THE ETHICS OF DEFENCE INVESTIGATION

5.7   Obtaining evidence in a manner that protects its integrity maximises the chance of it being admitted by the Court of Appeal. Being aware of potential ethical pitfalls is particularly important in appeal cases. Interviewing witnesses who gave evidence for the Crown at trial is a matter that often gives rise to particular concern. An unwillingness to speak to them often stems from a fear that the defence team could be accused of influencing the witness to change their evidence, particularly if the witness previously gave statements that are inconsistent with what they are now saying.[10]

5.8   These and other concerns can be minimised by following best practices and the relevant ethical rules that can be found in the solicitor's Code of Conduct.[11] The Law Society has published guidance to assist defence solicitors when dealing with defence witness notices, which has some application generally.[12] In particular, the investigator should:

(a)   create a careful file note of the meeting or significant conversation with a witness that lays out exactly what was said by all parties;

---

9   Currently Enquiry Agents guidance hourly rate is £25.60 outside London and £18.40 in London (https://assets.publishing.service.gov.uk/government/uploads/system/uploads/attachment_data/file/791497/Guidance_on_the_Remuneration_of_Expert_Witnesses_April2019.pdf).
10   Hannibal, M. and Mountford, L. (2013) *Criminal Litigation Handbook 2013/14*, Oxford: OUP, para 1.11.6, and for a recent refusal by the Court of Appeal to accept retraction evidence see *R v SB* [2019] EWCA Crim 565.
11   SRA Code of Conduct IB 5.10.
12   Law Society Practice Notes: Defence Witness Notices, 21 December 2015.

(b)   never misrepresent who they are, who they work for and why they are asking questions;[13]

(c)   take care not to pressurise a witness in any way and remember that it is the witness's prerogative to refuse to be interviewed;[14]

(d)   never take advantage of an unrepresented third party;[15]

(e)   never interview a represented person without the consent of their legal representative; and

(f)   never give legal advice where there is a conflict of interest.[16]

5.9   The defendant himself should not be involved in questioning potential witnesses nor should any other potential defence witnesses.

THE TECHNIQUES OF INVESTIGATION

Funding for an investigation

5.10   Where leave has not been applied for and the purpose of the investigation is to put the defence in a position to make an application for leave, funding can be requested from the Legal Aid Authority under the Advice and Assistance scheme. (See Chapter 8 for consideration of funding applications under the scheme.) If leave is granted the Court may grant a representation order to allow the appellant's solicitors to undertake particular tasks. (See 6.44 and 8.9–8.10.)

---

13   The people you are interviewing or asking for records from may ask you questions in return about what you are up to. This is part of the natural give and take of conversation and does not mean they are unwilling to talk to you. This does not mean you have to explain things that are confidential to the defendant or things that, strategically, you would rather not have in the public realm. You can simply explain that you are investigating for an appeal on behalf of a defendant, and that you want to hear everyone's side of the story.

14   This includes thinking carefully about who is the best person to do the interview, with reference to matters such as age, gender, race, etc. The suspicion that a witness's feeling of being intimidated stems from prejudice does not obviate the fact that they felt intimidated. Achieving Best Evidence (ABE) techniques and Special Measures can be employed when appropriate with vulnerable witnesses.

15   A lawyer has a duty to represent their client to the best of their ability, but they also have a duty not to take advantage of those who do not have legal representation in order to do so (Solicitors Regulation Authority Code of Conduct, Chapter 11, Outcome 11.1). One way of dealing with this situation may be to ensure that the potential witness has independent legal assistance before formalising what they have to say in a s 9 witness statement.

16   See the Solicitors Regulatory Authority Code of Conduct, Chapter 3, Outcome 3.5. If someone else wants to confess to the crime, or confess to previous perjury in the case, the defendant's lawyer cannot advise them of the legal implications of doing this. It is necessary to get the information from them about what they would tell the Court (because that is your duty to your client), but the defendant's lawyer can't advise them of the risks they face. They should obtain independent legal representative before they make any formal statement.

Conducting the investigation strategically

5.11   Planning an investigation involves:

(a)   knowing what evidence was before the jury and what evidence was available to both the prosecution and the defence at trial;

(b)   prioritising the leads to follow first (given the limited resources available);

(c)   working from the outside of the circle to the centre when approaching a sensitive issue or witness, so that as much information as possible is obtained before any evidence is removed from reach (such as a witness refusing to talk or a document being destroyed).

What you already know

5.12   It is always helpful to start by establishing what material is already in the hands of the defence. This will involve speaking to the defendant, their family and certainly their previous lawyers.[17] It is also important to gather as complete a case file as possible.

5.13   The following material should normally be sought:

(a)   records of arrest and pre-trial detention (especially as to defendant's state of mind and the circumstances of admissions);

(b)   the defendant's proof of evidence, comments on prosecution witnesses and defence case statement (and any character evidence);

(c)   the defence solicitor's police station attendance notes;

(d)   defence witness statements whether relied on or not and reasons why not called;

(e)   police statements, plus material the police relied on in writing their statements reports (such as contemporaneous notes especially first descriptions which they have a duty to record);

(f)   witness statements taken by the police;

(g)   news media reports (often available through internet search engines);

(h)   recordings of transcribed statements especially Achieving Best Evidence (ABE) recordings;

---

17   The Court of Appeal recently held that speaking with previous legal representatives 'will henceforth be necessary ... to ensure that facts are correct, unless there are in exceptional circumstances good and compelling reasons not to do so.' *R v McCook* [2014] EWCA Crim 734, para 11. See Chapter 6 for further discussion of the case.

(i)   other recorded evidence such as CCTV, copies of computer hard drives and any 999 calls;

(j)   expert reports plus any material experts relied on in reaching their conclusions for both prosecution and the defence (and whether relied upon);

(k)   unused material provided to the trial team by the CPS and defence section 8 CPIA applications;

(l)   trial solicitors' working file including notes, correspondence and billing (the latter is useful for working out when/whether material was actually read though the previous solicitor is not obliged to produce internal documents that do not relate to advice provided);[18]

(m)   trial exhibits/material that went before the jury especially admissions;

(n)   trial transcript (access limited – see below);

(o)   defence trial advocate's notebooks;

(p)   any previous grounds of appeal;

(q)   any previous applications to Criminal Cases Review Commission (CCRC) and any statement of reasons from the CCRC;

(r)   HMPPS prisoner records;[19]

(s)   prison and probation files, including OASYS reports and the most recent parole dossier from the National Offender Management Service (NOMS), which often contains historical documents that may have been destroyed by others including old court transcripts; and

(t)   prison healthcare records and medical records from the client's General Practitioner.

Whereas in older cases a request for case papers will generally result in many boxes of papers arriving at your doorstep, things have improved with the introduction of the Crown Court Digital Case System ('Caselines'), as now the previous solicitor can simply add you to the Caselines bundle which will give you access to the prosecution material, though you will still need to obtain the defence papers. As more solicitors work digitally, their files can increasingly be supplied in an electronic format. It is important to remember that only those prosecution documents which were put before the court will be on Caselines. Unused material and documents such as unused expert reports and the proof of evidence of the defendant are not uploaded to Caselines. When requesting a case file it is advisable to request these be added onto the Caselines bundle and for any other documents which were not uploaded. In addition, where

---

18   The Law Society has published a Practice Note: Who owns the file? 16 January 2019.
19   Obtainable from the Data Access and Compliance Unit (at the Branson Registry).

the defendant had co-defendants, there may be both an 'individual' and a 'joindered' Caselines bundle so you should ensure you are added to both of these; although a lot of the documents will be the same, there are often different documents on each of them.

5.14   Building an electronic file makes it easier and quicker to create a chronology of what happened, and who knew what and when, as well as an index of appeal issues, with each item linked back to the relevant pages of the file. A similar tagging of witness statements and police interviews is also helpful. There is increasingly sophisticated case analysis software to help with this task.[20]

5.15   In older cases the trial lawyers may no longer be in possession of the case file, as the obligation is only to keep the file for six years.[21] In these circumstances it may be necessary to reconstruct the trial solicitor's files from individual sources such as the Court, the CPS, the police, the defendant and their supporters. Sometimes the parole dossier may be all that is left as a source of relevant material.

5.16   A complete trial transcript is an invaluable guide to what occurred at trial but the cost of ordering one from the relevant transcription company can be prohibitively high. Generally, legal aid funding under advice and assistance (see Chapter 8) can be obtained for specific, necessary transcripts, such as the summing up, mitigation and sentencing hearings, or the evidence of specific witnesses, but the LAA will not grant funding for transcripts of whole proceedings. You will also need to obtain the permission of the resident judge at the Crown Court where it was tried (see 8.40).

Seeking additional material from the prosecution

5.17   Following conviction the prosecution's statutory duty to disclose relevant material ends.[22] There is a continuing common law duty of disclosure when material 'comes to light after the conclusion of the proceedings, which may cast doubt upon the safety of the conviction'.[23]

---

20 Useful software includes Devon Think for Mac, Masterfile for PCs and Case map for Lexis users, plus various cloud-based offerings.
21 The six-year requirement was originally set out in the Guide to Professional Conduct of Solicitors, Annex 12A, and it is now within the discretion of law firms to decide how long to retain closed cases.
22 Criminal Procedure and Investigations Act 1996, s 7A.
23 Attorney General's Guidelines on Disclosure, Attorney General's Office (2013), s 72; See also CPS Guidance on Disclosure of Material to Third Parties and the CPS Disclosure Manual (revised 26 February 2018).

5.18   In *R (on the application of Nunn) v Chief Constable of Suffolk Constabulary*[24] the Supreme Court held that whilst the prosecution should disclose material that may assist the defence in presenting a ground of appeal, 'there is no continuing right to indefinite re-investigation of cases following conviction.' The burden lies on the defence lawyers to make the case for further disclosure of documents in the prosecution or police files.

5.19   Attempts to obtain new material from the prosecution can start with written Subject Access Requests to the police, the Crown Prosecution Service or the relevant prosecuting authority which should[25]:

(a)   specify as clearly as possible what material is sought;

(b)   explain why it is sought with reference to any potential grounds of appeal;

(c)   state why you believe that they have the material in question; and

(d)   ask for full reasons to be given for any refusal to provide disclosure.

5.20   If the prosecutor refuses to provide further material, the Court of Appeal may order its disclosure but it will only consider doing so after an application for leave has been lodged with the Court (see Chapter 6). Therefore, until an application for leave is made, the only remedy is an application for judicial review of the prosecutor's refusal to disclose. This should start with a detailed letter setting out why the prosecution should exercise their discretion to provide access to the material in question.

Seeking new material

Subject Access Requests under the Data Protection Act 2018

5.21   Material which contains personal information about a particular person may be obtained through a 'Subject Access Request' (SAR) made to a 'competent authority'[26] under section 45(1) of the Data Protection Act 2018 (DPA 2018).[27] Such requests may be made to the agency that holds the information with the written authorisation of the person to whom the data relates, enabling the request to be made on their behalf by their lawyer.

---

24   [2014] UKSC 37.
25   It may be necessary to complete a specific Subject Access Request (SAR) on behalf of your client for that organisation – see 5.21.
26   Schedule 7 Data Protection Act 2018 sets out a list of competent authorities, which includes ministerial government departments, courts, police forces, the parole board, and prisons (including those which are privately run).
27   An SAR, is a request made for records that relate to the person making the request, or their representative.

5.22 *Defence investigations*

5.22   Access to personal data may be restricted, either wholly or partially, in order to:

(a)   avoid obstructing an official or legal inquiry, investigation or procedure;

(b)   avoid prejudicing the prevention, detection, investigation or prosecution of criminal offences or the execution of criminal penalties;

(c)   protect public security;

(d)   protect national security;

(e)   protect the rights and freedoms of others.

Any such a restriction to the right of access to personal data must be a necessary and proportionate measure, having regard to fundamental rights and legitimate interests of the individual, and only to the extent that, and for so long as, is necessary.[28] That exemption might apply on appeal cases when the information sought is still relevant to other investigations or prosecutions.

5.23   If the request is made by someone other than the subject, then a signed authorisation form will also be required which entitles the person making the request to obtain the documents they are requesting on behalf of the subject. This is so, even where the application form specifically states that the data subject must sign the form themselves. Where a person is in prison or detained, it is not necessary to comply with the requirement to provide identification documents, although this is stated on the majority of application forms. In this situation, it may assist if you can confirm the client's location via email with the National Offender Management Service (NOMS) prisoner location service and then send a PDF of this email along with the SAR.[29]

A difficulty sometimes arises where a client has previously been imprisoned but has been transferred to hospital under section 47 or section 49 of the Mental Health Act (MHA), as the NOMS prisoner location service records will state that the person has been released from prison. If this is the case, generally it is best to explain this situation to the Data Controller and see what other proof may be acceptable to them – for example, email confirmation from the detained person's treating clinician stating that they have been transferred to hospital under section 47 or section 49 MHA.

5.24   It is important to include the requestor's name and contact details, the data subject's full names and any relevant information that will help the agency concerned to locate the material that is sought. The information should be provided without undue delay and, in any event, within one month of them either receiving the full request (with all necessary information) or

---

28   Data Protection Act 2018, s 45(4); which mirrors the test for restricting a Convention right.
29   Prisoner Location Service (NOMS): Prisoner.Location.Service@noms.gsi.gov.uk.cjsm.net.

them obtaining the data which is requested.[30] Where an organisation fails to comply with this deadline, ultimately you can report them to the Information Commissioner's Office.

5.25 Since the DPA 2018 came into force, SARs should no longer involve the payment of any administration fee. As a result many organisations are struggling to comply with the guidelines as the number of requests has increased considerably. There is an exception to this, whereby a reasonable fee may be charged if the data subject has made 'manifestly unfounded or excessive requests'.[31] There is no example or definition of 'manifestly unfounded or excesive'. An excessive request may be one that merely repeats the substance of previous requests. For example, if you have already requested a client's prison healthcare records and require an update, you should request the records from the last date of the previous records onwards, rather than requesting all records, in order to avoid a request being viewed as excessive. The Information Commissioner's Office website provides a useful guide to making SARs and has examples of pro-forma request letters that can be followed. A large number of agencies and organisations, including the Metropolitan Police, have their own SAR application form available online.

If a client has been in prison for a long time, they may no longer be registered with a General Practitioner. If so, their medical records will have been sent to Primary Care Support England (PCSE), which is an NHS department responsible for storing residual medical records. These records can be obtained directly from PCSE by completing the application form available the PCSE website.

Requests under the Freedom of Information Act 2000

5.26 Applications for data held by public authorities that does not fall under section 7 of the Data Protection Act 1998 can be made under section 1 of the Freedom of Information Act 2000. Again, a clear and detailed guide to making such applications is to be found on the Information Commissioner's website.

5.27 Such applications can be a useful means of obtaining information that is important for understanding the evidence in the case, for example, how those with a role in the case are trained to do their jobs and the procedures that are followed by particular institutions. However, freedom of information requests cannot generally be used to bypass the requirements of disclosure in criminal proceedings and obtain material that is held by the prosecution in relation to the case. Material held for the purpose of a criminal investigation

---

30　Data Protection Act 2018, paras 45(3) and 54.
31　Data Protection Act 2018, s 53.

or prosecution is exempt from the requirements of section 1 to the extent that the information holder does not regard it as being in the public interest to disclose it.[32]

Records collection generally

5.28

(a)   It is important to follow up on requests sent out. A request may have to be sent several times. Further, fees for access to records via SAR are now generally not permitted under the DPA 2018 so many organisations are dealing with large increases in the numbers of requests.

(b)   If the investigator believes that a record exists, but the relevant agency states they cannot find it, or that it has been destroyed, it can be helpful to ask for a sworn statement from a representative of the agency or company attesting to what searches have been made, or to their personal knowledge of the destruction of that particular document.

(c)   It is always necessary (and beneficial) to be polite and courteous to the record-holders.

(d)   Although it is important to be specific about what records are sought, it is helpful to try to draft a request in such a way as to catch other potentially relevant documents that may be in the possession of the record holder.

(e)   The investigator should personally search any archived files if permitted to do so.

(f)   The investigator should think outside the box ('where else would copies of that missing record end up?').

(g)   Good records should be kept of all requests made, including follow-ups to the original request. This will become particularly relevant when submitting an application for an extension of time for leave to appeal as it will be necessary to justify any delay in making the application, which is often contributed to by delays in obtaining documents.

Visiting and recording the crime scene and other significant locations

5.29   Visiting the crime scene or another location that is significant to the case is something that the defence should consider as part of their preparation for trial. However, it is often overlooked. When investigating a case for a potential appeal one should not assume that site visits have

---

32   Freedom of Information Act 2000, s 30.

been done or that they could not now assist in any appeal. Even if site visits have already taken place, a fresh pair of eyes may notice something that has previously been missed. If a site visit is to take place, the following should be borne in mind:

(a)   It is useful to take cameras with the capacity to shoot both stills and moving footage. One film of a location can then be shot with a voiceover by the film-maker describing what can be seen and its relevance. A second film should be taken without the voiceover, so the ambient sound can be recorded. Stills of the same areas should also be taken.

(b)   Measurements should be taken where possible, using a tape measure or a rolling measuring wheel. This should be done after any film and stills have been taken.

(c)   If access to private property is required to make the recording, the owner should be asked, unless of course the owner or occupier is a complainant, in which case filming will have to be restricted to what can be seen from the street at a time when the complainant is not likely to be disturbed or upset. The relevant privacy, trespass, harassment or data protection laws should be consulted and followed if it appears that filming may give rise to legal issues.

Conducting interviews with potential witnesses

5.30   In addition to the ethical considerations already discussed, the following guidelines will help the investigator obtain useful evidence from potential witnesses:

(a)   Where possible, and provided it does not put the investigator at risk, the investigator should seek to conduct the interview in the witness's own home where they are likely to be more relaxed, less pressed for time and where there is a possibility of meeting other potential witnesses.

(b)   The investigator should be courteous and respectful at all times and dress appropriately for the meeting.

(c)   The investigator should prepare for the interview by reviewing all relevant materials in order to understand what the witness has already said. It may be useful for the investigator to take the materials with them, but care needs to be taken not to distract or influence the witness.

(d)   The investigator should be prepared to explain their role, the status of the case and what may happen next.

(e)   If questioned about their view of the case, the investigator should stay non-committal, objective and open.

(f)   The questions should generally be open-ended.

(g)   Close attention should be paid to what is said and the witness should be asked to clarify what they have said, if necessary. Notes should be taken to the extent that is possible without making the witness feel uncomfortable. A record should be typed up as soon as possible afterwards. Witnesses may be distrustful of recording equipment so it should be introduced with caution and only with the witnesses consent.

(h)   Pregnant pauses should be allowed to develop as often an uncomfortable silence is filled by the interviewee saying what is on their mind.

(i)   The contact details of the interviewee should be confirmed and they should be informed that the defence team may wish to contact them again.

(j)   Notes should be reviewed for coherence. It is important that anyone who reads the notes can understand what was said.

(k)   If the decision is made to take a statement from a witness, it should be done using the format required for admission of the statement under section 9 of the Criminal Justice Act 1967, which allows for the statement to be admitted before the Court without the witness needing to appear.

CO-OPERATING WITH OTHER INVESTIGATORY BODIES

Investigation by the Criminal Cases Review Commission

5.31   The CCRC can deploy powers and call upon trained investigators to carry out investigations that are unavailable to the defence. However, the CCRC has limited capacity to take on new cases. According to 2017/2018 figures, 75.32 per cent of cases are closed (with a final decision having been sent by the CCRC) within 12 months of the initial application.[33] Unlike in previous years [34] in its most recent annual report, the CCRC did not disclose the average time an applicant will have to wait while the Commission allocates, reviews and (if it decides to do so) investigates the case. The processing time is a substantial period of imprisonment that a defendant may be able to reduce if they or their lawyers are able to obtain and disclose material to the Commission. However, it should be borne in mind that the Commission has the distinct advantage of being able to appoint their own investigators (including an external police force) and also being able to examine public interest immunity material as well as the transcripts of closed hearings.

---

33   Criminal Case Review Commission Annual Report 2017–18, pp 18 and 85.
34   Criminal Case Review Commission Annual Report 2013/14 at p 15, in which the average time for a full review by the Commission, from receipt of application to final decision, was 72.8 weeks.

5.32 An application to the Commission which can provide material, give an account of the steps that have already been undertaken, and provide the Commission with the responses to any defence enquiry can greatly assist the speed and success of any investigation that the Commission itself decides to carry out and may assist in persuading the Commission that such an investigation is necessary.

5.33 For full consideration of applications to the Commission, see Chapter 9.

Journalistic investigations

5.34 Historically, print and broadcast journalists have done much of the heavy lifting when it comes to righting miscarriages of justice. They can play a vital role in uncovering evidence which the applicant's lawyers can later use in court.

5.35 However, it is necessary to exercise caution when co-operating with or seeking to enlist the help of journalists. Whilst the primary duty of a lawyer is to their client subject to their duty to the Court, the journalist's own overriding duty is to tell the truth as they see it. The interests of a defendant and a journalist's desire to expose the truth may coincide, but they may clash.

5.36 Therefore, in those cases where it is believed that co-operating with a journalist may lead to the uncovering of new evidence or may simply raise the profile of a case, it is important to consider the risks and benefits of doing so and ensure that the terms of the relationship are clear at the outset.

SUMMARY OF KEY POINTS

- Defence investigations can uncover vital material for an appeal against conviction or sentence.

- Investigations do not have to be carried out by the defendant's lawyers. However, they should be carried out under their direction.

- Following clear ethical guidelines when conducting any investigation will assist in any application to have evidence that has been obtained considered by the Court of Appeal.

- Investigations should be carefully planned. It is first necessary to establish what material the defence already have and what material the prosecution may already have that might be disclosed, before considering whether further material should be sought.

- Disclosure requests may be made to the prosecution and, if not complied with, orders for disclosure may be sought from the Court of Appeal

5.36 *Defence investigations*

when leave has been granted, or judicial review commenced where it has not. However, regard must be had to the limited disclosure duties of the prosecution following a conviction.

- Material may be sought from public authorities under the Data Protection Act 2018 and the Freedom of Information Act 2000.

- Interviewing witnesses, including those who gave evidence for the prosecution in the Crown Court, can be of vital importance but should be done with care, following clear ethical principles.

- Site visits should not be overlooked. It should not be assumed that they took place before trial or, even if they did, that another site visit would not yield further information.

- Informing the Criminal Cases Review Commission of the work that has been undertaken in any defence investigation and providing the Commission with any material obtained may help to persuade the Commission to conduct their own investigation and may assist them in doing so.

Chapter 6

Applying for leave to appeal

INTRODUCTION

6.1   There are two ways to appeal a conviction or sentence in the Crown Court to the Court of Appeal: either an application to the Crown Court judge for a certificate to appeal, or an application to the Court of Appeal for leave to appeal. As it is rare for a Crown Court judge to grant a certificate to appeal it is far more likely that the application will be direct to the Court of Appeal.

The application to the Court of Appeal is usually decided on the papers by a High Court judge (the 'single judge'). If the application is refused it may then be renewed orally by asking for a hearing before the full Court. In a small number of cases the Registrar may bypass the single judge and refer the application to the Court for a full hearing (see 6.51 below).

Before considering an application to the Court of Appeal the advocate should first consider whether the 'slip rule' can be used to avoid having to trouble the court at all. This is likely to arise in sentencing cases where a legal or factual error was made by the judge or the parties that should be brought to the sentencing judge's attention. As the time limit is short (56 days) and it needs to be dealt with by the same judge. This should be done quickly and if necessary can be dealt with in the defendant's absence.[1]

6.2   This chapter will focus on the usual route of applying for leave to appeal to the Court of Appeal, as well as renewing that application and withdrawing it ('abandonment').

6.3   The preparation and advocacy at the actual hearing before the full Court is considered separately in Chapter 7.

6.4   **Note on terminology and the procedural rules:** anyone applying for leave to appeal is referred to as the 'applicant' until leave is granted, when they become the 'appellant'. As with other areas of criminal litigation the relevant procedures on appeals are set out in detail in procedural rules, which

---

1   Powers of Criminal Court (Sentencing) Act 2000, s 155; *R v Warren* [2017] EWCA Crim 226.

should be closely followed. These are found in the relevant 'divisions' of the Criminal Practice Directions 2015 (CPD 2015) and the Criminal Procedure Rules (CrimPR).[2] Following these rules will help applicants and their lawyers navigate through the process of a criminal appeal. It will also enhance the chances of a favourable outcome. Ignoring them could seriously damage the applicant's prospects and may result in criticism by the court and even wasted costs.

ADVICE ON APPEAL

The trial lawyer's duty to advise promptly on appeal

6.5   The duty of lawyers to provide advice on appeal is set out in the HMCTS 'Guide to commencing proceedings in the Court of Appeal Criminal Division' ('The Guide'):[3]

> 'Provision for advice or assistance on appeal is included in the trial representation order issued by the Crown Court. Solicitors should not wait to be asked for advice by the defendant. Immediately following the conclusion of the case, the legal representatives should see the defendant and advocates should express orally a view as to the prospects of a successful appeal (whether against conviction or sentence or both). If there are reasonable grounds, grounds of appeal should be drafted, signed and sent to instructing solicitors as soon as possible bearing in mind the time limits that apply to lodging an appeal. Solicitors should immediately send a copy of the documents received from the advocate to the defendant.'[4]

6.6   The revised Guide no longer requires the advocate to confirm a negative advice in writing but warns them that they must only advise in favour of appeal if they conclude that there are 'arguable grounds' that they would be prepared to argue before the court, and not simply because they are 'instructed' to do so.[5] The solicitor should also confirm the advocate's advice in writing, whether positive or negative, and attach a copy, if there is a written one.

As the opinion of the defendant is generally irrelevant to whether there is a legal point to be argued, the lawyers may proceed with an appeal which has merit even when the defendant cannot be contacted because they have absconded or have been removed from the jurisdiction. In appeal cases it is law and ethics that determine what is the right advice, not the views of the client.[6]

---

2   Criminal Practice Direction (CPD) 2015 IX Appeals, para 29 A–G; Parts 36 and 39 CrimPR. See Appendix A – CPD 2015 and Appendix B – CrimPR.
3   Replaces the former guidance produced by the Registrar. See Appendix C – The Guide.
4   The Guide, A.1-1.
5   The Guide A.3-6; CPD IX Appeal, para 39 C.2.
6   *R v Okedare & Ors* [2014] EWCA Crim 228.

The defendant's right to seek a second opinion

6.7   A defendant should consider carefully the advice that they are given, but they are not bound to accept it. They may ask their solicitor to instruct a new advocate to advise on appeal (although whether to do so will be a matter for the solicitor). Alternatively, they may wish to seek assistance from new solicitors. There is a limited amount of publicly funded advice available. This is dependent on whether there is a good reason to provide the advice and whether the defendant has passed a very restrictive means test. Even if they do many criminal lawyers refuse to take on these cases as they are very poorly paid (see Chapter 8).

Such advice needs to be given promptly because the time limits for lodging an appeal are very short. It can take a considerable amount of time for a new defence team to get up to speed with the case afresh so they may not be able to lodge an appeal in time even if the advice is positive. This will add another hurdle as it means an application will be required for an extension of time. This has become slightly less of a problem with the introduction of the Digital Case System in the Crown Court, which has made it easier to access the prosecution case papers and some defence documents online by being invited on to the Crown Court case.

Time limits, extensions and the need for expedition

6.8   An application for leave to appeal must be lodged no later than 28 days after the decision which is being appealed.[7] It is a common mistake to assume that the time limit to appeal against a conviction runs from the date of sentence. In fact, the period for appeal runs from the date of what is being appealed. For conviction it starts at the date of the verdict, sentence runs from the date of sentence and a confiscation appeal runs from the date on which the confiscation order was made.

6.9   The court may grant an extension of time in which to appeal, either before or after the 28 days have expired.[8] It will usually only do so if it decides that there is merit in the application for leave itself. Even then, it is not bound to grant the extension but must take an overall view of what justice requires.[9] Whilst, there is power to grant an extension before expiry of the deadline, the Criminal Appeal Office prefers any application to be submitted with the appeal notice and the grounds so the judge can assess the merits of the substantive grounds at the same time as the extension application.[10]

---

7   CAA 1968, s 18(2).
8   CAA 1968, s 18(3).
9   *R v Thorsby* [2015] EWCA Crim 1.
10   The Guide, A.6-5; Part 36.4 CrimPR generally regarding extension of time applications.

6.10 The fact that the court does generally consider the merits of the application for leave to appeal when deciding whether to grant an extension should never lead the applicant or their lawyers to be complacent about time limits. If nothing else, it is more difficult for the court to consider an application in a sympathetic light if the applicant or their legal advisors appear to have done little or nothing for a significant period of time, than one in which they have clearly worked hard to ensure that the application is lodged as soon as possible. The longer the period of time that has elapsed since the 28-day period has expired, the greater the need to show why there has been a justifiable delay.[11]

6.11 When new lawyers are instructed to advise on appeal, unavoidable delays may well arise from the need to consider transcripts from the trial and contact previous lawyers before advising on the merits. The court will be more sympathetic to such delays if it can see that the delay was due to serious attempts being made to ensure the factual basis for the appeal was correct and that any new evidence or legal points were fully aired with the previous team. The court will want the fullest picture of what decisions were taken at the trial and what advice was provided and that the new team have fully complied with their *McCook* duties (see 6.13 and 6.14 below).[12] However, the court has made it clear that time limits will be taken seriously:

> 'Time limits are set for good reason and in the interests of justice. They must be strictly observed unless there are good and exceptional reasons for their not being so observed. As was made clear by Lord Taylor CJ in *R v Burley* – an unreported decision referred to in *Williams* [2010] EWCA Crim 3289 at paragraph 5 – the interests of justice as a whole require the strict observance of time limits.'[13]

The Practice Direction makes it clear that any late amendments will face an even higher hurdle.[14]

Obtaining transcripts for the purpose of advising on appeal

6.12 It will often be necessary for the advocate to have access to transcripts from the original trial in order to advise on whether there are arguable grounds to appeal. A quote for the relevant transcript will be needed to get prior authority from the Legal Aid Agency (LAA) (or to agree the disbursement with a privately paying client). This quote can be obtained from the transcription company for the court where the case was heard. The application form includes

---

11 *R v Wilson* [2016] EWCA Crim 65.
12 *R v McGill & Ors* [2017] EWCA Crim 1228.
13 *R v Roberts & Ors* [2016] EWCA Crim 71 at para 39.
14 CPD IX Appeals, para 39C.4 [f].

guidance with a list of the relevant transcription companies.[15] It is necessary to get permission from the judge who heard the case (or the resident judge) to authorise release of the transcript. This is done by completing a Form EX107 setting out what transcripts you need and why you want them, as well as specifying when you need them.[16] The funding for transcripts is considered in detail in Chapter 8, but in general terms, the cost of transcripts must be met by the LAA or the client prior to an application for leave as the Registrar will not obtain transcripts unless and until an application for leave is lodged.

Contacting trial lawyers – due diligence

McCook – the new regime

6.13   Anyone considering an appeal against conviction or sentence should note that there has been a significant change of culture in recent times. Having become dismayed by the volume of appeals from new legal teams raising novel points along with potential criticisms of decisions taken at trial, the court has made it clear that the new lawyers have a heavy burden to overcome to satisfy themselves that the proposed grounds are properly arguable and based on a sound history of the previous advice received and the instructions given.[17]

The new team should advise the applicant that the Registrar will expect a waiver of privilege (on previous advice received – not current advice being given) so the court can investigate what instructions or advice was provided at trial and any tactical decisions that were taken. If a suitable waiver is not forthcoming adverse inferences may be drawn.[18]

The Guide cautions:

> 'it is necessary for the fresh solicitors or advocate to approach the solicitors and/or advocate who previously acted to ensure that the facts upon which the grounds of appeal are premised are correct, unless there are exceptional circumstances and good and compelling reasons not to do so.'

This guidance has now been incorporated into the updated Practice Direction.[19] These directions are essential reading for any fresh team of lawyers, as failure to comply could easily lead to a wasted costs order and/or a loss of time direction.

---

15   https://assets.publishing.service.gov.uk/government/uploads/system/uploads/attachment_data/file/763958/ex107-gn-eng.pdf

16   Form EX107 has a declaration that you agree to pay the costs of the transcript.

17   *R v Davis and Thabagu* [2013] EWCA Crim 2424; *R v Achogbuo* [2014] EWCA Crim 567; *R v McCook* [2014] EWCA Crim 734.

18   The Guide A.4-1–4-3.

19   CPD IX Appeal, para 39 C.4 [c]–[h].

6.14   *Applying for leave to appeal*

Where a new defence team are advising they are warned that they must take account of the fact that their client should have already received advice on appeal and, if it was positive, the previous lawyers would have lodged any grounds of appeal. Bearing that in mind the new lawyers must comply with their duty of due diligence outlined in *McCook* and explain to their client that a waiver of privilege is very likely to be required. Any fresh grounds should be reviewed carefully once the original trial lawyers have responded to confirm that the proposed ones are 'reasonably arguable and particularly cogent'. Once lodged the Registrar will get transcripts and usually ask for a respondents' notice to address the fresh grounds.

These principles have been developed further to highlight:

(i)   the duty to obtain objective and independent evidence to establish the evidential basis for the new grounds;[20]

(ii)   the need for extensive enquiries of the previous team on all relevant matters;[21]

(iii) the waiver of privilege procedure for criticism of the previous team;[22]

(iv)   the waiver of privilege procedure for new evidence cases (see 6.31).[23]

Fresh and amended grounds procedure

6.14   Where the previous lawyers submitted grounds that were rejected by the single judge and the new lawyers want to put in fresh grounds, they will have to establish whether they need to vary the original appeal notice as well as applying for an extension of time to submit fresh grounds.

The principles to be applied were extensively discussed in *R v James* (per Hallett LJ, VP):[24]

'(i)   As a general rule, all the Grounds of Appeal an applicant wishes to advance should be lodged with the Notice of Appeal/Application; subject to their being perfected on receipt of transcripts from the Registrar.

(ii)   The filter mechanism provided by section 31 of the CAA 1968 (consideration of the application for leave by the single judge) is an important stage in the process and should not be "bypassed" solely on the basis that lawyers instructed post-conviction would have done

---

20   *R v Lee* [2014] EWCA Crim 2928.
21   *R v McGill & Ors* [2017] EWCA Crim 1228.
22   *R v JH* [2014] EWCA Crim 2618.
23   *R v Singh* [2017] EWCA Crim 466.
24   Above at 24.

or argued things differently from the trial lawyers. Fresh Grounds advanced by fresh counsel must be particularly cogent.

(iii) Once an application for leave has been considered by a single Judge, if the applicant wishes to advance fresh Grounds that have not in substance been considered by the single judge, they require the leave of the court. Applications to advance fresh Grounds must be accompanied by an application to "vary" the notice of appeal. If there is any doubt as to whether a Ground is 'fresh', an application to vary should be made.

(iv) The advocate should address in writing the relevant factors which the full Court is likely to consider in determining whether to allow variation of the notice of appeal and an extension of time for the renewal if required.

(v) In deciding whether to vary the Grounds of Appeal, the full Court will take into account the following (non-exhaustive) list of issues:

    (a) The extent of the delay in advancing the new ground/s;

    (b) The reason for the delay in advancing the new ground/s;

    (c) Whether the issues / facts giving rise to the new Grounds were known to the applicant's representative at the time he or she advised the applicant regarding any available Grounds of Appeal;

    (d) The overriding objective (Crim PR 1.1) namely acquitting the innocent and convicting the guilty and dealing with the case efficiently and expeditiously;

    (e) The interests of justice.

(vi) The application to vary would not require "exceptional leave" (by demonstrating substantial injustice) but the hurdle for the applicant is a high one. Counsel should remind themselves of the provisions of the PD. 39C.2 namely that "Advocates should not settle grounds unless they consider that they are properly arguable. Grounds should be carefully drafted." They should also bear very much in mind their duty to the court.

(vii) Advocates should also remind themselves of the rules relating to time limits. Leave will not be given to renew out of time unless the applicant can persuade the court that very good reasons exist. If the application to renew out of time is accompanied by an application to vary the Grounds the hurdle is higher.

(viii) For pragmatic reasons we suggest the application to vary should be considered by the full Court and not on the papers. An applicant would have a right to require a review of a decision not to vary if it were made by the Registrar or single Judge and a full Court hearing would in any event be required.

(ix) Assuming that the applicant will have received advice and assistance on appeal from his trial advocate, who will have advised that no grounds exist on which to challenge the safety of the conviction or settled the original Grounds of Appeal in the notice of appeal, fresh counsel should in every case be required to comply with the duty of due diligence as explained in *McCook* [2014] EWCA Crim 734. Waiver will almost certainly be required.

(x) Once the trial lawyers have responded, "fresh counsel" should again consider with great care their duty to the court and whether the "fresh grounds" should be advanced as properly arguable and particularly cogent.

(xi) The Registrar should obtain, in advance of the full Court hearing, transcripts relevant to the new Grounds and (where required) a Respondents' Notice relating to the new Grounds.

(xii) The Crim PR Committee may wish to consider formulating rules for the lodging of a Notice of Application to vary a notice of appeal.

(xiii) On any renewal the full Court when refusing an application to vary the notice of appeal has the power to make a loss of time order or order for costs in line with *R v Gray and Others*. By analogy with *R v Kirk* [2015] EWCA Crim 1764 (where the Court refused an extension of time) the Court has the power to order costs of obtaining the Respondent's Notice and or transcripts.'

The above procedure should be carefully followed and clients advised accordingly of the possible consequences.

TRIAL JUDGE'S CERTIFICATE

Whether to apply for a trial judge's certificate

6.15   The alternative to applying for leave is to apply to the judge who conducted the trial or imposed the sentence (depending on the nature of the decision being appealed) for a certificate that the conviction or sentence is fit for appeal.[25]

6.16   A certificate can only be granted in very exceptional circumstances[26] and it will only arise when the appeal involves a point of law:

---

25 CAA 1968, s 1(2)(b) in respect of conviction; CAA 1968, s 11(1A) in respect of sentence.
26 *R v Kalis* [2003] EWCA Crim 1080.

(a)   The procedure is governed by section 1(2)(b) of CAA 1968 and Part 39.4 CrimPR.

(b)   An oral application may be made immediately after the relevant decision or a written application must be made within 14 days providing similar information to an appeal notice.

(c)   If the judge decides to issue the certificate they must do so within 28 days of the decision. This statutory time limit may not be extended, unless it relates to insanity or unfitness to stand trial.[27]

(d)   The certificate is issued by the judge completing Form C and the Crown Court officer sending it to the Registrar – Part 36.8(5) CrimPR.

(e)   The refusal to grant a certificate may not be appealed.

(f)   If the certificate is granted, the Crown Court may also grant bail pending appeal. This should specify a condition of residence. The procedure for such applications is to be found in the relevant Practice Direction which adopts the general procedure set out in Part 14 CrimPR.[28]

(g)   If the certificate is granted there is no requirement to lodge grounds. However, a Form NG must still be lodged with the Court of Appeal.

THE GROUNDS OF APPEAL

Who may draft grounds of appeal?

6.17   The grounds may be drafted by the applicant, his solicitor or advocate. The Registrar will not accept grounds drafted by a third party unless they are expressly adopted by the applicant (except in exceptional cases, where the applicant lacks the capacity to do so).

The form and content of the grounds

6.18   The purpose of the grounds is to convince the High Court judge who will consider them ('the single judge') to grant leave to appeal. They should therefore be drafted with care so as to ensure that they are as clear, concise and persuasive as possible.

6.19   The Practice Direction makes it clear that the traditional practice of submitting short grounds and a separate advice on appeal should no longer be followed and advocates should not include their written advice to the lay

---

27   CAA 1968, s 16A(2)(b).
28   CPD III Custody and Bail, Para14 H5-6.

client.[29] The grounds must be lodged with the relevant appeal notice (with separate Form NGs for conviction/sentence/confiscation) and they must be signed and dated. The Practice Direction now specifies exactly how they should be drafted.[30] The Criminal Procedure Rules also provide detailed advice on the expected content of both the appeal notice (if there is no prescribed Form NG) and the grounds; including the precise requirements that they should be concise and drafted on A4-size portrait format (in not less than 12-point type with 1.5 spacing).[31]

6.20   The rules now prescribe how the grounds should be set out:

(a)   include in no more than the first two pages a summary of the grounds that makes what follows easy to understand;

(b)   in each ground of appeal identify the event or decision to which that ground relates;

(c)   in each ground of appeal summarise the facts relevant to that ground, but only to the extent necessary to make clear what is in issue;

(d)   concisely outline each argument in support of each ground;

(e)   number each ground consecutively, if there is more than one;

(f)   identify any relevant authority and—

(i)   state the proposition of law that the authority demonstrates, and

(ii)   identify the parts of the authority that support that proposition; and

(g)   where the Criminal Cases Review Commission refers a case to the court, explain how each ground of appeal relates (if it does) to the reasons for the reference.

PARTICULAR ISSUES

Appeals against conviction (evidence)

6.21   In an appeal against conviction it is important to identify the particular error at trial or fresh evidence that is relied upon. However, it is just as important to identify how this makes the conviction 'unsafe'. Whilst this should not involve a lengthy description of the evidence, it is helpful to set out the context in which the error is said to be significant. A common reason for refusing leave is the single judge's assessment that the evidence was so strong that the error, or new evidence, would have made no difference to the jury's

---

29   CPD IX Appeal, Para 39 C.1.
30   CPD IX Appeal, Para 39 C.2.
31   Part 39.3(2)(a)–(g) CrimPR; the Guide A.3-1 to 3-5.

decision. When the prosecution case appears to be strong, the grounds should anticipate this objection: was the case truly overwhelming? If not, why not? If it was overwhelming could the new evidence itself have created a doubt where none otherwise existed?

Appeal against sentence (general)

6.22   The grounds should set out the offence, the maximum sentence that was available for the offence, whether the plea was guilty or not guilty, details of previous convictions and any other order made by the judge when passing sentence. In a case involving several sentences it may be useful to include a table setting out this information in relation to each offence and specifying whether it was a concurrent or consecutive sentence.

Appeal against sentence (assistance provided to the police)

6.23   When a ground of appeal is that insufficient weight was given for assistance that the applicant had provided to the police, special considerations apply. As these cases involve sensitive information that may be damaging to the applicant (or others), should it become public, there is a particular procedure to be followed.[32] The grounds of appeal and Form NG should be lodged with the Court of Appeal in the usual way. They should make no mention of the fact that information had been given to the sentencing judge in the form of a 'text' about assistance that the applicant had been provided to the police. This means that if the only ground of appeal is the failure of the Crown Court to make a proper reduction in sentence for such assistance, the grounds will be a very short, bland document. A separate note should then be lodged with the grounds, marked for the attention of the Registrar. It should alert the Registrar to the existence of the text and might also include any arguments in relation to the text that the applicant wishes the court to consider. The Registrar will ensure that the text is obtained and provided to the single judge and if leave granted to the full Court with the necessary steps taken to prevent publicity.

CITATION OF AUTHORITIES

6.24   In *R v Erskine*[33] the court emphasised that the only authorities that should be cited are those which are strictly necessary to advance the case. Lord Judge CJ said at para 75:

> 'If it is not necessary to refer to a previous decision of the court, it is necessary not to refer to it.'

---

32   The Guide A.5-2.
33   *R v Erskine* [2009] EWCA Crim 1425.

6.25   In appeals against conviction the court emphasised that the authorities relied on, should be, those which establish a particular proposition, and not, those which do 'no more than illustrate or restate an established proposition.' (*Erskine*, para 78)

6.26   The Court was particularly concerned about unhelpful citation of authorities in sentencing cases:

> 'Advocates must expect to be required to justify the citation of any authority. In particular where a definitive Sentencing Guidelines Council guideline is available there will rarely be any advantage in citing an authority reached before the issue of the guideline, and authorities after its issue which do not refer to it will rarely be of assistance. In any event, where the authority does no more than uphold a sentence imposed at the Crown Court, the advocate must be ready to explain how it can assist the court to decide that a sentence is manifestly excessive or wrong in principle.' (*Erskine*, para. 80)

6.27   While it is important to follow this guidance it is also important that it should not cause such anxiety that an authority that is genuinely significant is not drawn to the court's attention. The golden rule must be that the advocate is able to justify reference to a particular authority in the light of the approach that *Erskine* requires. The definitive citation rules are now summarised in the Practice Direction concerning matters of general application to all aspects of advocacy.[34]

NEW ARGUMENTS

6.28   If the appeal is based on a legal argument that was not raised in the Crown Court, the court will want to know why it was not raised. If it is necessary to apologise for failing to spot a legal point, then apologising in the written grounds is more likely to disarm any criticism than having that concession extracted by judicial cross examination at the full hearing.

Failure to object to things said in the summing up

6.29   If the appeal concerns the judge's summing up the Court will want to know:

(a)   Did the judge give the advocate the opportunity to address them, before the summing up, on any matters about which the applicant now complains? If so, did the advocate raise the point that is now raised on appeal? If not, why not?

---

34   CPD XII General Application, paras D2–D7.

(b)   Did the advocate seek to address the judge at the conclusion of the summing up in relation to the matter? If not, why not?

Criticism of previous lawyers

6.30   This is subject to detailed guidance which must be followed (see 6.13). The client needs to be advised at an early stage that waiver of privilege will be expected so the previous lawyers can respond fully and the court will be able to look at the instructions given at the time of the trial and the advice provided. Any indication that the matter should have been pursued then or was deliberately avoided for tactical reasons will be likely to be fatal to the appeal.

FRESH EVIDENCE

6.31   At the leave stage the single judge should actively consider the reason why the evidence was not sought at the trial stage. This will involve asking whether there has been a waiver of privilege and if not why. A Respondent's Notice will be required and the single judge should direct one if none has been filed. Having considered the response of the trial representatives the single judge should consider whether admission of the fresh evidence is potentially arguable. If it is not then leave should be refused, but if it is, the single judge should refer the application to the full court with directions rather than grant leave. Once referred the parties should ask for further direction from the court.[35]

Once referred the matters to be considered include:[36]

(a)   The section 23(2) CAA considerations (as discussed in Chapter 3) need to be addressed.

(b)   If the applicant seeks to call evidence by way of live witnesses, Form W must be completed for each proposed witness.[37] In practice the court may well hear and decide the appeal without actually hearing any witnesses. Nonetheless, that is a decision for the court to take, and the lawyers preparing the appeal need to offer the court the option of hearing the evidence.

(c)   The court has the power to order the attendance of a witness.[38] This includes witnesses who would not be compellable to give evidence at

---

35   *R v Kunwar Singh* [2017] EWCA Crim 466, paras 52–55.
36   The Guide A.5.
37   Available on the Ministry of Justice website.
38   CAA 1968, s 23(1)(b).

trial, such as previous lawyers and jurors.[39] If such an order is required, the Form W should make that clear. The granting of such an order does not mean that the court will hear the evidence. That will be decided by the full court at the hearing.

(d)   The statements of the witnesses (in section 9 form) or the documents that constitute the fresh evidence, should all be attached.

(e)   There must be a '*Gogana*' statement[40] from the applicant's solicitor in section 9 form (or affidavit) setting out why the evidence was not available at trial and how it came to light. The Guide, points out 'This will implicitly require fresh representatives to comply with *McCook*'.[41]

(f)   Applications for any of the following orders should be made in accordance with the relevant Parts of the Criminal Procedure Rules.[42]

  (i)   written witness statements (Part 16 CrimPR);

  (ii)   measures to assist a witness or defendant to give evidence (Part 18 CrimPR);

  (iii)   hearsay evidence (Part 20 CrimPR);

  (iv)   evidence of bad character (Part 21 CrimPR);

  (v)   evidence of a complainant's previous sexual behaviour (Part 22 CrimPR).

If these issues are raised in the grounds then they should be addressed in the Respondent's Notice (RN) or if raised in the Respondent's Notice then the applicant has 14 days to respond. The court and the Registrar have powers to make directions without a hearing.[43]

The court can also make orders for the production of exhibits, documents or other material (Part 39.7(3) CrimPR); or the attendance of witnesses before the court, or an examiner on behalf of the court, provided the correct procedure is followed (Part 39.7(4)–(7) CrimPR).

CHANGE IN LAW APPEALS

6.32   Where the application is lodged in time (see 6.8) the test is whether the conviction is unsafe. Where the application is made out of time the then

---

39 Criminal Justice and Immigration Act 2008, Sch 8, para 10 introduced this amendment to CAA 1968, s 23.
40 *R v Gogana* (1999) *Times*, 12 July.
41 The Guide A.5-1.2.
42 Part 39.7(1) CrimPR.
43 Part 39.7(2) CrimPR.

exceptional leave will be required. This will only be granted if the applicant will suffer 'substantial injustice' due to the change in the law.[44]

Applying for extension of time within which to appeal

6.33   For those applications that are lodged after the end of the 28-day period there is a box to be ticked in the Form NG indicating that an application for an extension is being made. In addition to ticking the box it is essential that the reasons for delay should also be clearly explained either in the grounds or as a separate document.

6.34   In a case involving significant delay, particularly where that delay has been brought about by the time that it took fresh solicitors to prepare the appeal, the application should be accompanied by a chronology of the work that has been done in the lead up to lodging the application with particular reference to the timing of instructions and actions taken. (See 6.8–6.11 above, for consideration of time limits, extensions and the need for due diligence). The substantial injustice test may prevent leave being granted even where the appeal is unopposed or had substantial merit.[45]

Other documents to be lodged in support of the application

6.35   It is always worth considering what other documents might be needed for the court to understand the grounds. Examples would include the written directions to the jury if they are being criticised or a witness statement that was admitted in evidence by way of a hearsay ruling that is a ground of appeal. If there was relevant CCTV or other footage it should be supplied with a summary if it would assist. In appeals based on new material that relies on the applicant being a victim of trafficking, the Criminal Appeal Office will want the relevant material including the National Referral Mechanism (NRM) assessment and accompanying evidence to be lodged with the Form NG.

It makes sense to copy and attach such documents to avoid any delay caused by the Registrar later having to obtain them.

---

44   *R v Johnson & Ors* [2016] EWCA 1613; The Guide A.5-3.
45   *R v Ordu* [2017] EWCA Crim 4.

OTHER APPLICATIONS WHICH MAY BE MADE ALONG WITH THE APPLICATION FOR LEAVE

Applications for bail

6.36   The single judge does have the power to grant bail pending appeal. However, the court has held that bail pending appeal should only be granted in exceptional circumstances in which the court concludes that it is necessary in order to 'do justice in the case'.[46]

6.37   Bail cannot be applied for until an application for leave is lodged.[47] If a bail application is included with the application for leave then usually the single judge will consider it when they decide whether to grant leave.

6.38   The application for bail should be made with Form B, and served on the CPS (or the prosecuting authority). The rules for bail applications are at Part 39.8 CrimPR. If bail is granted with pre-conditions before release, such as a surety, the specific steps are outlined at Part 39.9.[48]

6.39   If the issue of bail is urgent because of the shortness of the sentence or ill-health of the applicant, a note should be sent to the Registrar making this clear. In extreme cases the Registrar may ask the single judge to consider bail before the application for leave is considered. However, the court only grants bail in exceptional circumstances so it is very unlikely to do so without consideration of the strength of the application for leave itself.

6.40   The granting of bail should not create an expectation that the applicant will not be returned to prison should the appeal fail.[49]

Request for an expedited hearing

6.41   As well as applying for bail or in cases where bail is unlikely to be granted the applicant can ask for an expedited hearing. There is no form to be submitted but a note attached to the application should make clear the reasons for urgency. If the Registrar can refer the case to the full court immediately for a rolled-up hearing of leave and, if granted, the appeal.

---

46   *R v Watton* (1979) 68 Cr App R 293.
47   *R v Suggett* (1985) 81 Cr App R 243.
48   The Guide A.13.
49   *R v Kalia* (1974) 60 Cr App R 200.

Requests for transcripts

6.42   Once an application for leave is lodged the Registrar will obtain a copy of the summing up (in an appeal against conviction), sentencing remarks (in an appeal on sentence) and prosecution opening facts (in a sentence following a guilty plea).[50]

6.43   If the applicant asks for a transcript of any other part of the trial (specific evidence, a judge's ruling or a legal argument) in the application for leave to appeal conviction, they should explain why it is necessary for the appeal and identify the date and, if possible, the time at which the relevant part of the trial commenced and concluded.[51] Transcripts can also be requested in an application for leave to appeal against sentence.[52]

Applications for funding

6.44   The Form NG contains a box to apply for a representation order. It will be granted if leave to appeal is granted. Usually it will be only be granted for an 'advocate alone' which will not cover the instructing solicitor. If the appeal requires work by the solicitor and they have a criminal legal aid contract an application can be made to the Registrar to extend the representation order. This can be done by letter and it will help if the advocate provides a supporting note confirming the work that needs to be done. If the Registrar does not grant the application to extend the order they will usually refer it to the single judge or the full court.

6.45   If the Crown Court representation order was for a junior and a leading junior or QC, the Court of Appeal will normally grant a representation order for a single advocate only on the basis that two advocates will not be needed for the presentation of the appeal.[53] Again, a letter explaining why it requires an additional advocate with a supporting note will need to be sent to the Registrar. See Chapter 8 for a detailed consideration of funding.

Disclosure of third-party material

6.46   If third-party material is needed for the appeal the applicant must provide a clear and compelling explanation why the material was not obtained

---

50   The Guide A.7-1 to 7-2.
51   Part 39.3(c) CrimPR; the Guide A.7.
52   The Guide A.7.3 to 7.5: the appellant may be ordered to pay for them and a privately funded one will be expected to.
53   The revised Form NG asks that a copy of the Crown Court representation order is attached if possible.

in the Crown Court.[54] The full court, the single judge and Registrar can order a third party to produce documents or other material, but they will only do so in exceptional cases.

6.47   An application for third-party material should contain:

(a)   completed Form W;

(b)   details of the material sought;

(c)   its relevance to the appeal;

(d)   details of the party against whom any order for production of the material is to be made; and

(e)   details of any refusal of the party to provide the material on a voluntary basis.

6.48   The application should be served on the party in question (and anyone the material relates to) so that they can raise any objections.[55] If there are objections the court may direct that there is a hearing so that the parties who are directly concerned can be heard, before deciding to make the order.

Request for an oral leave hearing

6.49   It is possible to apply for an oral leave hearing to argue the grounds before the single judge. This is rare given that the applicant will have a right to an oral hearing if they renew the refused application (on the papers).

LODGING THE GROUNDS – DIRECT LODGEMENT

6.50   The traditional practice of sending the grounds to the relevant Crown Court ended on 1 October 2018. There is a new Form NG for conviction, sentence and confiscation that should be completed separately for each. They should be sent by secure email to the Criminal Appeal Office. If that is not possible then they can be posted.[56]

6.51   When an application for leave is received by the Registrar, the Criminal Appeal Office's lawyer will:

(a)   check that the application for leave is in valid form;

---

54   *R v Niwar Doski* [2011] EWCA Crim 987.

55   *R (on the application of TB) v The Combined Courts at Stafford* [2006] EWHC 1645 (Admin).

56   criminalappealoffice.applications@hmcts.x.gsi.gov.uk; para 39C.5 CPD IX Appeal; the Guide A2-2.

(b)   if the application is out of time, check an application for extension of time has also been made;

(c)   contact the Crown Court to ensure that all relevant exhibits are retained until the conclusion of any appeal;

(d)   obtain the transcripts and any other documents that are necessary for the single judge to determine the application;

(e)   if relevant, check there is a waiver of legal privilege and contact previous lawyers for their comments on matters raised in the application;

(f)   if appropriate, ask the prosecution for their views, before the case is sent to the single judge.[57] If the prosecutor wishes to make observations on the appeal they will serve a Respondent's Notice (see 6.56).

6.52   The Registrar has the power to refer a case directly to the full court to deal with leave and any appeal as a rolled up hearing. There are a number of reasons why this might be done: if co-defendants have already been given leave to argue the point; if the need for a hearing is urgent or the question of law is particularly complicated; or if the Registrar is of the view that the application may be considered vexatious. However, this is unusual.

STEPS BEFORE THE CASE IS SENT TO THE SINGLE JUDGE

Perfecting the grounds

6.53   Before the case is considered by the single judge the Registrar will send the relevant transcripts from the trial to the applicant or their lawyers, if represented. This is so that the grounds can be reviewed or 'perfected'. The 'perfected' grounds should be a new document. It will replace the original grounds and should contain references to the page and paragraph number of the relevant passages in the transcripts.

6.54   The applicant will be given 14 days to perfect the grounds or they will need to apply for more time.[58] The advocate should include a list of any relevant case law with the perfected grounds along with copies of any unreported authorities (see 6.24 and 6.25).[59]

6.55   The Registrar may direct that the transcripts must be returned unmarked so a copy should be made and kept for any future hearings.

---

57   Part 39 CrimPR specifies when a prosecution response is required.
58   The Guide A.8 sets out the expectations.
59   Part 39.3(2)(g) CrimPR; the Guide A.8-5.

Responses from trial lawyers and the respondent

6.56   The applicant will be given the opportunity to respond to the observations from the trial lawyers to any additional questions asked by the Registrar. This can be made by amending the grounds or in a separate document. It may be unnecessary to add anything if it is already covered in the grounds.

6.57   The respondent should serve their response (Form RN) on the applicant.[60] However, they sometimes fail to. It is therefore worth contacting either the CPS Appeals Unit or prosecuting counsel directly in order to check if one has been completed. The Registrar will ask for a Form RN in the following cases:

(i)   where the grounds concern matters which were the subject of public interest immunity (PII);

(ii)   allegations of jury irregularity;

(iii)   criticisms of the prosecution or the conduct of the judge;

(iv)   complex frauds;

(v)   inconsistent verdicts;

(vi)   fresh evidence; and

(vii)   where the grounds claim that the wrong statute, rule or regulation was applied.

The prosecution will be invited to lodge a Form RN in the following cases:

(i)   all applications involving a fatality;

(ii)   all conviction applications involving rape, attempted rape or a serious sexual offence;

(iii)   all conviction applications where the CPS Complex Casework Unit dealt with the case;

(iv)   all conviction applications where the offence was perverting the course of justice.

6.58   The applicant should respond urgently to any new points in the Form RN as the papers will go to the single judge as soon as the Form RN is received.

---

60   Part 39.6(3)–(6) CrimPR; CPD IX Appeal, para 39D; the Guide A.9.

DECISION OF THE SINGLE JUDGE

6.59   Once the perfected grounds, the trial lawyers' comments and the Form RN are received, the papers will be sent to the single judge who may:

(a)   grant leave on some or all of the grounds that are arguable;

(b)   refuse leave on all grounds; or

(c)   refer the case to the full Court.

6.60   Other applications, including representation and any extensions of time, will also be considered. The reasons for the decisions will be set out in the Form SJ, which will be sent to the applicant. If the judge refuses leave they will also initial the 'loss of time box' if they believe the application is hopeless (see 6.65 and 6.66).

6.61   If leave is granted, then a representation order will be granted to the advocate to appear at the hearing to argue any grounds that have been given leave.

6.62   Waiting for the decision of the single judge can be frustrating because, once the papers have been sent to the judge, the Criminal Appeal Office cannot tell the applicant precisely how long it will take the judge to consider them. Often 'the papers are with the judge' is the only indication that will be given.

RENEWING AN APPLICATION FOR LEAVE

6.63   The applicant can renew the application for leave on any of the grounds that have been refused. The application must be lodged within 14 days of receipt of the Form SJ. This is done by completing the SJ Renewal Form that is on the reverse side of the Form SJ and sending it to the court. The 14-day period will only be extended in exceptional circumstances. Any application for extension will be referred to the full court with the renewal application.

6.64   If all of the grounds were refused, the application to renew will be heard by the full court. If leave has been granted on some grounds, the renewed application for leave for the remaining grounds can be argued at the full appeal hearing. However, when leave is partially granted the applicant will have to remember to complete the renewal form for any refused grounds that they want to re-argue at the appeal hearing.

6.65   The decision to renew is often difficult. It is not made any easier by the fact that legal aid will have come to an end. The advocate and their solicitor will need to reflect on the reasoning of the single judge when reviewing the strength of the grounds. On the one hand, the advocate should not have drafted grounds unless they thought that they were arguable, on the other a High Court judge has said the case is not arguable. The applicant will need to be advised on the risk of a 'loss of time' order and whether the advocate is prepared to act *pro bono* or, if not, the cost of renewing privately. The advocate will note the advice in the Guide that they should never act simply because they are instructed to do so, but only if there are reasonably arguable grounds (see 6.6). Having said that if the grounds are properly arguable the advocate should stand by them. Many appeals are allowed despite refusal of leave by the single judge. Indeed, some appeals have been allowed even when the single judge has initialled the loss of time box. If the advocate does act pro bono on the renewal and leave is granted by the court then usually a retrospective representation order will be granted to cover the hearing (see Chapter 8).

The risk of loss of time served and costs

6.66   The biggest risk for the applicant is that the court will direct that some of the time served whilst appealing should not count towards sentence.[61] The court should only do this if it thinks the application lacks any merit.

6.67   The initials of the single judge in the loss of time box on the Form SJ is an indication to the full court that it should consider making an order for loss of time. That creates a higher risk of a 'loss of time' order being made. Even if the box is not initialled there is still a risk.[62] An order can be made even when the applicant's advocate advised that there were arguable grounds of appeal.[63] The full court is becoming increasingly active in considering loss of time orders. As we are reminded in the Practice Direction:[64]

> 'unmeritorious renewal applications took up a wholly disproportionate amount of staff and judicial resources in preparation and hearing time. They also wasted significant sums of public money … The more time the Court of Appeal Office and the judges spent on unmeritorious applications, the longer the waiting times were likely to be … The only means the court has of discouraging unmeritorious applications which waste precious time and resources is by using the powers given to us by Parliament in the Criminal Appeal Act 1968 and the Prosecution of Offenders Act 1985.'[65]

In the end the decision to renew must be the applicant's, but they will rely heavily on the advice they receive and whether the advocate will agree to act *pro bono*. Even if a loss of time direction cannot be made because the applicant

---

61   CAA 1968, s 29.
62   Para 39 E.1 CPD IX Appeal; the Guide A.16.
63   *R v Hart* [2006] EWCA Crim 3239; CPD IX Appeal, para 39E.3.
64   CPD IX Appeal, para 39E.2.
65   *R v Gray & Others* [2014] EWCA Crim 2372.

has been released from detention the single judge should additionally consider whether to indicate that an adverse costs direction should be considered by the full court.[66]

Renewing when considering taking the case to the European Court of Human Rights

6.68 Where the applicant wants to take a point to the European Court of Human Rights they should considering renewing the application.[67] Otherwise there is a danger that, by not renewing, it could later be said that the domestic remedies had not been exhausted, which can be a bar to the European Court considering the application. Where compatibility with a Convention right arises the Registrar will give notice the any party potentially affected.[68]

Renewing other applications

6.69 On renewing an application for leave the applicant can also renew other applications, including bail. These applications are renewed on the same SJ Renewal Form to renew the leave application. They need to be made within 14 days of receipt of the SJ decision. They will be considered by the full court at the renewal hearing.

ABANDONING AN APPLICATION FOR LEAVE

6.70 Any application will be considered by the court unless it is abandoned by the applicant. The decision to abandon is made by lodging a Form A with the court prior to the hearing. The Form A needs to be signed by the applicant or their lawyer. Abandonment can be made at the hearing, but only with the leave of the court.[69] The main reasons to abandon are to avoid the risk of a loss of time or costs order.

6.71 Once an appeal is abandoned no new appeal against the same decision may be brought, unless the case is referred to the court by the Criminal Cases Review Commission. Abandonment cannot be withdrawn. Therefore, by abandoning a case the appellant is effectively signing away his appeal rights.

---

66   *R v Terence Nolan* [2017] EWCA Crim 2449; CPD IX Appeal, para 39E.4.
67   See the discussion in Chapter 11.
68   Part 36.12(2) CrimPR.
69   Part 36.13(2) CrimPR.

Abandonment as a nullity

6.72   Abandonment may only be challenged on the basis that an apparent abandonment is a nullity. Abandonment will be a nullity when the Court concludes that the mind of the applicant did not go along with the act of abandonment (*R v Medway*).[70] The clearest example of this would be where the applicant signed a notice of abandonment thinking that he was signing a different type of document.[71]

Bad legal advice giving rise to nullity

6.73   The court may accept that the abandonment was a nullity if it was based on bad legal advice (*R v L*[72]), but only if that advice was positively wrong, not if it was advice on a difficult point with which some might agree and others disagree (*R v Smith (Paul James)*[73]).

Making an application for reinstatement

6.74   If the Court agrees the abandonment was a nullity it will reinstate the application. An application to reinstate an appeal or application for leave following abandonment is heard before the full court and the applicant must satisfy the court that it was a nullity.[74] The procedure is contained in Part 36.13 CPR.[75]

Skeleton arguments

6.75   It may be useful to serve a skeleton prior to the hearing especially if there is a novel point to argue or it involves a complex sentence.[76] Any skeleton must be served at least 21 days before the hearing and any response at least 14 days before the hearing unless the court says otherwise.[77] Skeletons should be no more than a numbered list of points that the advocate wants to cover for each ground using no more than one or two sentences. The document should have the CAO reference and the date it was served on the header and the advocate's name on the footer.[78] The advocate should

---

70   (1976) 62 Cr App R 85.
71   As happened in *R v Mohamed* [2010] EWCA Crim 2464.
72   [2013] EWCA Crim 1913.
73   [2013] EWCA Crim 2388.
74   *R v Medway* (1976) 62 Cr App R 85; *R v Zabotka* [2016] EWCA Crim 1771.
75   The Guide A.17.
76   CPD IX Appeal, para 39F.1.
77   CPD IX Appeal, para 39F.2.
78   CPD IX Appeal, para 39F.3; See general guidance at CPD XII General Application, para D17-23.

double check that list of authorities is correct and the bundle complies with the general Practice Direction.[79]

The hearing

6.76   Normal case management duties apply to appeals just as in any criminal matter.[80] The Registrar and the single judge have extensive statutory powers that apply to efficient management of the case and obtaining evidence.[81] If the Registrar refuses to make a procedural direction there is a right of appeal to the single judge.[82]

The judges hearing the appeal will have the papers prepared by the lawyers at the Criminal Appeal Office. These consist of a case summary which comes in two parts. Part 1 goes to the advocate (or unrepresented appellant). They can be shown to the lay and professional client but they are not for wider circulation and should not be copied without permission. Part 1 consists of:

(i)   a summary of the proceedings in the Crown Court including names of the representatives and any co-defendants;

(ii)   a history of the proceedings in the Court of Appeal;

(iii)   a summary of the case drafted by the lawyer in the Criminal Appeal Office based on the appeal documents,

(iv)   the transcripts and trial statements or exhibits;

(v)   the submissions, rulings, summing up and sentencing remarks.

The case summary is a matter for the lawyer drafting it but an advocate can raise relevant matters to their attention as it is meant to be an objective document.

Part 2 is for the court only and consists of:

(i)   a summary of the grounds

(ii)   in a sentence case the antecedent history of the applicant or appellant and any pre-sentence report, medical report or other reports for sentencing.

The advocate should note that the court will have access to the source material so they can refer them to it.[83] Generally the hearings are to be conducted in public but there are limited exceptions.[84] Reasonable notice of hearings should

---

79   CPD XII General Application, para D.11-16.
80   Part 36.2 CrimPR; the Guide A.18.
81   CAA 1968, s 23(1)(a), s 31.
82   CAA 1968, s 31A(4).
83   CPD IX Appeal, Para 39G.
84   CrimPR, Part 36.6.

be given to anyone affected by the judgment.[85] An appellant who is in custody (but not an applicant), has a general right to attend the full hearing. That is unless the court directs that it is only a point of law or the appellant was found to lack capacity. This attendance will generally be by way of a prison video link (PVL).[86] Therefore, it is important, especially in sentencing renewals, to confirm with the client in advance that they will waive this right to appear at the appeal hearing if the renewal is successful and the court wishes to proceed to a full appeal hearing immediately. This is generally good advice as a successful renewal is more likely to lead to a successful appeal with the same judges rather than taking the chance it will be adjourned and then heard by less receptive ones. It will also save time and costs, which will be well received. The advocate can expect to be asked if they have instructions to proceed.[87]

The judgment

6.77   Unless the court made a specific direction, the draft judgment is provided to the lawyers about three working days before being handed down. Any observations should be directed to the judge's clerk. It should not be circulated to the parties until two hours before being handed down. Any breach of these directions will be treated as contempt.[88]

Miscellaneous appeals

6.78   The above outlines the general procedures in everyday appeals against conviction, sentence and confiscation. Chapters 12, 13 and 14 look at more specialist appeals and there is detailed guidance on the specific procedure or forms required for these miscellaneous appeals against interlocutory rulings, ancillary orders or costs in the HMCTS Guide.[89]

SUMMARY OF KEY POINTS

- Appeals from the Crown Court against conviction or sentence require leave from the single judge or full court except in rare cases where it might be appropriate to apply to the Crown Court for a certificate of fitness for appeal.

- Application for leave to appeal must be lodged within 28 days of the decision which is challenged.

---

85   CrimPR, Part 36.7.
86   CAA 1968, s 22 (c) gives the court the power to direct PVL.
87   Part 39.11 CrimPR.
88   Para C1-14 CPD XII General Application.
89   The Guide, paras B–E.

- The court has the power to extend the time either before or after the 28 days expire. However, the application to extend must contain an explanation for the delay.

- The application must be made using the specified Form NG and in accordance with the requirements of Part 39.3 CPR.

- All other applications, including extension of time, bail and any application for a representation order should be lodged with the grounds.

- The application must be lodged at the Criminal Appeal Office unless it relates to a preparatory, terminatory or similar trial ruling, or is an AG reference, in which case it is lodged at the Crown Court.[90]

- The Registrar's office will prepare the case in order to either send it to the single judge or refer it directly to the full court for consideration.

- If leave on any ground is refused by the single judge it may be renewed. The application for renewal must be lodged within 14 days of the decision.

- The court may consider exercising its power to loss of time order if an application for leave is renewed that the court regards as being 'wholly without merit'. If the single judge has indicated on the Form SJ that the court should consider this then there is a strong chance that it will do so.

- If leave has been granted on some grounds, renewal needs to be made within 14 days on any remaining grounds that need to be re-argued at the final hearing.

- Other applications that were refused by the single judge may also be renewed before the court.

---

90 See summary: www.justice.gov.uk/courts/procedure-rules/criminal/docs/october-2015/2018-appeal-forms/guidance-lodging-appeals-september-2018.pdf

Chapter 7

Preparing for hearings in the Court of Appeal

INTRODUCTION

7.1   Every advocate who has appeared before the Court of Appeal will have had the experience of preparing the case thoroughly and arguing it passionately only to sit down and listen to the Court deliver a judgment that had clearly been written before the hearing commenced. It is tempting to ask what was the point in arguing it at all?

7.2   Before the hearing the Court will often have formed a preliminary view of the case. However, just as every advocate will have had the experience of failing to change the Court's collective mind, judges attest to occasions when the Court was convinced by effective oral advocacy.

7.3   If belief in one's ability to persuade is the first principle of advocacy in the Court of Appeal, the second is that the task of persuading the Court does not begin with the hearing itself. As the Court inevitably forms a preliminary view of the case, it is important to try to influence its thinking as early as possible by effective drafting, ensuring that important documents are lodged in good time and that the relevant authorities are drawn to the Court's attention.

7.4   This chapter covers the preparation for and presentation of the hearing. The topics covered apply to both appeals with leave and oral applications for leave to appeal. When different considerations apply to each type of hearing, this is made clear.

PREPARING FOR THE HEARING

Considering the Court bundle

7.5   The Registrar (in practice the lawyer at the Criminal Appeal Office who has been assigned to the case) is responsible for compiling the bundle of material that will be considered by the judges. It will be sent to the parties in advance of the hearing. It should be read with care. This is the case that the Court will read. In particular it is necessary to do the following:

Ensure that all the relevant documents are included

7.6   If either of the parties wish the Court to consider any document that is not in the bundle, they should write to the Registrar, enclosing the document, stating its relevance and asking that it be included. Alternatively, try phoning the lawyer at the Criminal Appeal Office (whose details and direct number are normally to be found in the correspondence) to discuss the contents of the judges' bundles.

Consider the case summary

7.7   Within the bundle will be the case summary that will have been prepared by the lawyer in the Criminal Appeal Office. It will contain what the writer considers to be the significant information about the facts of the case and its procedural history.

7.8   It should be considered carefully. It is vital that it is accurate and that it refers to the facts that are significant to the appeal. They are usually both accurate and comprehensive but if there is an amendment that should be made, the Registrar should be written to and asked to include it. Whether to make the amendment sought is a matter for the judgment of the summary writer. If it is decided not to include that matter in the case summary, the Court will be provided with the document that requested its inclusion.[1]

7.9   Advocates can (unless the Registrar states otherwise) show the summary to their clients but it should not be copied or reproduced.

Check the time estimate that has been given to the case

7.10   The summary writer's view of the likely time estimate will be on the front page. It will be used to list the case. The Court will expect hearings to be concluded within the time estimate. Therefore, if it is thought that the time estimate is inadequate, the Registrar should be written to[2] and told why; bear in mind, before doing so, that the hearing will be conducted by three experienced judges who will have already read into the case.

---

1   Practice Direction 39G.3.
2   Practice Direction 39B.4.

Skeleton arguments

7.11   The Practice Direction provides:

'39F.1 Advocates should always ensure that the court, and any other party as appropriate, has a single document containing all of the points that are to be argued. The appeal notice must comply with the requirements of CrimPR 39.3. In cases of an appeal against conviction, advocates must serve a skeleton argument when the appeal notice does not sufficiently outline the grounds of the appeal, particularly in cases where a complex or novel point of law has been raised. In an appeal against sentence it may be helpful for an advocate to serve a skeleton argument when a complex issue is raised.

39F.2 The appellant's skeleton argument, if any, must be served no later than 21 days before the hearing date, and the respondent's skeleton argument, if any, no later than 14 days before the hearing date, unless otherwise directed by the Court.

39F.3 A skeleton argument, if provided, should contain a numbered list of the points the advocate intends to argue, grouped under each ground of appeal, and stated in no more than one or two sentences. It should be as succinct as possible. Advocates should ensure that the correct Criminal Appeal Office number and the date on which the document was served appear at the beginning of any document and that their names are at the end.'

7.12   It may well be helpful to draft a skeleton in a case that is to be presented in a different way before the full Court to the way in which it was first presented in the grounds (for example, if particular grounds are not going to be advanced before the full Court, or more recent authorities relied on).

New grounds of appeal

7.13   The appellant must obtain leave to advance any new ground that was not in the application for leave. Whilst the advocate should not be afraid to pursue a powerful new ground, the Court has profoundly discouraged this course; see *R v James and Others*.[3]

Authorities

7.14   Guidance from the Registrar on how authorities should be provided to the Court will be set out in a letter from the Registrar with each case. The general position is that a list of reported cases, with case references, should have been supplied to the Criminal Appeal Office with the Perfected Grounds

---

3   [2018] EWCA Crim 285.

of Appeal with copies of any unreported cases.[4] If, when preparing for the appeal, the advocate discovers a further authority, the Registrar should be told as soon as possible. The Court is unlikely to flatly refuse to look at a further case at the hearing, but it would be foolhardy to ask them to do so without having ready at least an apology and, better still, a reasonable explanation for asking them to do so.

7.15   In deciding what authorities (if any) to rely on, it is important to bear in mind what the Court said in *Erskine* about not placing unnecessary authorities before the Court and, in particular, not relying on sentencing cases that pre-date a sentencing guideline or guideline case, unless there is very good reason to do so. (See 6.24–6.27 for full details.)

LISTING THE HEARING

7.16   The Court of Appeal Listing Office is responsible for fixing a date for hearing, of which the parties are notified. It will consider applications for a hearing to be moved but will generally not move a case because the advocate has another case in a lower Court. Appearances in the Court of Appeal must take precedence.[5]

THE HEARING

Presence of the appellant/applicant

Hearings with leave

7.17   An appellant who is in custody has the right to be produced at his full hearing, unless he suffers from insanity or a disability; this will almost always be by way of a video link, and the Court now has video conference facilities. There is no right to be present at a preparatory hearing although production can be requested.[6]

7.18   If the appellant does not wish to be produced, the appeal can take place in his absence.[7] For this to take place the Registrar may require his consent to be in writing.

---

4   Part 39.3(2)(g)) CrimPR.
5   Practice Direction 39B.2.
6   CAA 1968, s 22.
7   CAA 1968, s 22(4).

Renewed applications for leave

7.19   Applicants have no right to be present at renewed applications for leave. If an application for leave to appeal against conviction is successful then the full hearing will generally take place at a later date at which an appellant who is in custody will then be produced. However, if the application for leave to appear against sentence is successful, the Court will usually proceed to determine the appeal at the same hearing, in the absence of the appellant. If this takes place, the Registrar will then write to the appellant informing him of the result of the hearing and of his right to have a further hearing at which he will be present but that the Court will only consider new submissions at such a hearing if the applicant presents new material (*R v Spruce and Anwar*).[8]

7.20   In order to avoid this taking place the applicant's solicitors should, in advance of the hearing, obtain their client's instructions on whether he would wish to be present at the full hearing. In any event, it is often the practice of the Court to produce the applicant from custody in cases where the effect of granting leave and allowing the appeal against sentence would be his immediate release.

When the appellant has absconded

7.21   If the appellant has absconded whilst in custody or on bail, the Court may dismiss the appeal, hear it in the absence of the appellant or adjourn the case pending his being returned to custody. The Court has held that it is only in exceptional cases that the Court will hear the appeal.[9] An important factor will be whether the appellant had given his lawyers instructions that are sufficiently clear and detailed for them to be able to properly advance his case in his absence.[10]

When the appellant has died

7.22   Section 44A of CAA 1968 provides that an appeal can continue when an eligible person can be identified and approved by the Court to take over his case. The categories of eligible persons are:

(a)   the widow or widower, or surviving civil partner, of the dead person;

(b)   a person who is the personal representative (within the meaning of section 55(1)(xi) of the Administration of Estates Act 1925) of the dead person; or

---

8   [2005] EWCA Crim 1090. See also CPR, r 68.12.
9   *R v Gooch* [1998] 2 Cr App R 130 (CA), confirmed in *R v Salloum* [2010] EWCA Crim 312.
10   *R v Okedare* [2014] EWCA Crim 228.

(c)   any other person appearing to the Court of Appeal to have, by reason of a family or similar relationship with the dead person, a substantial financial or other interest in the determination of a relevant appeal relating to him.

7.23   Except in the case of an appeal on a reference by the Criminal Cases Review Commission, an application for such approval may not be made after the end of the period of one year beginning with the date of death.

Whether the prosecution will be represented at the hearing

7.24   The prosecution will be represented in appeals against conviction. They may choose or be asked by the Court to appear in appeals against sentence. They may also choose or be asked by the Court to appear at a renewed application for leave.

Orders restricting public access or reporting of hearings

The public right to attend court hearings

7.25   The general rule is that the Court should hear appeals in public but it may order that a hearing take place in private. The opposite approach applies when the Court is hearing a Public Interest Immunity application which must be held in private, unless the Court decides to hold it in public.[11]

7.26   An order that a hearing take place in private may be made under the Court's inherent power[12], but only in exceptional circumstances where the Court concludes that a public hearing would frustrate the administration of justice. An order may also be made under the following statutory powers:

(a)   in any appeal against a review of sentence (section 75(2) of the Serious Organised Crime and Police Act 2005 in relation to appeals pursuant to section 74(12));

(b)   where a witness under the age of 18 is giving evidence (section 37 Children and Young Person's Act 1933) (note: such an order cannot apply to members of the press);

(c)   where the Court hears evidence in relation to a sexual offence (section 25 of the Youth Justice and Criminal Evidence Act 1999) (with, once more, an exception for the press).

---

11   Part 36.6(2) CrimPR.
12   Part 36.6(1) Crim PR.

Reporting restrictions

7.27   The press are entitled to report, in full, the Court's proceedings unless it makes an order placing a restriction upon the reporting of a particular case or unless one of the following three automatic statutory reporting restrictions applies:

(a)   The Sexual Offences (Amendment) Act 1992 gives the victim of a sexual offence lifetime anonymity in respect of their identification. The types of offences covered by this section are set out in section 2 of the Act (as amended by subsequent legislation) and includes the majority of sexual offences.

(b)   Section 12 of the Criminal Justice Act 1987 and section 37 of the Criminal Procedure and Investigations Act 1996 provide limitations to the facts that may be reported in an appeal in relation to a preparatory hearing.

(c)   Section 71 of the Criminal Justice Act 2003 provides that reporting restrictions apply to prosecution appeals against a preparatory ruling.

7.28   The Court may make an order restricting the reporting of a case under its inherent power but it also has a number of statutory powers to do so. Part 6 of the CPR sets out the proper approach to the making of reporting restrictions and also contains a complete schedule of all statutory powers to make such an order.

7.29   In all cases where a reporting restriction might be appropriate, for example one involving children,[13] the parties should check with the Clerk of the Court whether any restrictions are in place. Any application should be made at the commencement of the hearing.

Hearing appeals regarding public immunity applications

7.30   In *R v McDonald, Rafferty and O'Farrell*[14] the Court set out the principles that should govern appeals in which the conduct of a Public Interest Immunity hearing in the Crown Court is the subject of challenge.

Televised Court hearings

7.31   An order has been made which allows television companies to broadcast legal arguments and judgments from the Court of Appeal, for the

---

13   Children and Young Persons Act 1933, s 39.
14   [2004] EWCA Crim 2614.

purpose of news reporting only.[15] Witnesses, victims and appellants must not be shown.

The procedure at the hearing

Appeals with leave

7.32   The case commences with the appellant being identified on the video link. The appellant's advocate will make submissions. The advocate for the respondent (if the respondent is represented) will then make submissions. There is a final reply from the appellant. The judges frequently adopt an interventionist approach and will not be slow to ask the advocate about a particular point that concerns or interests them or to indicate that they think that an argument is a bad one.

7.33   If there is evidence to be called, the appellant will generally be expected to call the witness and examine him and the respondent to cross-examine in the normal way. However, when, if at all, that evidence is to be called is a matter to be determined by the Court.

7.34   Unless there is a clear indication, in advance of the hearing, that the Court does not wish to hear from a particular witness, or the prosecution agree the witness, the witness should be at Court and in a position to give evidence if called.

7.35   In most cases the Court gives judgment at the end of the hearing. In more complex cases it may give a reserved judgment and the parties will be informed of the date of a further hearing for judgment to be pronounced.

Renewed applications for leave

7.36   The hearings follow the same procedure as full hearings. Successful renewed applications for leave to appeal against conviction usually result in the Court listing the case for a full hearing on another occasion at which the appellant (if in custody) can be produced and the prosecution can be represented.

7.37   However, if a renewed application for leave to appeal against sentence is successful, the Court will generally proceed to determine the appeal at the same hearing.

---

15   The Crime and Courts Act 2013, s 32, which provides that the Lord Chancellor may, with the concurrence of the Lord Chief Justice, make an order allowing for filming in particular courts. The general ban on filming and recording in court is contained within the Criminal Justice Act 1925, s 41 and the Contempt of Court Act 1981, s 9.

Suggestions for advocacy

7.38   When preparing:

(a)   Re-read everything.

(b)   Identify the strongest point (or points) and be prepared to argue it concisely but with conviction. Not to do so is to throw away the opportunity that is presented by oral advocacy.

(c)   Search out the difficulties in your case. Every case has them. The Court will identify them and ask the advocate about them.

(d)   Clearly tab up the significant parts of the transcript so that they can be found quickly in Court.

(e)   If it is intended to rely on authorities that have not been lodged with the Court or that were lodged late (and may not have reached the judges), three additional copies should be brought to court (along with an explanation for not having provided them earlier).

7.39   In Court:

(a)   When a judge sits in the Court of Appeal he or she is always addressed as My Lord or My Lady.

(b)   The Court will expect an advocate to introduce his opponent.

(c)   The Court will not expect the advocate to tell it about the facts of the case. It should be assumed that the relevant facts are in the papers and that the judges will have read the papers.

(d)   It should not be assumed that the Court will be bound by the views of the single judge. Although it is wise to carefully consider the reasons of the single judge for granting or refusing, it is unwise to place reliance on the fact that leave has been given in the submissions themselves.

(e)   If there are apologies that may have to be offered (if an argument was missed at trial) or concessions that are going to have to be made (if the judge got the law right once, and the grounds rely on his getting it wrong at some other stage), it is often best to make them immediately. It is more attractive to hear an advocate face up to a problem, admit it and then go straight on to argue why nonetheless the appeal should be allowed, than to witness the Court having to cross examine him into an admission he should have made at once.

(f)   When making an application for leave that is out of time the advocate should not forget that the application to extend time must also be made. It is sometimes sensible to mention at the outset when the advocate proposes to deal with it (it usually makes sense to address it at the conclusion of the substantive arguments on the grounds, unless the Court wants it to be addressed immediately) so that the Court is aware that the advocate has not forgotten the need to do so.

APPLICATIONS AT THE CONCLUSION OF THE CASE

Applying for leave to appeal to the Supreme Court

7.40   If the appeal is dismissed, the appellant has 28 days to apply to the Court of Appeal to:

(a)   certify a point of law of general public importance; and

(b)   grant leave to appeal on the point to the Supreme Court.[16]

7.41   The Court of Appeal rarely certifies a point of law and almost never grants permission to appeal.

7.42   If the Court certifies a point and refuses leave to appeal, the appellant then has 28 days to apply to the Supreme Court for permission to appeal. However, if the Court refuses to certify a point of law the appellant cannot apply to the Supreme Court. This is frustrating for appellants and their lawyers who feel there is a good legal argument that deserves further consideration, but both the Court of Appeal and the ECtHR have held that section 33 of CAA 1968, which, in effect, allows the Court of Appeal Criminal Division to terminate any further domestic appeal, is compatible with Article 6 of the Convention.[17]

7.43   A certified point is in the form of a question which should be framed in a way that identifies a particular legal issue that arose in the appeal but also indicates its wider importance.

7.44   If the Court has given judgment on the day of the hearing, the application to certify and for leave to appeal can be made orally, immediately after the judgment. However, it can be useful to reflect and draft a question with some care.

Applying to certification when considering an application to the European Court of Human Rights

7.45   If the appellant wishes to take the case to the ECtHR, it is advisable to make the application to the Court for leave and certification or the appellant may later face a difficulty in satisfying the ECtHR that he has complied with the requirement to exhaust all domestic remedies. (See 11.6 and 11.7 for full discussion.)

---

16   CAA 1968, s 34.
17   *R v Dunn* [2010] EWCA Crim 1823 and application 62793/10 (declaration of inadmissibility, by a majority).

Costs

7.46 Orders for costs are not routinely made in the Court of Appeal and the law governing such payments has been greatly restricted in recent years.

7.47 The law in relation to costs is to be found in Criminal Practice Directions 2015 Division X.

Costs from central funds for the successful applicant/appellant

7.48 The only residual power to award costs from central funds relates to appeals about insanity[18].

Costs against an unsuccessful appellant or applicant

7.49 The Court can award costs against an unsuccessful appellant or applicant[19], but only when satisfied he or she has sufficient means to pay the order, and not on the basis the money could be raised after release from prison or by a third party[20]. The CPR also sets out the process that should be followed when the prosecution seeks costs.

Costs for unnecessary or improper expenses

7.50 If the Court is satisfied that a party's unreasonable or improper act or omission has put another party to expense, it may order that party to pay some or all of the other party's costs.[21] The Court may make such an order on the application of a party or on its own initiative. An application should be made in accordance with the requirements of rule 45.8 of the CPR in writing, as soon as practical after becoming aware of the grounds for doing so. A copy should be served on the Registrar and one on the other parties.

Wasted costs orders against representatives

7.51 'Wasted costs' are defined by section 19(1) of the Prosecution of Offences Act 1985 as any cost incurred 'as a result of an unnecessary or improper act or omission by, or on behalf of, another party to the proceedings'.

7.52 The Court may make a wasted costs order against a legal representative or 'other representative', defined in the act as a person who is exercising a

---

18 CPD X Costs 2.4.4.
19 Prosecution of Offences Act 1985, s 18(2).
20 CrimPR 45.6(8) and CPD. See 8.19.
21 Prosecution of Offences Act 1985, s 19(1).

right of audience or right to conduct litigation on behalf of any party to the proceedings[22]. 'Wasted costs' in that section is defined as:

(a)   as a result of any improper, unreasonable, or negligent act or omission on the part of any representative or any employee of a representative; or

(b)   which, in the light of any such act or omission occurring after they were incurred, the court considers it is unreasonable to expect that party to pay.

7.53   The guidance for making a wasted costs order is to be found at paragraph 4.1.1. of the Costs Practice Direction. Further guidance is to be found in *Re P (A Barrister)*.[23]

7.54   As an alternative to making a wasted costs order the Court may, when the appellant is funded by a representation or costs are to be paid out of central funds, make adverse observations about the representative's conduct of the case, for use in a costs assessment.[24]

Costs against a third party

7.55   The Court may make an order for costs against a third party when the Court considers that there had been serious misconduct by that party.[25] Guidance on the use of that section is at rule 4.7 of the CPR (2015, Division X). It is noted that such orders can only be made either of the Court's own volition or on the application of a party to the case.

Applications for a representation order following successful applications for leave

7.56   In successful applications for leave to appeal an application for a representation order may be requested at the conclusion of the hearing. It is a good idea to be specific, so if the preparation *and* presentation of the appeal was all unfunded, asking for 'a representation order for the preparation and presentation of the appeal' will avoid any danger of the Registrar later taking the view that only the work on the day of the hearing was covered by the order obtained.

SUMMARY OF KEY POINTS

●   It is important to carefully read the appeal bundle to ensure that:

---

22   Prosecution of Offences Act 1985, s 19A.
23   [2001] EWCA Crim 1728.
24   CPD X Costs 4.3. See 8.19.
25   Prosecution of Offences Act 1985, s 19B.

- ○ it contains all the documents that are important to the appeal;
- ○ that the case summary is accurate and covers the points that are important to the appeal;
- ○ that the time estimate that has been given for the hearing is accurate.

- Whether to lodge a skeleton argument is a matter for the advocate, but the Court does not encourage advocates to provide skeleton arguments when the case is already fully set out in the appeal notice.

- Lists of any reported authorities and bundles of any unreported authorities should be lodged with the grounds or perfected grounds. The guidance in *Erskine* should be considered when determining what authorities to rely on.

- Leave of the Court will be needed in order to argue any ground that was not contained in the original grounds that were considered by the single judge.

- The appellant has a right to be present at all appeals with leave, normally by video link, but not at renewed applications for leave. If the Court, having given leave to appeal against sentence, goes on to allow the appeal at the same hearing at which the appellant has not been produced, he will be written to asking if he wishes to have a hearing at which he will be produced.

- When an appellant or applicant has absconded, the Court has a discretion as to whether to hear the case, adjourn or dismiss the appeal.

- If the appellant dies before the hearing, the case may proceed if an approved person can be appointed to continue the case on his behalf.

- The prosecution will be represented at appeals against conviction. They may be represented at appeals against sentence or renewed applications for leave depending on whether the Court requests it or the prosecuting authority themselves decide to be represented.

- The Court's hearings are open to the public unless an order is made that a particular hearing be held in private. Certain reporting restrictions may automatically apply or be made by the Court depending on the nature of the case. In a case in which the parties believe that an order restricting public access of press reporting of the case should be made, it should be applied for at the commencement of the hearing.

- In straightforward appeals the Court will give judgment at the conclusion of the hearing. In complex cases judgment may be reserved to another date.

- At the conclusion the advocate should remember to make any necessary application for a representation order or to certify a point of law of general public importance for the Supreme Court.

Chapter 8

Public funding and pro bono assistance

INTRODUCTION

Three distinct types of funding

8.1   There is publicly funded appeals advice available to those who are
unable to afford a lawyer. This comes in three varieties of 'legal aid'. The first
two are different types of 'advice and assistance' (out-of-court advice) and the
third is 'representation' ('advocacy') in court.[1]

As with all forms of state assistance, the rules for accessing this advice and
claiming for the work are labyrinthine and scattered across various statutory
sources. The overarching statutory framework for all types of legal aid is
now set out in the Legal Aid, Sentencing and Punishment of Offenders Act
2012 (LASPO 2012).[2] However, the important detail is contained in various
statutory regulations which include: the Criminal Legal Aid (General)
Regulations 2013 (SI 2013/09) ('General Regulations'), the Criminal
Legal Aid (Remuneration) Regulations 2013 (SI 2013/435) ('Remuneration
Regulations'),[3] and the Criminal Legal Aid (Financial Resources) Regulations
2013 (SI 2013/471) ('Means Regulations').[4]

Advice and assistance under the Crown Court Representation Order

8.2   A limited amount of advice and assistance is provided for by the
defendant's Crown Court Representation Order. The defendant's lawyers (the

---

1   Criminal Legal Aid (General) Regulations 2013 (SI 2013/09) 'General Regulations', Reg 2
     provides that 'criminal legal aid' means 'advice, assistance and representation made available
     under s.13, 15 and 16 of the Act' (LASPO); General Regulations, Reg 33(c) provides that
     'advice & assistance' includes 'an appeal or potential appeal against the outcome of criminal
     proceedings'.
2   LASPO, ss 14–19 set out the statutory basis for legal aid in criminal proceedings including
     advice and assistance.
3   Remuneration Regulations, Reg 6 refers to Sch 3, which sets out what can be claimed and the
     fees for both advice and assistance and advocacy under a representation order.
4   Means Regulations specify who qualifies financially for advice.

solicitor assigned on the order and their instructed advocate) can provide brief advice at the end of the Crown Court case. If that advice is positive it will also cover preparing the grounds to lodge at the Court of Appeal.

Advice and assistance under the Standard Criminal Contract

8.3   If the defendant asks a solicitor who is not assigned under the Crown Court Representation Order to advise then they may be able to provide 'freestanding' advice and assistance under the 2017 Standard Criminal Contract (SCC). The important contract rules are set out in the Standard Terms and the Specification to the contract. There is also important guidance produced by the Legal Aid Agency (LAA) in the Criminal Bills Assessment Manual (CBAM).[5]

Any organisation who has a General Crime Contract can carry out work under the SCC. The rules for advice on appeal is covered in section 11 of the Specification headed 'Appeals and Reviews Class'. As it happens, only a minority of the organisations holding a contract actually do provide freestanding advice and assistance on appeals. This is because the work is seen as specialist and badly paid. They will advise those who they have represented in the Crown Court under their representation order, but will not provide fresh advice to defendants who say they have been wrongly advised, or not advised at all.

Partly that is also to do with the widespread assumption that the original trial lawyers will have provided a full written advice addressing any concerns the defendant has raised at the end of the Crown Court case. The continued stagnation of legal aid fees for Crown Court work makes that assumption less reliable. As advocates and litigators are not actually paid anything extra to provide a negative advice in writing some do a minimal amount of work at the end of the case. This is unsurprising given the fixed fee for the Crown Court work is often very low. This means it can be difficult for aggrieved defendants and their families to obtain a comprehensive advice explaining precisely why they do not have an appeal. Often their only option is to pay privately. The potential problems are exacerbated by the parlous state of publicly funded fees currently paid to both prosecutors and defence advocates, which means that there may be even greater need to check that the original lawyers got it right first time round at the trial.

---

5   The contract documents can be found at: www.gov.uk/government/publications/standard-crime-contract-2017

Representation under the Court of Appeal Representation Order

8.4   If leave to appeal is granted then the Court of Appeal will usually grant a representation order if it is requested on the Form NG. The funding regime under the Court of Appeal representation order is very similar to that under the original Crown Court representation order. The major difference is that the order usually extends only to the advocate who drafted the grounds and does not include a solicitor.[6] However, an application can be made to extend its scope to include a solicitor to do specific work and, if necessary, more than one advocate.

Actual representation replaces advice and assistance

8.5   Once the Court of Appeal has assigned an advocate under a representation order it will replace the original Crown Court order so the advice and assistance on appeal under the previous order will cease. For the avoidance of doubt, the SCC makes it clear that advice and assistance also available under the SCC cannot be used as an alternate or supplement to the court's powers to grant legal representation, where only an advocate has been authorised.[7]

Pro bono assistance

8.6   There are also a small number of organisations who provide free assistance or representation for appeal work. The limited availability of legal aid means that these can be a vital backstop for those who seek to challenge their sentence or conviction. The assistance that they may provide is considered at the end of this chapter.

WORK UNDER A CROWN COURT OR COURT OF APPEAL REPRESENTATION ORDER

The funding rules

8.7   As already discussed at 8.2 above, the usual starting point for advice on appeal is the representation order in the Crown Court. That order includes

---

6   The Court of Appeal exercised the power in LASPO, s 19(1) to grant representation and the Criminal Legal Aid (Determination by a Court and Choice of Representative) Regulations 2013 (SI 2013/614) allow the Court of Appeal to grant representation of its own motion or on an application.

7   SCC, para 11.40.

advice and assistance on any appeal.[8] The scheme of funding for representation orders is set out in LASPO (which refers to the grant of funding by the court as a 'determination').[9] The rates of pay are set out in the Remuneration Regulations.[10]

To appreciate how legal aid works in the Crown Court it is important to bear in mind that the vast majority of Crown Court work is paid by way of fixed fees. These are the Litigator Graduated Fee Scheme (LGFS) for solicitors and the Advocates Graduated Fee Scheme (AGFS) for advocates. The fixed fee is based on four factors: the type of offence; the outcome; the page count; and the number of witnesses. No additional fee is paid for a negative advice on appeal at the end of the case as that work is included in the fixed fee.

However, if the appeal advice is positive and grounds are lodged at the Court of Appeal, then an additional claim can be made for the advice and grounds by both the solicitor and the advocate from the Court of Appeal. If the single judge refuses leave then a claim for the fees for that additional work is made by sending it to the Registrar's costs office.[11]

If the single judge grants leave, or he or she refers the application to the full court, then a representation order will usually be only granted for the advocate who drafted the grounds. They will then be able to claim a further fee for their preparation and advocacy at the full hearing. If additional work needs to be done by the solicitor an application needs to be made to the Registrar to extend the order to cover the solicitor for any specific tasks. It is rare for the Registrar to agree to extend the order generally to cover a solicitor, but it can be done if a lot of work is required.

You will find most of the relevant rules and guidance for advice on appeals under a representation order in the Practice Directions (CPD 2015),[12] the Criminal Procedure Rules (CrimPR)[13] and the Remuneration Regulations (see 8.1).

---

8   Legal Aid, Sentencing and Punishment of Offenders Act 2012, s 42; 'representation' includes 'advice and assistance as to any appeal'.
9   LASPO, s 16.
10   Given the number of changes in fees in recent years you will need to carefully check the relevant Remuneration Regulations at the date of the representation order you are providing advice under. The old rate applies pre-20/03/14; the current rate (with a 8.75% cut) applies from 20 March 2014 to 1 July 2015, then full 17.5% cut from 1 July 2015 to 31 March 2016 before returning to current rate thereafter.
11   The claim is made on the old ex post facto claim form – see COA Bill of Costs at Appendix E.
12   See Appendix A.
13   See Appendix B.

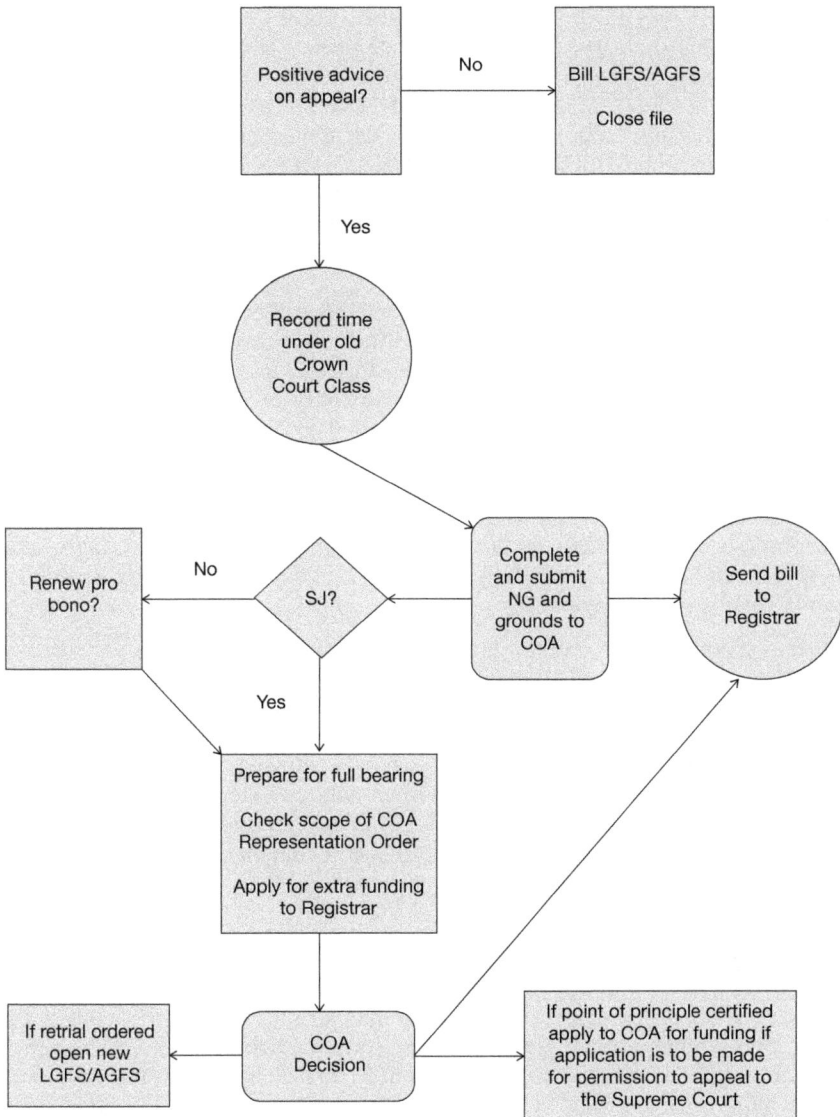

Figure 8.1   Flowchart for appeals under the Crown Court representation order

What advice is covered?

8.8   The best place to look at what work will be allowed is the Guide to advocates produced by Her Majesty's Courts & Tribunals Service's 'Guide to commencing proceedings in the Court of Appeal Criminal Division' ('The Guide')[14]. This indicates what work the Registrar will be likely to authorise and what his or her costs team will consider necessary and reasonable when they assess the work done on the bill. The Guide instructs the advocate to provide basic advice as soon as the Crown Court case finishes under the Crown Court order. If exceptional work needs to be done under a Court of Appeal representation order, then it is best to lodge provisional grounds with the Criminal Appeal Office and send a note to the Registrar setting out why a representation order should be granted to cover that additional work.[15]

8.9   The Registrar will not usually extend the order to allow work by a solicitor unless he or she is persuaded that there is good reason to do so. This is because the Registrar will assume that the appeal involves a discrete point of law which can be dealt with adequately by the advocate alone. If the solicitor can show an extension is needed to do specific work, such as instructing an expert or taking a witness statement, then they should write to the Registrar explaining why and include a full supporting note from the advocate. If an extension is granted it will clearly set out the limited purpose(s) for which the solicitor is assigned on the actual order. Therefore, it is important to check carefully what work is authorised and if necessary apply for further extensions.

Once a representation order is granted the Registrar will send a form to the appellant asking them to confirm their means remain the same as they were when the Crown Court representation order was granted.

8.10   If there is any doubt about what is allowed, clarification can be obtained from the Criminal Appeal Office and an extension obtained. This must be done before carrying out the work. There is no set form of application. It can be made by letter and it should always include a supporting note from the assigned advocate setting out why it is needed.

Effect of refusal by single judge

8.11   If the single judge refuses leave they will also refuse the application for a representation order. This means any further advice will have to be either privately funded or *pro bono*. The original Crown Court order does not cover renewal and the unavailability of legal aid for renewal to the full court does not breach Article 6 of the ECHR.[16] Depending on the comments of the single judge, and particularly whether they have initialled the 'loss of time' box on

---

14   Note at time of writing the current Practice Direction CPD X Costs, Part 8.1 still makes reference to the former Guide produced by the Registrar of Criminal Appeals, but this guidance has been updated and replaced by the HMCTS one (latest version August 2018).
15   The Guide A.1-4.
16   *R v Oates* [2002] EWCA Crim 1071.

the Form SJ, the advocate may be prepared to renew the application *pro bono* before the full court. If the renewal of the application for leave is successful the full court will grant a representation order even if ultimately the substantive appeal fails. That order will cover the preparation and advocacy for the full hearing, but it will not usually cover the work done by the solicitor unless it is specifically requested at the renewal hearing and the court agrees.

Post-SJ refusal advice

8.12   As the court can grant retrospective representation when they grant leave on a renewed application then it may be worthwhile asking the court to consider extending the representation order to cover not just the advocate but also the solicitor who worked on the renewal. As this will be unusual it will require exceptional justification, but it is possible and should be considered in preparation for the renewal hearing. It is useful if the solicitor can provide a schedule of work done so that the advocate can fully argue it.[17]

CLAIMING FOR WORK DONE IN THE COURT OF APPEAL

All claims

8.13   The rules for claiming fees for work done in the Court of Appeal are mainly contained in Remuneration Regulations.[18]

The claim for cost must be submitted within three months from the conclusion of the case.[19] The time limit may be extended by the Criminal Appeal Office if there is 'good reason', but any costs allowed may be a reduced if there is not a good reason for the delay and it is reasonable to reduce them. If the assessor proposes to reduce the fees they must give the solicitor or advocate the opportunity to make submissions and they can appeal to the Costs Judge if there are unsatisfied by the reasons given for the reduction.[20]

The claim 'must be in such a manner and form as the appropriate officer may direct' and sent to the costs team at the Criminal Appeal Office.[21] It should include a copy of the representation order and any receipts or vouchers for any disbursements.

---

17 CBAM, para 6.9.4; *Regina v Gibson (Ivano)* [1983] 1 WLR 1038.
18 Remuneration Regulations, Reg 6 refers to the fees set out in Sch 3.
19 Remuneration Regulations, Sch 3, paras 2 and 5.
20 Remuneration Regulations, Reg 31.
21 SCC, para 5.25; see Appendix F for the current version of the claim form.

All assessments are based on:

'all the relevant circumstances of the case including the nature, importance, complexity or difficulty of the work and;

the time involved and allow a reasonable amount in respect of all work actually and reasonably done.'[22]

The solicitor and advocate should draft a full note justify each item of work and the time spent with the claim. This should also point to any special circumstances of the case and provide as much information as possible to assist the costs team in assessing the claim with reference to the above test.

Solicitors' claims

8.14   The costs assessor has to take account of the 'class of work done'. The assessment will look at whether the work done was reasonable and the time spent.[23]

Solicitors' work in the Court of Appeal is broken down into five classes:

(i)   preparation (which includes all the general work a solicitor will do on a case);

(ii)   advocacy;

(iii)   attending at court with the advocate;

(iv)   travelling and waiting; and

(v)   dealing with routine letters and telephone calls.[24]

The claim should group these classes of work separately and set out the date it was done, the time taken and amount claimed (and whether it was done for more than one assisted person).

The claim must specify the level of fee-earner and set out any work done for more than one indictment.[25] It must also set out why any enhancement is claimed (see 8.15).[26] If a claim is made under a retrospective representation order (see 8.11), the claim must confirm that none of the fees have been claimed under a defence costs order from central funds. As costs from central funds can no longer include legal fees in the Court of Appeal this is unlikely.[27]

---

22   Remuneration Regulations, Sch 3, para 1(2); CBAM, the general principles in para 2.4 also would apply.
23   Remuneration Regulations, Sch 3, para 3(2).
24   Remuneration Regulations, Sch 3, para 3(1).
25   Remuneration Regulations, Sch 3, para 2(3).
26   Remuneration Regulations, Sch 3, para 3(2); CBAM, para 3.1 applies to all assessments
27   Prosecution of Offences Act, s 16A.

The level of fee earner will be either:

(i)   Grade A, which is a senior solicitor (this is normally 10 years post qualification experience 'PQE' or eight years' specialist experience);

(ii)   Grade B, which is a non-senior solicitor or an experienced legal executive; or

(iii) Grade C, which is a trainee or paralegal.

The rates that can be claimed are set out in the Remuneration Regulations.[28] These are fairly modest and have remained pretty much unchanged since the mid-1990s. The assessor will look at the level of fee-earner for each item on the bill and firstly decide if that person was the right grade of fee-earner for that task. Therefore, it is important that the note that is sent with the claim makes it clear why a solicitor carried out any routine work which could have been delegated or why a senior solicitor was used. It may well be the case that as that fee-earner dealt with the original case and knows the history and the client then overall that will have saved time and this can be used to justify the overall time as reasonable. You may be able to show that a more experienced fee-earner has accomplished a task quicker than a less experienced one would and that this has reduced the claim overall or that a less experienced one would have needed to do additional work getting up to speed with the case.

Enhancement

8.15   Given the low basic hourly rates for solicitors it is vital that 'enhanced' rates are claimed whenever possible.[29] If allowed, the hourly rate will usually double as it will be enhanced by 100%. Usually it will only apply to non-routine work as, by definition, it must be exceptional, but sometimes if there is an exceptional amount of travel or waiting because of the location of the client or the nature of the case. This would be very rare. Enhanced rates can be claimed for any of the specified offences.[30]

To claim enhanced hourly rates the solicitor must show:

(a)   the work was done with exceptional competence, skill or expertise;

(b)   the work was done with exceptional despatch; or

(c)   the case involved exceptional complexity or other exceptional circumstances.

---

28   Schedule 3, para 7.
29   Remuneration Regulations, Sch 3, paras 8(2).
30   Remuneration Regulations. Sch 1, Part 7 provides a list of the specified offences A, B, C, D, G, I, J and K.

If made out the appropriate uplift will depend on:

(i)   the degree of responsibility accepted by the fee-earner;

(ii)   the care, speed and economy with which the case was prepared; and

(iii)   the novelty, weight and complexity of the case.

The usual uplift is up to 100% and for a solicitor based in London the appropriate uplift should be the full 100% taking account of the local Senior Courts' Costs Office (SCCO) rates.[31] If it is a very complex or serious fraud it can be up to 200%.[32] The test of 'exceptional' means simply 'unusual or out of the ordinary' for the *general type* of case, it does not mean exceptional for *that type* of case.[33] A claim for enhancement may be more likely to persuade the assessor if the solicitor or advocate focuses on the particular tasks that meet the enhancement criteria rather than claiming a blanket enhancement across the board.

To maximise the chances of being successful in claiming an enhancement all actual work which can be shown to be reasonable and necessary to provide advice on appeal should be clearly recorded. Exceptional 'competence, skill or expertise' may be shown by the standard of work carried out or the favourable outcome. Exceptional 'despatch' will require real urgency. This may be because of late service of papers or the need to consider a large volume of work in a short period of time which meant rearranging or cancelling other work. It will assist if you can point to the need to rearrange other work to accommodate the urgency of the task and point out any evening or weekend work. The general factors that may have made the original case exceptional are set out in CBAM. These include the character of the defendant (including any vulnerability); if the case was particularly weighty or complex; the type of case or degree of public interest; significant expert issues; difficulties with defence witnesses; or the exceptional length of trial.[34] They may or may not apply at the appeal level, which will be on a narrow legal issue so enhancement submissions will need to focus on the appeal aspects to the work. However, it is unusual for the Registrar to assign a solicitor so that is a good starting point for submissions.

The bill will be assessed by a member of the costs team at the Criminal Appeal Office who will not necessarily be aware of the details of the case so it is helpful to carefully set out the factors in the case that justify both the level of fee-earner who worked on the case and any grounds for enhancement with detailed reference to the individual circumstances of the case and the client. If

---

31   These are local guideline hourly rates for general litigation approved by the SCCO and they are much higher than the rates for publicly funded work.

32   CBAM 2018 (June) para 9.1.

33   *R v the Legal Aid Board ex parte RM Broudie* [1994] 138 SJ 94.

34   CBAM, para 9.1.3.

the time spent on a piece of work is longer than one would expect that should be clearly explained in the note with the claim.

Disbursements

8.16   Disbursements that are abnormally large because of the distance travelled from the solicitor's office to the court or the client may be reduced if not sufficiently justified. The cost of Crown Court transcripts that were not obtained through the Registrar may also be disallowed unless reasonable.[35] The fees for experts are set out in Schedule 5 of the Remuneration Regulations. These prescribed rates can be increased if justified in exceptional circumstances.

Advocate's claim

8.17   The advocate submits their claim on the same form as the litigator and the matters they are required to set out are much the same apart from the level of fee-earner as that will be either junior counsel or QC depending on the representation order. They set out almost identical information including the date of the work, the time spent and whether it was for more than one assisted person. They should also draw the assessor's attention to any special circumstances.[36]

The Remuneration Regulations set out the type of work that can be claimed and the applicable hourly rates, basic fees, refreshers and subsidiary fees. There are minimum and maximum amounts for subsidiary fees and the assessor should take account of the hourly rates when assessing the fees. The rates are separate for QC and junior work.[37]

The advocate can also claim for a fee higher than the specified rate if the exceptional circumstances mean that the set fees would not provide 'reasonable remuneration' for the work done.[38] The factors set out at 8.15 would equally apply to the advocate's claim.

Appealing the assessment

8.18   If the costs are not allowed in full, then further representations can be made within 21 days of the initial assessment. If those representations are not completely successful an appeal can be submitted to the Costs Judge at the Senior Courts' Costs Office (SCCO).[39] If the appeal to the Costs Judge is

---

35   Remuneration Regulations, Sch 3, para 4.
36   Remuneration Regulations, Sch 3, para 5; see COA Claim Form at Appendix F.
37   Schedule 3, paras 9(1)–(3).
38   Remuneration Regulations, Sch 3, para 9(4).
39   Remuneration Regulations, Sch 3, para 11.

successful, even in part, the judge will usually order the additional costs of preparing and attending the costs appeal.

Other costs orders

8.19   If the court makes an adverse observation about the conduct of the case by either the litigator or advocate, the appropriate officer may reduce the fees. If they intend to do so they must give the person affected an opportunity to make representations as to whether the fee should be reduced and the extent of any reduction.[40] The Practice Direction addresses this in detail.[41] The Court of Appeal can also order an unsuccessful defendant to pay the costs of another party and any legal aid costs. It should not be done as a penalty and exceptions apply.[42]

FUNDING UNDER THE 2017 STANDARD CRIMINAL CONTRACT (SCC)

What work can be done?

8.20   The SCC sets out the types of advice that can be provided by organisations who hold a contract with the LAA (and referred to as 'providers'). The SCC is a detailed set of rules which need to be read with the LAA guidance in CBAM. This sets out the LAA's approach to the types of work it will allow providers to do and how funding requests will be viewed by the LAA. The rules and guidance go into minute detail as to what can and cannot be done. It should be remembered that the guidance is just that and may be departed from if justified. The SCC Specification is structured into sections: 1–8 apply generally to all classes of criminal work; and sections 9–13 refer to specific areas of work. Appeals and Reviews are covered at section 11.[43] If there is a conflict between any terms then the general sections take precedence over the specific ones.[44] CBAM also has general and specific sections.[45] If there is a conflict between the SCC and CBAM, then SCC takes precedence.[46] In addition there are Points of Principle of General Importance, generally referred to as 'PoPs', that set out general principles which have arisen from appeals to the LAA Costs Committee. There is a PoP Manual containing useful decisions that can be used to support funding applications.

---

40   Remuneration Regulations, Reg 26.
41   CPD X Costs, para 4.3.
42   CPD X Costs, para 3.
43   SCC, para 11 deals specifically with Appeals and Reviews.
44   SCC, para 1.4.
45   CBAM, para 12 deals with Appeals and Reviews.
46   CBAM, para 1.1.

Advantages of using the SCC

8.21   If a new team of lawyers are instructed after conviction they could, in theory, apply to transfer the Crown Court representation order and provide advice and assistance under the Crown Court order. That would involve an application to the Crown Court where the matter was heard.[47] Given the strict criteria for transfer it is unlikely to be successful unless there has been a complete breakdown in the relationship between the defendant and the trial lawyers. In any event the new team will be reluctant to have the order transferred to them before they can assess the merits because there is no additional payment for a negative advice under the LGFS and AGFS. Therefore, a better solution is to see whether the work qualifies under the 'Appeals and Reviews' class of work in the SCC. This 'Appeal and Reviews' class of work covers both applications for leave to the Court of Appeal and requests to the Criminal Cases Review Commission (CCRC) to review the conviction or sentence. It is important to gather as much information from the prospective client at the outset in order to be able to assess whether the case meets the initial sufficient benefits test and is likely to pass the means test. This can be done using a detailed New Client Appeals Enquiry Form, which captures sufficient information.[48]

Disadvantages of using SCC – costs limits and audit compliance

8.22   There are separate costs limits for applications to the Court of Appeal and the CCRC.[49] Once these limits are reached any additional costs or disbursements will require a specific costs extension by the LAA. As the work up to the first extension is self-authorised by the provider it is essential that there are clear file notes complying with both the SCC and the guidance in CBAM. Apart from the applications for extensions to the upper limit, none of the work on the file will be subject to any ongoing checks by the LAA unless the file is requested for an audit, so it is essential that the solicitor checks the evidence on the file to ensure the contract requirements on application forms, evidence of means and file notes are in perfect order. Indeed, the further extensions by the LAA assume that the provider has followed the contract to the letter at the self-authorisation stage and, if not, those LAA extensions will be in jeopardy on any audit of being invalidated and all the money being recouped. In appeals cases lasting many years this can mean substantial costs can be run up on a longstanding and complex advice file, which may be subject to minute scrutiny on a LAA audit after the case has concluded. Most of these costs will have been paid (or be contractually due) to an external advocates or expert(s). The LAA will audit a selection of files every year. These audits are thorough and will result in contract notices and recoupment of any monies paid

---

47   The Legal Aid Manual, ch 7.
48   An example can be seen at Appendix F.
49   For Court of Appeal cases it is currently £273.75 and for CCRC applications £456.25.

where there is a lack of evidence of compliance with the contract requirements. That is irrespective of whether the work was necessary and reasonably done or indeed authorised by the LAA retrospectively as all authorities must be granted *before* the work is done. This bureaucracy and the fact that there is no means to obtain payment of disbursements before the case concludes, are severe disincentives to taking on this type of work. On audit, the main pitfalls are: incorrect or incomplete application forms, a lack of adequate evidence of means, or inadequate file notes recording decisions. Files will also be examined by the LAA to check the costs limit was extended before the work was done. Payments made when the rules are not complied with or when the limits are exceeded will be recouped.[50] Contract audits can be appealed, and while many successfully are, it is time-consuming and unpaid work so it is better to try to avoid them by having tight supervision from the start.

Who can advise under the SCC?

8.23   All organisations holding a current general crime contract or a specific 'appeals only' contract are authorised to provide advice and assistance on Appeals and Reviews. However, if there is an existing representation order then the LAA will expect advice to be given under that order (see 8.6 above) by the existing litigator and advocate unless there has been a justifiable change of provider. In that case the new provider should carefully consider the advice the client has already received and whether fresh advice at the public's expense is justified.[51] If the solicitor who has provided advice under the original order is asked to readvise under the SCC they may do so but they should consider whether they should make an application to the Court of Appeal for a representation order.[52]

The general supervisor requirements in the SCC apply.[53] Where the organisation holds an appeals only contract there is an additional supervisor requirement that the supervisor must have held a non-conditional practising certificate for three years or they must have undertaken a minimum of 350 hours' casework in Appeals and Reviews in the past 12 months (or, if part-time, 1050 hours in the past five years).[54] The supervisor is required to sign a declaration to confirm that. They can supervise a maximum of four designated fee-earners.[55] Any advocate instructed to provide an opinion must be independent to the instructing litigator unless they are undertaking the advocacy:

---

50   SCC, para 5.19.
51   SCC, paras 11.3–11.5.
52   SCC, para 11.7.
53   SCC, paras 2.1–2.31.
54   SCC, para 2.26.
55   SCC, para 2.30.

'An in-house advocate instructed by you to give an opinion must be from a different organisation from your instructing Solicitor unless undertaking advocacy on the same case. The use of such an advocate who must not be a partner in, or employed by, or a consultant to your organisation will ensure that any opinion obtained is independent and objective (in the same way that an external opinion would be).'[56]

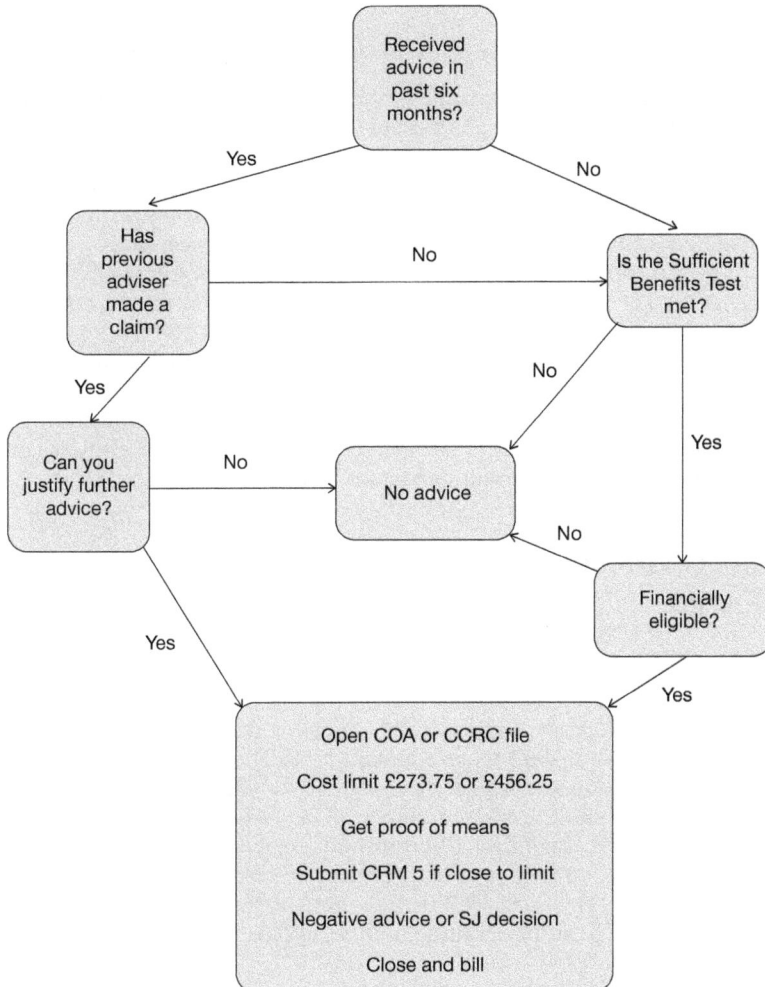

Figure 8.2   Flowchart for advice on appeal to COA or CCRC under SCC 2017 Appeals and Reviews Class

---

56   SCC, para 4.17.

Bars to advising – previous advice and assistance

8.24   You cannot advise a client under this scheme if they have received advice from another provider within the past six months unless:

(a)   there is a gap in time and circumstances have changed materially between the first and second occasions when the advice and assistance was sought;

(b)   the client has reasonable cause to transfer from the first provider; or

(c)   the first provider has confirmed that they will be making no claim for the payment for the advice and assistance.[57]

8.25   The six-month rule does not apply if the previous advice was given under a representation order.[58] However, as that advice was likely to be negative, the justification for fresh advice will need to be carefully considered. Generally, you will need to wait at least six months before providing fresh advice. After six months you may provide advice if the means test and the merits test, which is known as the sufficient benefit test (SBT), are passed (see 8.32). The request will not pass the SBT if the previous advice dealt adequately with the matters the client is now raising. Providers will be expected to filter out these requests without opening an advice file. It will be easier for the case to pass the SBT if the client is in custody so it relates to their liberty or the conviction is having an ongoing impact on their life.[59]

PRE-CONDITIONS – FINANCIAL ELIGIBILITY (MEANS)

The Means Regulations

8.26   The SCC adopts the eligibility rules for financial eligibility that are contained in Part 2 of the Means Regulations.[60] The LAA will enforce them strictly when auditing any appeal files so it is vital that the information on the file complies with the LAA requirements. They will look at the guidance in CBAM at Annex B: Financial Eligibility. If evidence is not satisfactory the LAA can issue a contract notice and recoup any costs and disbursements that were already paid. This may well include hefty disbursements to third parties that the provider will still be contractually liable for.

---

57   SCC, para 11.26.
58   CBAM, para 12.2.1.
59   CBAM, paras 12.2.2 and 12.2.3.
60   SCC, para 11.9.

Deemed eligibility

8.27   There is 'deemed' financial eligibility if the individual (or their partner) is in receipt of the following benefits:

(a)   a 'qualifying benefit': income support; income-based jobseeker's allowance; guaranteed state pension credit; income-related employment and support allowance; and universal credit;[61] or

(b)   they currently receive either:

   (i)   any working tax credit payable under Part 1 of the 2002 Act claimed together with child tax credit payable under Part 1 of that Act; or

   (ii)   any working tax credit payable under Part 1 of the 2002 Act with a disability element or severe disability element (or both).

And in the case of (i) or (ii) the individual's total income from all sources for the year before signing the CRM1/2 is not more than £14,213, otherwise the full eligibility calculation must be carried out.

If relying on a qualifying benefit you must keep satisfactory evidence on the file.[62] It will passport them straight through to the sufficient benefit test (see 8.27).

Partner

8.28   If the client has a partner their resources need to be taken into account.

"'Partner" means –

(a)   'an individual's spouse or civil partner, from whom the individual is not separated due to a breakdown in the relationship which is likely to be permanent;

(b)   a person with whom the individual lives as a couple; or

(c)   a person with whom the individual ordinarily lives as a couple, from whom they are not separated due to a breakdown in the relationship that is likely to be permanent'

This means that a client serving a custodial sentence may be separated from their partner physically but still in a relationship. You must not assume they are single because they are in prison.[63]

---

61   Means Regulations, Regs 14 and 2.
62   SCC, para 3.5.
63   CBAM, para 13.3.4.

The financial resources of the individual's partner must be treated as the individual's financial resources unless:

(a)   the individual's partner has a contrary interest in the matter in respect of which the individual is seeking advice and assistance; or

(b)   the Director of Legal Aid Casework considers that, in all the circumstances of the case, it would be inequitable or impractical to do so.[64]

Disposable income

8.29   For those who are not deemed eligible, their 'disposable' income cannot exceed £99 and 'disposable' capital must be no more than £1,000.[65]

The period of calculation is the seven days up to and including the date on which the CRM1 and CRM2 was signed.[66]

Although CBAM does not deal with specific evidence of means in the Appeals and Reviews chapter it does in the Prison Law chapter, which must also apply to appeals files. It warns providers not to assume that prisoners have no income (or capital). However, noting their prison income on the CRM1/2 will be sufficient and you are not required to provide further evidence of their prison income.[67]

To work out disposable income the following amounts can be deducted:

(a)   income tax;

(b)   National Insurance contributions;

(c)   attendance allowance including constant attendance allowance in addition to a disability pension;

(d)   disability living allowance and any payments out of the Social Fund;

(e)   any back-to-work bonus treated as jobseeker's allowance;

(f)   any direct payments under the Health and Social Care Act 2001 or section 17A of the Children Act 1989;

(g)   any reasonable living expenses provided as an exception to a restraint order under section 41 of the Proceeds of Crime Act 2002; and

(h)   any personal independent payment paid under Part 4 of the Welfare Reform Act 2012.[68]

---

64   Means Regulations, reg 9.
65   Means Regulations, reg 8.
66   Means Regulations, reg 2.
67   CBAM, paras 13.2.2 and 13.2.5.
68   Means Regulations, reg 11.

If the individual has dependents then there are fixed deductions of £33.65 for a partner and £47.45 for each child. There is also a list of deductions for maintenance.[69]

Disposable capital

8.30   To calculate 'disposable' capital deductions can be made:

(a)   the value of the individual's (i) household furniture and effects; (ii) clothes; and (iii) tools and implements of the individual's trade; and

(b)   any back-to-work bonus received payable by way of a jobseeker's allowance.

The value of any interest in land is the sale value less the amount of any mortgage debt or hereditable security secured on that land, to a maximum of £100,000. There is a capital disregard of the first £100,000 of the value of the property where the applicant resides.

Where the client lives with a partner or dependents there is a capital deduction of £335 for the first, £200 for the second and £100 for each of the rest.[70]

Usually the proof of financial eligibility needs to be provided before any work is started unless it is impractical to do so. If it is not subsequently obtained then any claim is limited to two hours work unless in exceptional circumstances it can be shown that the personal circumstances of the client make it impracticable to obtain the proof at any point during the matter. In that case a note can be made justifying it but generally it will be very risky to proceed without acceptable proof.[71]

Children

8.31   A child is a client who is under 18 at the date the application is signed.[72] The general rule in the SCC is that you should deal with the parent, guardian or other person responsible for the child.[73] However, you may accept instructions directly from a child where there is a good reason provided the child is old enough to give instructions and understand the nature of the advice and proceedings.[74] In that case the child must sign the form and you must decide 'whether it is just and equitable not to aggregate the Child's means with those of the person liable to maintain him or her'. There is a presumption

---

69   Means Regulations, reg 12.
70   Means Regulations, reg 13.
71   SCC, paras 3.5–3.7.
72   Means Regulations, reg 2.
73   SCC, para 4.25.
74   SCC, para 4.28 (c).

that the means should be aggregated, but this can be rebutted if you decide it would not be equitable and this is more likely to be the case where there is a conflict between the child and the person liable to maintain them. It should be easy to justify taking instructions direct from the child. The Law Society Guidance encourages solicitors to view the child as the client as the wishes or views of the parent are often in conflict with those of the child. As children in criminal proceedings do not have an independent guardian to act for them there is a heavier burden on the solicitor to manage potential conflicts between the child and those who appear to be responsible for them. There will often be a potential conflict. Indeed, often the child will be in detention, which would make the Local Authority ultimately responsible in any event which is another factor that would justify not aggregating the means.

All work – the sufficient benefits test (merits)

8.32   This is the key test that must be satisfied in order to provide advice and assistance under the SCC:

> 'Advice and Assistance may only be provided on legal issues concerning English (or Welsh) law and where there is sufficient benefit to the Client, having regard to the circumstances of the matter, including the personal circumstances of the Client, to justify work or further work being carried out.'[75]

8.33   The same test applies to any application to any extension of funding under the scheme. As the provider is exercising a delegated function they are protected by the general principle that the assessor should only depart from that decision if it was 'manifestly unreasonable', which means no reasonably competent solicitor could have concluded that the SBT was met.[76] A clear file note should prevent any audit issues.[77] It applies to all extensions as well which must be noted on the file [78] (see 8.34 below).

8.34   It is a broad test, but it requires the issue to be a legal one which has a realistic prospect of success. You must consider the benefit to the client and the cost involved. Often the test comes down to whether a private paying client of moderate means would fund the step. This will be easier to justify if they are in custody or it has an impact on their everyday life. In a case in which trial lawyers have advised negatively, it is not sufficient that the client wishes to obtain a second opinion. The LAA will expect the new solicitors to show that there has been a change of circumstances or grounds for concluding that the advice may have been incorrect or incomplete. The LAA has indicated the

---

75 SCC, paras 3.10 and 12.5; CBAM, para 13.4.
76 CBAM, para 2.4.5, CLA 56.
77 SCC, para 12.7, else it will result in nil assessment.
78 SCC, paras 5.14 and 12.6; CBAM, para 8.3.2.

minimum information they expect the provider to record on the file to show they have properly considered the SBT. This includes details of the offence(s), whether the client pleaded or was convicted, the name of their trial lawyers and any advice, the court and the date the case concluded, the date and length of sentence and, perhaps most importantly, why the client says the conviction is unsafe or the sentence is wrong.[79] There is an assumption that previous advice was adequate unless rebutted so the LAA will require extra justification if previous advice was given and if it appears that the previous advice addressed the issues raised by the client the provider will have to point to an ongoing substantive issue or a material development since that advice.[80]

PRACTICAL ISSUES

Completing CRM 1 and CRM 2

8.35   The relevant application forms are currently known as CRM 1 and CRM 2. The general rule is that the client must be within the jurisdiction of England and Wales and sign the completed form in your presence.[81] A 'copy' of the completed application form must be kept on your file for audit purposes; if you work digitally it can be a scanned or electronic copy without keeping the wet ink copy.[82]

As most prospective clients will be serving prisoners it is unlikely that you will be able to invite them to your office to complete and sign the forms. Instead you will want to send them the forms by post to complete. In that case you are allowed to send the forms to them as an exception to the general rule above. If this is the case, you will need to note this on the CRM2 form, by ticking to indicate that you have accepted a postal application and setting out the justification for this, as per the relevant sections of the SCC.[83] Alternatively you are allowed to claim the travel to visit them in order to complete the forms (see 8.37 below).

Once these forms have been completed the provider will need to check them for consistency. One area where particular care needs to be taken is whether there is a 'partner' whose income or capital needs to be taken into account (see 8.23 above). Prospective clients will often tick 'single' or 'separated' on the forms and at the same time supply other information that suggests they are married or in a long-term relationship. The fact that they may be separated due to the client's incarceration does not mean the partner's financial resources can be ignored unless that has brought about an end to the emotional relationship.

---

79   CBAM, para 12.2.4.
80   CBAM, paras 12.2.5 and 12.2.7.
81   SCC, paras 4,21 and 4.24.
82   SCC, para 4.2.
83   SCC, paras 11.11–11.12.

The LAA will look at factors such as whether the partner was providing any regular financial support and/or visiting the client on a regular basis. Sharing the same address will be taken into consideration when a client is not in custody, but it may not mean they are in a subsisting relationship as they may be living together as separate households. If there is any contradictory information it needs to be addressed before the file is opened and there should be a clear file note supporting your decision if you have exercised your discretion.

Filtering requests

8.36   You are required to filter requests for advice by checking whether the client has received negative advice already. If that advice appears to be sound then you will not be able to accept the case.[84]

Outward travel or postal applications

8.37   Often clients will be unable to attend the solicitor's office as they will be in custody, so you can give advice and travel to a client before the forms are actually signed. Solicitors can also accept postal applications where there is good reason.[85] If they are outside the European Union special rules apply.[86] Telephone advice can also be provided to the client before signature. This work can be claimed provided the client completes the CRM 1 and CRM 2 and qualifies for advice. The reason must be noted on the file.[87] Unless you are visiting the prison or detention centre for some other reason that is already funded, generally it is safer for a solicitor to send the application forms to the client to complete and return. This is because prison visits are often cancelled or ineffective for reasons outside your control and if, as a result, the forms do not get signed you will be unable to claim for your time.

Is further advice justified?

8.38   Further advice can be justified if there appears to be new evidence or there is an issue with the conviction or sentence that was not addressed adequately in the previous advice. The LAA will want the file to show that there are substantive issues outstanding or there has been a material development.[88] They suggest up to three hours' work should be sufficient to investigate these further and instruct an advocate.[89]

---

84   SCC, para 11.5; this can be done using a detailed New Enquiry Form – see Appendix F.
85   SCC, para 4.31.
86   SCC, para 4.31.
87   SCC, paras 11.11–11.15.
88   CBAM, para 12.2.7.
89   SCC, para 11.6.

Applications to extend funding

8.39   The initial costs limits are modest.[90] If there is a substantive issue with either the sentence or the conviction you will need apply to extend the upper limit. This is best approached in stages. Each stage will set out the minimum work that needs to be done till the next stage is reached. The LAA will expect you to have carried out all the work authorised before reapplying. This can create practical problems if you do not carry out the anticipated work, but there is other unanticipated work that needs to be carried out. There is no procedure for amending the extension once it is granted so you can either do the work and make a clear note for audit purposes or email the LAA for advice. If you can show it is reasonable to do the work it should be allowed on an audit assessment.[91] The solicitor must then apply for extensions using a CRIM 5 eForm via the LAA portal.[92] The application should set out a breakdown of the work using the correct rates specified in the Criminal Legal Aid (Remuneration) Regulations 2013.[93] The CRIM 5 application will be considered by a specialist team at the LAA. Extensions cannot be obtained retrospectively.[94] The time spent making the application to extend can be claimed so it should be factored into the next stage of work as part of the CRIM 5 application as it will be necessary to spend time drafting a further CRIM 5 for any follow on application for a further extension.[95] Applications for extensions will set out the estimate of time for the litigator's work at the applicable hourly rates.[96] The application should show that the proposed work is reasonable and the SBT continues to be met.[97] The application will include any disbursements that will need to be authorised. The figures should not include VAT.[98] There is general guidance in CBAM on the disbursements that will be allowed under the SCC.[99]

It is important to note that it will be the actual costs that have been already incurred and not the previous limit extension that will be taken as the starting point for the new application. This means that any excess in your previous upper limit is lost when a new application is submitted. In certain exceptional circumstances, where it is necessary to urgently apply for further funding, the LAA may allow you to treat the remainder of the upper limit which not yet been used as having already been incurred, but this is unusual and it should be assumed that this will usually not be allowed. A detailed note of any communication with the LAA regarding this should be kept on file.

---

90   Currently for Court of Appeal cases £273.75 and for CCRC applications £456.25.
91   SCC, para 5.19.
92   SCC, para 5.10.
93   CBAM, para 5.15; SCC, para 8.2.
94   SCC, para 5.13; CBAM, para 8.3.
95   CBAM, paras 3.3.4 and 7.1.11.
96   Remuneration Regulations Part 8, Sch 4. Routine items: London £3.51, national £3.38; preparation: London £45.35, national £42.80; travel and waiting £24.00.
97   CBAM, para 8.3.
98   SCC, para 8.18.
99   SCC, paras 5.37–5.49; CBAM para 7.

The LAA assessor may return the CRM5 application with queries about the contents. A response with clarification can be sent back electronically via a text box on the eForms portal. This response must be provided within five working days of the query.

If an application for an extension is refused, submissions can be made to the crime finance team at the LAA. If these are unsuccessful then the usual appeals procedure applies. Any request must be made within 28 days of the decision. The matter is referred to an Independent Costs Assessor (ICA). Submissions to the ICA should succinctly address the LAA's reasons for refusal and these are more likely to succeed if they contain specific references to relevant sections of the SCC, CBAM and the PoP Manual. The ICA should look at the issues completely afresh and they can confirm, increase or decrease the previous assessment. The solicitor and advocate can request an oral hearing if the issues are complex though the vast majority of appeals are dealt with on paper.[100] If you are still dissatisfied the only remedy would be judicial review. It should be noted that, when an application is made to the ICA it is not only the current application which can be reconsidered. The ICA has the power to reconsider any previous application for extensions of the upper limit and reduce or remove any prior authorities which had been previously granted.

SPECIFIC APPLICATIONS AND APPEALS AGAINST REFUSALS

8.40   The usual applications will include:

(a)   Transcripts – These can be obtained for the relevant parts of the proceedings. In a sentence case this will be the sentencing remarks and possibly the prosecution opening and mitigation. In a conviction case it will usually be the relevant parts of the summing up or the rulings in issue. If you may need evidential transcripts, you should consider whether the summary of the evidence in the summing up is sufficient without the actual transcript of the evidence.[101] In CCRC cases that have already been to the single judge or full Court it is worth checking if there are any transcripts on the court file. Also in CCRC cases you should obtain a transcript of the full Court of Appeal judgment to show that new issues are being raised on the application to the CCRC that were not previously raised on the appeal.

(b)   The EX107 Form procedure must be followed for Crown Court transcripts.[102]. This is a two-part process: the first is to get a quote by

---

100 CBAM, paras 8.19–8.29 and 4.4.
101 CBAM, para 12.3.5.
102 For Court of Appeal transcripts it is not necessary to request the permission of the court – this is automatically granted. The completed EX107 must simply be sent to the transcribers directly.

completing and sending the Form EX107 to the Crown Court via email, copying in the transcription company, and the second is to complete and send the Form EX107 to the court.[103] There is a list of transcribers for the different Crown Courts set out in the EX107 guidance. The request must be approved by a judge, who will sign a section of the form to confirm their approval of a transcript being obtained. Once approved, the Court will send the completed EX107 to the defence team and to the transcription company, who will then provide a quote. The Form EX107 has a declaration that you agree to be responsible for the costs. However, there is a section of the form where you can indicate that you require a quote to be provided and approved by you before they will begin the transcription. Once a quote has been obtained you will need to apply to the LAA for an extension to cover the estimate provided. Often the actual cost will be less than that quoted, but if it is more you will need to apply for a further extension. (b) Advocate's advice – Once a realistic appeal point has been identified an advocate will need to be instructed for an advice and, if it is positive, to draft the grounds. This will usually be an external advocate given the restrictions on advice by an in-house advocate and the additional requirement that they must also be the advocate in the case, which is not always possible to guarantee (see 8.18 above). The going rate for a junior advocate is £80 per hour for drafting and advising. This should include a breakdown of the hours needed to advise. For sentence this will usually involve four to six hours' reading and drafting, though this will be very case-dependent. While care should be taken to avoid unnecessary reading of documents that can be passed to the advocate to read, the litigator is not just a post box for the advocate.[104] For more complex cases, especially CCRC applications involving expert issues, the number of hours could be 20–30 or more. These applications will be carefully scrutinised by the LAA and if not granted in full despite further representations, they may need an appeal to the ICA (see 8.34 above). The SCC recognises that specialist advice will be needed in CCRC applications.[105] They will allow a higher hourly rate of £120 per hour for 'exceptional' cases, as these will usually involve a QC, but the fact that you have instructed a QC to advise on a case does not necessarily mean that the LAA will agree to grant the higher rate as it is difficult to persuade the LAA that the higher rate is justified.[106]

(c)   Expert opinion – it is often necessary to instruct an expert. There is general guidance on what factors the LAA will look at when assessing

---

103 Guidance at: https://assets.publishing.service.gov.uk/government/uploads/system/uploads/attachment_data/file/763958/ex107-gn-eng.pdf
104 CBAM, para 7.2.
105 SCC, paras 11.24–11.25.
106 The current guidance the LAA employ appears to consider 'exceptional' as meaning for that type of case which is contrary to the guidance in Broudie that it should be compared to cases in general (see 8.15).

an application to pay their assistance.[107] The application may be stronger if supported by an advice from an advocate explaining the need for one. However, you should bear in mind that will lead to further costs so it may be better to apply without one in a straightforward case. The LAA may ask for at least two quotes in less straightforward cases, but often an expert you have used before for LAA work will be approved. Generally the rates payable to experts are those set out in the regulations.[108] In exceptional cases the LAA may agree to increase these rates. If the expert is in a very specialist field and you cannot find a suitable one for LAA approved rates it can be useful to get the expert to provide details of other recent publicly funded cases they have done for either the prosecution or the defence where their higher rate was paid. There is a presumption that a further report will not be paid for so if you are unhappy with the first one, you will face resistance from the LAA to any application for a new one.[109]

(d)   Travel – The LAA take a starting point that any return travel time over two hours will be disallowed unless justified. Good reason may be that your client has made several requests for advice from local providers without any response or that this is a complex matter and there are no solicitors with specialist criminal appeal experience who are closer to the client. Another good reason might be that you have significant knowledge of the case or the client. Generally, return travel over four hours will not be granted unless exceptional. The usual exception relied upon would be that your specific knowledge of the client or the case means it would not be cost-effective to instruct a firm closer to the prison or detention centre. That would be because it would take more preparation or attendance time for the new provider get up to speed than the additional amount of travel being asked for. Likewise, if your client is transferred to a different prison that is further away from your office it is possible to justify additional travel time being granted on this basis.

Criminal Cases Review Commission applications – special considerations

8.41   There are some obvious distinctions between an application for permission to appeal to the Court of Appeal and an application to the CCRC. The tests are different and usually the applicant will have to have already unsuccessfully appealed the conviction or sentence. As that is a pre-requisite to making an application unless exceptional circumstance apply (see Chapter 9) the first question is to check whether an application for permission has already

---

107 CBAM, para 7.2.
108 The Criminal Legal Aid (Remuneration) Regulations 2013 (SI 2013/435) (updated version), Sch 5.
109 CBAM, para 7.2.8.

refused by the single judge or the full Court. If leave has not been refused the advice you are providing will not be about an application to the CCRC but the normal application to the Court of Appeal. In that case a file needs to be opened for that advice bearing in mind the guidance (see 8.24 and 8.25 above).

In a small number of cases the exceptional circumstances test might be met for an application direct to the CCRC bypassing the Court of Appeal; this may because a lot of investigative work needs to be done which you will need the assistance of the CCRC and their extensive powers (see Chapter 9). These types of cases may include developments in forensic science, concerns about credibility of witnesses or police conduct, PII issues or undisclosed material which you would not have the resources or powers to pursue adequately. Another issue that often arises at the outset which will affect funding is whether to renew an application for permission to the full Court when it was refused by the single judge. Usually that will be a better option as an application to the Commission is the last resort which the client will still have if the full Court refuses permission. The SCC recognises these initial considerations apply.[110] If the CCRC is the correct option then your file opening note showing the SBT has been met should say why you think the CCRC referral criteria was met.[111]

8.42   The LAA recognises that it is not easy to show that the referral criteria are met without some investigation of the history of the appeal. You will generally be able to open a file if the case potentially passes the referral test.[112] A lawyer coming to the case afresh will be unable to decide immediately whether the case is likely to meet the referral criteria so you are allowed to provide 'initial case screening' to an eligible client who it appears may have an application.[113] The LAA expects the lawyer to obtain a statement from the client to carry this out and it suggests that this will 'normally' take two hours for a client in the locality of the office.[114] It is useful to have a detailed enquiry form for prospective clients to complete with questions covering the specific details you will need to consider. There is an example in the Annex.[115] Often it will take longer and, as with all work in this area, file notes should justify the time spent. In making an assessment 'the provider should initially take instructions and ascertain whether the case is both suitable to be heard by the Commission and whether the case meets the referral criteria applied by the Commission'. Often this work will give rise to difficult decisions as to whether the costs of further investigation are justified. The LAA expects the lawyer to make these decisions 'in light of the available information and using your professional skill and common sense'.[116]

---

110 SCC, para 11.19.
111 SCC, para 11.20.
112 SCC, para 11.22.
113 SCC, para 11.21.
114 SCC, para 11.22; CBAM, para 12.3.4.
115 See Appendix F.
116 SCC, para 11.21.

8.43   It may be necessary to obtain transcripts of the evidence but you should check whether any were already obtained by the Court of Appeal or are adequately covered by the Summing Up if already available.[117] The LAA acknowledge the need to get the opinion of an advocate in these cases.[118] The reality is that these cases are often grave and complex. They can involve novel and complex areas of legal interpretation which may require advice from a leading advocate. The LAA will be reluctant to incur the costs of a leading advocate especially if a junior advocate has already advised. Therefore, the solicitor must decide whether to involve a QC from the start and ask them to justify the higher rate or instruct a junior advocate and see whether they feel the issues are within their competence. Often if the higher rate is refused the QC will agree to work for a lesser rate, though in principle if a case justifies the instruction of a QC the higher rate should be applied for and, if refused without good reason, the decision should be appealed to the ICA. Sometimes the ICA refuse these appeals on the basis that the higher rate is above that quoted in the general criminal regulations, but as the majority of general crime work is paid by the way of fixed fees the comparison is not helpful and should be challenged. The test is whether the case justifies a much more experienced advocate.

8.44   It may be necessary to obtain, prior to the referral, expert evidence where there is an issue that is crucial to the safety of the conviction, although the LAA expects the defence lawyers to bear in mind that the CCRC can obtain or pay for expert reports.[119] It should be noted that if the CCRC obtain expert reports, these will not normally be disclosed to the applicant's lawyers during the CCRC's assessment and review process. This means that it is not possible to make representations to the CCRC on behalf of your client until the provisional statement of reasons is provided by the CCRC referencing any expert advice they have obtained. At that stage you may request sight of any expert opinion referred to in the CCRC's provisional conclusions so you can address the issues. They may agree to provide it though it is often preferable to instruct your own expert at an earlier stage so you are in control of the issues.

8.45   Once a case is referred back to the Court of Appeal by the CCRC the Registrar will usually grant a representation order to include an advocate and litigator. As soon as that is granted you should close and bill your advice and assistance file.

Claiming for work done under the advice and assistance scheme

8.46   You cannot advise under freestanding advice and assistance where there is a representation order in the proceedings and advice on appeal or

---

117 CBAM, para 12.3.5–12.3.7.
118 SCC, para 11.24.
119 CBAM, para 12.3.3.

sentence can be claimed under that representation order, except where the client has changed provider since the original proceedings.[120] However, this means you are allowed to advise and claim under freestanding advice and assistance for any *fresh* issue that arises subsequently. If that relates to an issue that you have not previously advised on regarding either a possible appeal to the Court of Appeal or a CCRC referral then an Appeals and Reviews matter can be opened as there is no other way to claim for this work under the original representation order. Of course, if it is a matter that you *should* have advised on originally, or it relates to an error or omission by you, you will need to consider whether a conflict of interest arises and whether the client should be advised to instruct a new team. If the point now raised was due to a questionable legal decision taken by the original external advocate, it may be possible to continue to act but with a new advocate instructed.

8.47   A claim should only be submitted when:[121]

(a)   the matter has concluded;

(b)   it is known that no further work will be undertaken for the client in the same matter;

(c)   it is unclear whether further work will be undertaken and at least one month has elapsed since the last work was undertaken; or

(d)   in the case of a claim for advice and assistance on an appeal against conviction or sentence, including an appeal by way of case stated or an application to vary a sentence, where a determination has been made by the relevant court as soon as the representation order has been issued.

Often in CCRC cases you will want to close and bill your file under condition (c) as soon as the application is acknowledged by the CCRC as it will be a long time before you will hear from them again. Once you have received their provisional reasons you can then re-open the file and start to record time again (see 8.48 below).

Further instructions after a matter ends or a claim has been submitted

8.48   Once you have closed and billed your file any subsequent advice and assistance in relation to the same matter will require a new application but will be subject to the previous upper limit. This can only be done if there are substantive issues outstanding from the first occasion or there has been a material development or change in the client's circumstances such that further advice is now required. The client must complete a further CRM 1 and CRM 2

---

120 SCC, para 11.40.
121 SCC, para 11.4.

and the means test and SBT must be passed. The same unique reference number (UFN) must be used and the second file should include a reference to the first and kept together for audit purposes.[122]

ALTERNATIVE SOURCES OF ADVICE AND ASSISTANCE

8.49   There are limitations to the type of work that the LAA may be willing to fund. Funding is rarely extended to complex cases or lengthy investigations. Moreover, the availability of funding does not guarantee that there will be competent lawyers who will be willing to undertake the work in question. Not only are the number of solicitors firms who undertake work in this area threatened by cuts to legal aid, but the limitations in the extent of funding may mean that competent firms who do have LAA contracts may feel that they cannot justify extensive work on complex cases for the limited funding that is available.

8.50   Whilst it is always open to a defendant with the means to pay for their legal representation, this is not an option for many of those who have been convicted of serious crimes, particularly when the conviction is followed by a substantial custodial sentence. It may, therefore, be necessary for the defendant to consider alternative means of advice or assistance.

Innocence projects

8.51   Innocence projects were first established in the USA. They are university-based projects in which students, under an academic supervisor and often also with the assistance of practising lawyers, investigate potential miscarriages with a view to obtaining evidence that is capable of proving the innocence of the convicted person. In the USA many of the projects have had success in obtaining the evidence that leads to the overturning of convictions.

8.52   The innocence projects that are based in England and Wales have been established more recently than many of their US counterparts and they have yet to achieve the success of which many US projects can boast. The first UK project was established at Bristol University in 2005 and there are now approximately 30 located at various universities.[123] Until 2014 many operated as affiliates to the Innocence Network UK, which was run by the founders of the Bristol University project and provided training and support for other

---

122 SCC, para 11.36–38.
123 Article by Lee Glendinning, *Guardian*, 3 September 2004. See: www.theguardian.com/uk/2004/sep/03/ukcrime.prisonsandprobation/print.

projects.[124] Despite this activity, the work of the UK innocence projects has yet to lead to the overturning of a single conviction. Certain projects, particularly Bristol and Cardiff, have had successes in getting cases are referred back to the Court of Appeal by the CCRC as a result of evidence that they have uncovered. But in 2013 a lawyer from the CCRC remarked in a speech that the number of referrals that they had received from innocence projects was very low (17 in ten years from a total of five universities).[125]

8.53   There a number of limitations to the innocence project model. The fact that they will usually only assist those who proclaim their total non-involvement with their alleged offence (precluding, for example, assistance being given to the defendant convicted of murder who claims to have suffered from provocation or diminished responsibility that would render them guilty of manslaughter) acts as a limit on the number of people that innocence projects can assist. However, it is the experience of lawyers that prisons are not short of prisoners who proclaim their innocence and seek to have their convictions overturned. It seems that there are limitations to what students, who lack legal training and can give neither full-time nor long-term commitment to a particular case can achieve.

8.54   They may be no substitute for qualified legal assistance but innocence projects can supplement the work of lawyers, particularly in undertaking the investigative work for which funding may not be available. For those who seek to prove their innocence and cannot find a lawyer to take on their case, innocence projects may, for months or years, be their sole source of assistance.

The Centre for Criminal Appeals

8.55   The Centre for Criminal Appeals is a charitable organisation that was founded, on the model of American civil rights-era non-profit legal practices in order to assist those who wish make an application to the CCRC and/or appeal a conviction in the Court of Appeal but lack the means to pay for their own representation. As a charity the Centre can raise private funds and have access to pro bono experts and advocates that will enable its lawyers to focus solely on appeals and overcome the limitations imposed by the public funding regime. The Centre takes on carefully selected cases which they believe will have strategic impact upon the criminal appeals system. Their model of work includes substantial hands-on investigative work to uncover new evidence, a methodology which is not generally achievable by legal aid funding. The

---

124 See the Innocence Network UK website at www.innocencenetwork.org.uk for the history of the organisation and its present role.
125 Article by Jon Robbins, *Guardian*, 20 November 2013. See: www.theguardian.com/law/2013/nov/20/appeal-court-innocence-projects-dwaine-george.

Centre provides valuable advice and assistance, particularly in those cases requiring significant investigation work and a long-term commitment by the legal team.[126]

Advocate (formerly known as the Bar Pro Bono Unit)

8.56 A number of advocates are prepared to provide advice and assistance in particular cases for free. The best chance of obtaining such assistance is through Advocate, which can obtain the details of a particular case and forward it to advocates who may have the experience and willingness to assist. However, it is not altogether clear that an advocate would have the willingness or the best professional expertise to undertake the type of extensive work for which funding would not be available under the advice and assistance scheme.

SUMMARY OF KEY POINTS

- The three regimes for public funding are: representation orders that are granted by the Crown Court; representation orders granted by the Court of Appeal; and funding for advice and assistance under the Standard Crime Contract. These sources of funding are mutually exclusive.

- Positive advice and assistance in lodging an appeal can be claimed by both the trial litigator and the advocate under the Crown Court representation order. No claim can be made for a negative advice.

- Funding for advice and assistance under the Standard Crime Contract will enable lawyers who did not represent the defendant at trial to provide advice and assistance (but not representation). It is subject to the criteria of means and merits. An application may not be made until six months have elapsed since the client was last advised under the scheme. The scheme also allows the original lawyers to look at a fresh issue that arises later provided they are not being criticised.

- Application for funding for advice and assistance is by way of CRM 1 and CRM 2. Each application for an extension of funds, including funding to cover the advice of an independent advocate, transcript, experts' reports or extensive work by defence solicitors, must be made through CRIM 5.

- It will assist an application for extension of funding if it is supported by an advocate's advice that explains why the funding that is sought is necessary to the case.

- The merits criteria must be satisfied in respect of each application for extension of funding. In order to meet the merits criteria the application

---

126 See the Centre for Criminal Appeals Project website at www.criminalappeals.org.uk. It should be noted that lawyers from the Centre contributed to Chapter 5 of this book.

must provide some reason to show that the work could benefit the client. It is not sufficient simply to suggest that there should be a second opinion.

- For those cases which involve extensive work for which funding may not be granted, the defendant may wish to seek the assistance of an innocence project or the Centre for Criminal Appeals.

Part 3
Applications from the Court of Appeal

Chapter 9

The Criminal Cases Review Commission

INTRODUCTION

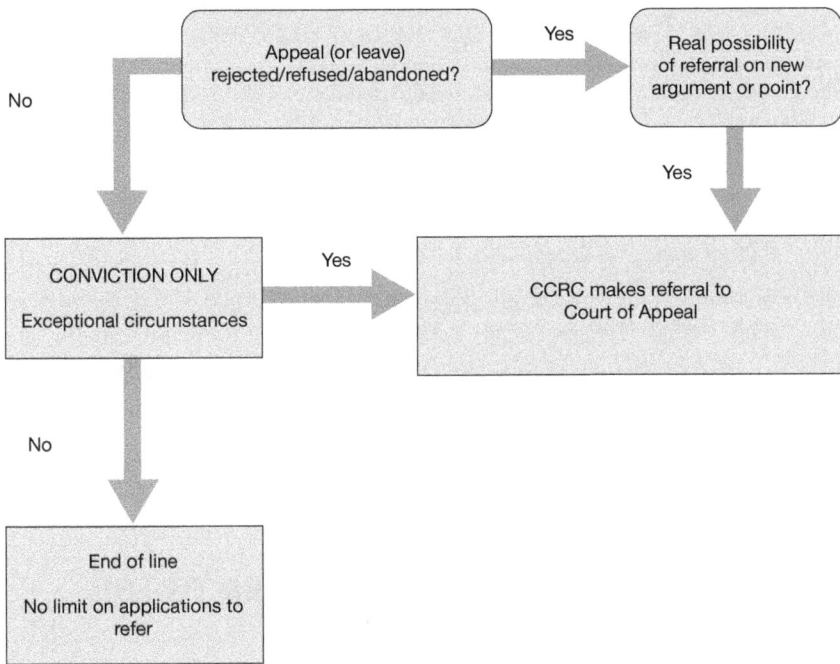

Figure 9.1   Flowchart for referrals by the CCRC

9.1   The Court of Appeal will not allow a second application for leave to appeal conviction or sentence after a previous such appeal has been dismissed. The only route back to a second appeal to the Court of Appeal is by way of a reference back by the Criminal Cases Review Commission.

9.2   In addition to its power to send cases back to the Court of Appeal, the Criminal Cases Review Commission (CCRC) can investigate convictions and has powers beyond those otherwise available to a convicted person and their lawyers. The CCRC can use those powers either when considering an application by a convicted person to refer a case to the Court of Appeal or, more rarely, when the Court of Appeal directs it to do so.

THE ESTABLISHMENT AND ROLE OF THE CRIMINAL CASES REVIEW COMMISSION

9.3　For many years, the only route back to the Court of Appeal, Criminal Division, for a second appeal was a reference by the Home Secretary; such references were rare and the process by which applications were considered was slow and opaque. After a series of miscarriages of justice in the late 1980s and early 1990s,[1] a Royal Commission[2] recommended the power to refer possible miscarriages of justice be removed from the Home Secretary and placed in the hands of an independent body. Parliament enacted those recommendations through the Criminal Appeal Act 1995 (CAA 1995), which established the CCRC as an independent, non-governmental body[3] with the following powers:

(a) to refer any sentence or conviction in the Crown Court to the Court of Appeal if the Commission is of the opinion that there is a real possibility that an appeal will be allowed;

(b) to conduct any investigation that the Court of Appeal may direct it to undertake in order to assist the Court in the determination of an appeal;

(c) to refer, on the same basis, any sentence or conviction in the Magistrates Court to the Crown Court;

(d) to assist the Home Secretary by providing an opinion on whether to recommend the exercise of Her Majesty's prerogative of mercy in relation to a conviction.[4]

THE COMMISSION'S POWER TO REFER TO THE COURT OF APPEAL

9.4　The Commission has a power to refer a conviction or sentence to the Court of Appeal where a person has been convicted of an offence on indictment

---

1　The late 1980s and early 1990s saw the exposure of a series of miscarriages of justice, related to wrongful convictions for terrorist crimes, which culminated with the 'Birmingham Six' appeal in 1991.

2　The Royal Commission on Criminal Justice, commonly referred to as the 'Runciman Commission', was established by the Home Secretary in March 1991 and reported in July 1993.

3　CAA 1995, s 8 establishes its constitution.

4　CAA 1995, s 16(1). The Commission has never been called upon to make a recommendation under this section.

in England, Wales or Northern Ireland.[5] The power extends to a verdict of not guilty by reason of insanity and a finding that a person was under a disability when they did an act or made an omission.[6]

9.5   It may refer following an application or of its own motion where no application has been made.[7] A referral will be treated as an appeal, with leave, under CAA 1968 and must be heard by the Court.[8]

9.6   Although the CCRC only refers a small percentage of applications that it receives, there is a high success rate.[9]

THE TEST FOR REFERRAL

9.7   Section 13 of CAA 1995 provides that no reference shall be made unless the Commission considers that there is a 'real possibility' that:

(a)   the conviction, verdict or finding under appeal would not be upheld because of an argument, or evidence, not raised in the proceedings which led to it (or on any appeal or application for leave against it); or

(b)   in the case of a sentence, because of an argument on a point of law or information not so raised; and

(c)   an appeal against the conviction, verdict, finding or sentence has been determined or leave to appeal has been refused.

9.8   However, section 13 gives the Commission the power to refer even when (a) or (c) do not apply if there are 'exceptional circumstances' which justify making it; thus, there can be a reference back even where there is no new evidence or argument and/or when there has not been a previous appeal. The 'no new point' exception, however, only applies to an appeal against conviction, so for a sentence appeal there must be a new argument.

The discretion whether to refer

9.9   It is important to note that the Commission has discretion not to refer even if the test under section 13 is satisfied. For example, if the conviction is

---

5   CAA 1995, s 9. By virtue of s 12A it has also been extended to include references of convictions and sentences by the Court Martial to the Court Martial Appeal Court and by the Service Civilian Court to the Court Martial.

6   CAA 1995, s 9(5), (6).

7   CAA 1995, s 14(1).

8   CAA 1995, s 9(2), (3).

9   Of the six referrals decided by the appeal courts in 2017/2018, four appeals were allowed and two dismissed (CCRC Annual Report and Accounts, 2017/2018).

likely to be quashed but only to be substituted by an alternative conviction, allowing the original conviction to stand may cause no real injustice to the applicant.[10] The appellate courts have been robust in protecting the CCRC's use of this discretion, no doubt fearing the opening of flood gates such as would drown the Court of Appeal in further cases, were the CCRC's 'gatekeeper' role undermined.

APPLYING TO THE COMMISSION FOR A REFERRAL

Who may apply?

9.10   An application does not have to be made by the defendant him or herself. This means that a family member with a substantial interest in the outcome of an appeal could make an application on behalf of someone who had died after conviction. However, when a defendant has died, the Commission will only consider the application if an 'approved person'[11] (such as a family member) can be identified in whose name any application for leave might be made.

When to apply

9.11   Normally an application should be made to the Commission only if:

(a)   an appeal has been considered and refused by the Court of Appeal; or

(b)   leave has been refused by the single judge (it need not have been renewed before the full Court); or

(c)   an application for leave or an appeal with leave has been abandoned; and

(d)   there is argument, evidence or information in the terms of section 13(a) or (b) that was not considered by the Court of Appeal in that initial appeal.

9.12   What counts as 'new argument' is a matter to be considered in each case. However, a change in the law will not itself be regarded as giving rise to new argument that raises a real possibility of an appeal being allowed. Section 16C of CAA 1968[12] now provides that the Court may dismiss any reference based solely on the change of law where, had the application for extension of time been made by the defendant, that application would have been refused. The Commission should now only refer cases involving a change

---

10   *Smith (Duncan Wallace)* [2004] EWCA Crim 631.
11   CCA 1968, s 46A makes the nomination of an approved person following the death of a defendant a pre-condition for a valid appeal.
12   As inserted by the Criminal Justice and Immigration Act 2008, s 42.

in the law where the test of a change in the law giving rise to 'substantial injustice'(*R v Fletcher; R v Cottrell*)[13] may be said to be met. The Commission has published guidance on this aspect of its discretion.[14]

9.13 There are no time limits for making an application, but this does not mean that the applicant should delay making it. There is no formal restriction on reapplying; indeed a recent successful referral was made at the third time of asking where fresh DNA evidence further undermined questionable identification evidence.[15] However, applications which are substantially the same as those which have already been refused should clearly not be made.

'Exceptional circumstances'

9.14 As indicated, the Commission may, in exceptional circumstances, make a reference to the Court of Appeal even if there was no previous appeal. Whilst there is no statutory definition of 'exceptional circumstances', the Commission's own guidance sets out a number of non-exhaustive situations in which exceptional circumstances may be made out.[16]

9.15 Among them are cases where there may be an arguable appeal but this will depend on further investigations being carried out and third party material being obtained and considered. If the Commission concludes that it is not possible for the applicant and their legal representatives to carry out this investigation but that it might be carried out by the Commission, then this might give rise to exceptional circumstances. However, the Court has stressed that the mere existence of relevant third party material should not necessarily be regarded as giving rise to exceptional circumstances.[17]

Making the application

9.16 The Commission's website contains guidance for the making of an application.[18] In addition, it has published individual memoranda on various aspects of its work describing how it deals with common issues. These can be found in the 'casework' section of the website.

---

13   [2007] EWCA Crim 2016.
14   CCRC Formal Memorandum – Discretion in Referrals (including applications based on a change in the law), Version 1.
15   *Regina v Victor Nealon* [2014] EWCA Crim 574.
16   CCRC Formal Memorandum – Exceptional Circumstances
17   *R v Gerald* [1999] Crim LR 315.
18   www.justice.gov.uk/downloads/about/criminal-cases-review/policies-and-procedures/ccrc-q-and-a.pdf.

9.17   It is advisable, although not necessary, that an application be made with the assistance of a lawyer. Funding may be available for legal representation under the 'Advice and Assistance' scheme (see 8.36–8.40 for details). While there have been a number of successful references back to the Court of Appeal by applicants in person, the involvement of a lawyer will (or at least, should) weed out the bad points, set out more clearly the good and thereby make the CCRC's task easier and increase the chances of a successful application.

9.18   The application should be made using the Commission's application form. However, applicants are likely to benefit by submitting additional grounds which should set out the legal and factual issues that are relevant to the application, address the relevant statutory questions and include all material that may be of assistance to the Commission in making its decision.

Requesting an investigation

9.19   If an applicant wishes the Commission to carry out an investigation, it is important to explain why the material sought is of importance to the application. It is also important to explain what steps the applicant and their lawyers have already taken to obtain the material sought and the outcome of any such enquiries.

9.20   There has been increasing demand for the Commission to use its powers to investigate the adequacy of legal advice given to those who may have been prosecuted in contravention of international conventions or pleaded guilty in ignorance of a defence, in particular section 31 of the Immigration and Asylum Act 1999.[19] The Commission has published specific guidance for potential applicants who may be refugees or the victims of trafficking.[20]

The decision-making process

9.21   An initial screening takes place to ensure that the application is valid. Early steps are taken to secure potentially relevant material that is held by a public body. Certain cases will be given priority.[21] The case will then be allocated to a case review manager who will examine the issues raised in the application to see if there might be anything that could give grounds for referring the case. The Commission is allowed to consider any representations

---

19 In *Regina v Mateta* [2013] EWCA Crim 1372 the Commission referred a number of cases to the Court concerning the defence under s 31.

20 www.justice.gov.uk/downloads/about/criminal-cases-review/policies-and-procedures/ccrc-seeker-refugee-leaflet.pdf.

21 For example, if the applicant is serving a sentence that is soon to expire or is suffering from a potentially fatal illness.

and any matters that appear to be relevant.[22] Investigations are carried out when they are appropriate. Most are carried out by Commission staff. However, investigators may be appointed to assist in carrying out enquiries. If necessary, the Commission can, at any stage, ask the Court of Appeal to provide an opinion on a relevant matter of law.[23]

9.22   When the review is complete it is considered by either a single commissioner or a committee of three commissioners. A single commissioner may decide not to make a referral. However, only a committee of three commissioners can make a referral.[24] If they are of the view that a referral is justified then a final statement of reasons will be completed and sent to the applicant and the Court of Appeal. If it is decided not to refer, a provisional statement of reasons is drafted.

The provisional statement of reasons

9.23   The applicant and their lawyers will be sent a copy of the provisional statement of reasons and be given the opportunity to respond to any points made or to provide further information. The correspondence will usually indicate that any response must be received by a particular date. If more time is needed it should be requested with an explanation.

The final decision

9.24   The final decision will be contained in the 'Final Statement of Reasons' which will be provided to the applicant and their legal representative. The decision must be clear and fully reasoned in order that the applicant can understand how it has been reached. Fairness may require the disclosure of information that the Commission has taken into account when reaching its decision *(R v Secretary of State for the Home Department, ex p Hickey (No. 2))*.[25]

Likely timeframe for a decision

9.25   The CCRC reports the timings of its process in two stages: the time between an application being received and assigned to a case review manager (CRM); and the time then taken to reach a provisional view to either refer or to refuse to refer the case to the Court of Appeal. In 2017/18 the average time from receipt to allocation was 15.9 weeks for custody and at liberty cases, and 23.3

---

22   CAA 1995, s 14(2).
23   CAA 1995, s 14(3).
24   CAA 1995, Sch 1, para 6(3).
25   [1995] 1 WLR 734 (DC).

weeks for liberty cases. In the same period, the average time from allocation to a CRM to a provisional view being taken was 32.6 weeks.[26] The CCRC has ambitions to lower both waiting times but for the present, an applicant would need to be advised that the average wait from application to decision is in the region of a year. However, the length of time can vary from weeks to many months depending on, amongst other things, whether the Commission needs to undertake any investigations.

CHALLENGING A REFUSAL TO MAKE A REFERENCE

9.26   A decision not to refer the case may be challenged by way of judicial review. As with any judicial review, the Court will not be concerned with whether the decision was right but only whether it was lawful and reasonable (*Ex p Pearson*).[27] The Administrative Court has indicated that a high threshold will have to be crossed to persuade it that a decision of the Commission not to refer should be quashed (*Cleeland v CCRC*).[28]

THE PROCEDURE FOLLOWING A REFERENCE BEING MADE TO THE COURT OF APPEAL

9.27   The procedure, which is largely governed by section 14 of CAA 1995 and Part 39 of the CPR, can be summarised as follows:

(a)   If the Commission decides to make a reference to the Court of Appeal it must send that decision to every person who is likely be party to the appeal.[29]

(b)   The decision is also passed to the Registrar of Criminal Appeals who must also serve notice of the decision on the appellant and 'any party directly affected by the appeal' (which obviously includes the Respondent).[30]

(c)   The Registrar is likely at this stage to grant representation orders for solicitors and counsel for the purpose of preparing the appeal.

(d)   A Form NG should be served by the legal representatives of the appellant within 28 days of receipt of the Registrar's notice of appeal (application to extend that time can be made) on the Registrar, not the Crown Court.[31]

---

26   The CCRC Annual Report and Accounts 2017/2018.
27   [2000] 1 Cr App R 141.
28   [2009] EWHC 474 (Admin), para 48.
29   CAA 1995, s 14(4)(b).
30   Part 39.6 CrimPR.
31   Part 39. 2 CrimPR.

(e) Permission of the Court is required if the appellant seeks to advance grounds that are not related to the reasons given in the reference.[32] The term 'related to', however, gives some latitude provided the grounds advanced are founded on one of the points on which the CCRC has sent the case back.

(f) Directions may be made for a particular case. However, the Court in *R v Siddall and Brooke*[33] suggested a timetable that parties should adhere to and indicated delay caused by a failure to adhere to the timetable may give rise to a risk of a wasted costs order being made.

AN OVERVIEW OF THE COMMISSION'S INVESTIGATORY POWERS

9.28 The Commission's investigatory powers are largely contained in sections 17 to 25 of CAA 1995. The law in relation to those powers can be summarised as follows:

(a) The Commission is authorised to obtain access to (and copy) all documents and material from public bodies if it believes it may assist the investigation. The duty of the public body to comply with a request is not affected by any obligation of secrecy or other limitation on disclosure and therefore will often include material not disclosed or available to the defence at trial,[34] for example social services' files or other sensitive information.

(b) The power includes a power to direct that such material is preserved in an unaltered state until the Commission further directs.[35] This may be important if there is a risk that efforts may be made to conceal or alter potentially relevant material.

(c) However, the person providing information to the Commission may withhold consent for it to be disclosed to another party if an obligation of secrecy would otherwise have prevented disclosure to the Commission and it is reasonable to do so.[36]

(d) Although the public body is required to provide such material to the Commission as it requests, there is no formal sanction for any failure to do so, although the Commission may seek a remedy by way of judicial review.

---

32 CAA 1995, s 14(4A), (4B); and see *Regina v Hallam* [2012] EWCA Crim 1158.
33 [2006] EWCA Crim 1353.
34 CAA 1995, s 17(4).
35 CAA 1995, s 17(2).
36 CAA 1995, s 25.

(e)   In addition to carrying out its own investigations, the Commission may require the appointment of an investigating officer to carry out inquiries on its behalf. Such a person may be from a public body or (more usually) from the police. The Commission can direct that particular individuals are not appointed or that police officers should not be from the police force that carried out the original investigation.[37]

(f)   With the two exceptions set out in (g) and (h) below, the Commission is empowered only to obtain material from public bodies, not from private corporations. The meaning of 'public body' is narrowly defined.[38]

(g)   As a 'relevant public body'[39] the Commission may, in accordance with the provisions of the Regulation of Investigatory Powers Act 2000, obtain communication data from private individuals and bodies.

(h)   If police officers are appointed to carry out an investigation, they may employ their powers under the Police and Criminal Evidence Act 1984 to obtain material from private individuals or bodies.

(i)   It is a criminal offence under section 23 of CAA 1995 for present or former members or employees of the Commission, or investigating officers appointed by the Commission, to disclose information obtained in the course of the investigation save for one of the purposes contained in section 24 of CAA 1995.

(j)   There is no obligation to disclose all material obtained in an investigation to an applicant or appellant. Indeed, there may be material which should not be disclosed. However, the Commission should provide the applicant with sufficient disclosure to enable them to properly present their best case (*Ex p Hickey (No 2)*).[40]

9.29   As can be seen from the powers listed above, the CCRC have far wider powers than those available to applicants and their lawyers. In many cases the CCRC have obtained social services records and/or material that would be withheld from any defendant as being subject to public interest immunity. While the CCRC guard their discretion to choose which enquiries they make, it is always worthwhile considering where fruitful material might be found when drafting an application.

---

37   CAA 1995, s 19. *R v Hallam* [2012] EWCA Crim 1158 is a recent example of the successful use of s 19 to investigate a police investigation.
38   CAA 1995, s 22(1).
39   By virtue of the Regulation of Investigatory Powers (Communications Data) (Additional Functions and Amendment) Order 2006 (SI 2006/1878).
40   [1995] 1 WLR 734 (DC).

COMMISSION INVESTIGATIONS AT THE DIRECTION OF THE COURT OF APPEAL

9.30   On any appeal against conviction the Court of Appeal may direct the Commission to investigate and report to the Court on any matter, if it appears to the Court that:

(a)   the matter is relevant to the determination of the case and ought, if possible, to be resolved before the case is determined;

(b)   an investigation of the matter by the Commission is likely to result in the Court being able to resolve it; and

(c)   the matter cannot be resolved by the Court without an investigation by the Commission.[41]

9.31   The Court may direct the Commission to carry out such an investigation if any of the potential grounds turn on alleged irregularity in a jury's deliberations.[42] Serious failures by the prosecution in their duties of disclosure have also been the subject of investigations at the direction of the Court.[43] However, the only limits to the type of matter that the Court may ask the Commission to investigate are those in (a) to (c) above.

9.32   The procedure for such investigations is governed by section 23A of CAA 1968 and section 15 of CAA 1995, which provide as follows:

(a)   The Court may, at any time, either before leave[44] is considered or after it is granted, make such a direction. However, a direction may not be given by a single judge.[45]

(b)   The copies of direction must also be made available to the appellant and respondent.[46]

(c)   The investigation must be carried out 'in such manner as the Commission sees fit'.[47]

(d)   In doing so it may investigate any related matter that it believes to be relevant to the determination of the case by the Court, which ought to be and can be resolved by the Court.[48]

---

41   CAA 1995, s 15(1).
42   *Regina v Shabir Ahmed* [2014] EWCA Crim 619; *Regina v Emma Mitchell* [2013] EWCA Crim 1072; *Regina v Ian Lewis* [2013] EWCA Crim 776.
43   For example, *R v Joof* [2012] EWCA Crim 1475.
44   CAA 1968, s 23A(1)(aa), inserted by CJA 2003, s 313.
45   CAA 1968, s 23A(1A).
46   CAA 1968, s 23A(5).
47   CAA 1995, s 15(1).
48   CAA 1995, s 15(2).

(e)   The Commission must keep the Court informed of the progress of the investigation[49] and must file a report either at the conclusion of the investigation or when directed to do so by the Court.[50] The report should detail the enquiries that were pursued[51] and should be accompanied by any statements and opinions received by the Commission in the investigation.[52]

(f)   The Court must notify the appellant and the respondent that the Commission has reported and may make available to them the report of the Commission and any statements, opinions and reports which accompanied it.[53]

TOO HIGH A TEST?

9.33   The CCRC has not been without its critics. Many lawyers who regularly advise would-be appellants and applicants argue that over the course of its existence the Commission has grown more conservative and less willing to refer cases back to the Court of Appeal. Another common observation is that the outcome of a particular application may depend not just on the merits but on which of the various CRMs is assigned to consider it. For all such criticisms, however, the CCRC remains an intellectually rigorous organisation staffed by well-intentioned individuals who do their best to deal with the problems and challenges that they face. On any view, it remains a vast improvement on what went before.

SUMMARY OF KEY POINTS

•   The Commission has the power to refer appeals against sentence or conviction from the Crown Court to the Court of Appeal or from the Magistrates' Court to the Crown Court when it is of the view that there is a real possibility that the appeal will be allowed.

•   It normally makes referrals following a failed or abandoned appeal if there is new evidence or arguments not originally advanced. However, it has discretion, in exceptional circumstances, to refer a conviction even when there was no initial appeal.

---

49   CAA 1995, s 15(3).
50   CAA 1995, s 15(4).
51   CAA 1995, s 15(5).
52   CAA 1995, s 15(6). However, the Commission need not include any reports that were made to the Commission by an investigating officer, pursuant to s 20(6).
53   CAA 1968, s 23A(4).

- The effect of a referral is that the case will be returned to the Court to be heard as an appeal with leave. However, the Court may dismiss such an appeal when the only ground for a referral is a change in the law.

- In determining whether to refer the Commission may carry out such investigations as it deems necessary.

- It must carry out an investigation when directed to do so by the Court of Appeal in relation to an appeal or an application for leave to appeal against sentence or conviction.

- In carrying out these investigations it has extensive powers to obtain material in the hands of public bodies and, in accordance with the relevant provisions of the Regulation of Investigatory Powers Act 2000, communication data in the hands of private bodies or individuals.

- It may carry out investigations itself or appoint police officers or members of other public bodies to do so.

Chapter 10

Appealing to the Supreme Court

INTRODUCTION

10.1   On 1 October 2009 the Supreme Court was established by the Constitutional Reform Act 2005 (CRA 2005). Its jurisdiction corresponds to that of the Appellate Committee of the House of Lords, which it replaced as the final court of appeal.[1]

10.2   The Supreme Court rarely grants leave to appeal from the Court of Appeal (Criminal Division). The effect of this is that when leave is granted the appellant's lawyers may be faced with a procedure that is entirely new to them. Supreme Court procedure has its own terminology and imposes upon the parties a number of exacting procedural requirements. However, there are a number of reasons why case preparation should not be as daunting as it might at first appear:

(a)   Section 33 of the Criminal Appeal Act 1968 sets out the decisions of the Court of Appeal which may and may not be appealed to the Supreme Court.

(b)   Rules relevant to the procedure for appealing to the Supreme Court are set out in the Criminal Procedure Rules Part 43.

(c)   The Supreme Court also has its own Rules and Practice Directions (PD) which are clear and detailed. Practice Directions 1–11 and 13 governing civil proceedings apply to criminal proceedings in the Supreme Court subject to any modifications or additional provisions made by Practice Direction 12, which applies only to criminal proceedings.

(d)   The staff of the Registry, which is headed by the Registrar of the Supreme Court, are usually helpful and tend to have more time to devote to a particular case than the staff in lower courts.

(e)   A representation order for a leading advocate is routinely granted, even if there was none in the Court of Appeal. Earlier instruction of an experienced leading advocate should assist.

---

1   CRA 2005, s 40, Sch 9.

(f)   The mystery that always surrounded appeals to the House of Lords has not attached itself to the Supreme Court because from the outset its proceedings have been broadcast. An appellant or his lawyers who want to know what to expect can turn on and see the judges who are likely to hear their case at work on another.[2]

10.3   Note on terminology: The right of appeal to the Supreme Court exists by virtue of section 33 of CAA 1968 which speaks of 'leave' to appeal. The Court's own Rules and Practice Directions, which apply also to civil appeals, use the term 'permission' to appeal. This chapter follows the statute and uses the term 'leave'.

THE TYPES OF CASES FOR WHICH LEAVE IS GIVEN

10.4   The test set for granting leave to appeal to the Supreme Court is that a point of law of general public importance is involved in the decision and it appears to the Court of Appeal or the Supreme Court (as the case may be) that the point is one which ought to be considered by the Supreme Court.[3]

10.5   The Supreme Court does hear a number of appeals that arise out of criminal litigation, but the number of appeals from the Court of Appeal Criminal Division is low. In 2018 the Court delivered only two judgments in appeals from the Court of Appeal Criminal Division.[4]

10.6   The reason for this low number is not hard to discern. The job of the Court of Appeal is to develop and clarify the criminal law. It is presided over by the Lord Chief Justice, the head of the judiciary, who can and does identify those cases that involve important questions of law and may allocate them to a Court of seven judges. There will be a limited number of cases that then justify further consideration.

10.7   Leave to appeal from the Court of Appeal appears to be given not simply to those cases which involve issues of particular importance but to those cases which involve genuinely difficult points of law and raise wide questions of principle which justify the sustained consideration and analysis that the Supreme Court provides.

---

2   Hearings may be viewed by accessing the website of the Supreme Court or Sky Supreme Court Live.
3   CAA 1968, s 33.
4   *R v Sally Lane and John Letts (AB and CD)* [2018] UKSC 36 (interpretation of s 17 Terrorism Act 2000); *R v Mackinlay and others* [2018] UKSC 42 (ambit of requirement to declare election expenses).

10.8   Application for leave should seek to awaken the interest of the justices in the point of public importance which the Court of Appeal has certified, indicating why the point is sufficiently rich in its implications and calls for a depth of analysis that justifies consideration by the Supreme Court.

APPLYING FOR LEAVE

10.9   Before an application for leave to appeal can be made to the Supreme Court, an application for leave and for a certificate of a point of law of public importance must already have been made to the Court of Appeal within 28 days of the relevant decision (or 14 days where the appeal is against the decision on an appeal by the Attorney-General against sentence).[5] The application for leave to appeal will usually be refused. However, it can only be made again before the Supreme Court if the Court of Appeal has certified a point of law of public importance.

10.10   The applicant has 28 days from the refusal of leave by the Court of Appeal to apply to the Supreme Court for leave.[6] The procedure for making such an application is contained in Part 3 of the Supreme Court Practice Direction.

10.11   However, if the applicant wishes to apply for funding to cover the cost of making the application for leave, an application for a representation order must be made to the Court of Appeal.[7] If a copy of the application for a representation order and the decision that is being appealed is then sent to the Registry of the Supreme Court, the 28-day time limit will stop running until the application for a representation order is determined.[8] If granted it will usually cover only solicitors and junior advocate at the leave stage and will be extended to cover the instruction of a leading advocate if leave is granted.

10.12   Additional papers can be lodged within seven days of the application for leave.[9] If the respondent wishes to make any objections it must do so within 14 days of the application having been lodged.[10]

10.13   The application is considered by a panel of Supreme Court justices. They may decide to hold an oral hearing but decisions are generally made on the papers.

---

5   CAA 1968, s 34; para 43.2 CrimPR.
6   Supreme Court Rules 2009 (SI 2009/1603), r 11.
7   PD 12.3.6.
8   PD 8.12.
9   Supreme Court Rules 2009 (SI 2009/1603), r 14.2.
10   Supreme Court Rules 2009 (SI 2009/1603), r 13.

PREPARING THE CASE FOLLOWING LEAVE

10.14   Once leave has been granted it is necessary to get to grips with the process of preparing the case for hearing. There is no substitute for acquainting oneself with the relevant practice directions that apply at each stage of the case.

10.15   However, the drafting is an exercise in advocacy as much as in rule compliance. Therefore, the leading advocate should be involved at each stage.

The form and content of Supreme Court documents

10.16   The following paragraphs of the Practice Direction provide the guidance as to the form and contents of the significant documents:

- The form of all documents to be presented to the Court: PD 5.1.2.

- The form and content of the statement of facts and issues: PD 5.1.3.

- The form and content of the appendix: PD 5.1.4 and 5.1.5.

- The form and content of authorities: PD 6.5.2 to 6.5.9.

- The form of core volumes: PD 6.4 (electronic form PD 14).

Timetable following the granting of leave by the Supreme Court

10.17   If leave is granted,[11] the steps required and timetable for preparation are set out in Parts 4 to 6 of the PD. Of particular note are the following requirements:

(a)   The appellant must, within 14 days, file a notice of intention to proceed.[12] When the notice is filed, the application for leave to appeal will be re-sealed and the appellant must then serve a copy on each respondent, on any recognised intervener (that is, an intervener whose submissions have been taken into account under rule 15) and on any intervener in the court below; and file seven copies.[13]

(b)   In a case in which a declaration of incompatibly with the European Convention on Human Rights is sought, Form 1 or 3 must be completed and served and filed along with the notice.

---

11   Separate rules apply when permission has already been granted by a lower Court; see Supreme Court Rules 2009 (SI 2009/1603), r 19.

12   PD 4.1.1.

13   Supreme Court Rules 2009 (SI 2009/1603), r 18(2).

(c)   The statement of facts and issues and the appendix must be filed by the appellant within 112 days after the filing of the notice. If the appellant is unable to comply with the relevant time limit, an application for an extension of time must be made.[14]

(d)   Within seven days after the filing of the statement of facts and issues and the appendix, the parties must notify the Registrar that the appeal is ready to list and specify the number of hours that their respective counsel estimate to be necessary for their oral submissions.[15]

(e)   No later than six weeks before the proposed date of the hearing, the appellants must file at the Registry the original and two copies of their case and serve it on the respondents.[16]

(f)   No later than four weeks before the proposed date of the hearing, the respondents must serve on the appellants a copy of their case in response and file at the Registry the original and two copies of their case, as must any other party filing a case (for example, an intervener or advocate to the court).[17]

(g)   As soon as the parties' cases have been exchanged, and in any event not later than 14 days before the date fixed for the hearing, the appellant must file ten bound core volumes in accordance with PD 6.4.3 and (if necessary) additional volumes containing further parts of the appendix and ten copies of every case filed by the parties or any intervener. These copies of the cases must contain cross-references (in a footnote or in the body of the text) to the appendix and authorities volumes.[18]

(h)   Ten copies of all authorities that may be referred to during the hearing must be filed by the appellant at the same time as the core volumes.[19]

HEARINGS

10.18   Cases are generally heard by a panel of five justices. In particular cases the Justices may sit as a larger panel. It is only in 'wholly exceptional circumstances'[20] that the Court would sit in private. Most hearings take place in public and are broadcast. The average time for a hearing is two days. Judgments are reserved. PD 6.6.1 to 6.6.10 should be consulted for further details.

---

14   Supreme Court Rules 2009 (SI 2009/1603), r 5 and PD 5.2.3.
15   PD 6.2.1 and Supreme Court Rules 2009 (SI 2009/1603), r 22(3).
16   PD 6.3.9.
17   PD 6.3.10.
18   PD6.4.1.
19   PD 6.4.2.
20   PD 6.6.4.

PARTICULAR ISSUES

Bail

10.19   Bail is not determined by the Supreme Court but by the Court of Appeal.[21]

Attendance of the appellant

10.20   There is no right for an appellant to be present at the hearing. The effect of this is that whilst an applicant on bail can attend, and is usually required to do so in order to surrender,[22] an appellant who is in custody will not be produced unless the Court deems it necessary.[23]

Costs

10.21   The Court 'may make such orders as it considers just in respect of the costs of any appeal, application for permission to appeal, or other application to or proceeding before the Court'.[24] PD 13.4 gives specific guidance on the making of costs against publically funded parties. PD 13.6 sets out the circumstances in which costs may be claimed against a party who made an unsuccessful application for leave. The subsequent parts of PD 13 provide detailed guidance on costs assessment.

Death of a party

10.22   In the event of the death of a party, the power to appoint an approved person to continue an appeal following the death of the party applies to appeals from the Court of Appeal (Criminal Division) to the Supreme Court.[25]

SUMMARY OF KEY POINTS

- The Supreme Court is the highest court of the land having been established by the Constitutional Reform Act 2005 to replace the House of Lords.

- It hears appeals from the Court of Appeal (Criminal Division) although permission to appeal from that Court is rarely granted.

---

21   CAA 1968, s 36.
22   PD 12.13.2.
23   PD 12.13.2.
24   Supreme Court Rules 2009 (SI 2009/1603), r 46(1).
25   CAA 1968, s 44A(2)(b).

- An application for leave can only be made if the Court of Appeal has first certified a point of law of public importance. The applicant generally has 28 days to apply to the Supreme Court itself for leave. The time will be extended if application is made to the Court of Appeal for a representation order.

- That application must be made in accordance with the Rules of the Supreme Court.

- If leave is granted there is a particular procedure to be followed for the preparation of the case, which is clearly set out in the Supreme Court Rules and Practice Directions.

- All documents lodged must be in a form that is prescribed by the Rules and Practice Directions.

- A representation order to allow for the instruction of the leading advocate will usually be granted only if leave is granted.

- Bail may be granted by the Court of Appeal.

- Hearings take place in public and may be broadcast live. The average length of a hearing is two days.

- The appellant has no right to be present at the hearing. Therefore, appellants will not generally be produced from custody.

- The Supreme Court has the power to award costs on such terms as it considers just.

Chapter 11

Applications to the European Court of Human Rights

INTRODUCTION

11.1   Making an application to the European Court of Human Rights is for those who are prepared to play a long game in order to keep alive their chances of achieving a favourable result.

11.2   It is not part of the appeal process. The ECtHR cannot quash a conviction or reduce a sentence. However, the impact of a finding by the ECtHR that a conviction or sentence was obtained in a manner that breached an applicant's rights under the European Convention on Human Rights can have a profound impact on the appeal process. It may provide a reason for the Criminal Cases Review Commission (CCRC) to refer the case to the Court of Appeal.

11.3   However, the fact that the ECtHR has found that there has been a violation of Convention rights does not necessarily require the CCRC to make a reference (*Dowsett v Criminal Cases Review Commission*[1]). A violation of a Convention right, even of the right to a fair trial under Article 6, does not necessarily render a conviction unsafe (see Chapter 3). Moreover, the domestic courts are not bound to agree with the ECtHR on what Article 6 requires.

11.4   However, the Convention has proved to be a powerful force in shaping the criminal law in significant and often unpredictable ways. A ruling from the ECtHR may lead the Commission and ultimately the Court of Appeal to consider familiar issues in a new light and so open up the possibility of a successful appeal.

WHETHER TO APPLY

11.5   Before embarking on litigation that may take years to conclude, a potential applicant should consider carefully what he wants to gain from

---

1   [2007] EWHC 1923 (Admin).

the process. Does he want the satisfaction of a finding that his rights were violated? If so, it is necessary to consider the case law of the ECtHR in order to determine the prospects of obtaining such a finding. Does he want to be paid compensation? If so, it is also important to consider the level of compensation that might be awarded (remembering that sometimes the ECtHR decides not to award compensation at all) in the event that the application succeeds. Does he want to challenge the conviction or sentence? If so, it is necessary to consider whether there is a real chance that a finding by the ECtHR that the applicant's rights were violated will lead the Commission to refer the case to the Court of Appeal. This final point must be considered in the light of the time that it is likely to take for an application to be determined. A sentence of three years or less is likely to have been completed by the time that the ECtHR makes a finding that the applicant's rights were violated.

APPLYING TO THE ECTHR

Exhaustion of domestic remedies

11.6   The ECtHR 'may only deal with the matter after all domestic remedies have been exhausted'.[2] However, the domestic remedies must be available and effective. The applicant does not need to exhaust domestic remedies that have no reasonable prospect of success.

11.7   Applying this approach to the criminal appeal process:

(a)   The applicant must have lodged an application for leave to appeal to the Court of Appeal.

(b)   If that application was refused by the single judge and not renewed before the full Court, the ECtHR may well find the applicant had not exhausted his remedies (*Reilly v UK*).[3]

(c)   If a renewed application for leave was refused by the full Court, the domestic remedies will normally have been exhausted (although see (e), below).

(d)   If the Court of Appeal heard and dismissed an appeal, it may be held that domestic remedies would only be exhausted once an application for leave to appeal to the Supreme Court had been sought. In *Selvanayagam v UK*,[4] the ECtHR accepted that domestic remedies had been exhausted when the applicant presented the separate opinions of a number of counsel that appeal to the House of Lords (the predecessor of the Supreme

---

2   Convention, Art 35(1).
3   App No 53731/00 (Dec) 26 June 2003.
4   App No 57981/00 (Dec) 12 December 2002.

Court) would not have succeeded. However, it may be better not to take a risk and, in a case in which an application to the ECtHR may be made, apply for leave to appeal to the Supreme Court, notwithstanding the unlikelihood of the application being granted.

(e) An application to the CCRC will not usually be regarded as giving rise to an available remedy but may do in unusual cases where it was highly likely that the Commission would have referred the case to the Court of Appeal. Such a situation might arise where a number of references had been made in similar cases (see *Tucka v UK (No. 1)*[5]).

Time limits for lodging an application

11.8 The current time limit for lodging an application with the ECtHR is six months from the date of the final decision by the UK courts which exhausted the process of seeking domestic remedies.[6] This period is due to be reduced to four months when all member states have ratified Protocol 15.[7] The time limit is strict and there is no discretion to extend it. It stops running when the application is physically received by the Court, with all the required supporting documents. It is therefore important when preparing the application to dispatch it by recorded delivery and to allow time for any potential delays and for the possibility that the Registry of the ECtHR will indicate that a further document is required.

Standing

11.9 Domestic rules on standing will not be decisive.[8] An individual or organisation may bring an action on behalf of another if they have clear written authority to act on their behalf. An application cannot be made on behalf of a deceased person.[9] However, if an applicant dies before the case is determined, the ECtHR usually permits a spouse or close relative to continue the proceedings on his behalf.

Drafting the application

11.10 Rule 47 of the Rules of the European Court of Human Rights sets out the information that needs to be included with the application. A failure to comply with its requirements will at best add to the delays that are a pronounced feature of proceedings before the ECtHR. At worst it will lead the Registry

---

5   App No 34566/10 (Dec) 18 January 2011.
6   Convention, Art 35.
7   App No 53731/00 (Dec) 26 June 2003.
8   *Scozzai v Italy*, 13 July 2000, ECHR 2000-VIII, paras 138–139.
9   *Dupin v Croatia*, App No 363868/03 (Dec) 7 July 2009.

to refuse to register the application and, if a second, properly completed, application is then lodged too late, to declare the application inadmissible through being out of time.

11.11   All the documents that are required should be supplied as copies, not originals. The exception is the requirement for an original dated and signed authority from the applicant authorising his lawyer to act on his behalf in the ECtHR proceedings.

11.12   The application form is to be found on the ECtHR website along with the technical requirements, such as page size, font size, spacing, and the like. Three sections of the form require careful drafting:

(a)   the statement of the facts;

(b)   the alleged violation(s) of the Convention and the relevant arguments;

(c)   confirmation of the exhaustion of domestic remedies and that the final domestic decision was made not more than six months before the application was made.

11.13   The statement of facts needs to be concise. It must not mislead or omit crucial unhelpful facts, but it is perfectly proper to focus on matters that support the argument that there has been a violation of the applicant's Convention rights.

11.14   The 'alleged violations' section of the application form allows several pages for submissions. An additional 20 pages can be appended. In drafting this section every lawyer will follow his own style and preferences. However, the following points should be borne in mind:

(a)   The ECtHR is not concerned with whether the UK courts have complied with UK law, practice and precedent, but whether the outcome is such as to breach Convention rights. Therefore, although the domestic law must be accurately stated, it is best to focus on the practical effect of the events in the UK courts and to contrast those effects with the guarantees of the Convention as amplified and explained by decisions of the ECtHR.

(b)   Each of the 47 member states of the Council of Europe has its own legal system, so the enforcement of human rights has to be flexible in its application. The ECtHR is concerned with substance not form. In an Article 6 argument, it is concerned with fairness not with technicalities.

(c)   The judges of the Court will not necessarily speak English as their first language. To allow for this, submissions about violations of Convention rights are best drafted in clear and direct language. An application has to deal with technical legal matters, but the excessive use of legalistic terms or national jargon or idiom may not help the application find favour further down the judicial line.

11.15   Once the application has been posted and received, the Registry will send the applicant's lawyers a letter giving the application number and, of late, a set of printed bar codes. The number and the bar codes can then be used in all future correspondence.

11.16   Then the applicant has to wait. At the time of writing that wait can be a few months or even a few years. Delay has been a persistent feature of proceedings before the ECtHR, although it is taking significant steps to reduce it.[10]

Progress of the application

11.17   Once they are received by the ECtHR applications may be allocated to a single judge, a committee of three judges or a Chamber.

11.18   The application will be allocated to a single judge if it appears on its face to be inadmissible.[11] The judge may declare it inadmissible, a decision from which there is no appeal. Alternatively he may forward it to a committee of three judges or to a Chamber.

11.19   A committee has the power to declare a case inadmissible or may declare it admissible and go on to deliver judgment on the merits if the underlying question in the case is already the subject of well-established case law.[12]

11.20   A Chamber is composed of seven judges, one of whom must be from the state against whom the application is brought.[13] If a Chamber does not, at the outset, conclude that the case is inadmissible, it will make a 'communication' of the complaint to the government of the state which stands accused of violating the applicant's rights. This is an invitation to the government to answer a series of questions, both about the admissibility and the merits of the application. These will often be directly taken from the application, and will directly address the matter in issue. For example, 'Was the [event at trial that is complained about] a violation of the Applicant's right to a fair trial under Article 6?'

11.21   The fact a communication is made is, of course, an encouraging sign. However, many cases in which a communication takes place are later declared inadmissible or no violation of the Convention is found.

---

10   Changes to Rule 47 in 2014 and the introduction of Protocols 14 and 15.
11   Convention, Art 27.
12   Convention, Art 28.
13   Convention, Art 29.

11.22   The applicant has a right of reply to any response from the government. In this way, the case is argued on paper and the Chamber will often make final determinations of admissibility and merits on the papers without an oral hearing.

11.23   In a small number of cases Chambers do decide to hold a hearing before determining a case. It will set a date for both sides to travel to the Court and present brief, time-limited, oral arguments, followed by questions from the Court. The Registry supplies full and helpful directions about what is required of the lawyers on these occasions.

11.24   It is the normal practice of Chambers to make a final determination of admissibility and merits in the same judgment, having considered all the representations from the parties.

Referral to a Grand Chamber

11.25   If either party wishes to challenge a judgment they can apply, within three months of judgment being given, for referral to a Grand Chamber, which is composed of 17 judges.[14] A panel of five judges will decide whether to accept the referral. If it is accepted the case will be considered afresh by the Grand Chamber as a complete re-determination. The Grand Chamber almost always holds an oral hearing before reaching its determination. In addition, a Chamber that is hearing the application may transfer it to the Grand Chamber, as long as neither party objects.[15]

A 'friendly settlement' in criminal litigation

11.26   In the course of the correspondence the Registry will offer the two parties the chance to discuss a 'friendly settlement'. Such a settlement involves an agreement by the government to pay compensation and, in some cases, to vary its policies or its actions towards an applicant so as to remove the event or conduct that is claimed to amount to a violation. This mechanism will almost never provide a means of resolving a claim arising out of a sentence or conviction, as the government can obviously not agree to ignore a judicial finding or order, such as a conviction or prison sentence.

11.27   An exception might arise in a case where an applicant has a good claim that the time taken for his trial is too long to comply with Article 6. In such cases, the UK government may sometimes offer to make a payment. It

---

14   Convention, Art 43.
15   Convention, Art 30.

may be worth considering accepting such an offer as the chances of such a violation leading to a conviction being quashed may be slim.

Representation

11.28   There is no requirement that an application be submitted by a lawyer. However, if the application is communicated to the respondent government the ECtHR requires an applicant to be represented by an advocate who is qualified within one of the 47 signatory states. [16] There is no right to self-representation nor is there a right to be represented by a lawyer or another from outside the contracting territories. Any request for self-representation or representation from someone outside the contracting territories must be made in writing to the president of the ECtHR. [17]

Legal aid

11.29   The right to legal aid does not arise unless and until a communication is made to the government of the state which is accused of violating the applicant's Convention rights. At that point means forms may be sent out to the applicant to be completed and returned to the ECtHR. Legal aid is granted only if the ECtHR is satisfied that the applicant does not have the means to pay for all or part of his own representation. [18] Although legal aid is paid by the ECtHR, it asks the domestic legal aid authority to conduct an assessment of means on the basis of the information the applicant provided. It is the practice of the ECtHR to only pay for work undertaken by one lawyer. Reasonable travel expenses will be reimbursed if the advocate is required to attend an oral hearing.

THE CONSEQUENCES OF A SUCCESSFUL OUTCOME

The judgment

11.30   For the applicant who wants to return to the domestic courts to appeal his conviction or sentence, the most important outcome is a ruling that contains a finding that his rights have been violated. It will need to be studied with care in order to determine whether it provides the basis for an application to the Commission for a reference.

---

16   Rules of the Court, r 36(2), (3).
17   *Manoussos v Czech Republic*, App No 46488/99 (Dec) 7 September 2002.
18   Rules of the Court, r 101(b).

Compensation

11.31   Even if the ECtHR finds that there has been a violation of the applicant's Convention rights, it will not necessarily order financial compensation. The finding of breach is often considered to be a sufficient remedy. If it does decide to award compensation it may do so on the basis of pecuniary and non-pecuniary loss. However, an application for compensation may be made within two months of the application being declared admissible.

Costs

11.32   There is no provision for the applicant to pay costs to the responding government in the event that the application is withdrawn or dismissed. However, a successful applicant may be awarded his costs, to be paid by the government. It is, therefore, a good idea to keep a record of the tasks completed by solicitors, senior and junior counsel, the hours worked and the hourly rate charged. This should be submitted with the applicant's reply to the government's observations as there is no separate costs stage of proceedings. Although the ECtHR will seek submissions from the government on the applicant's costs, it will generally award what seems to the Court to be a reasonable amount for the work undertaken; often this will be less than claimed, but is always better than nothing. Costs, if awarded, have to be paid within three months of the judgment becoming final.

SUMMARY OF KEY POINTS

- An application to the ECtHR may only be made after domestic remedies have been exhausted.

- It must be received by the Registry within six months of the decision of the domestic courts that exhausted the domestic remedies.

- A finding by the ECtHR that the conviction or sentence gave rise to a breach of Convention rights may lead the Criminal Cases Review Commission to refer the case back to the Court of Appeal, but only if it was capable of leading the Court of Appeal to conclude that a conviction was unsafe or the sentence wrong and should be reduced on appeal.

- The requirement to exhaust domestic remedies does not involve an obligation to pursue those remedies that have no realistic prospect of success. A failure to lodge an application for leave to appeal will be a failure to exhaust domestic remedies, so may a failure to renew an application for leave before the full Court. Whether an application for leave to appeal to the Supreme Court was required, following an unsuccessful appeal in the Court of Appeal, may depend on the facts of the case. The ECtHR would not normally find that the applicant should have made an application to the Criminal Cases Review Commission for a reference, but may do in certain circumstances.

- The application should be made using the forms available on the ECtHR website. Copies of all the documents required by Rule 47 must be included or the application may not be considered.

- The application will be allocated to a single judge, committee or Chamber, any one of whom may make a declaration of inadmissibility.

- Should the Court not take the view that the application is clearly inadmissible it will issue a communication to the relevant government. It will give the applicant the right of reply to any response from the government.

- Both the final determination of admissibility and the merits of the case are likely to be made on the basis of these documents in a single judgment.

- The Chamber occasionally conducts oral hearings before making its judgment.

- The Chamber can send the case to the Grand Chamber (of 17 judges) for a determination. Alternatively, an unsuccessful party can request a re-hearing before the Grand Chamber (a request that is considered by a panel of five judges).

- Legal aid may be available after a communication has been made to the government of the state that is accused of breaching the applicant's rights.

- A successful applicant may apply for costs and compensation but the Court has no power to order costs to a responding government in the event that the application is withdrawn or dismissed.

Part 4
Other Rights of Appeal

Chapter 12

Appeals against interlocutory rulings

INTRODUCTION

12.1   The right of appeal most commonly arises at the conclusion of the case. However, Parliament has created a number of exceptions in which appeals may be brought against interlocutory rulings. One of those exceptions, the right of prosecution to appeal against certain rulings, is considered in Chapter 13.

12.2   Other exceptions include the following appeals:

(a)   appeals against rulings made at preparatory hearings in serious or complex fraud cases;

(b)   appeals against rulings at preparatory hearings in complex, serious or lengthy cases;

(c)   appeals against a ruling that a case should be tried by a judge alone because of the risk of jury tampering;

(d)   appeals against a decision of the trial judge to discharge a jury and continue to try the case alone;

(e)   appeals against a ruling that certain counts on an indictment should be tried by judge alone, following a conviction by a jury on sample counts.

12.3   The procedures in relation to each appeal are very similar. They follow, in truncated form, the procedures for appealing against conviction and sentence. They are all governed by Part 37 of the Criminal Procedure Rules as well as their own specific statutory provisions. However, with the exception of appeals against rulings against a decision of the judge to discharge a jury and try the case alone, those statutory provisions replicate or adopt the statutory scheme for appeals from preparatory hearings in complex or lengthy fraud cases that were introduced in the Criminal Justice Act 1987 (CJA 1987).

APPEALS AGAINST RULINGS MADE AT PREPARATORY HEARINGS IN SERIOUS OR COMPLEX FRAUD CASES

12.4   If a judge has made a wrongful ruling at the beginning of a complex or lengthy case, it would be a waste of time and money for the case to proceed for weeks or months on an incorrect footing when the matter might be immediately appealed and the matter corrected so that the trial can proceed on a correct basis (*R v Hedworth*[1]).

12.5   Such was the thinking behind section 9 of CJA 1987 which established a right of appeal from a ruling of the judge made in serious or complex fraud cases.

The circumstances in which a ruling may be appealed

12.6   Section 7(1) of CJA 1987 provides that:

'Where it appears to a judge of the Crown Court that the evidence on an indictment reveals a case of fraud of such seriousness or complexity that substantial benefits are likely to accrue from a hearing (in this Act referred to as a "preparatory hearing") before the jury are sworn, for the purpose of –

(a)   identifying issues which are likely to be material to the verdict of the jury;

(b)   assisting their comprehension of any such issues;

(c)   expediting the proceedings before the jury; or

(d)   assisting the judge's management of the trial,

he may order that such a hearing shall be held.'

12.7   The right of appeal to the Court of Appeal arises in relation to any ruling made by the judge, in the course of a preparatory hearing on:

(a)   a question arising under section 6 of the Criminal Justice Act 1993 (relevance of external law to certain charges of conspiracy, attempt and incitement);

(b)   any question as to the admissibility of evidence; and

(c)   any other question of law relating to the case.[2]

---

1   [1997] 1 Cr App R 421.
2   CJA 1987, s 9(3).

12.8   Such a ruling may be appealed to the Court of Appeal.[3]

12.9   In *R v H*[4] the House of Lords held that whilst it was open to a judge to determine disclosure applications at the preparatory hearing, rulings in relation to disclosure were not questions of law within the meaning of section 9(3)(b) of CJA 1987 and could not, therefore, be subject to an interlocutory appeal.

Appealing a ruling

12.10   The procedure for appealing is as follows:

(a)   Leave is needed from the trial judge or the Court of Appeal.[5] Application for leave from the trial judge must be made orally immediately after, or in writing within two days, of the decision having been made.[6]

(b)   Application for leave to the Court of Appeal must be made in writing not more than five business days either after the decision that is the subject of the appeal or after the Crown Court judge refuses to give leave.[7] This time limit may be extended on application to the Court, by the Court, single judge or Registrar. The Registrar should be asked to exercise his or her power to refer a case directly to the full Court due to its urgency, and the advocate should set out the reasons why.

(c)   An application for leave to appeal is made on Form NG(Prep).

(d)   The application must be served on the Crown Court, the Registrar and any party directly affected by the application.[8]

(e)   It must be made in the terms prescribed in rule 37.3 of the Criminal Procedure Rules.

(f)   If the application is opposed, a respondent's notice (Form RN) should be served within five days of the application having been made.[9]

(g)   It is considered by the single judge. If refused it may be renewed before the full court within five days of refusal.[10]

(h)   Once leave is granted the preparatory hearing can continue but trial of facts must not take place until it is determined or abandoned.[11] The party

---

3   CJA 1987, s 9(11).
4   [2007] UKHL 7.
5   CJA 1987, s 9(11); CPIA 1996, s 35(1).
6   Part 37.4 CrimPR.
7   Part 37.2 CrimPR.
8   Part 37.2 CrimPR.
9   Part 37.5 CrimPR.
10   Part 37.7 CrimPR.
11   CJA 1987, s 9(13); CPIA 1996, s 35(2).

in custody has the right to attend; this will often be a virtual attending by way of a video link.[12]

(i) The Court can confirm, vary or reverse the decision that is the subject of the appeal.[13] A right of appeal lies from the Court of Appeal to the Supreme Court.[14]

(j) Funding for the proceedings will generally be covered by the existing Crown Court representation order.

Reporting restrictions on appeals from preparatory hearings

12.11 Section 11(1) of CJA 1987 restricts the reporting of an appeal from a preliminary ruling to those matters specified within that section, which contains lists of the basic information about the case. However, the Court of Appeal may make an order to remove or amend them.[15]

APPEALS UNDER SECTION 35 OF THE CRIMINAL PROCEDURE AND INVESTIGATIONS ACT 1996

12.12 Section 29 of the Criminal Procedure and Investigations Act 1996 ('CPIA 1996') provides that a preparatory hearing may be held where the judge determines that the case is likely to be of such length, seriousness or complexity that there will be significant benefits from holding a hearing in order to:

(a) identify issues that are likely to be material to the determinations and findings that are likely to be required during the trial;

(b) if there is to be a jury, assist their comprehension of those issues and expedite the proceedings before them;

(c) determine an application to which section 45 of the Criminal Justice Act 2003 ('CJA 2003') applies (where the prosecution have applied, under section 43 or 44 of CJA 2003 for the trial to take place without a jury);

(d) assist the judge's management of the trial;

(e) consider questions as to the severance or joinder of charges.

12.13 In addition the judge must order a preparatory hearing in a terrorist case.[16]

---

12 Part 37.8 CrimPR.
13 CJA 1987, s 9(14); CPIA 1996, s 13(3).
14 CAA 1968, s 33.
15 CJA 1987, s 11(5).
16 CPIA 1996, s 29(1C), (6).

12.14   The right of appeal exists against ruling, made at the preparatory hearing, in relation to:

(i)   any question as to the admissibility of evidence;

(ii)   any other question of law relating to the case;

(iii)   any question as to the severance or joinder of charges.

12.15   In *R v I (C)*[17] the Court of Appeal confirmed that the principles established in *R v H* regarding disclosure rulings (see 12.9 above) applied to appeals under section 35 of CPIA 1996.

The procedure for appealing

12.16   The procedures for appealing a ruling under section 35 of CPIA 1996 are the same as for the appeals against rulings in serious or complex fraud cases set out in 12.10 and 12.11, above. The relevant references for appeals under section 35 are contained in the footnotes.

Reporting restrictions

12.17   Section 37(1) of CPIA 1996 mirrors section 11 of CJA 1987 in creating an automatic reporting restriction (which may be removed or varied by the Court of Appeal) that applies to appeals against rulings made under section 35 and restricts reporting to certain basic facts.

APPEALS AGAINST A RULING THAT A CASE SHOULD BE TRIED BY A JUDGE AND NOT A JURY WHEN THERE IS A RISK OF JURY TAMPERING

12.18   A judge may, following an application by the prosecution, order that a trial take place without a jury in a case where there is a risk of jury tampering.[18] If such an application is made, a preparatory hearing must be held at which the application may be determined. The Court must be satisfied to the criminal standard (section 46(3) of CJA 2003) that the following criteria is made out:

'(4)   The first condition is that there is evidence of a real and present danger that jury tampering would take place.

---

17   [2009] EWCA Crim 1793.
18   CJA 2003, s 44.

(5)   The second condition is that, notwithstanding any steps (including the provision of police protection) which might reasonably be taken to prevent jury tampering, the likelihood that it would take place would be so substantial as to make it necessary in the interests of justice for the trial to be conducted without a jury.'

The procedure

12.19   Section 45 of CJA 2003 amends the relevant provisions of CJA 1987 and CPIA 1996 so as to ensure that the procedure for preparatory hearings and subsequent appeals applies to the decision of the judge as to whether to order that a trial take place without a jury under section 44. Therefore, the procedure for appeals and powers of the Court and reporting restrictions as set out at 12.10 and 12.11, above apply to appeals against such an order.

APPEALS AGAINST A DECISION TO ORDER A TRIAL WITHOUT A JURY WHERE JURY TAMPERING HAS TAKEN PLACE

12.20   If, after a trial has commenced, the trial judge is satisfied of the following;

(a)   that jury tampering has taken place, and

(b)   that to continue the trial without a jury would be fair to the defendant or defendants,

the judge may discharge the jury and proceed to try the case alone.[19]

12.21   However, if the judge decides that it is necessary in the interests of justice for the trial to be terminated, he must instead terminate the trial.[20]

12.22   Before determining whether the above test is satisfied, the judge must inform the parties of his grounds for concern and allow them to make representations.

12.23   Such an order may be appealed to the Court of Appeal. The Court may confirm or revoke the order.

12.24   As an order does not take place within the context of a preparatory hearing, the relevant powers of the Court of Appeal in relation to appeals from preparatory hearings do not apply to appeals against a decision. However, rule

---

19   CJA 2003, s 47.
20   CJA 2003, s 47(4).

37.1 of the Criminal Procedure Rules applies to appeals against a decision under section 46 of CJA 2003.

12.25 For this reason, what is said above about appeals from preparatory hearings applies also to appeals against decisions made under section 46, with the following exceptions:

(a) Leave may be given by the trial judge or the full court,[21] but because it may not be given by the single judge, there is no procedure for renewing the application for leave.

(b) The power of the Court is simply to confirm or revoke the order.[22]

(c) The right to appeal to the Supreme Court against the decision of the Court of Appeal arises under section 47(6), which inserts the right into section 33(1) of CAA 1968.

RULING THAT A JUDGE SHOULD TRY CERTAIN COUNTS ALONE FOLLOWING CONVICTION BY A JURY ON SAMPLE COUNTS

12.26 In a case involving multiple counts the prosecution may apply to the Crown Court for an order that certain counts are to be tried by a judge alone in the absence of a jury. If such an order is made, the trials without jury may only take place if a jury has first tried and convicted the defendant of counts which are to properly be regarded as sample counts of those which may be tried by the judge.

12.27 The conditions of the making of such an order are set out in section 17(3) to (5) of the Domestic Violence, Crime and Victims Act 2004.

12.28 Such an order may only be made at a preparatory hearing and may be appealed to the Court of Appeal. The Domestic Violence, Crime and Victims Act 2004 amends the relevant sections of CJA 1987 and CPIA 1996 so as to ensure that appeals from decisions under section 17 are subject to their statutory regime. Therefore, the powers of the Court of Appeal and the procedure for appealing are as set out at 12.10, above.

SUMMARY OF KEY POINTS

- There are a number of situations in which an appeal against an interlocutory ruling may be brought.

---

21   CJA 2003, s 47(2).
22   CJA 2003, s 47(4).

12.28 *Appeals against interlocutory rulings*

- These appeal rights largely follow the procedures set down in relation to appeals against rulings at preparatory hearings that were established by CJA 1987 in relation to appeals against rulings in serious or complex fraud cases.

- The procedure for such appeals is contained in Part 37 of the CrimPR, which sets out a truncated version of the procedure for appealing against conviction or sentence.

- Applications should be made using adapted forms for appeals against conviction and sentence.

- There are restrictions on the reporting of such appeals, which can, on application, be removed or amended by the Court of Appeal.

Chapter 13

Responding to prosecution appeals

INTRODUCTION

13.1   This chapter sets out the circumstances in which the prosecution may appeal to the Court of Appeal against a decision of the lower Court and then moves on to focus on responding to two common types of prosecution appeal:

(a)   Appeals under section 58 of CJA 2003 against a trial judge's ruling (often misleadingly referred to as appeals against 'terminating rulings').

(b)   Appeals against sentences known as 'Attorney-General's References'.

THE PROSECUTION'S RIGHTS OF APPEAL

13.2   The prosecution's rights of appeal are far more restricted than those of the defence. The principle of the finality of the jury's verdict is respected and there is no general right of appeal against an acquittal. However, Parliament has established the following rights of appeal by the prosecution:

1   Appeals against rulings

(a)   Appeals against interlocutory rulings: these are considered in Chapter 12.

(b)   Appeals against a ruling of the trial judge pursuant to section 58 of CJA 2003 (see paras 13.3 to 13.19 below).

(c)   Appeals against evidentiary rulings in relation to qualifying offences pursuant to section 62 of CJA 2003. However, section 62 is yet to be brought into force. At the time of writing it is understood there are no plans to do so.

(d)   A reference by the Attorney-General of a point of law to the Court of Appeal following an acquittal on indictment pursuant to section 36(1) of the Criminal Justice Act 1972. The acquittal will be unaffected by the Court of Appeal's decision but the judgment of the Court will be available for the benefit of future cases.

2   Appeals against acquittals

    (a)   Section 54 of CPIA 1996 gives the prosecution the right to appeal to the High Court against an acquittal when there has been a conviction for interference or intimidation of a witness or juror in the proceedings that lead to the acquittal and there is a real possibility that the acquittal would not have taken place but for the interference or intimidation.

    (b)   Under Part 10 of CJA 2003 the prosecution may apply to the Court of Appeal to quash an acquittal in England and Wales and order a re-trial or for a ruling that a foreign acquittal should be no bar to the defendant being tried for the same offence. This is the exception to the double jeopardy rule and the application will only be granted where there is 'new or compelling evidence'.

3   Appeals against sentence

    (a)   The prosecution have a right to appeal against a refusal to make a confiscation order under the Proceeds of Crime Act 2002 (see 4.52–4.53).

    (b)   Under section 14A(5A) of the Football Spectators Act 1989 the prosecution have a right to appeal against the refusal to make a banning order.

    (c)   Under sections 35 and 36 of the Criminal Justice Act 1988 the Attorney-General may refer a sentence to the Court of Appeal on the basis that it is unduly lenient (see paras 13.20 onwards, below).

PROSECUTION APPEALS AGAINST RULINGS UNDER SECTION 58 OF CJA 2003

13.3   Section 58 of CJA 2003 gives the prosecution the right of appeal against a trial judge's ruling. This is often referred to as a right to appeal against a 'terminating' ruling but the Court of Appeal has deprecated the use of the term (*R v Arnold*[1]). It is misleading because the prosecution can appeal against a ruling even when it will not necessarily result in the defendant's acquittal. If, for example, a judge were to exclude a significant part of the evidence, the prosecution could appeal even if there was still some evidence remaining such as might enable the case to continue past a later submission of 'no case to answer'.

13.4   That said, the defining feature of these appeals is that the prosecution may only seek leave to appeal if it is prepared to accept that the defendant will

---

1   [2008] EWCA Crim 1034.

be acquitted of the count that is the subject of the appeal if it fails. For this reason it will most usually be deployed where the ruling either does terminate the case on that count, or where it is comes close to doing so.

When an appeal under section 58 may be brought

13.5 Leave to appeal may only be sought if the following conditions are met:

(a) The appeal must be against a ruling that was made before the summing up.[2]

(b) It must not be a ruling to discharge the jury.[3]

(c) There must be no other right of appeal available to the prosecution – it follows that where an appeal may be brought under the regime for appeals against interlocutory rulings it must be brought under those provisions.[4]

(d) The prosecution must have given notice of intention to appeal after the ruling was given or have applied for an adjournment in order to consider whether to appeal.[5]

(e) The prosecution must have given a valid acquittal agreement at the time when the indication of intention to appeal is given (section 58(8)).

13.6 The Court of Appeal has interpreted these preconditions strictly. If they are not met the appeal will be refused (*R v Arnold*[6]).

What is an acquittal agreement?

13.7 Section 58(8) of CJA 2003 requires the prosecution to give the undertaking that in the event of leave to appeal being refused or the appeal being abandoned, they will agree to the defendant being acquitted.[7] The undertaking has to be given *at or before* the time that the prosecution notifies the Crown Court of its intention to appeal; a failure to give the undertaking at that time will be fatal to the appeal (*R v Arnold*[8]).

---

2   See s 74(1) for the broad definition given to ruling; s 58(13) for the requirement that it be before the summing up.
3   CJA 2003, s 57(2)(a).
4   CJA 2003, s 57(2)(b).
5   CJA 2003, s 58(4).
6   [2008] EWCA Crim 1034.
7   CJA 2003, s 61(3).
8   [2008] EWCA Crim 1034; see also LSA [2008] EWCA Crim 1034. NT [2010] EWCA Crim 711; *B* [2014] EWCA Crim 2078.

13.8   If the defendant cannot be formally 'acquitted' because of the stage the case has reached, no such undertaking can be given and therefore the right of appeal does not arise. This has the effect of precluding an appeal under this section against a ruling made before arraignment (*R v Thompson*[9]).

The procedure for appealing

13.9   The procedure for applications for leave and subsequent appeals is to be found in Part 38 of the Criminal Procedure Rules. The General Rules found in Part 36 also apply.

13.10   The prosecution must inform the Court that it intends to appeal or request an adjournment to consider whether to appeal,[10] which, if granted, will be until the next business day.[11] The Judge has discretion to so adjourn if there is a real reason for doing so.[12] The prosecution must give the undertaking in relation to an acquittal agreement at the time when it informs the Court of its intention to appeal. Once a decision has been taken, a notice and application to appeal[13] must be served on the Crown Court, Registrar and every defendant affected by the ruling the next business day if the trial Judge expedites the appeal or otherwise five business days of giving notice of the intent to appeal.[14]

13.11   Permission to appeal is required and may be granted either by the trial judge or by the Court of Appeal.[15] Application for permission to the trial judge must be made orally immediately after the ruling is given or in writing at the expiry of the time given for consideration of whether to appeal. The trial judge must hear representations from the defence and generally reach a decision on permission the same day that the application is made.[16]

13.12   Leave should be granted only where the trial judge considers there is a real prospect of success and not to speed up the hearing of the appeal.[17]

The respondent's notice

13.13   Once a notice of appeal has been lodged the defendant, now the respondent must within five days (or one day if the appeal is expedited) serve

---

9   [2006] EWCA Crim 2849.
10   CJA 2003, s 58(4).
11   Part 38.2(2) CrimPR.
12   *H* [2008] EWCA Crim 483.
13   See Part 38.8 CrimPR for the relevant requirements of the notice.
14   Part 38.3 CrimPR.
15   CJA 2003, s 57(4).
16   Part 38.5 CrimPR.
17   *JG* [2006] EWCA Crim 3276.

a respondent's notice including grounds of opposition, if it wishes to make any representations or if directed to do so by the Court.[18]

13.14 The requirements of the form and service of the respondent's notice are set out in Crim PR 38.7.The notice should be served on the prosecution, the Crown Court, the Registrar, and any co-defendants who are also the subject of the application to appeal within five days (or no later than the next business day if the appeal is expediated).

13.15 The respondent's notice must:

'(a) give the date on which the respondent was served with the appeal notice;

(b) identify each ground of opposition on which the respondent relies, numbering them consecutively (if there is more than one), concisely outlining each argument in support and identifying the ground of appeal to which each relates;

(c) summarise any relevant facts not already summarised in the appeal notice;

(d) identify any relevant authorities;

(e) include or attach any application for the following, with reasons –

(i) an extension of time within which to serve the respondent's notice,

(ii) a direction to attend in person any hearing that the respondent could attend by live link, if the respondent is in custody;

(f) identify any other document or thing that the respondent thinks the court will need to decide the appeal.'

The Hearing

13.16 The defendant has the right to attend the appeal hearing, though the Registrar can direct that this occurs via a video link.[19] There is an automatic restriction on the reporting of appeals which may be lifted or varied by the Court.[20]

13.17 Resisting an appeal will often involve persuading the Court to rely on the trial judge's experience and any advantages the trial judge had in hearing live

---

18 Part 38.7 CrimPR.
19 Part 38.11 CrimPR.
20 CJA 2003, s 71.

evidence in the case. In *R v B*[21] Lord Judge CJ laid emphasis on the trial judge's experience and reputation and indicated that the decision had to be shown to be clearly wrong before the Court of Appeal would think it right to interfere.

13.18 The Court of Appeal's powers in such an appeal are wider than simply to uphold or overturn a trial level ruling. Section 61 of CJA 2003 also permits the Court to vary a ruling. Where the ruling by the trial judge is difficult to defend in its precise terms the respondent may wish to argue that the overall merits of the ruling should lead the Court to uphold the ruling in modified terms.

13.19 Either party may appeal to the Supreme Court, subject to the Court of Appeal certifying a point of law of general public importance.

ATTORNEY-GENERAL'S REFERENCES

13.20 Section 36 of the Criminal Justice Act 1988 (CJA 1988) permits the Attorney-General to appeal against unduly lenient sentences in certain serious cases. The offences in relation to which the sentence may be appealed under section 36 include all indictable-only offences and any other offence set out in the relevant statutory instrument made under the Act:[22]

Grounds for an appeal

13.21 Section 36(1) makes it clear that the overarching basis upon which the Attorney-General can appeal is that the sentence passed was 'unduly lenient'. Section 36(2) goes on to specify that the test of undue leniency may be met where a sentencing judge has either erred in law as to his powers of sentencing or failed to pass one of the minimum sentences required by statute.

The procedure

13.22 The procedure is governed by Part 41 of the CrimPR. The general rules contained in Part 36 also apply.

Notification of an appeal and reply

13.23 Schedule 3 to CJA 1988 allows 28 days for the prosecution to lodge an application for leave to refer a sentencing case. The CrimPR impose

---

21 [2008] EWCA Crim 1144.
22 See CJA 1988 s 35 and Criminal Justice Act 1988 (Reviews of Sentencing) Order 2006 (SI 2006/1116) Sch 1.

requirements as to the form and content of the application.[23] In practice the prosecution will usually send out a standard letter with supporting documents within 28 days of the sentence being passed.

13.24   The Registrar will serve those papers on the respondent who must make any represenations within 14 days. Most respondents will be keen to do so. The CrimPR impose requirements as to the form, content and service of the respondent's notice.[24]

Funding for respondent's representation

13.25   Representation Orders are granted by the Registrar in order to enable the defendant to respond to an Attorney-General's Reference.

Permission and full hearings

13.26   Attorney-General's References require leave from the Court but the practice is to list the case and allow the Court to consider both leave and, if leave is given, to deal with the substantive appeal all in one hearing.

13.27   A respondent who is in custody has the right to attend at the substantive hearing though this may be by video link if the Registrar directs.[25] There is no right to be produced at any permission or other incidental hearings.

The Court's approach to Attorney-General's References

13.28   The Court must first decide whether the sentence was unduly lenient. In doing so, it has frequently made clear that sentencing judges are entitled to depart from sentencing guidelines provided there is a rational and justifiable basis to do so. Lord Phillips CJ emphasised in *Attorney-General's Reference (No. 8 of 2007)*[26] that a judge who took such a decision should not waver from it for fear of a reference. The power to allow an appeal is for sentences that are *unduly* lenient, not just lenient. The test is a high one and is intend to capture those sentences which cause public concern and affect the confidence in the criminal justice system (*Attorney-General's Reference (Nos 3 and 5 of 1989)*).[27]

---

23   Parts 41.2 and 41.3 CrimPR.
24   Part 41.4 CrimPR.
25   Part 41.6 CrimPR.
26   [2007] EWCA Crim 922.
27   (1990) 90 Cr App R 358.

13.29   In the event that the Court decides that the sentence was unduly lenient, it must then go on to consider whether and to what extent to reduce or vary the sentence. This is a matter that is within the discretion of the Court; there is no statutory guidance on the exercise of that discretion and the Court has been known to take into account a wide range of factors.

13.30   In determining whether the sentence was unduly lenient, the Court considers the facts as they were before the sentencing judge. It will not take account of new material (see *Attorney-General's Reference (No. 19 of 2005)*[28]). The Court has, however, been prepared to look at new material in deciding what the new sentence should be *(Attorney-General's Reference (No. 74 of 2010)*[29]; Att-Gen's Reference (No 79 of 2015)[30]. In both those cases, the new material in question consisted of probation reports but the Court's approach has wider application; in the event that the Court decides that a sentence was unduly lenient it will often consider material in relation to the progress of the respondent from the time when the sentence was passed in order to assist in determining whether to interfere with it.

13.31   Difficulties have occurred where a defendant has been given reasons to expect a certain sentence, most commonly when a *Goodyear*[31] indication has been given. The fact that an indication was given does not necessarily mean that the Court will not interfere with the sentence, nor does the fact that the prosecution at the time raised no objection to the indicated sentence (see *A-G's Refs (Nos 86 and 87 of 1999).*[32] However, the prosecution's seeming consent may be a powerful reason not to increase a sentence, especially if the offender acted in reliance on the indication that was given (see *Attorney-General's References (Nos 25 and 26 of 2008)*[33]). In the more recent case of *Powell*,[34] where prosecution counsel had agreed to an erroneous categorisation under the aggravated burglary sentencing guideline, the court ruled that the sentence was unduly lenient, but it would not be just to permit the Attorney-General to go so far behind what was said to the sentencing judge as to raise the case to a higher category.

Discount for double jeopardy

13.32   Double jeopardy is the term used for the fear and distress that arises from being sentenced a second time. When, following a finding of undue leniency, the Court considers what new sentence to impose, it will often make a

---

28   [2006] EWCA Crim 785.
29   [2011] EWCA Crim 873.
30   [2016] EWCA Crim 448
31   *R v Goodyear* [2005] EWCA Crim 888.
32   [2001] 1 Cr App R (S) 141 (505).
33   [2008] EWCA Crim 2665.
34   [2018] 1 Cr App R (S).

discount from what would have been the correct sentence, had it been imposed at first instance, to take account of this.

13.33   In *Attorney-General's References (Nos 14 and 15 of 2006)*,[35] the Court reviewed the authorities in relation to double jeopardy. It concluded that deductions at or near the top of the range which was 30 per cent might be made in relation to: offenders who faced a custodial sentence when one had not originally been passed; offenders who had committed the offence in question when young and immature; and those offenders who were about to be released from prison. In relation to those cases where the offender had a lengthy determinate sentence to serve or was serving a discretionary life sentence it was not necessarily wrong to make deductions for double jeopardy. However, those deductions would generally be smaller and in some cases no deduction would need to be made. In *Att-Gen's Reference (No 45 of 2014)*[36] the Court of Appeal explained that cases in which the principle is likely to arise are now rare by reason of a number of factors: the changes in the sentencing regime, including greater clarity and uniformity in relation to sentencing for most offences as a result of sentencing guidelines, such that advocates can advise of the risk of a reference where a judge has departed from the guidelines without explanation or good reason; the rapid consideration by the Attorney General of sentences, leading to quick references to the court; and an approach to sentencing that has become more victim-oriented since 2006. For rare, recent examples of the Court of Appeal making an allowance on for double jeopardy, see *Att-Gen's Reference (R v Ferizi)*[37] and *R v Phelps*.[38]

13.34   Under section 36A of CJA 1988 the Court should not make any allowance for double jeopardy when the reference relates to a minimum term for a mandatory life sentence under section 269(2) of CJA 2003.

13.35   If and when it comes into force (no date has yet been fixed) section 46 of the Criminal Justice and Immigration Act 2008 will amend section 36A of CJA 1988 so as to extend its application to discretionary life sentences.

Responding to the appellant's case

13.36   The respondent may seek to persuade the Court both that the sentence was not unduly lenient and that, even if it was, the Court should exercise its discretion not to increase the sentence. In cases where the correctness of the original sentence is very difficult to justify, the focus of the submissions should often be on the latter point.

---

35   [2006] EWCA Crim 1335.
36   [2014] EWCA Crim 1566.
37   [2016] EWCA Crim 2022.
38   [2017] EWCA Crim 2403.

13.37   In seeking to persuade the Court that the sentence is not unduly lenient, arguments that are commonly advanced include:

(a)   the high threshold that must be passed for a sentence to be regarded as unduly excessive;

(b)   the fact that the judge was experienced (if true) and the advantage that the judge had of having heard the evidence (if sentence was imposed after trial or *voire dire*);

(c)   the particular facts of the case which justified the judge in departing from the guidelines or the usual sentencing practice.

13.38   In certain cases, the problem may be not that the judge passed an unjustifiable sentence but that he failed to justify it in his sentencing remarks. The appellant will seek to set out the facts of the case which justify the sentence that was imposed.

13.39   When seeking to persuade the Court not to increase sentence, the respondent will wish to focus on double jeopardy, any significant progress that the respondent has made in the completion of the sentence or any significant change of circumstances that has occurred since sentence was passed that would make it wrong to now increase it.

Appeal to the Supreme Court

13.40   Either party can appeal to the Supreme Court, subject to certification of a point of general public importance and permission. The period for applying to the Court of Appeal for certification and permission is 14 days and a subsequent application for permission to the Supreme Court must be brought within 14 days after refusal of permission by the Court of Appeal.[39]

SUMMARY OF KEY POINTS

- Parliament has established a number of prosecution rights of appeal. The most commonly used are the right to appeal against rulings under section 58 of CJA 2003 and the Attorney-General's right to appeal against a sentence that is unduly lenient.

- The procedure for appealing under section 58 of CJA 2003 is governed by Part 38 of the CrimPR. Attorney-General's References are governed by Part 41. Part 36 applies to both.

---

39   CJA 1988, s 36 and Sch 3.

- There are a number of preconditions on the right to appeal against a ruling, including a requirement that the prosecution provides an agreement that it will seek the acquittal of the defendant if the appeal fails.

- Such an undertaking must be given at the time an indication of an intention to appeal is given.

- Leave to appeal under section 58 may be given by the trial judge or the Court of Appeal.

- In respect of an Attorney-General's Reference, leave must be granted by the Court of Appeal. However, it is the normal practice of the Court to hold a single permission/appeal hearing.

- In these appeals the defendant becomes the respondent who must, if he wishes to be heard, serve and lodge a respondent's notice.

- In both types of appeal either party has the right to appeal to the Supreme Court.

Chapter 14

Appeals in relation to defendants suffering from a mental disorder

INTRODUCTION

14.1   As a matter of principle, once a defendant is found to be suffering either from a disability that makes him unfit to be tried or from insanity, the case is no longer a criminal case.

Appeals against findings of a disability or insanity are covered in this chapter. These are appeals where the mental incapacity was raised at the time of trial. This type of appeal is in contrast to those where the incapacity was not identified at the time of trial. Those appeals are covered by Chapters 3 and 6, which include common issues for appeal lawyers arising in murder cases where a partial defence may be available that reduces culpability from murder to involuntary manslaughter.[1] Those cases raise issues of fresh expert evidence. They will inevitably involve criticism of the previous lawyers and an application to admit fresh evidence (see especially 6.28, 6.30 and 6.31). Likewise, in any case where the appeal lawyer identifies the issue of non-insane automatism as a potential defence that should have been considered at the original trial, the same considerations will apply. In sentencing cases similar issues can arise where the court shoud have considered a hospital order or a 'hybrid' order.[2] However, this chapter is concerned with the reverse scenario as it looks at the means of appealing a trial finding of incapacity.

A finding that the defendant committed the act with which he is charged does not amount to a conviction nor should a hospital or supervision order made against such a defendant be regarded as a sentence (*R v H*).[3] However, the procedures for dealing with those suffering from mental disorders who commit criminal acts closely follow criminal law procedures. Appeals are no exception.

---

1   Partial defences are available to murder under s 2 Homicide Act 1957 for offences before 4 October 2010 and since under s 52; s 54 and 55 Coroners and Justice Act 2009 (diminished responsibility and loss of control); and under s 4 Homicide Act 1957 as part of a suicide pact or under s .1 Infanticide Act 1938.
2   See *R v Vow*les [2015] EWCA Crim 45; *R v Edwards* [2018] EWCA Crim 595.
3   [2003] UKHL 1.

14.2   *Appeals in relation to defendants suffering from a mental disorder*

The Criminal Appeal Act 1968 (CCA 1968) establishes the following rights of appeal from decisions of the Crown Court, the procedures for which follow the procedural scheme for appeals against conviction or sentence:

(a)   A finding of unfitness to be tried may be appealed under section 15 of CAA 1968.

(b)   A defendant who has been found to be unfit to be tried did the act or made the omission with which he is charged may appeal under section 15 of CAA 1968.

(c)   A verdict of not guilty by reason of insanity may be appealed under section 12 of CAA 1968.

(d)   A hospital or supervision order that was imposed following a finding under (b) or (c), above may be appealed under section 16A of CAA 1968.

14.2   The test to be applied and the powers of disposal which the Court may exercise following a successful appeal differ for appeals under each of the above provisions (and are considered at 14.6–14.19 below). However, appeals under these provisions share a number of common features. The law in relation to who has the right to appeal, the availability of public funding and the procedures to be followed are the same for each and are considered first.

Who may appeal

14.3   These are defence, not prosecution appeals. Given the nature of the disabilities in question, the rights of appeal can be exercised by a defendant's lawyer without the need for the defendant's consent. In *R v Antoine (Pierre Harrison)*[4] the Court held that counsel who had appeared in the Crown Court had the authority to settle grounds, lodge notice of appeal and present the appeal on behalf of a defendant who suffered from a mental disability such that he was incapable of giving instructions.

Funding

14.4   There is no statutory provision for the granting of representation orders in respect of any of these appeals. The successful appellant may apply for a defendant's costs order. Moreover, advocates who are instructed by the Court to represent a defendant who suffers from a mental disorder may claim costs from central funds (see *Antoine*, above).

---

4   [1999] 2 Cr App R 225.

The appeal process

14.5   The procedure for these appeals follows that for appeals against conviction or sentence. They are contained in the particular provisions of CAA 1968 that apply to each appeal. In addition, Part 36 and 398 of the CPR apply to all of them. The main features of the process are:

(a)   An application for certification of fitness to appeal may be made to the trial judge within 28 days of the decision which is the subject of challenge (but see 14.7 below in relation to when the 28-day period runs in appeals under section 15).

(b)   An application for leave to the Court of Appeal must be made using Form NG within 28 days of the decision but may be extended on application. Leave may be granted by the single judge or the full Court.

(c)   An application for leave that is refused may be renewed orally before the Court.

(d)   The defendant who is in custody as a result of a finding of unfitness to stand trial or insanity does not have a right to be present at the hearing.

(e)   An appeal or application for leave may be abandoned using Form A.

(f)   Under section 33 of CAA 1968 there is a right of appeal from the Court of Appeal to the Supreme Court, which involves the usual requirements of certification and leave.

APPEALS AGAINST FINDINGS OF UNFITNESS TO PLEAD AND FINDINGS THAT THE ACCUSED MADE THE ACT OR OMISSION CHARGED

14.6   Sections 4 and 4A of the Criminal Procedure (Insanity) Act 1964 set out a two-stage procedure whereby the Crown Court must first determine whether an accused, who appears to be suffering from some mental illness or disorder, is fit to stand trial and, if found not to be fit, must go on to determine whether he did the acts of which he is accused.

14.7   Under section 15 of CAA 1968 an appeal may be brought against both or either of these findings. The procedural requirements contained in section 15 are as set out at 14.3–14.5 above. The 28-day period for lodging an appeal is calculated from the date of the decision against which leave is sought. However, the trial judge may only grant a certificate of fitness to appeal within 28 days of the finding that the accused did the act or made the omission charged.[5]

---

5   CAA 1968, s 15(2)(b).

14.8   The test for an appeal under section 15 is whether the finding that is the subject of the appeal is unsafe. If the Court allows an appeal against a finding of disability, it may order that a trial take place and may make orders that are necessary and expedient for custody or release on bail.[6]

14.9   The Court's powers to dispose of an appeal under section 15 are contained in section 16. If the Court allows an appeal against a finding that the defendant committed the act or made the omission in question, it must quash the order and direct that a verdict of acquittal be recorded.

14.10   The Court has no power to order a retrial. However, where the Court finds that there has been a procedural irregularity such as to render the proceedings in the Crown Court a nullity, it may, instead of allowing the appeal, issue a writ of *venire de novo* (discussed more fully in Chapter 3) and order that the case be remitted for fresh proceedings to take place. It did so in *R v D (David Michael)*[7] when it transpired that one of the doctors upon whose opinion the finding of unfitness had been based was not qualified.

14.11   There is no appeal against a finding that the accused is fit to be tried. If such a finding is made and the accused goes on to be convicted, leave to appeal against conviction may be applied for in the usual way. If, in the course of that appeal, the Court is satisfied on the requisite evidence[8] that the convicted person is not fit but did carry out the acts or make the omission charged, then it may not quash the conviction but must substitute one of the orders under section 5 of the Criminal Procedures (Insanity) Act 1964 (see 14.16, below) for any sentence that had been imposed.

APPEALS AGAINST A VERDICT OF NOT GUILTY BY REASON OF INSANITY

14.12   Section 2 of the Trial of Lunatics Act 1883 allows a jury to return a special verdict of not guilty by reason of insanity. Appeal against such an order may be brought under section 12 of CAA 1968 and follows the procedures set out at 14.3–14.5, above. The test is whether the special verdict is unsafe.[9]

14.13   The Court's powers to dispose of an appeal are contained in section 13 of CAA 1968. If the Court finds that the verdict of insanity was unsafe but that the proper verdict would have been guilty of the offence charged or any

---

6   CAA 1968, s 16(3)(a), (b).
7   [2001] EWCA Crim 911.
8   The written or oral evidence of two medical practitioners, one of whom must be duly approved (Criminal Procedure (Insanity) Act 1964, s 4(5), (6)).
9   CAA 1968, s 13.

other offence for which the jury might have found the accused guilty, it may substitute a verdict of guilty of that offence for the verdict of not guilty by reason of insanity.

14.14   If the Court finds that the verdict of insanity is unsafe but that, on the evidence of appropriately qualified and approved practitioners,[10] the accused suffered from a disability within the meaning of sections 4 and 4A of the Criminal Procedure (Insanity) Act 1964 and that he made the act or omission charged, it may make an order under section 5 of the Criminal Procedure (Insanity) Act 1964.

14.15   In all other cases in which an appeal is allowed the Court must substitute a verdict of acquittal.

APPEALS AGAINST AN ORDER MADE UNDER SECTION 5 OF THE CRIMINAL PROCEDURE (INSANITY) ACT 1964

14.16   Following a verdict of insanity or a finding that the defendant did the act or omission with which he is charged, the Crown Court may make one of the following orders under section 5 of the Criminal Procedure (Insanity) Act 1964. Those orders are:

(a)   a hospital order (with or without a restriction order);

(b)   a supervision order; or

(c)   an absolute discharge.

14.17   Under section 16A of CAA 1968[11] an appeal may be brought against such an order (although it is not clear when a defendant would seek to appeal an order for an absolute discharge). The procedural requirements for such an appeal are as set out at 14.3–14.5, above. If it allows the appeal, the Court may vary the order or may quash it and substitute it for another order under section 5.

14.18   The test on appeal is simply whether the Court 'considers that the appellant should be dealt with differently to the way in which the Court below dealt with him'.[12]

---

10   See fn 8 above.
11   As inserted by the Domestic Violence, Crime and Victims Act 2004, s 25.
12   CAA 1968, s 16B(1).

14.19 *Appeals in relation to defendants suffering from a mental disorder*

14.19 If the Court of Appeal disposes of an appeal by making an interim hospital order or a supervision order, that order may be revoked or varied by the Crown Court. The Crown Court also has the power to revoke or vary an interim hospital order or a supervision order when an appeal against that order is still pending.[13]

---

13 CAA 1968, s 16B(2)–(5).

Appendix A

Criminal Practice Directions, Division IX

DIVISION IX
APPEAL

34A: *Appeals to the Crown Court*

34A.1   On an appeal against conviction CrimPR 34.3 requires the appellant and respondent to supply information needed for the effective case management of the appeal, but allows the Crown Court to relieve the appellant – not the respondent – of that obligation, in whole or part.

34A.2   The court is most likely to exercise that discretion in an appellant's favour where he or she is not represented and is unable, without assistance, to provide reliable such information. The notes to the standard form of appeal notice invite the appellant to answer the relevant questions in that form to the extent that he or she is able, explaining that while the appellant may not be able to answer all those questions nevertheless any answers that can be given will assist in making arrangements for the hearing of the appeal. Where an appellant uses the prescribed form of easy read appeal notice the court usually should assume that the appellant will not be able to supply case management information, and that form contains no questions corresponding with those in the standard appeal notice. In such a case relevant information will be supplied by the respondent in the respondent's notice and may be gleaned from material obtained from magistrates' court records by Crown Court staff.

34B: *Appeal to the Crown Court: Information from the magistrates' court*

34B.1   CrimPR 34.4 applies when a defendant appeals to the Crown Court against conviction or sentence and specifies the information and documentation that must be made available by the magistrates' court.

34B.2   In all cases magistrates' court staff must ensure that Crown Court staff are notified of the appeal as soon as practicable: CrimPR 34.4(2)(b).

Appendix A   *Criminal Practice Directions, Division IX*

In most cases Crown Court staff will be able to obtain the other information required by CrimPR 34.4(3) or (4) by direct access to the electronic records created by magistrates' court staff. However, if such access is not available then alternative arrangements must be made for the transfer of such information to Crown Court staff by electronic means. Paper copies of documents should be created and sent only as a last resort.

34B.3   On an appeal against conviction, the reasons given by the magistrates for their decision should not be included with the documents; the appeal hearing is not a review of the magistrates' court's decision but a re-hearing. There is no requirement for the Notice of Appeal form to be redacted in any way; the judge and magistrates presiding over the rehearing will base their decision on the evidence presented during the rehearing itself.

34B.4   On an appeal solely against sentence, the magistrates' court's reasons and factual finding leading to the finding of guilt should be included, but any reasons for the sentence imposed should be omitted as the Crown Court will be conducting a fresh sentencing exercise. Whilst reasons for the sentence imposed are not necessary for the rehearing, the Notice of Appeal form may include references to the sentence that is being appealed. There is no requirement to redact this before the form is given to the judge and magistrates hearing the appeal.

39A   Appeals against conviction and sentence – the provision of notice to the prosecution

39A.1   When an appeal notice served under CrimPR 39.2 is received by the Registrar of Criminal Appeals, the Registrar will notify the relevant prosecution authority, giving the case name, reference number and the trial or sentencing court.

39A.2   If the court or the Registrar directs, or invites, the prosecution authority to serve a respondent's notice under CrimPR 39.6, prior to the consideration of leave, the Registrar will also at that time serve on the prosecution authority the appeal notice containing the grounds of appeal and the transcripts, if available. If the prosecution authority is not directed or invited to serve a respondent's notice but wishes to do so, the authority should request the grounds of appeal and any existing transcript from the Criminal Appeal Office. Any respondent's notice received prior to the consideration of leave will be made available to the single judge.

39A.3   The Registrar of Criminal Appeals will notify the relevant prosecution authority in the event that:

(a)   leave to appeal against conviction or sentence is granted by the single Judge; or

(b)   the single Judge or the Registrar refers an application for leave to appeal against conviction or sentence to the Full Court for determination; or

(c)   there is to be a renewed application for leave to appeal against sentence only.

If the prosecution authority has not yet been served with the appeal notice and transcript, the Registrar will serve these with the notification, and if leave is granted, the Registrar will also serve the authority with the comments of the single judge.

39A.4   The prosecution should notify the Registrar without delay if they wish to be represented at the hearing. The prosecution should note that the Registrar will not delay listing to await a response from the Prosecution as to whether they wish to attend. Prosecutors should note that occasionally, for example, where the single Judge fixes a hearing date at short notice, the case may be listed very quickly.

39A.5   If the prosecution wishes to be represented at any hearing, the notification should include details of Counsel instructed and a time estimate. An application by the prosecution to remove a case from the list for Counsel's convenience, or to allow further preparation time, will rarely be granted.

39A.6   There may be occasions when the Court of Appeal Criminal Division will grant leave to appeal to an unrepresented applicant and proceed forthwith with the appeal in the absence of the appellant and Counsel. The prosecution should not attend any hearing at which the appellant is unrepresented. *Nasteska v. The former Yugoslav Republic of Macedonia* (Application No.23152/05) As a Court of Review, the Court of Appeal Criminal Division would expect the prosecution to have raised any specific matters of relevance with the sentencing Judge in the first instance.

39A.7   Where there is a renewed application for leave to appeal against a sentence imposed for an offence involving a fatality, the Crown Prosecution Service has indicated that it wishes to be represented at all sentence appeals in order to ensure that they are in a position, if appropriate, to make representations as to the impact of the offence upon the victim and their family. In those circumstances, if the court is minded to grant the application for leave to appeal the court should consider adjourning the hearing of the appeal to allow prosecution counsel to attend and for the victim's family to be notified and attend if they so wish.

39B   Listing of appeals against conviction and sentence in the Court of Appeal Criminal Division (CACD)

39B.1   Arrangements for the fixing of dates for the hearing of appeals will be made by the Criminal Appeal Office Listing Officer, under the superintendence of the Registrar of Criminal Appeals who may give such directions as he deems necessary.

39B.2   Where possible, regard will be had to an advocate's existing commitments. However, in relation to the listing of appeals, the Court of Appeal takes precedence over all lower courts, including the Crown Court. Wherever practicable, a lower court will have regard to this principle when making arrangements to release an advocate to appear in the Court of Appeal. In case of difficulty the lower court should communicate with the Registrar. In general an advocate's commitment in a lower court will not be regarded as a good reason for failing to accept a date proposed for a hearing in the Court of Appeal.

39B.3   Similarly when the Registrar directs that an appellant should appear by video link, the prison must give precedence to video-links to the Court of Appeal over video-links to the lower courts, including the Crown Court.

39B.4   The copy of the Criminal Appeal Office summary provided to advocates will contain the summary writer's time estimate for the whole hearing including delivery of judgment. It will also contain a time estimate for the judges' reading time of the core material. The Listing Officer will rely on those estimates, unless the advocate for the appellant or the Crown provides different time estimates to the Listing Officer, in writing, within 7 days of the receipt of the summary by the advocate. Where the time estimates are considered by an advocate to be inadequate, or where the estimates have been altered because, for example, a ground of appeal has been abandoned, it is the duty of the advocate to inform the Court promptly, in which event the Registrar will reconsider the time estimates and inform the parties accordingly.

39B.5   The following target times are set for the hearing of appeals. Target times will run from the receipt of the appeal by the Listing Officer, as being ready for hearing.

39B.6

NATURE OF APPEAL	FROM RECEIPT BY LISTING OFFICER TO FIXING OF HEARING DATE	FROM FIXING OF HEARING DATE TO HEARING	TOTAL TIME FROM RECEIPT BY LISTING OFFICER TO HEARING
Sentence Appeal	14 days	14 days	28 days
Conviction Appeal	21 days	42 days	63 days
Conviction Appeal where witness to attend	28 days	52 days	80 days

39B.7 Where legal vacations impinge, these periods may be extended. Where expedition is required, the Registrar may direct that these periods be abridged.

39B.8 'Appeal' includes an application for leave to appeal which requires an oral hearing.

39C Appeal notices containing grounds of appeal

39C.1 The requirements for the service of notices of appeal and the time limits for doing so are as set out in CrimPR Part 39. The Court must be provided with an appeal notice as a single document which sets out the grounds of appeal. Advocates should not provide the Court with an advice addressed to lay or professional clients. Any appeal notice or grounds of appeal served on the Court will usually be provided to the respondent.

39C.2 Advocates should not settle grounds unless they consider that they are properly arguable. Grounds should be carefully drafted; the court is not assisted by grounds of appeal which are not properly set out and particularised in accordance with CrimPR 39.3. The grounds must:

i.   be concise; and

ii.   be presented in A4 page size and portrait orientation, in not less than 12 point font and in 1.5 line spacing.

Appellants and advocates should keep in mind the powers of the court and the Registrar to return for revision, within a directed period, grounds that do not comply with the rule or with these directions, including grounds that are so prolix or diffuse as to render them incomprehensible. They should keep in mind also the court's powers to refuse permission to appeal on any ground that is so poorly presented as to render it unarguable and thus to exclude it from consideration by the court: see CrimPR 36.14. Should leave to amend the grounds be granted, it is most unlikely that further grounds will be entertained.

39C.3 Where the appellant wants to appeal against conviction, transcripts must be identified in accordance with CrimPR 39.3(1)(c). This includes specifying the date and time of transcripts in the notice of appeal. Accordingly, the date and time of the summing up should be provided, including both parts of a split summing-up. Where relevant, the date and time of additional transcripts (such as rulings or early directions) should be provided. Similarly, any relevant written materials (such as route to verdict) should be identified.

39C.4 Where the appellant wants to rely on a ground of appeal that is not identified by the appeal notice, an application under CrimPR 36.14(5) is required. In *R v James and Others* [2018] EWCA Crim 285 the Court of

Appendix A   *Criminal Practice Directions, Division IX*

Appeal identified as follows the considerations that obtain and the criteria that the court will apply on any such application:

(a)   as a general rule all the grounds of appeal that an appellant wishes to advance should be lodged with the appeal notice, subject to their being perfected on receipt of transcripts from the Registrar.

(b)   the application for permission to appeal under section 31 of the Criminal Appeal Act 1968 is an important stage in the process. It may not be treated lightly or its determination in effect ignored merely because fresh representatives would have done or argued things differently to their predecessors. Fresh grounds advanced by fresh representatives must be particularly cogent.

(c)   as well as addressing the factors material to the determination of an application for an extension of time within which to renew an application for permission to appeal, if that is required, on an application under CrimPR 36.14(5) the appellant or his or her representatives must address directly the factors which the court is likely to consider relevant when deciding whether to allow the substitution or addition of grounds of appeal. Those factors include (but this list is not exhaustive):

    (i)   the extent of the delay in advancing the fresh ground or grounds;

    (ii)   the reasons for that delay;

    (iii)   whether the facts or issues the subject of the fresh ground were known to the appellant's representatives when they advised on appeal;

    (iv)   the interests of justice and the overriding objective in Part 1 of the Criminal Procedure Rules.

(d)   on the assumption that an appellant will have received advice on appeal from his or her trial advocate, who will have settled the grounds of appeal in the original appeal notice or who will have advised that there are no reasonably arguable grounds to challenge the safety of the conviction:

    (i)   fresh representatives should comply with the duty of due diligence explained in *McCook* [2014] EWCA Crim 734. Waiver of privilege by the appellant is very likely to be required.

    (ii)   once the trial lawyers have responded, the fresh representatives should again consider with great care their duty to the court and whether the proposed fresh grounds should be advanced as reasonably arguable and particularly cogent.

    (iii)   the Registrar will obtain, before the determination of the application under CrimPR 36.14(5), transcripts relevant to the fresh grounds and, where required, a respondents' notice relating to the fresh grounds.

(e)   while an application under CrimPR 36.14(5) will not require 'exceptional leave', and hence the demonstration of substantial injustice should it not be granted, the hurdle for the applicant is a high one nonetheless. Representatives should remind themselves of the provisions of paragraph 39C.2 above.

(f)   permission to renew out of time an application for permission to appeal is not given unless the applicant can persuade the court that very good reasons exist. If that application to renew out of time is accompanied by an application to vary the grounds of appeal, the hurdle will be higher still.

(g)   any application to substitute or add grounds will be considered by a fully constituted court and at a hearing, not on the papers.

(h)   on any renewal of an application for permission to appeal accompanied by an application under CrimPR 36.14(5), if the court refuses those applications it has the power to make a loss of time order or an order for costs in line with *R v Gray and Others* [2014] EWCA Crim 2372. By analogy with *R v Kirk* [2015] EWCA Crim 1764 (where the court refused an extension of time) the court has the power to order payment of the costs of obtaining the respondent's notice and any additional transcripts.

Direct Lodgement

39C.5   With effect from 1st October 2018, Forms NG and Grounds of Appeal which are covered by Part 39 of the Criminal Procedure Rules (appeal to the Court of Appeal about conviction or sentence) are to be lodged directly with the Criminal Appeal Office and not with the Crown Court where the appellant was convicted or sentenced. This Practice Direction must be read alongside the detailed guidance notes that have been produced to accompany the new forms. They are available: http://www.justice.gov.uk/courts/procedure-rules/criminal/forms. From this date the Crown Court will no longer accept Forms NG and will return them to the sender. Forms NG and Grounds of Appeal should only be lodged once. They should, where possible, be lodged by email. Applications should not be lodged directly onto the Digital Case System. Applications must be lodged at the following address: criminalappealoffice.applications@hmcts.x.gsi.gov.uk

If you do not have access to an email account, you should post Form NG and the Grounds of Appeal to:

The Registrar, Criminal Appeal Office, Royal Courts of Justice, Strand, London WC2A 2LL.

Once an application has been effectively lodged, the Registrar will confirm receipt within 7 days.

Service

39C.6 Legal representatives should make sure they provide their secure email address for the purposes of correspondence and service of document. The date of service for new applications lodged by email will be the day on which it is sent, if that day is a business day and if sent no later than 2:30pm on that day, otherwise the date of service will be on the next business day after it was sent.

Completing the Form NG

39C.7 All applications must be compliant with the relevant Criminal Procedure Rules, particularly those in Part 39. A separate Form NG should be completed for each substantive application which is being made. Each application (conviction, sentence and confiscation order) has its own Form NG and must be drafted and lodged as a stand-alone application.

39D   Respondents' notices

39D.1 The requirements for the service of respondents' notices and the time limits for doing so are as set out in CrimPR Part 39. Any respondent's notice served should be in accordance with CrimPR 39.6. The Court does not require a response to the respondent's notice.

39E   Loss of time

39E.1 Both the Court and the single judge have power, in their discretion, under the Criminal Appeal Act 1968 sections 29 and 31, to direct that part of the time during which an applicant is in custody after lodging his notice of application for leave to appeal should not count towards sentence. When leave to appeal has been refused by the single judge, it is necessary to consider the reasons given by the single judge before making a decision whether to renew the application. Where an application devoid of merit has been refused by the single judge he may indicate that the Full Court should consider making a direction for loss of time on renewal of the application. However, the Full Court may make such a direction whether or not such an indication has been given by the single judge.

39E.2 The case of *R v Gray & Others* [2014] EWCA Crim 2372 makes clear 'that unmeritorious renewal applications took up a wholly disproportionate amount of staff and judicial resources in preparation and hearing time. They also wasted significant sums of public money... The more time the Court of Appeal Office and the judges spent on unmeritorious applications, the longer the waiting times were likely to be....The only means the court has of discouraging unmeritorious applications which waste precious time and resources is by using the powers given to us by Parliament in the Criminal Appeal Act 1968 and the Prosecution of Offenders Act 1985.'

39E.3   Further, applicants and counsel are reminded of the warning given by the Court of Appeal in *R v Hart and Others* [2006] EWCA Crim 3239, [2007] 1 Cr. App. R. 31, [2007] 2 Cr. App. R. (S.) 34 and should 'heed the fact that this court is prepared to exercise its power ... The mere fact that counsel has advised that there are grounds of appeal will not always be a sufficient answer to the question as to whether or not an application has indeed been brought which was totally without merit.'

39E.4   Where the single judge has not indicated that the Full Court should consider making a Loss of Time Order because the defendant has already been released, the case of *R v Terence Nolan* [2017] EWCA Crim 2449 indicates that the single judge should consider what, if any, costs have been incurred by the Registrar and the Prosecution and should make directions accordingly. Reference should be made to the relevant Costs Division of the Criminal Practice Direction.

39F   Skeleton arguments

39F.1   Advocates should always ensure that the court, and any other party as appropriate, has a single document containing all of the points that are to be argued. The appeal notice must comply with the requirements of CrimPR 39.3. In cases of an appeal against conviction, advocates must serve a skeleton argument when the appeal notice does not sufficiently outline the grounds of the appeal, particularly in cases where a complex or novel point of law has been raised. In an appeal against sentence it may be helpful for an advocate to serve a skeleton argument when a complex issue is raised.

39F.2   The appellant's skeleton argument, if any, must be served no later than 21 days before the hearing date, and the respondent's skeleton argument, if any, no later than 14 days before the hearing date, unless otherwise directed by the Court.

39F.3   Paragraphs XII D.17 to D.23 of these Practice Directions set out the general requirements for skeleton arguments. A skeleton argument, if provided, should contain a numbered list of the points the advocate intends to argue, grouped under each ground of appeal, and stated in no more than one or two sentences. It should be as succinct as possible. Advocates should ensure that the correct Criminal Appeal Office number and the date on which the document was served appear at the beginning of any document and that their names are at the end.

Appendix A *Criminal Practice Directions, Division IX*

39G Criminal Appeal Office summaries

39G.1   To assist the Court, the Criminal Appeal Office prepares summaries of the cases coming before it. These are entirely objective and do not contain any advice about how the Court should deal with the case or any view about its merits. They consist of two Parts.

39G.2   Part I, which is provided to all of the advocates in the case, generally contains:

(a)   particulars of the proceedings in the Crown Court, including representation and details of any co-accused,

(b)   particulars of the proceedings in the Court of Appeal (Criminal Division),

(c)   the facts of the case, as drawn from the transcripts, appeal notice, respondent's notice, witness statements and / or the exhibits,

(d)   the submissions and rulings, summing up and sentencing remarks.

39G.3   The contents of the summary are a matter for the professional judgment of the writer, but an advocate wishing to suggest any significant alteration to Part I should write to the Registrar of Criminal Appeals. If the Registrar does not agree, the summary and the letter will be put to the Court for decision. The Court will not generally be willing to hear oral argument about the content of the summary.

39G.4   Advocates may show Part I of the summary to their professional or lay clients (but to no one else) if they believe it would help to check facts or formulate arguments, but summaries are not to be copied or reproduced without the permission of the Criminal Appeal Office; permission for this will not normally be given in cases involving children, or sexual offences, or where the Crown Court has made an order restricting reporting.

39G.5   Unless a judge of the High Court or the Registrar of Criminal Appeals gives a direction to the contrary, in any particular case involving material of an explicitly salacious or sadistic nature, Part I will also be supplied to appellants who seek to represent themselves before the Full Court, or who renew to the full court their applications for leave to appeal against conviction or sentence.

39G.6   Part II, which is supplied to the Court alone, contains

(a)   a summary of the grounds of appeal and

(b)   in appeals against sentence (and applications for such leave), summaries of the antecedent histories of the parties and of any relevant pre-sentence, medical or other reports.

39G.7   All of the source material is provided to the Court and advocates are able to draw attention to anything in it which may be of particular relevance.

44A References to the European Court of Justice

44A.1   Further to CrimPR 44.3 of the Criminal Procedure Rules, the order containing the reference shall be filed with the Senior Master of the Queen's Bench Division of the High Court for onward transmission to the Court of Justice of the European Union. The order should be marked for the attention of Mrs Isaac and sent to the Senior Master:

c/o Queen's Bench Division Associates Dept Room WG03 Royal Courts of Justice Strand London WC2A 2LL

44A.2   There is no longer a requirement that the relevant court file be sent to the Senior Master. The parties should ensure that all appropriate documentation is sent directly to the European Court at the following address:

The Registrar Court of Justice of the European Union Kirchberg L-2925 Luxemburg

44A.3   There is no prescribed form for use but the following details must be included in the back sheet to the order:

i.   Solicitor's full address;

ii.   Solicitor's and Court references;

iii.   Solicitor's e-mail address.

44A.4   The European Court of Justice regularly updates its Recommendation to national courts and tribunals in relation to the initiation of preliminary ruling proceedings. The current Recommendation is 2012/C 338/01: http://eurlex.europa.eu/LexUriServ/LexUriServ.do?uri=OJ:C:2012:338:00 01:0006:EN:PDF

44A.5   The referring court may request the Court of Justice of the European Union to apply its urgent preliminary ruling procedure where the referring court's proceedings relate to a person in custody. For further information see Council Decision 2008/79/EC [2008] OJ L24/42: http://eurlex.europa.eu/LexUriServ/LexUriServ.do?uri=OJ:L:2008:024:00 42:0043:EN:PDF

44A.6   Any such request must be made in a document separate from the order or in a covering letter and must set out:

iv.   The matters of fact and law which establish the urgency;

v.   The reasons why the urgent preliminary ruling procedure applies; and

vi.   In so far as possible, the court's view on the answer to the question referred to the Court of Justice of the European Union for a preliminary ruling.

44A.7   Any request to apply the urgent preliminary ruling procedure should be filed with the Senior Master as described above.

Appendix B

The Criminal Procedure Rules, Parts 36 to 44

CRIMINAL PROCEDURE RULES 2015

SI 2015/1490

PART 36
APPEAL TO THE COURT OF APPEAL: GENERAL RULES

36.1. When this Part applies

(1)   This Part applies to all the applications, appeals and references to the Court of Appeal to which Parts 37, 38, 39, 40, 41 and 43 apply.

(2)   In this Part and in those, unless the context makes it clear that something different is meant 'court' means the Court of Appeal or any judge of that court.

[Note. See rule 2.2 for the usual meaning of 'court'.

Under section 53 of the Senior Courts Act 1981, the criminal division of the Court of Appeal exercises jurisdiction in the appeals and references to which Parts 37, 38, 39, 40 and 41 apply.

Under section 55 of that Act, the Court of Appeal must include at least two judges, and for some purposes at least three.

For the powers of the Court of Appeal that may be exercised by one judge of that court or by the Registrar, see sections 31, 31A, 31B, 31C and 44 of the Criminal Appeal Act 1968; section 49 of the Criminal Justice Act 2003; the Criminal Justice Act 2003 (Mandatory Life Sentences: Appeals in Transitional Cases) Order 2005; the Serious Organised Crime and Police Act 2005 (Appeals under section 74) Order 2006; the Serious Crime Act 2007 (Appeals under Section 24) Order 2008; and the power conferred by section 53(4) of the 1981 Act.]

36.2.   Case management in the Court of Appeal

(1)   The court and the parties have the same duties and powers as under Part 3 (Case management).

(2)   The Registrar—

    (a)   must fulfil the duty of active case management under rule 3.2; and

    (b)   in fulfilling that duty may exercise any of the powers of case management under—

        (i)   rule 3.5 (the court's general powers of case management),

        (ii)   rule 3.10(3) (requiring a certificate of readiness), and

        (iii)   rule 3.11 (requiring a party to identify intentions and anticipated requirements)

    subject to the directions of the court.

(3)   The Registrar must nominate a case progression officer under rule 3.4.

36.3.   Power to vary requirements

The court or the Registrar may—

    (a)   shorten a time limit or extend it (even after it has expired) unless that is inconsistent with other legislation;

    (b)   allow a party to vary any notice that that party has served;

    (c)   direct that a notice or application be served on any person;

    (d)   allow a notice or application to be in a different form, or presented orally.

[Note. The time limit for serving an appeal notice—

    (a)   under section 18 of the Criminal Appeal Act 1968 on an appeal against conviction or sentence, and

    (b)   under section 18A of that Act on an appeal against a finding of contempt of court

may be extended but not shortened: see rule 39.2.

The time limit for serving an application for permission to refer a sentencing case under section 36 of the Criminal Justice Act 1988 may be neither extended nor shortened: see [rule 41.2(4)][1].

The time limits in rule 43.2 for applying to the Court of Appeal for permission to appeal or refer a case to the Supreme Court may be extended or shortened only as explained in the note to that rule.]

Amendment

1   Substituted by the Criminal Procedure (Amendment) Rules 2018, SI 2018/132, rr 2, 15(a).

36.4. Application for extension of time

A person who wants an extension of time within which to serve a notice or make an application must—

(a) apply for that extension of time when serving that notice or making that application; and

(b) give the reasons for the application for an extension of time.

36.5. Renewing an application refused by a judge or the Registrar

(1) This rule applies where a party with the right to do so wants to renew—

(a) to a judge of the Court of Appeal an application refused by the Registrar; or

(b) to the Court of Appeal an application refused by a judge of that court.

(2) That party must—

(a) renew the application in the form set out in the Practice Direction, signed by or on behalf of the applicant;

(b) serve the renewed application on the Registrar not more than 14 days after—

(i) the refusal of the application that the applicant wants to renew; or

(ii) the Registrar serves that refusal on the applicant, if the applicant was not present in person or by live link when the original application was refused.

[Note. The time limit of 14 days under this rule is reduced to 5 days where Parts 37, 38 or 40 apply: see rules 37.7, 38.10 and 40.7.

For the right to renew an application to a judge or to the Court of Appeal, see sections 31(3), 31C and 44 of the Criminal Appeal Act 1968, the Criminal Justice Act 2003 (Mandatory Life Sentences: Appeals in Transitional Cases) Order 2005, the Serious Organised Crime and Police Act 2005 (Appeals under section 74) Order 2006 and the Serious Crime Act 2007 (Appeals under Section 24) Order 2008.

A party has no right under section 31C of the 1968 Act to renew to the Court of Appeal an application for procedural directions refused by a judge, but in some circumstances a case management direction might be varied: see rule 3.6.

If an applicant does not renew an application that a judge has refused, including an application for permission to appeal, the Registrar will treat it as if it had been refused by the Court of Appeal.

Under section 22 of the Criminal Appeal Act 1968, the Court of Appeal may direct that an appellant who is in custody is to attend a hearing by live link.]

36.6.   Hearings

(1)   The general rule is that the Court of Appeal must hear in public—

    (a)   an application, including an application for permission to appeal; and

    (b)   an appeal or reference,

but it may order any hearing to be in private.

(2)   Where a hearing is about a public interest ruling, that hearing must be in private unless the court otherwise directs.

(3)   Where the appellant wants to appeal against an order restricting public access to a trial, the court—

    (a)   may decide without a hearing—

        (i)   an application, including an application for permission to appeal, and

        (ii)   an appeal; but

    (b)   must announce its decision on such an appeal at a hearing in public.

(4)   Where the appellant wants to appeal or to refer a case to the Supreme Court, the court—

    (a)   may decide without a hearing an application—

        (i)   for permission to appeal or to refer a sentencing case, or

        (ii)   to refer a point of law; but

    (b)   must announce its decision on such an application at a hearing in public.

[(5)   Where a party wants the court to reopen the determination of an appeal—

    (a)   the court—

        (i)   must decide the application without a hearing, as a general rule, but

        (ii)   may decide the application at a hearing; and

    (b)   need not announce its decision on such an application at a hearing in public.][1]

[(6)]² A judge of the Court of Appeal and the Registrar may exercise any of their powers—

(a)   at a hearing in public or in private; or

(b)   without a hearing.

[Note. For the procedure on an appeal against an order restricting public access to a trial, see Part 40.

[For the procedure on an application to reopen the determination of an appeal, see rule 36.15.]¹]

Amendments

1   Inserted by the Criminal Procedure (Amendment) Rules 2018, SI 2018/132, rr 2, 15(b)(ii), (iii).
2   Substituted by the Criminal Procedure (Amendment) Rules 2018, SI 2018/132, rr 2, 15(b)(i).

36.7. Notice of hearings and decisions

(1)   The Registrar must give as much notice as reasonably practicable of every hearing to—

(a)   the parties;

(b)   any party's custodian;

(c)   any other person whom the court requires to be notified; and

(d)   the Crown Court officer, where Parts 37, 38 or 40 apply.

(2)   The Registrar must serve every decision on—

(a)   the parties;

(b)   any other person whom the court requires to be served; and

(c)   the Crown Court officer and any party's custodian, where the decision determines an appeal or application for permission to appeal.

(3)   But where a hearing or decision is about a public interest ruling, the Registrar must not—

(a)   give notice of that hearing to; or

(b)   serve that decision on,

anyone other than the prosecutor who applied for that ruling, unless the court otherwise directs.

36.8. Duty of Crown Court officer

(1)   The Crown Court officer must provide the Registrar with any document, object or information for which the Registrar asks, within such period as the Registrar may require.

(2)   Where someone may appeal to the Court of Appeal, the Crown Court officer must keep any document or object exhibited in the proceedings in the Crown Court, or arrange for it to be kept by some other appropriate person, until—

    (a)   6 weeks after the conclusion of those proceedings; or

    (b)   the conclusion of any appeal proceedings that begin within that 6 weeks,

unless the court, the Registrar or the Crown Court otherwise directs.

(3)   Where Part 37 applies (Appeal to the Court of Appeal against ruling at preparatory hearing), the Crown Court officer must as soon as practicable serve on the appellant a transcript or note of—

    (a)   each order or ruling against which the appellant wants to appeal; and

    (b)   the decision by the Crown Court judge on any application for permission to appeal.

(4)   Where Part 38 applies (Appeal to the Court of Appeal against ruling adverse to prosecution), the Crown Court officer must as soon as practicable serve on the appellant a transcript or note of—

    (a)   each ruling against which the appellant wants to appeal;

    (b)   the decision by the Crown Court judge on any application for permission to appeal; and

    (c)   the decision by the Crown Court judge on any request to expedite the appeal.

(5)   Where Part 39 applies (Appeal to the Court of Appeal about conviction or sentence), the Crown Court officer must as soon as practicable [serve on or make available to the Registrar][1]—

    ...[2]

    [(a)][1] any Crown Court judge's certificate that the case is fit for appeal;

    [(b)][1] the decision on any application at the Crown Court centre for bail pending appeal;

    [(c)][1] such of the Crown Court case papers as the Registrar requires; and

    [(d)][1] such transcript of the Crown Court proceedings as the Registrar requires.

(6)   Where Part 40 applies (Appeal to the Court of Appeal about reporting or public access) and an order is made restricting public access to a trial, the Crown Court officer must—

    (a)   immediately notify the Registrar of that order, if the appellant has given advance notice of intention to appeal; and

(b)   as soon as practicable provide the applicant for that order with a transcript or note of the application.

[Note. See also section 87(4) of the Senior Courts Act 1981 and rules 5.5 (Recording and transcription of proceedings in the Crown Court), 36.9 (duty of person transcribing record of proceedings in the Crown Court) and 36.10 (Duty of person keeping exhibit).]

Amendments

1   Substituted by the Criminal Procedure (Amendment No. 2) Rules 2018, SI 2018/847, rr 2, 10(a)(i), (iii).
2   Revoked by the Criminal Procedure (Amendment No. 2) Rules 2018, SI 2018/847, rr 2, 10(a)(ii).

36.9.   Duty of person transcribing proceedings in the Crown Court

A person who transcribes a recording of proceedings in the Crown Court under arrangements made by the Crown Court officer must provide the Registrar with any transcript for which the Registrar asks, within such period as the Registrar may require.

[Note. See also section 32 of the Criminal Appeal Act 1968 and rule 5.5 (Recording and transcription of proceedings in the Crown Court).]

36.10.   Duty of person keeping exhibit

A person who under arrangements made by the Crown Court officer keeps a document or object exhibited in the proceedings in the Crown Court must—

(a)   keep that exhibit until—

(i)   6 weeks after the conclusion of the Crown Court proceedings, or

(ii)   the conclusion of any appeal proceedings that begin within that 6 weeks,

unless the court, the Registrar or the Crown Court otherwise directs; and

(b)   provide the Registrar with any such document or object for which the Registrar asks, within such period as the Registrar may require.

[Note. See also rule 36.8(2) (Duty of Crown Court officer).]

36.11.   Registrar's duty to provide copy documents for appeal or reference

Unless the court otherwise directs, for the purposes of an appeal or reference—

(a)   the Registrar must—

(i)   provide a party with a copy of any document or transcript held by the Registrar for such purposes, or

     (ii)   allow a party to inspect such a document or transcript,

on payment by that party of any charge fixed by the Treasury; but

    (b)   the Registrar must not provide a copy or allow the inspection of—

     (i)   a document provided only for the court and the Registrar, or

     (ii)   a transcript of a public interest ruling or of an application for such a ruling.

[Note. Section 21 of the Criminal Appeal Act 1968 requires the Registrar to collect, prepare and provide documents needed by the court.]

36.12. Declaration of incompatibility with a Convention right

(1)   This rule applies where a party—

    (a)   wants the court to make a declaration of incompatibility with a Convention right under section 4 of the Human Rights Act 1998; or

    (b)   raises an issue that the Registrar thinks may lead the court to make such a declaration.

(2)   The Registrar must serve notice on—

    (a)   the relevant person named in the list published under section 17(1) of the Crown Proceedings Act 1947; or

    (b)   the Treasury Solicitor, if it is not clear who is the relevant person.

(3)   That notice must include or attach details of—

    (a)   the legislation affected and the Convention right concerned;

    (b)   the parties to the appeal; and

    (c)   any other information or document that the Registrar thinks relevant.

(4)   A person who has a right under the 1998 Act to become a party to the appeal must—

    (a)   serve notice on—

     (i)   the Registrar, and

     (ii)   the other parties,

if that person wants to exercise that right; and

    (b)   in that notice—

     (i)   indicate the conclusion that that person invites the court to reach on the question of incompatibility, and

> (ii) identify each ground for that invitation, concisely outlining the arguments in support.

(5) The court must not make a declaration of incompatibility—

  (a) less than 21 days after the Registrar serves notice under paragraph (2); and

  (b) without giving any person who serves a notice under paragraph (4) an opportunity to make representations at a hearing.

36.13. bandoning an appeal

(1) This rule applies where an appellant wants to—

  (a) abandon—

    (i) an application to the court for permission to appeal, or

    (ii) an appeal; or

  (b) reinstate such an application or appeal after abandoning it.

(2) The appellant—

  (a) may abandon such an application or appeal without the court's permission by serving a notice of abandonment on—

    (i) the Registrar, and

    (ii) any respondent

    before any hearing of the application or appeal; but

  (b) at any such hearing, may only abandon that application or appeal with the court's permission.

(3) A notice of abandonment must be in the form set out in the Practice Direction, signed by or on behalf of the appellant.

(4) On receiving a notice of abandonment the Registrar must—

  (a) date it;

  (b) serve a dated copy on—

    (i) the appellant,

    (ii) the appellant's custodian, if any,

    (iii) the Crown Court officer, and

    (iv) any other person on whom the appellant or the Registrar served the appeal notice; and

  (c) treat the application or appeal as if it had been refused or dismissed by the Court of Appeal.

(5)   An appellant who wants to reinstate an application or appeal after abandoning it must—

    (a)   apply in writing, with reasons; and

    (b)   serve the application on the Registrar.

[Note. The Court of Appeal has power only in exceptional circumstances to allow an appellant to reinstate an application or appeal that has been abandoned.]

[36.14.   Grounds of appeal and opposition

(1)   If the court gives permission to appeal then unless the court otherwise directs the decision indicates that—

    (a)   the appellant has permission to appeal on every ground identified by the appeal notice; and

    (b)   the court finds reasonably arguable each ground on which the appellant has permission to appeal.

(2)   If the court gives permission to appeal but not on every ground identified by the appeal notice the decision indicates that—

    (a)   at the hearing of the appeal the court will not consider representations that address any ground thus excluded from argument; and

    (b)   an appellant who wants to rely on such an excluded ground needs the court's permission to do so.

(3)   An appellant who wants to rely at the hearing of an appeal on a ground of appeal excluded from argument by a judge of the Court of Appeal when giving permission to appeal must—

    (a)   apply [for permission to do so][1], with reasons, and identify each such ground;

    (b)   serve the application on—

        (i)   the Registrar, and

        (ii)   any respondent;

    (c)   serve the application not more than 14 days after—

        (i)   the giving of permission to appeal, or

        (ii)   the Registrar serves notice of that decision on the applicant, if the applicant was not present in person or by live link when permission to appeal was given.

[(4)   Paragraph (5) applies where one of the following Parts applies—

    (a)   Part 37 (Appeal to the Court of Appeal against ruling at preparatory hearing);

(b)   Part 38 (Appeal to the Court of Appeal against ruling adverse to prosecution);

(c)   Part 39 (Appeal to the Court of Appeal about conviction or sentence); or

(d)   Part 40 (Appeal to the Court of Appeal about reporting or public access restriction).

(5)   An appellant who wants to rely on a ground of appeal not identified by the appeal notice must—

(a)   apply for permission to do so and identify each such ground;

(b)   in respect of each such ground—

(i)   explain why it was not included in the appeal notice, and

(ii)   where Part 39 applies, comply with rule 39.3(2);

(c)   serve the application on—

(i)   the Registrar, and

(ii)   any respondent;

(d)   serve the application—

(i)   as soon as reasonably practicable, and in any event

(ii)   at the same time as serving any renewed application for permission to appeal which relies on that ground.][2]

[(6)][1] Paragraph (5) applies where a party wants to abandon—

(a)   a ground of appeal on which that party has permission to appeal; or

(b)   a ground of opposition identified in a respondent's notice.

[(7)][1] Such a party must serve notice on—

(a)   the Registrar; and

(b)   each other party,

before any hearing at which that ground will be considered by the court.

[Note. In some legislation, including the Criminal Appeal Act 1968, permission to appeal is described as 'leave to appeal'.

Under rule 36.5 (Renewing an application refused by a judge or the Registrar), if permission to appeal is refused the application for such permission may be renewed within the time limit (14 days) set by that rule.]][3]

Amendments

1   Substituted by the Criminal Procedure (Amendment No. 2) Rules 2018, SI 2018/847, rr 2, 10(b)(i), (ii).

2   Inserted by the Criminal Procedure (Amendment No. 2) Rules 2018, SI 2018/847, rr 2, 10(b)(iii).
3   Substituted by the Criminal Procedure (Amendment) Rules 2017, SI 2017/144, rr 2, 9(a).

[36.15.   Reopening the determination of an appeal

(1)   This rule applies where—

    (a)   a party wants the court to reopen a decision which determines an appeal or reference to which this Part applies (including a decision on an application for permission to appeal or refer);

    (b)   the Registrar refers such a decision to the court for the court to consider reopening it.

(2)   Such a party must—

    (a)   apply in writing for permission to reopen that decision, as soon as practicable after becoming aware of the grounds for doing so; and

    (b)   serve the application on the Registrar.

(3)   The application must—

    (a)   specify the decision which the applicant wants the court to reopen; and

    (b)   explain—

        (i)   why it is necessary for the court to reopen that decision in order to avoid real injustice,

        (ii)   how the circumstances are exceptional and make it appropriate to reopen the decision notwithstanding the rights and interests of other participants and the importance of finality,

        (iii)   why there is no alternative effective remedy among any potentially available, and

        (iv)   any delay in making the application.

(4)   The Registrar—

    (a)   may invite a party's representations on—

        (i)   an application to reopen a decision, or

        (ii)   a decision that the Registrar has referred, or intends to refer, to the court; and

    (b)   must do so if the court so directs.

(5)   A party invited to make representations must serve them on the Registrar within such period as the Registrar directs.

(6)   The court must not reopen a decision to which this rule applies unless each other party has had an opportunity to make representations.

[Note. The Court of Appeal has power only in exceptional circumstances to reopen a decision to which this rule applies.]][1]

Amendment

1   Inserted by the Criminal Procedure (Amendment) Rules 2018, SI 2018/132, rr 2, 15(c).

PART 37
APPEAL TO THE COURT OF APPEAL AGAINST RULING AT PREPARATORY HEARING

37.1. When this Part applies

(1)   This Part applies where a party wants to appeal under—

(a)   section 9(11) of the Criminal Justice Act 1987 or section 35(1) of the Criminal Procedure and Investigations Act 1996; or

(b)   section 47(1) of the Criminal Justice Act 2003.

(2)   A reference to an 'appellant' in this Part is a reference to such a party.

[Note. Under section 9(11) of the Criminal Justice Act 1987 (which applies to serious or complex fraud cases) and under section 35(1) of the Criminal Procedure and Investigations Act 1996 (which applies to other complex, serious or long cases) a party may appeal to the Court of Appeal against an order made at a preparatory hearing in the Crown Court.

Under section 47(1) of the Criminal Justice Act 2003 a party may appeal to the Court of Appeal against an order in the Crown Court that because of jury tampering a trial will continue without a jury or that there will be a new trial without a jury.

Part 3 contains rules about preparatory hearings.

The rules in Part 36 (Appeal to the Court of Appeal: general rules) also apply where this Part applies.]

37.2. Service of appeal notice

(1)   An appellant must serve an appeal notice on—

(a)   the Crown Court officer;

(b)   the Registrar; and

(c)   every party directly affected by the order or ruling against which the appellant wants to appeal.

(2)   The appellant must serve the appeal notice not more than 5 business days after—

    (a)   the order or ruling against which the appellant wants to appeal; or

    (b)   the Crown Court judge gives or refuses permission to appeal.

37.3.   Form of appeal notice

(1)   An appeal notice must be in the form set out in the Practice Direction.

(2)   The appeal notice must—

    (a)   specify each order or ruling against which the appellant wants to appeal;

    (b)   identify each ground of appeal on which the appellant relies, numbering them consecutively (if there is more than one) and concisely outlining each argument in support;

    (c)   summarise the relevant facts;

    (d)   identify any relevant authorities;

    (e)   include or attach any application for the following, with reasons—

        (i)   permission to appeal, if the appellant needs the court's permission,

        (ii)   an extension of time within which to serve the appeal notice,

        (iii)   a direction to attend in person a hearing that the appellant could attend by live link, if the appellant is in custody;

    (f)   include a list of those on whom the appellant has served the appeal notice; and

    (g)   attach—

        (i)   a transcript or note of each order or ruling against which the appellant wants to appeal,

        (ii)   all relevant skeleton arguments considered by the Crown Court judge,

        (iii)   any written application for permission to appeal that the appellant made to the Crown Court judge,

        (iv)   a transcript or note of the decision by the Crown Court judge on any application for permission to appeal, and

        (v)   any other document or thing that the appellant thinks the court will need to decide the appeal.

[Note. An appellant needs the court's permission to appeal in every case to which this Part applies unless the Crown Court judge gives permission.]

37.4. Crown Court judge's permission to appeal

(1) An appellant who wants the Crown Court judge to give permission to appeal must—

    (a) apply orally, with reasons, immediately after the order or ruling against which the appellant wants to appeal; or

    (b) apply in writing and serve the application on—

        (i) the Crown Court officer, and

        (ii) every party directly affected by the order or ruling

    not more than 2 business days after that order or ruling.

(2) A written application must include the same information (with the necessary adaptations) as an appeal notice.

[Note. For the Crown Court judge's power to give permission to appeal, see section 9(11) of the Criminal Justice Act 1987, section 35(1) of the Criminal Procedure and Investigations Act 1996 and section 47(2) of the Criminal Justice Act 2003.]

37.5. Respondent's notice

(1) A party on whom an appellant serves an appeal notice may serve a respondent's notice, and must do so if—

    (a) that party wants to make representations to the court; or

    (b) the court so directs.

(2) Such a party must serve the respondent's notice on—

    (a) the appellant;

    (b) the Crown Court officer;

    (c) the Registrar; and

    (d) any other party on whom the appellant served the appeal notice.

(3) Such a party must serve the respondent's notice not more than 5 business days after—

    (a) the appellant serves the appeal notice; or

    (b) a direction to do so.

(4) The respondent's notice must be in the form set out in the Practice Direction.

(5) The respondent's notice must—

    (a) give the date on which the respondent was served with the appeal notice;

(b)   identify each ground of opposition on which the respondent relies, numbering them consecutively (if there is more than one), concisely outlining each argument in support and identifying the ground of appeal to which each relates;

(c)   summarise any relevant facts not already summarised in the appeal notice;

(d)   identify any relevant authorities;

(e)   include or attach any application for the following, with reasons—

(i)   an extension of time within which to serve the respondent's notice,

(ii)   a direction to attend in person any hearing that the respondent could attend by live link, if the respondent is in custody;

(f)   identify any other document or thing that the respondent thinks the court will need to decide the appeal.

37.6.   Powers of Court of Appeal judge

A judge of the Court of Appeal may give permission to appeal as well as exercising the powers given by other legislation (including these Rules).

[Note. See section 31 of the Criminal Appeal Act 1968 and section 49 of the Criminal Justice Act 2003.]

37.7.   Renewing applications

Rule 36.5 (Renewing an application refused by a judge or the Registrar) applies with a time limit of 5 business days.

37.8.   Right to attend hearing

(1)   A party who is in custody has a right to attend a hearing in public.

(2)   The court or the Registrar may direct that such a party is to attend a hearing by live link.

[Note. See rule 36.6 (Hearings).]

PART 38
APPEAL TO THE COURT OF APPEAL AGAINST RULING ADVERSE TO PROSECUTION

38.1.   When this Part applies

(1)   This Part applies where a prosecutor wants to appeal under section 58(2) of the Criminal Justice Act 2003.

(2)   A reference to an 'appellant' in this Part is a reference to such a prosecutor.

[Note. Under section 58(2) of the Criminal Justice Act 2003 a prosecutor may appeal to the Court of Appeal against a ruling in the Crown Court. See also sections 57 and 59 to 61 of the 2003 Act.

The rules in Part 36 (Appeal to the Court of Appeal: general rules) also apply where this Part applies.]

38.2.   Decision to appeal

(1)   An appellant must tell the Crown Court judge of any decision to appeal—

(a)   immediately after the ruling against which the appellant wants to appeal; or

(b)   on the expiry of the time to decide whether to appeal allowed under paragraph (2).

(2)   If an appellant wants time to decide whether to appeal—

(a)   the appellant must ask the Crown Court judge immediately after the ruling; and

(b)   the general rule is that the judge must not require the appellant to decide there and then but instead must allow until the next business day.

[Note. If the ruling against which the appellant wants to appeal is a ruling that there is no case to answer, the appellant may appeal against earlier rulings as well: see section 58(7) of the Criminal Justice Act 2003.

Under section 58(8) of the 2003 Act the appellant must agree that a defendant directly affected by the ruling must be acquitted if the appellant (a) does not get permission to appeal or (b) abandons the appeal.

The Crown Court judge may give permission to appeal and may expedite the appeal: see rules 38.5 and 38.6.]

38.3.   Service of appeal notice

(1)   An appellant must serve an appeal notice on—

(a)   the Crown Court officer;

(b)   the Registrar; and

(c)   every defendant directly affected by the ruling against which the appellant wants to appeal.

(2)   The appellant must serve the appeal notice not later than—

(a)   the next business day after telling the Crown Court judge of the decision to appeal, if the judge expedites the appeal; or

(b)   5 business days after telling the Crown Court judge of that decision, if the judge does not expedite the appeal.

[Note. If the ruling against which the appellant wants to appeal is a public interest ruling, see rule 38.8.]

38.4.   Form of appeal notice

(1)   An appeal notice must be in the form set out in the Practice Direction.

(2)   The appeal notice must—

    (a)   specify each ruling against which the appellant wants to appeal;

    (b)   identify each ground of appeal on which the appellant relies, numbering them consecutively (if there is more than one) and concisely outlining each argument in support;

    (c)   summarise the relevant facts;

    (d)   identify any relevant authorities;

    (e)   include or attach any application for the following, with reasons—

        (i)   permission to appeal, if the appellant needs the court's permission,

        (ii)   an extension of time within which to serve the appeal notice,

        (iii)   expedition of the appeal, or revocation of a direction expediting the appeal;

    (f)   include a list of those on whom the appellant has served the appeal notice;

    (g)   attach—

        (i)   a transcript or note of each ruling against which the appellant wants to appeal,

        (ii)   all relevant skeleton arguments considered by the Crown Court judge,

        (iii)   any written application for permission to appeal that the appellant made to the Crown Court judge,

        (iv)   a transcript or note of the decision by the Crown Court judge on any application for permission to appeal,

        (v)   a transcript or note of the decision by the Crown Court judge on any request to expedite the appeal, and

        (vi)   any other document or thing that the appellant thinks the court will need to decide the appeal; and

    (h)   attach a form of respondent's notice for any defendant served with the appeal notice to complete if that defendant wants to do so.

[Note. An appellant needs the court's permission to appeal unless the Crown Court judge gives permission: see section 57(4) of the Criminal Justice Act 2003. For 'respondent's notice' see rule 38.7.]

38.5. Crown Court judge's permission to appeal

(1) An appellant who wants the Crown Court judge to give permission to appeal must—

    (a) apply orally, with reasons, immediately after the ruling against which the appellant wants to appeal; or

    (b) apply in writing and serve the application on—

        (i) the Crown Court officer, and

        (ii) every defendant directly affected by the ruling

    on the expiry of the time allowed under [rule 38.2]¹ to decide whether to appeal.

(2) A written application must include the same information (with the necessary adaptations) as an appeal notice.

(3) The Crown Court judge must allow every defendant directly affected by the ruling an opportunity to make representations.

(4) The general rule is that the Crown Court judge must decide whether or not to give permission to appeal on the day that the application for permission is made.

[Note. For the Crown Court judge's power to give permission to appeal, see section 57(4) of the Criminal Justice Act 2003.

Rule 38.5(3) does not apply where the appellant wants to appeal against a public interest ruling: see rule 38.8(5).]

Amendment
1   Substituted by the Criminal Procedure (Amendment) Rules 2016, SI 2016/120, rr 2, 12.

38.6. Expediting an appeal

(1) An appellant who wants the Crown Court judge to expedite an appeal must ask, giving reasons, on telling the judge of the decision to appeal.

(2) The Crown Court judge must allow every defendant directly affected by the ruling an opportunity to make representations.

(3) The Crown Court judge may revoke a direction expediting the appeal unless the appellant has served the appeal notice.

[Note. For the Crown Court judge's power to expedite the appeal, see section 59 of the Criminal Justice Act 2003.

Rule 38.6(2) does not apply where the appellant wants to appeal against a public interest ruling: see rule 38.8(5).]

38.7. Respondent's notice

(1)   A defendant on whom an appellant serves an appeal notice may serve a respondent's notice, and must do so if—

    (a)   the defendant wants to make representations to the court; or

    (b)   the court so directs.

(2)   Such a defendant must serve the respondent's notice on—

    (a)   the appellant;

    (b)   the Crown Court officer;

    (c)   the Registrar; and

    (d)   any other defendant on whom the appellant served the appeal notice.

(3)   Such a defendant must serve the respondent's notice—

    (a)   not later than the next business day after—

        (i)   the appellant serves the appeal notice, or

        (ii)   a direction to do so

    if the Crown Court judge expedites the appeal; or

    (b)   not more than 5 business days after—

        (i)   the appellant serves the appeal notice, or

        (ii)   a direction to do so

    if the Crown Court judge does not expedite the appeal.

(4)   The respondent's notice must be in the form set out in the Practice Direction.

(5)   The respondent's notice must—

    (a)   give the date on which the respondent was served with the appeal notice;

    (b)   identify each ground of opposition on which the respondent relies, numbering them consecutively (if there is more than one), concisely outlining each argument in support and identifying the ground of appeal to which each relates;

    (c)   summarise any relevant facts not already summarised in the appeal notice;

(d)   identify any relevant authorities;

(e)   include or attach any application for the following, with reasons—

       (i)   an extension of time within which to serve the respondent's notice,

       (ii)   a direction to attend in person any hearing that the respondent could attend by live link, if the respondent is in custody;

(f)   identify any other document or thing that the respondent thinks the court will need to decide the appeal.

38.8.   Public interest ruling

(1)   This rule applies where the appellant wants to appeal against a public interest ruling.

(2)   The appellant must not serve on any defendant directly affected by the ruling—

(a)   any written application to the Crown Court judge for permission to appeal; or

(b)   an appeal notice,

if the appellant thinks that to do so in effect would reveal something that the appellant thinks ought not be disclosed.

(3)   The appellant must not include in an appeal notice—

(a)   the material that was the subject of the ruling; or

(b)   any indication of what sort of material it is,

if the appellant thinks that to do so in effect would reveal something that the appellant thinks ought not be disclosed.

(4)   The appellant must serve on the Registrar with the appeal notice an annex—

(a)   marked to show that its contents are only for the court and the Registrar;

(b)   containing whatever the appellant has omitted from the appeal notice, with reasons; and

(c)   if relevant, explaining why the appellant has not served the appeal notice.

(5)   Rules 38.5(3) and 38.6(2) do not apply.

[Note. Rules 38.5(3) and 38.6(2) require the Crown Court judge to allow a defendant to make representations about (i) giving permission to appeal and (ii) expediting an appeal.]

38.9.   Powers of Court of Appeal judge

A judge of the Court of Appeal may—

(a)   give permission to appeal;

(b)   revoke a Crown Court judge's direction expediting an appeal; and

(c)   where an appellant abandons an appeal, order a defendant's acquittal, his release from custody and the payment of his costs,

as well as exercising the powers given by other legislation (including these Rules).

[Note. See section 73 of the Criminal Justice Act 2003.]

38.10.   Renewing applications

Rule 36.5 (Renewing an application refused by a judge or the Registrar) applies with a time limit of 5 business days.

38.11.   Right to attend hearing

(1)   A respondent who is in custody has a right to attend a hearing in public.

(2)   The court or the Registrar may direct that such a respondent is to attend a hearing by live link.

[Note. See rule 36.6 (Hearings).]

PART 39
APPEAL TO THE COURT OF APPEAL ABOUT CONVICTION OR SENTENCE

39.1.   When this Part applies

(1)   This Part applies where—

(a)   a defendant wants to appeal under—

(i)   Part 1 of the Criminal Appeal Act 1968,

(ii)   section 274(3) of the Criminal Justice Act 2003,

(iii)   paragraph 14 of Schedule 22 to the Criminal Justice Act 2003, or

(iv)   section 42 of the Counter Terrorism Act 2008;

(b)   the Criminal Cases Review Commission refers a case to the Court of Appeal under section 9 of the Criminal Appeal Act 1995;

(c)   a prosecutor wants to appeal to the Court of Appeal under section 14A(5A) of the Football Spectators Act 1989;

(d)   a party wants to appeal under section 74(8) of the Serious Organised Crime and Police Act 2005;

(e)   a person found in contempt of court wants to appeal under section 13 of the Administration of Justice Act 1960 and section 18A of the Criminal Appeal Act 1968; or

(f)   a person wants to appeal to the Court of Appeal under—

(i)   section 24 of the Serious Crime Act 2007, or

(ii)   regulation 3C or 3H of The Costs in Criminal Cases (General) Regulations 1986.

(2)   A reference to an 'appellant' in this Part is a reference to such a party or person.

[Note. Under Part 1 (sections 1 to 32) of the Criminal Appeal Act 1968, a defendant may appeal against—

(a)   a conviction (section 1 of the 1968 Act);

(b)   a sentence (sections 9 and 10 of the 1968 Act);

(c)   a verdict of not guilty by reason of insanity (section 12 of the 1968 Act);

(d)   a finding of disability (section 15 of the 1968 Act);

(e)   a hospital order, interim hospital order or supervision order under section 5 or 5A of the Criminal Procedure (Insanity) Act 1964 (section 16A of the 1968 Act).

See section 50 of the 1968 Act for the meaning of 'sentence'.

Under section 274(3) of the 2003 Act, a defendant sentenced to life imprisonment outside the United Kingdom, and transferred to serve the sentence in England and Wales, may appeal against the minimum term fixed by a High Court judge under section 82A of the Powers of Criminal Courts (Sentencing) Act 2000 or under section 269 of the 2003 Act.

Under paragraph 14 of Schedule 22 to the Criminal Justice Act 2003 a defendant sentenced to life imprisonment may appeal against the minimum term fixed on review by a High Court judge in certain cases.

Under section 42 of the Counter Terrorism Act 2008 a defendant may appeal against a decision of the Crown Court that an offence has a terrorist connection.

See section 13 of the Criminal Appeal Act 1995 for the circumstances in which the Criminal Cases Review Commission may refer a conviction, sentence, verdict or finding to the Court of Appeal.

Under section 14A(5A) of the Football Spectators Act 1989 a prosecutor may appeal against a failure by the Crown Court to make a football banning order.

Under section 74(8) of the Serious Organised Crime and Police Act 2005 a prosecutor or defendant may appeal against a review by a Crown Court judge of a sentence that was reduced because the defendant assisted the investigator or prosecutor.

Under section 13 of the Administration of Justice Act 1960 a person in respect of whom an order or decision is made by the Crown Court in the exercise of its jurisdiction to punish for contempt of court may appeal to the Court of Appeal.

Under section 24 of the Serious Crime Act 2007 a person who is the subject of a serious crime prevention order, or the relevant applicant authority, may appeal to the Court of Appeal against a decision of the Crown Court in relation to that order. In addition, any person who was given an opportunity to make representations in the proceedings by virtue of section 9(4) of the Act may appeal to the Court of Appeal against a decision of the Crown Court to make, vary or not vary a serious crime prevention order.

Under regulation 3C of the Costs in Criminal Cases (General) Regulations 1986, a legal representative against whom the Crown Court makes a wasted costs order under section 19A of the Prosecution of Offences Act 1985 and regulation 3B may appeal against that order to the Court of Appeal.

Under regulation 3H of the Costs in Criminal Cases (General) Regulations 1986, a third party against whom the Crown Court makes a costs order under section 19B of the Prosecution of Offences Act 1985 and regulation 3F may appeal against that order to the Court of Appeal.

The rules in Part 36 (Appeal to the Court of Appeal: general rules) also apply where this Part applies.]

[39.2. Service of appeal notice

The appellant must serve an appeal notice on the Registrar—

  (a) not more than 28 days after—

  (i) the conviction, verdict, or finding,

  (ii) the sentence,

  (iii) the order (subject to paragraph (b)), or the failure to make an order, or

  (iv) the minimum term review decision under section 274(3) of, or paragraph 14 of Schedule 22 to, the Criminal Justice Act 2003

  about which the appellant wants to appeal;

  (b) not more than 21 days after the order in a case in which the appellant appeals against a wasted or third party costs order;

(c) not more than 28 days after the Registrar serves notice that the Criminal Cases Review Commission has referred a conviction to the court.

[Note. The time limit for serving an appeal notice (a) on an appeal under Part 1 of the Criminal Appeal Act 1968 and (b) on an appeal against a finding of contempt of court is prescribed by sections 18 and 18A of the Criminal Appeal Act 1968. It may be extended, but not shortened.

For service of a reference by the Criminal Cases Review Commission, see rule 39.5.]]¹

Amendment

1 Substituted by the Criminal Procedure (Amendment No. 2) Rules 2018, SI 2018/847, rr 2, 11(a).

39.3. Form of appeal notice

…¹

[(1)]² [An appeal notice]² must—

(a) specify—

   (i) the conviction, verdict, or finding,

   (ii) the sentence, or

   (iii) the order, or the failure to make an order

about which the appellant wants to appeal;

[(b) identify each ground of appeal on which the appellant relies (and see paragraph (2));]²

(c) identify the transcript that the appellant thinks the court will need, if the appellant wants to appeal against a conviction;

(d) identify the relevant sentencing powers of the Crown Court, if sentence is in issue;

[(e) include or attach any application for the following, with reasons—

   (i) permission to appeal, if the appellant needs the court's permission,

   (ii) an extension of time within which to serve the appeal notice,

   (iii) bail pending appeal,

   (iv) a direction to attend in person a hearing that the appellant could attend by live link, if the appellant is in custody,

   (v) the introduction of evidence, including hearsay evidence and evidence of bad character,

       (vi)   an order requiring a witness to attend court,

       (vii) a direction for special measures for a witness,

       (viii) a direction for special measures for the giving of evidence by the appellant;

    (f)   identify any other document or thing that the appellant thinks the court will need to decide the appeal.][2]

...[1]

...[3]

[(2) The grounds of appeal must—

    (a)   include in no more than the first two pages a summary of the grounds that makes what then follows easy to understand;

    (b)   in each ground of appeal identify the event or decision to which that ground relates;

    (c)   in each ground of appeal summarise the facts relevant to that ground, but only to the extent necessary to make clear what is in issue;

    (d)   concisely outline each argument in support of each ground;

    (e)   number each ground consecutively, if there is more than one;

    (f)   identify any relevant authority and—

       (i)   state the proposition of law that the authority demonstrates, and

       (ii) identify the parts of the authority that support that proposition; and

    (g)   where the Criminal Cases Review Commission refers a case to the court, explain how each ground of appeal relates (if it does) to the reasons for the reference.][4]

[Note. [The Practice Direction sets out [forms of appeal notice][5] for use in connection with this rule.][4]

In some legislation, including the Criminal Appeal Act 1968, permission to appeal is described as 'leave to appeal'.

An appellant needs the court's permission to appeal in every case to which this Part applies, except where—

    (a)   the Criminal Cases Review Commission refers the case;

    (b)   the appellant appeals against—

       (i)   an order or decision made in the exercise of jurisdiction to punish for contempt of court, or

       (ii) a wasted or third party costs order; or

(c)   the Crown Court judge certifies under sections 1(2)(a), 11(1A), 12(b), 15(2)(b) or 16A(2)(b) of the Criminal Appeal Act 1968, under section 81(1B) of the Senior Courts Act 1981, under section 14A(5B) of the Football Spectators Act 1989, or under section 24(4) of the Serious Crime Act 2007, that a case is fit for appeal.

A judge of the Court of Appeal may give permission to appeal under section 31 of the Criminal Appeal Act 1968.

[See also rule 39.7 (Introducing evidence).][6]]

Amendments

1   Revoked by the Criminal Procedure (Amendment) Rules 2018, SI 2018/132, rr 2, 16(a)(i), (v).
2   Substituted by the Criminal Procedure (Amendment) Rules 2018, SI 2018/132, rr 2, 16(a)(ii)-(v).
3   Revoked by the Criminal Procedure (Amendment No. 2) Rules 2018, SI 2018/847, rr 2, 11(b)(i).
4   Inserted by the Criminal Procedure (Amendment) Rules 2018, SI 2018/132, rr 2, 16(a)(vi), (vii).
5   Substituted by the Criminal Procedure (Amendment No. 2) Rules 2018, SI 2018/847, rr 2, 11(b)(ii).
6   Inserted by the Criminal Procedure (Amendment) Rules 2017, SI 2017/144, rr 2, 10(a).

39.4.   Crown Court judge's certificate that case is fit for appeal

(1)   An appellant who wants the Crown Court judge to certify that a case is fit for appeal must—

    (a)   apply orally, with reasons, immediately after there occurs—

        (i)   the conviction, verdict, or finding,

        (ii)   the sentence, or

        (iii)   the order, or the failure to make an order

    about which the appellant wants to appeal; or

    (b)   apply in writing and serve the application on the Crown Court officer not more than 14 days after that occurred.

(2)   A written application must include the same information (with the necessary adaptations) as an appeal notice.

[Note. The Crown Court judge may certify that a case is fit for appeal under sections 1(2)(b), 11(1A), 12(b), 15(2)(b) or 16A(2)(b) of the Criminal Appeal Act 1968, under section 81(1B) of the Senior Courts Act 1981, under section 14A(5B) of the Football Spectators Act 1989 or under section 24(4) of the Serious Crime Act 2007.

See also rule 39.2 (service of appeal notice required in all cases).]

39.5.   Reference by Criminal Cases Review Commission

(1)   The Registrar must serve on the appellant a reference by the Criminal Cases Review Commission.

(2)   The court must treat that reference as the appeal notice if the appellant does not serve such a notice under rule 39.2.

39.6.   Respondent's notice

(1)   The Registrar—

   (a)   may serve an appeal notice on any party directly affected by the appeal; and

   (b)   must do so if the Criminal Cases Review Commission refers a conviction, verdict, finding or sentence to the court.

(2)   Such a party may serve a respondent's notice, and must do so if—

   (a)   that party wants to make representations to the court; or

   (b)   the court or the Registrar so directs.

(3)   Such a party must serve the respondent's notice on—

   (a)   the appellant;

   (b)   the Registrar; and

   (c)   any other party on whom the Registrar served the appeal notice.

(4)   Such a party must serve the respondent's notice—

   (a)   not more than 14 days after the Registrar serves—

      (i)   the appeal notice, or

      (ii)   a direction to do so; or

   (b)   not more than 28 days after the Registrar serves notice that the Commission has referred a conviction.

(5)   The respondent's notice must be in the form set out in the Practice Direction.

(6)   The respondent's notice must—

   (a)   give the date on which the respondent was served with the appeal notice;

   (b)   identify each ground of opposition on which the respondent relies, numbering them consecutively (if there is more than one), concisely outlining each argument in support and identifying the ground of appeal to which each relates;

   (c)   identify the relevant sentencing powers of the Crown Court, if sentence is in issue;

   (d)   summarise any relevant facts not already summarised in the appeal notice;

(e)   identify any relevant authorities;

(f)   include or attach any application for the following, with reasons—

    (i)   an extension of time within which to serve the respondent's notice,

    (ii)   bail pending appeal,

    (iii)   a direction to attend in person a hearing that the respondent could attend by live link, if the respondent is in custody,

    (iv)   the introduction of evidence, including hearsay evidence and evidence of bad character,

    (v)   an order requiring a witness to attend court,

    (vi)   a direction for special measures for a witness; and

(g)   identify any other document or thing that the respondent thinks the court will need to decide the appeal.

[Note. The Practice Direction sets out the circumstances in which the Registrar usually will serve a defendant's appeal notice on the prosecutor.

[See also rule 39.7 (Introducing evidence).][1]]

Amendment

1   Inserted by the Criminal Procedure (Amendment) Rules 2017, SI 2017/144, rr 2, 10(b).

[39.7. Introducing evidence

(1)   The following Parts apply with such adaptations as the court or the Registrar may direct—

(a)   Part 16 (Written witness statements);

(b)   Part 18 (Measures to assist a witness or defendant to give evidence);

(c)   Part 19 (Expert evidence);

(d)   Part 20 (Hearsay evidence);

(e)   Part 21 (Evidence of bad character); and

(f)   Part 22 (Evidence of a complainant's previous sexual behaviour).

(2)   But the general rule is that—

(a)   a respondent who opposes an appellant's application or notice to which one of those Parts applies must do so in the respondent's notice, with reasons;

(b)   an appellant who opposes a respondent's application or notice to which one of those Parts applies must serve notice, with reasons, on—

    (i)   the Registrar, and

(ii)   the respondent

not more than 14 days after service of the respondent's notice; and

(c)   the court or the Registrar may give directions with or without a hearing.

(3)   A party who wants the court to order the production of a document, exhibit or other thing connected with the proceedings must—

(a)   identify that item; and

(b)   explain—

(i)   how it is connected with the proceedings,

(ii)   why its production is necessary for the determination of the case, and

(iii)   to whom it should be produced (the court, appellant or respondent, or any two or more of them).

(4)   A party who wants the court to order a witness to attend to be questioned must—

(a)   identify the proposed witness; and

(b)   explain—

(i)   what evidence the proposed witness can give,

(ii)   why that evidence is capable of belief,

(iii)   if applicable, why that evidence may provide a ground for allowing the appeal,

(iv)   on what basis that evidence would have been admissible in the case which is the subject of the application for permission to appeal or appeal, and

(v)   why that evidence was not introduced in that case.

(5)   Where the court orders a witness to attend to be questioned, the witness must attend the hearing of the application for permission to appeal or of the appeal, as applicable, unless the court otherwise directs.

(6)   Where the court orders a witness to attend to be questioned before an examiner on the court's behalf, the court must identify the examiner and may give directions about—

(a)   the time and place, or times and places, at which that questioning must be carried out;

(b)   the manner in which that questioning must be carried out, in particular as to—

(i)   the service of any report, statement or questionnaire in preparation for the questioning,

        (ii)   the sequence in which the parties may ask questions, and

        (iii)   if more than one witness is to be questioned, the sequence in which those witnesses may be questioned; and

  (c)   the manner in which, and when, a record of the questioning must be submitted to the court.

(7)   Where the court orders the questioning of a witness before an examiner, the court may delegate to that examiner the giving of directions under paragraph (6)(a), (b) and (c).

[Note. An application to introduce evidence or for directions about evidence must be included in, or attached to, an appeal notice or a respondent's notice: see [39.3(1)(e)(v), (vi)]¹ and 39.6(6)(f)(iv), (v).

Under section 23 of the Criminal Appeal Act 1968, the Court of Appeal may order the production of a document, exhibit or other thing, may order a witness to attend to be examined before the court and may allow the introduction of evidence that was not introduced at trial. Under section 23(4), if it thinks it necessary or expedient in the interests of justice the court may order the examination of a witness to be conducted before any judge, court officer or other person, and allow the admission of a record of that examination as evidence before the court.]]²

Amendments

1   Substituted by the Criminal Procedure (Amendment) Rules 2018, SI 2018/132, rr 2, 16(b).
2   Substituted by the Criminal Procedure (Amendment) Rules 2017, SI 2017/144, rr 2, 10(c).

39.8. Application for bail pending appeal or retrial

(1)   This rule applies where a party wants to make an application to the court about bail pending appeal or retrial.

(2)   That party must serve an application in the form set out in the Practice Direction on—

  (a)   the Registrar, unless the application is with the appeal notice; and

  (b)   the other party.

(3)   The court must not decide such an application without giving the other party an opportunity to make representations, including representations about any condition or surety proposed by the applicant.

(4)   This rule and rule 14.16 (Bail condition to be enforced in another European Union member State) apply where the court can impose as a condition of bail pending retrial a requirement—

  (a)   with which a defendant must comply while in another European Union member State; and

  (b)   which that other member State can monitor and enforce.

[Note. See section 19 of the Criminal Appeal Act 1968, section 3(8) of the Bail Act 1976 and regulations 77 to 84 of the Criminal Justice and Data Protection (Protocol No. 36) Regulations 2014. An application about bail or about the conditions of bail may be made either by an appellant or respondent.

Under section 81(1) of the Senior Courts Act 1981, a Crown Court judge may grant bail pending appeal only (a) if that judge gives a certificate that the case is fit for appeal (see rule 39.4) and (b) not more than 28 days after the conviction or sentence against which the appellant wants to appeal.

See also rule 14.16. Under the 2014 Regulations, where an appellant or respondent is to live or stay in another European Union member State pending his or her trial in England and Wales, the court may grant bail subject to a requirement to be monitored and enforced by the competent authority in that other state. The types of requirement that can be monitored and enforced are set out in Article 8 of EU Council Framework Decision 2009/829/JHA. A list of those requirements is at the end of Part 14.]

39.9.   Conditions of bail pending appeal or retrial

(1)   This rule applies where the court grants a party bail pending appeal or retrial subject to any condition that must be met before that party is released.

(2)   The court may direct how such a condition must be met.

(3)   The Registrar must serve a certificate in the form set out in the Practice Direction recording any such condition and direction on—

    (a)   that party;

    (b)   that party's custodian; and

    (c)   any other person directly affected by any such direction.

(4)   A person directly affected by any such direction need not comply with it until the Registrar serves that person with that certificate.

(5)   Unless the court otherwise directs, if any such condition or direction requires someone to enter into a recognizance it must be—

    (a)   in the form set out in the Practice Direction and signed before—

        (i)   the Registrar,

        (ii)   the custodian, or

        (iii)   someone acting with the authority of the Registrar or custodian;

    (b)   copied immediately to the person who enters into it; and

    (c)   served immediately by the Registrar on the appellant's custodian or vice versa, as appropriate.

(6) Unless the court otherwise directs, if any such condition or direction requires someone to make a payment, surrender a document or take some other step—

    (a) that payment, document or step must be made, surrendered or taken to or before—

        (i) the Registrar,

        (ii) the custodian, or

        (iii) someone acting with the authority of the Registrar or custodian;

    (b) the Registrar or the custodian, as appropriate, must serve immediately on the other a statement that the payment, document or step has been made, surrendered or taken, as appropriate.

(7) The custodian must release the appellant where it appears that any condition ordered by the court has been met.

(8) For the purposes of section 5 of the Bail Act 1976 (record of decision about bail), the Registrar must keep a copy of—

    (a) any certificate served under paragraph (3);

    (b) a notice of hearing given under rule 36.7(1); and

    (c) a notice of the court's decision served under rule 36.7(2).

(9) Where the court grants bail pending retrial the Registrar must serve on the Crown Court officer copies of the documents kept under paragraph (8).

39.10. Forfeiture of a recognizance given as a condition of bail

(1) This rule applies where—

    (a) the court grants a party bail pending appeal or retrial; and

    (b) the bail is subject to a condition that that party provides a surety to guarantee that he will surrender to custody as required; but

    (c) that party does not surrender to custody as required.

(2) The Registrar must serve notice on—

    (a) the surety; and

    (b) the prosecutor,

of the hearing at which the court may order the forfeiture of the recognizance given by that surety.

(3) The court must not forfeit a surety's recognizance—

    (a) less than 7 days after the Registrar serves notice under paragraph (2); and

(b)   without giving the surety an opportunity to make representations at a hearing.

[Note. If the purpose for which a recognizance is entered is not fulfilled, that recognizance may be forfeited by the court. If the court forfeits a surety's recognizance, the sum promised by that person is then payable to the Crown.]

39.11.   Right to attend hearing

A party who is in custody has a right to attend a hearing in public unless—

(a)   it is a hearing preliminary or incidental to an appeal, including the hearing of an application for permission to appeal; ...[1]

[(b)   it is the hearing of an appeal and the court directs that—

(i)   the appeal involves a question of law alone, and

(ii)   for that reason the appellant has no permission to attend; or][2]

[(c)][3] that party is in custody in consequence of—

(i)   a verdict of not guilty by reason of insanity, or

(ii)   a finding of disability.

[Note. See rule 36.6 (Hearings) and section 22 of the Criminal Appeal Act 1968. There are corresponding provisions in the Criminal Justice Act 2003 (Mandatory Life Sentences: Appeals in Transitional Cases) Order 2005, the Serious Organised Crime and Police Act 2005 (Appeals under section 74) Order 2006 and the Serious Crime Act 2007 (Appeals under Section 24) Order 2008. Under section 22 of the 1968 Act and corresponding provisions in those Orders, the court may direct that an appellant who is in custody is to attend a hearing by live link.]

Amendments

1   Revoked by the Criminal Procedure (Amendment) Rules 2017, SI 2017/144, rr 2, 10(e)(i).
2   Inserted by the Criminal Procedure (Amendment) Rules 2017, SI 2017/144, rr 2, 10(e)(ii).
3   Substituted by the Criminal Procedure (Amendment) Rules 2017, SI 2017/144, rr 2, 10(e)(iii).

39.12.   Power to vary determination of appeal against sentence

(1)   This rule applies where the court decides an appeal affecting sentence in a party's absence.

(2)   The court may vary such a decision if it did not take account of something relevant because that party was absent.

(3)   A party who wants the court to vary such a decision must—

(a)   apply in writing, with reasons;

(b)   serve the application on the Registrar not more than 7 days after—

(i)   the decision, if that party was represented at the appeal hearing, or

(ii)   the Registrar serves the decision, if that party was not represented at that hearing.

[Note. Section 22(3) of the Criminal Appeal Act 1968 allows the court to sentence in an appellant's absence. There are corresponding provisions in the Criminal Justice Act 2003 (Mandatory Life Sentences: Appeals in Transitional Cases) Order 2005 and in the Serious Organised Crime and Police Act 2005 (Appeals under Section 74) Order 2006.]

39.13.   Directions about re-admission to hospital on dismissal of appeal

(1)   This rule applies where—

    (a)   an appellant subject to—

        (i)   an order under section 37(1) of the Mental Health Act 1983 (detention in hospital on conviction), or

        (ii)   an order under section 5(2) of the Criminal Procedure (Insanity) Act 1964 (detention in hospital on finding of insanity or disability)

        has been released on bail pending appeal; and

    (b)   the court—

        (i)   refuses permission to appeal,

        (ii)   dismisses the appeal, or

        (iii)   affirms the order under appeal.

(2)   The court must give appropriate directions for the appellant's—

    (a)   re-admission to hospital; and

    (b)   if necessary, temporary detention pending re-admission.

39.14.   Renewal or setting aside of order for retrial

(1)   This rule applies where—

    (a)   a prosecutor wants a defendant to be arraigned more than 2 months after the court ordered a retrial under section 7 of the Criminal Appeal Act 1968; or

    (b)   a defendant wants such an order set aside after 2 months have passed since it was made.

(2)   That party must apply in writing, with reasons, and serve the application on—

(a)   the Registrar;

(b)   the other party.

[Note. Section 8(1) and (1A) of the Criminal Appeal Act 1968 set out the criteria for making an order on an application to which this rule applies.]

PART 40
APPEAL TO THE COURT OF APPEAL ABOUT REPORTING OR PUBLIC ACCESS RESTRICTION

40.1. When this Part applies

(1)   This Part applies where a person directly affected by an order to which section 159(1) of the Criminal Justice Act 1988 applies wants to appeal against that order.

(2)   A reference to an 'appellant' in this Part is a reference to such a party.

[Note. Section 159(1) of the Criminal Justice Act 1988 gives a 'person aggrieved' (in this Part described as a person directly affected) a right of appeal to the Court of Appeal against a Crown Court judge's order—

(a)   under section 4 or 11 of the Contempt of Court Act 1981;

(b)   under section 58(7) of the Criminal Procedure and Investigations Act 1996;

(c)   restricting public access to any part of a trial for reasons of national security or for the protection of a witness or other person; or

(d)   restricting the reporting of any part of a trial.

See also Part 6 (Reporting, etc. restrictions) and Part 18 (Measures to assist a witness or defendant to give evidence).

The rules in Part 36 (Appeal to the Court of Appeal: general rules) also apply where this Part applies.]

40.2. Service of appeal notice

(1)   An appellant must serve an appeal notice on—

(a)   the Crown Court officer;

(b)   the Registrar;

(c)   the parties; and

(d)   any other person directly affected by the order against which the appellant wants to appeal.

(2)   The appellant must serve the appeal notice not later than—

    (a)   the next business day after an order restricting public access to the trial;

    (b)   10 business days after an order restricting reporting of the trial.

40.3.   Form of appeal notice

(1)   An appeal notice must be in the form set out in the Practice Direction.

(2)   The appeal notice must—

    (a)   specify the order against which the appellant wants to appeal;

    (b)   identify each ground of appeal on which the appellant relies, numbering them consecutively (if there is more than one) and concisely outlining each argument in support;

    (c)   summarise the relevant facts;

    (d)   identify any relevant authorities;

    (e)   include or attach, with reasons—

        (i)   an application for permission to appeal,

        (ii)   any application for an extension of time within which to serve the appeal notice,

        (iii) any application for a direction to attend in person a hearing that the appellant could attend by live link, if the appellant is in custody,

        (iv)   any application for permission to introduce evidence, and

        (v)   a list of those on whom the appellant has served the appeal notice; and

    (f)   attach any document or thing that the appellant thinks the court will need to decide the appeal.

[Note. An appellant needs the court's permission to appeal in every case to which this Part applies.

A Court of Appeal judge may give permission to appeal under section 31(2B) of the Criminal Appeal Act 1968.]

40.4.   Advance notice of appeal against order restricting public access

(1)   This rule applies where the appellant wants to appeal against an order restricting public access to a trial.

(2)   The appellant may serve advance written notice of intention to appeal against any such order that may be made.

(3)   The appellant must serve any such advance notice—

    (a)   on—

        (i)   the Crown Court officer,

        (ii)   the Registrar,

        (iii)   the parties, and

        (iv)   any other person who will be directly affected by the order against which the appellant intends to appeal, if it is made; and

    (b)   not more than 5 business days after the Crown Court officer displays notice of the application for the order.

(4)   The advance notice must include the same information (with the necessary adaptations) as an appeal notice.

(5)   The court must treat that advance notice as the appeal notice if the order is made.

40.5.   Duty of applicant for order restricting public access

(1)   This rule applies where the appellant wants to appeal against an order restricting public access to a trial.

(2)   The party who applied for the order must serve on the Registrar—

    (a)   a transcript or note of the application for the order; and

    (b)   any other document or thing that that party thinks the court will need to decide the appeal.

(3)   That party must serve that transcript or note and any such other document or thing as soon as practicable after—

    (a)   the appellant serves the appeal notice; or

    (b)   the order, where the appellant served advance notice of intention to appeal.

40.6.   Respondent's notice on appeal against reporting restriction

(1)   This rule applies where the appellant wants to appeal against an order restricting the reporting of a trial.

(2)   A person on whom an appellant serves an appeal notice may serve a respondent's notice, and must do so if—

    (a)   that person wants to make representations to the court; or

    (b)   the court so directs.

(3)   Such a person must serve the respondent's notice on—

    (a)   the appellant;

(b)   the Crown Court officer;

(c)   the Registrar;

(d)   the parties; and

(e)   any other person on whom the appellant served the appeal notice.

(4)   Such a person must serve the respondent's notice not more than 3 business days after—

(a)   the appellant serves the appeal notice; or

(b)   a direction to do so.

(5)   The respondent's notice must be in the form set out in the Practice Direction.

(6)   The respondent's notice must—

(a)   give the date on which the respondent was served with the appeal notice;

(b)   identify each ground of opposition on which the respondent relies, numbering them consecutively (if there is more than one), concisely outlining each argument in support and identifying the ground of appeal to which each relates;

(c)   summarise any relevant facts not already summarised in the appeal notice;

(d)   identify any relevant authorities;

(e)   include or attach any application for the following, with reasons—

(i)   an extension of time within which to serve the respondent's notice,

(ii)   a direction to attend in person any hearing that the respondent could attend by live link, if the respondent is in custody,

(iii)   permission to introduce evidence; and

(f)   identify any other document or thing that the respondent thinks the court will need to decide the appeal.

40.7.   Renewing applications

Rule 36.5 (Renewing an application refused by a judge or the Registrar) applies with a time limit of 5 business days.

40.8.   Right to introduce evidence

No person may introduce evidence without the court's permission.

[Note. Section 159(4) of the Criminal Justice Act 1988 entitles the parties to give evidence, subject to procedure rules.]

40.9.   Right to attend hearing

(1)   A party who is in custody has a right to attend a hearing in public of an appeal against an order restricting the reporting of a trial.

(2)   The court or the Registrar may direct that such a party is to attend a hearing by live link.

[Note. See rule 36.6 (Hearings). The court may decide an application and an appeal without a hearing where the appellant wants to appeal against an order restricting public access to a trial: rule 36.6(3).]

PART 41
REFERENCE TO THE COURT OF APPEAL OF POINT OF LAW OR UNDULY LENIENT SENTENCING

41.1.   When this Part applies

This Part applies where the Attorney General wants to—

(a)   refer a point of law to the Court of Appeal under section 36 of the Criminal Justice Act 1972; or

(b)   refer a sentencing case to the Court of Appeal under section 36 of the Criminal Justice Act 1988.

[Note. Under section 36 of the Criminal Justice Act 1972, where a defendant is acquitted in the Crown Court the Attorney General may refer to the Court of Appeal a point of law in the case.

Under section 36 of the Criminal Justice Act 1988, if the Attorney General thinks the sentencing of a defendant in the Crown Court is unduly lenient he may refer the case to the Court of Appeal: but only if the sentence is one to which Part IV of the 1988 Act applies, and only if the Court of Appeal gives permission. See also section 35 of the 1988 Act and the Criminal Justice Act 1988 (Reviews of Sentencing) Order 2006.

The rules in Part 36 (Appeal to the Court of Appeal: general rules) also apply where this Part applies.]

[41.2.   Service of notice of reference and application for permission

(1)   The Attorney General must serve any notice of reference and any application for permission to refer a sentencing case on—

(a)   the Registrar; and

(b)   the defendant.

(2)   Where the Attorney General refers a point of law—

(a) the Attorney must give the Registrar details of—

    (i) the defendant affected,

    (ii) the date and place of the relevant Crown Court decision, and

    (iii) the relevant verdict and sentencing; and

(b) the Attorney must give the defendant notice that—

    (i) the outcome of the reference will not make any difference to the outcome of the trial, and

    (ii) the defendant may serve a respondent's notice.

(3) Where the Attorney General applies for permission to refer a sentencing case, the Attorney must give the defendant notice that—

(a) the outcome of the reference may make a difference to that sentencing, and in particular may result in a more severe sentence; and

(b) the defendant may serve a respondent's notice.

(4) The Attorney General must serve an application for permission to refer a sentencing case on the Registrar not more than 28 days after the last of the sentences in that case.

[Note. The time limit for serving an application for permission to refer a sentencing case is prescribed by paragraph 1 of Schedule 3 to the Criminal Justice Act 1988. It may be neither extended nor shortened.]]¹

Amendment
1   Substituted by the Criminal Procedure (Amendment) Rules 2018, SI 2018/132, rr 2, 17(a).

41.3.   Form of notice of reference and application for permission

[(1) A notice of reference and an application for permission to refer a sentencing case must give the year and number of that reference or that case.]¹

(2) A notice of reference of a point of law must—

(a) specify the point of law in issue and indicate the opinion that the Attorney General invites the court to give;

(b) identify each ground for that invitation, numbering them consecutively (if there is more than one) and concisely outlining each argument in support;

(c) exclude any reference to the defendant's name and any other reference that may identify the defendant;

(d) summarise the relevant facts; and

      (e)   identify any relevant authorities.

(3)   An application for permission to refer a sentencing case must—

      (a)   give details of—

            (i)   the defendant affected,

            (ii)   the date and place of the relevant Crown Court decision, and

            (iii)   the relevant verdict and sentencing;

      (b)   explain why that sentencing appears to the Attorney General unduly lenient, concisely outlining each argument in support; and

      (c)   include the application for permission to refer the case to the court.

(4)   A notice of reference of a sentencing case must—

      (a)   include the same details and explanation as the application for permission to refer the case;

      (b)   summarise the relevant facts; and

      (c)   identify any relevant authorities.

(5)   Where the court gives the Attorney General permission to refer a sentencing case, it may treat the application for permission as the notice of reference.

Amendment

1   Substituted by the Criminal Procedure (Amendment) Rules 2018, SI 2018/132, rr 2, 17(b).

[41.4][1]. Respondent's notice

(1)   [A defendant on whom the Attorney General serves a notice of reference][1] or an application for permission to refer a sentencing case may serve a respondent's notice, and must do so if—

      (a)   the defendant wants to make representations to the court; or

      (b)   the court so directs.

(2)   Such a defendant must serve the respondent's notice on—

      (a)   the Attorney General; and

      (b)   the Registrar.

(3)   Such a defendant must serve the respondent's notice—

      (a)   where the Attorney General refers a point of law, not more than 28 days after—

            (i)   the [Attorney][1] serves the reference, or

            (ii)   a direction to do so;

    (b)   where the Attorney General applies for permission to refer a sentencing case, not more than 14 days after—

        (i)   the [Attorney]¹ serves the application, or

        (ii)   a direction to do so.

(4)   Where the Attorney General refers a point of law, the respondent's notice must—

    [(a)   give the date on which the respondent was served with the notice of reference;]²

    [(b)]¹ identify each ground of opposition on which the respondent relies, numbering them consecutively (if there is more than one), concisely outlining each argument in support and identifying the Attorney General's ground or reason to which each relates;

    [(c)]¹ summarise any relevant facts not already summarised in the reference;

    [(d)]¹ identify any relevant authorities; and

    [(e)]¹ include or attach any application for the following, with reasons—

        (i)   an extension of time within which to serve the respondent's notice,

        (ii)   permission to attend a hearing that the respondent does not have a right to attend,

        (iii)   a direction to attend in person a hearing that the respondent could attend by live link, if the respondent is in custody.

(5)   Where the Attorney General applies for permission to refer a sentencing case, the respondent's notice must—

    [(a)   give the date on which the respondent was served with the application;]²

    [(b)]¹ say if the respondent wants to make representations at the hearing of the application or reference; and

    [(c)]¹ include or attach any application for the following, with reasons—

        (i)   an extension of time within which to serve the respondent's notice,

        (ii)   permission to attend a hearing that the respondent does not have a right to attend,

        (iii)   a direction to attend in person a hearing that the respondent could attend by live link, if the respondent is in custody.

Amendments

1   Substituted by the Criminal Procedure (Amendment) Rules 2018, SI 2018/132, rr 2, 17(d), (e) (i)-(iii), (v).

2   Inserted by the Criminal Procedure (Amendment) Rules 2018, SI 2018/132, rr 2, 17(e)(iv), (vi).

[41.5][1].   Variation or withdrawal of notice of reference or application for permission

(1)   This rule applies where the Attorney General wants to vary or withdraw—

    (a)   a notice of reference; or

    (b)   an application for permission to refer a sentencing case.

(2)   The Attorney General—

    (a)   may vary or withdraw the notice or application without the court's permission by serving notice on—

        (i)   the Registrar, and

        (ii)   the defendant

    before any hearing of the reference or application; but

    (b)   at any such hearing, may only vary or withdraw that notice or application with the court's permission.

Amendment

1   Substituted by the Criminal Procedure (Amendment) Rules 2018, SI 2018/132, rr 2, 17(d).

[41.6][1].   Right to attend hearing

(1)   A respondent who is in custody has a right to attend a hearing in public unless it is a hearing preliminary or incidental to a reference, including the hearing of an application for permission to refer a sentencing case.

(2)   The court or the Registrar may direct that such a respondent is to attend a hearing by live link.

[Note. See rule 36.6 (Hearings) and paragraphs 6 and 7 of Schedule 3 to the Criminal Justice Act 1988. Under paragraph 8 of that Schedule, the Court of Appeal may sentence in the absence of a defendant whose sentencing is referred.]

Amendment

1   Substituted by the Criminal Procedure (Amendment) Rules 2018, SI 2018/132, rr 2, 17(d).

[41.7][1].   Anonymity of defendant on reference of point of law

Where the Attorney General refers a point of law, the court must not allow anyone to identify the defendant during the proceedings unless the defendant gives permission.

Amendment

1   Substituted by the Criminal Procedure (Amendment) Rules 2018, SI 2018/132, rr 2, 17(d).

PART 42
APPEAL TO THE COURT OF APPEAL IN CONFISCATION AND RELATED PROCEEDINGS

General rules

42.1. Extension of time

(1) An application to extend the time limit for giving notice of application for permission to appeal under Part 2 of the Proceeds of Crime Act 2002 must—

   (a) be included in the notice of appeal; and

   (b) state the grounds for the application.

(2) The parties may not agree to extend any date or time limit set by this Part or by the Proceeds of Crime Act 2002 (Appeals under Part 2) Order 2003.

42.2. Other applications

Rule 39.3(2)(h) (Form of appeal notice) applies in relation to an application—

   (a) by a party to an appeal under Part 2 of the Proceeds of Crime Act 2002 that, under article 7 of The Proceeds of Crime Act 2002 (Appeals under Part 2) Order 2003, a witness be ordered to attend or that the evidence of a witness be received by the Court of Appeal; or

   (b) by the defendant to be given permission by the court to be present at proceedings for which permission is required under article 6 of the 2003 Order,

   as it applies in relation to applications under Part I of the Criminal Appeal Act 1968 and the form in which rule 39.3 requires notice to be given may be modified as necessary.

42.3. Examination of witness by court

Rule 36.7 (Notice of hearings and decisions) applies in relation to an order of the court under article 7 of the Proceeds of Crime Act 2002 (Appeals under Part 2) Order 2003 to require a person to attend for examination as it applies in relation to such an order of the court under Part I of the Criminal Appeal Act 1968.

42.4. Supply of documentary and other exhibits

Rule 36.11 (Registrar's duty to provide copy documents for appeal or reference) applies in relation to an appellant or respondent under Part 2 of the Proceeds of Crime Act 2002 as it applies in relation to an appellant and respondent under Part I of the Criminal Appeal Act 1968.

42.5.   Registrar's power to require information from court of trial

The Registrar may require the Crown Court to provide the Court of Appeal with any assistance or information which it requires for the purposes of exercising its jurisdiction under Part 2 of the Proceeds of Crime Act 2002, the Proceeds of Crime Act 2002 (Appeals under Part 2) Order 2003 or this Part.

42.6.   Hearing by single judge

Rule [36.6(6)]¹ (Hearings) applies in relation to a judge exercising any of the powers referred to in article 8 of the Proceeds of Crime Act 2002 (Appeals under Part 2) Order 2003 or the powers in rules 42.12(3) and (4) (Respondent's notice), 42.15(2) (Notice of appeal) and 42.16(6) (Respondent's notice), as it applies in relation to a judge exercising the powers referred to in section 31(2) of the Criminal Appeal Act 1968.

Amendment
1   Substituted by the Criminal Procedure (Amendment) Rules 2018, SI 2018/132, rr 2, 18(a).

42.7.   Determination by full court

Rule 36.5 (Renewing an application refused by a judge or the Registrar) applies where a single judge has refused an application by a party to exercise in that party's favour any of the powers listed in article 8 of the Proceeds of Crime Act 2002 (Appeals under Part 2) Order 2003, or the power in rule 42.12(3) or (4) as it applies where the judge has refused to exercise the powers referred to in section 31(2) of the Criminal Appeal Act 1968.

42.8.   Notice of determination

(1)   This rule applies where a single judge or the Court of Appeal has determined an application or appeal under the Proceeds of Crime Act 2002 (Appeals under Part 2) Order 2003 or under Part 2 of the Proceeds of Crime Act 2002.

(2)   The Registrar must, as soon as practicable, serve notice of the determination on all of the parties to the proceedings.

(3)   Where a single judge or the Court of Appeal has disposed of an application for permission to appeal or an appeal under section 31 of the 2002 Act, the Registrar must also, as soon as practicable, serve the order on a court officer of the court of trial and any magistrates' court responsible for enforcing any confiscation order which the Crown Court has made.

42.9.   Record of proceedings and transcripts

Rule 5.5 (Recording and transcription of proceedings in the Crown Court) and rule 36.9 (Duty of person transcribing proceedings in the Crown Court) apply in relation to proceedings in respect of which an appeal lies to the Court of

Appeal under Part 2 of the Proceeds of Crime Act 2002 as they apply in relation to proceedings in respect of which an appeal lies to the Court of Appeal under Part I of the Criminal Appeal Act 1968.

42.10.   Appeal to the Supreme Court

(1)   An application to the Court of Appeal for permission to appeal to the Supreme Court under Part 2 of the Proceeds of Crime Act 2002 must be made—

    (a)   orally after the decision of the Court of Appeal from which an appeal lies to the Supreme Court; or

    (b)   in the form set out in the Practice Direction, in accordance with article 12 of the Proceeds of Crime Act 2002 (Appeals under Part 2) Order 2003 and served on the Registrar.

(2)   The application may be abandoned at any time before it is heard by the Court of Appeal by serving notice in writing on the Registrar.

(3)   Rule [36.6(6)][1] (Hearings) applies in relation to a single judge exercising any of the powers referred to in article 15 of the 2003 Order, as it applies in relation to a single judge exercising the powers referred to in section 31(2) of the Criminal Appeal Act 1968.

(4)   Rule 36.5 (Renewing an application refused by a judge or the Registrar) applies where a single judge has refused an application by a party to exercise in that party's favour any of the powers listed in article 15 of the 2003 Order as they apply where the judge has refused to exercise the powers referred to in section 31(2) of the 1968 Act.

(5)   The form in which rule 36.5(2) requires an application to be made may be modified as necessary.

Amendment

1   Substituted by the Criminal Procedure (Amendment) Rules 2018, SI 2018/132, rr 2, 18(b).

Confiscation: appeal by prosecutor or by person with interest in property

42.11.   Notice of appeal

(1)   Where an appellant wishes to apply to the Court of Appeal for permission to appeal under section 31 of the Proceeds of Crime Act 2002, the appellant must serve a notice of appeal in the form set out in the Practice Direction on—

    (a)   the Crown Court officer; and

    (b)   the defendant.

(2)   When the notice of a prosecutor's appeal about a confiscation order is served on the defendant, it must be accompanied by a respondent's notice in the form set out in the Practice Direction for the defendant to complete and a notice which—

(a)   informs the defendant that the result of an appeal could be that the Court of Appeal would increase a confiscation order already imposed, make a confiscation order itself or direct the Crown Court to hold another confiscation hearing;

(b)   informs the defendant of any right under article 6 of the Proceeds of Crime Act 2002 (Appeals under Part 2) Order 2003 to be present at the hearing of the appeal, although in custody;

(c)   invites the defendant to serve any notice on the Registrar—

(i)   to apply to the Court of Appeal for permission to be present at proceedings for which such permission is required under article 6 of the 2003 Order, or

(ii)   to present any argument to the Court of Appeal on the hearing of the application or, if permission is given, the appeal, and whether the defendant wishes to present it in person or by means of a legal representative;

(d)   draws to the defendant's attention the effect of rule 42.4 (Supply of documentary and other exhibits); and

(e)   advises the defendant to consult a solicitor as soon as possible.

(3)   The appellant must provide the Crown Court officer with a certificate of service stating that the appellant has served the notice of appeal on the defendant in accordance with paragraph (1) or explaining why it has not been possible to do so.

42.12.   Respondent's notice

(1)   This rule applies where a defendant is served with a notice of appeal under rule 42.11.

(2)   If the defendant wishes to oppose the application for permission to appeal, the defendant must, not more than 14 days after service of the notice of appeal, serve on the Registrar and on the appellant a notice in the form set out in the Practice Direction—

(a)   stating the date on which the notice of appeal was served;

(b)   summarising the defendant's response to the arguments of the appellant; and

(c)   specifying the authorities which the defendant intends to cite.

(3)   The time for giving notice under this rule may be extended by the Registrar, a single judge or by the Court of Appeal.

(4)   Where the Registrar refuses an application under paragraph (3) for the extension of time, the defendant is entitled to have the application determined by a single judge.

(5)   Where a single judge refuses an application under paragraph (3) or (4) for the extension of time, the defendant is entitled to have the application determined by the Court of Appeal.

42.13.   Amendment and abandonment of appeal

(1)   The appellant may amend a notice of appeal served under rule 42.11 or abandon an appeal under section 31 of the Proceeds of Crime Act 2002—

(a)   without the permission of the court at any time before the Court of Appeal has begun hearing the appeal; and

(b)   with the permission of the court after the Court of Appeal has begun hearing the appeal,

by serving notice in writing on the Registrar.

(2)   Where the appellant serves a notice abandoning an appeal under paragraph (1), the appellant must send a copy of it to—

(a)   the defendant;

(b)   a court officer of the court of trial; and

(c)   the magistrates' court responsible for enforcing any confiscation order which the Crown Court has made.

(3)   Where the appellant serves a notice amending a notice of appeal under paragraph (1), the appellant must send a copy of it to the defendant.

(4)   Where an appeal is abandoned under paragraph (1), the application for permission to appeal or appeal must be treated, for the purposes of section 85 of the 2002 Act (Conclusion of proceedings), as having been refused or dismissed by the Court of Appeal.

Appeal about compliance, restraint or receivership order

42.14.   Permission to appeal

(1)   Permission to appeal to the Court of Appeal under section 13B, section 43 or section 65 of the Proceeds of Crime Act 2002 may only be given where—

(a)   the Court of Appeal considers that the appeal would have a real prospect of success; or

(b)   there is some other compelling reason why the appeal should be heard.

(2)   An order giving permission to appeal may limit the issues to be heard and be made subject to conditions.

42.15. Notice of appeal

(1)   Where an appellant wishes to apply to the Court of Appeal for permission to appeal under section 13B, 43 or 65 of the Proceeds of Crime Act 2002 Act, the appellant must serve a notice of appeal in the form set out in the Practice Direction on the Crown Court officer.

(2)   Unless the Registrar, a single judge or the Court of Appeal directs otherwise, the appellant must serve the notice of appeal, accompanied by a respondent's notice in the form set out in the Practice Direction for the respondent to complete, on—

    (a)   each respondent;

    (b)   any person who holds realisable property to which the appeal relates; and

    (c)   any other person affected by the appeal,

as soon as practicable and in any event not later than 5 business days after the notice of appeal is served on the Crown Court officer.

(3)   The appellant must serve the following documents with the notice of appeal—

    (a)   four additional copies of the notice of appeal for the Court of Appeal;

    (b)   four copies of any skeleton argument;

    (c)   one sealed copy and four unsealed copies of any order being appealed;

    (d)   four copies of any witness statement or affidavit in support of the application for permission to appeal;

    (e)   four copies of a suitable record of the reasons for judgment of the Crown Court; and

    (f)   four copies of the bundle of documents used in the Crown Court proceedings from which the appeal lies.

(4)   Where it is not possible to serve all of the documents referred to in paragraph (3), the appellant must indicate which documents have not yet been served and the reasons why they are not currently available.

(5)   The appellant must provide the Crown Court officer with a certificate of service stating that the notice of appeal has been served on each respondent in accordance with paragraph (2) and including full details of each respondent or explaining why it has not been possible to effect service.

42.16. Respondent's notice

(1) This rule applies to an appeal under section 13B, 43 or 65 of the Proceeds of Crime Act 2002.

(2) A respondent may serve a respondent's notice on the Registrar.

(3) A respondent who—

(a) is seeking permission to appeal from the Court of Appeal; or

(b) wishes to ask the Court of Appeal to uphold the decision of the Crown Court for reasons different from or additional to those given by the Crown Court,

must serve a respondent's notice on the Registrar.

(4) A respondent's notice must be in the form set out in the Practice Direction and where the respondent seeks permission to appeal to the Court of Appeal it must be requested in the respondent's notice.

(5) A respondent's notice must be served on the Registrar not later than 14 days after—

(a) the date the respondent is served with notification that the Court of Appeal has given the appellant permission to appeal; or

(b) the date the respondent is served with notification that the application for permission to appeal and the appeal itself are to be heard together.

(6) Unless the Registrar, a single judge or the Court of Appeal directs otherwise, the respondent serving a respondent's notice must serve the notice on the appellant and any other respondent—

(a) as soon as practicable; and

(b) in any event not later than 5 business days,

after it is served on the Registrar.

42.17. Amendment and abandonment of appeal

(1) The appellant may amend a notice of appeal served under rule 42.15 or abandon an appeal under section 13B, 43 or 65 of the Proceeds of Crime Act 2002—

(a) without the permission of the court at any time before the Court of Appeal has begun hearing the appeal; and

(b) with the permission of the court after the Court of Appeal has begun hearing the appeal,

by serving notice in writing on the Registrar.

(2) Where the appellant serves a notice under paragraph (1), the appellant must send a copy of it to each respondent.

42.18. Stay

Unless the Court of Appeal or the Crown Court orders otherwise, an appeal under section 13B, 43 or 65 of the Proceeds of Crime Act 2002 does not operate as a stay of any order or decision of the Crown Court.

42.19. Striking out appeal notices and setting aside or imposing conditions on permission to appeal

(1)   The Court of Appeal may—

  (a)   strike out the whole or part of a notice of appeal served under rule 42.15; or

  (b)   impose or vary conditions upon which an appeal under section 13B, 43 or 65 of the Proceeds of Crime Act 2002 may be brought.

(2)   The Court of Appeal may only exercise its powers under paragraph (1) where there is a compelling reason for doing so.

(3)   Where a party is present at the hearing at which permission to appeal was given, that party may not subsequently apply for an order that the Court of Appeal exercise its powers under paragraph (1)(b).

42.20. Hearing of appeals

(1)   This rule applies to appeals under section 13B, 43 or 65 of the Proceeds of Crime Act 2002.

(2)   Every appeal must be limited to a review of the decision of the Crown Court unless the Court of Appeal considers that in the circumstances of an individual appeal it would be in the interests of justice to hold a re-hearing.

(3)   The Court of Appeal may allow an appeal where the decision of the Crown Court was—

  (a)   wrong; or

  (b)   unjust because of a serious procedural or other irregularity in the proceedings in the Crown Court.

(4)   The Court of Appeal may draw any inference of fact which it considers justified on the evidence.

(5)   At the hearing of the appeal a party may not rely on a matter not contained in that party's notice of appeal unless the Court of Appeal gives permission.

PART 43
APPEAL OR REFERENCE TO THE SUPREME COURT

43.1. When this Part applies

(1)   This Part applies where—

    (a)   a party wants to appeal to the Supreme Court after—

        (i)   an application to the Court of Appeal to which Part 27 applies (Retrial following acquittal), or

        (ii)   an appeal to the Court of Appeal to which applies Part 37 (Appeal to the Court of Appeal against ruling at preparatory hearing), Part 38 (Appeal to the Court of Appeal against ruling adverse to prosecution), or Part 39 (Appeal to the Court of Appeal about conviction or sentence); or

    (b)   a party wants to refer a case to the Supreme Court after a reference to the Court of Appeal to which Part 41 applies (Reference to the Court of Appeal of point of law or unduly lenient sentencing).

(2)   A reference to an 'appellant' in this Part is a reference to such a party.

[Note. Under section 33 of the Criminal Appeal Act 1968, a party may appeal to the Supreme Court from a decision of the Court of Appeal on—

    (a)   an application to the court under section 76 of the Criminal Justice Act 2003 (prosecutor's application for retrial after acquittal for serious offence). See also Part 27.

    (b)   an appeal to the court under—

        (i)   section 9 of the Criminal Justice Act 1987 or section 35 of the Criminal Procedure and Investigations Act 1996 (appeal against order at preparatory hearing). See also Part 37.

        (ii)   section 47 of the Criminal Justice Act 2003 (appeal against order for non-jury trial after jury tampering.) See also Part 37.

        (iii)   Part 9 of the Criminal Justice Act 2003 (prosecutor's appeal against adverse ruling). See also Part 38.

        (iv)   Part 1 of the Criminal Appeal Act 1968 (defendant's appeal against conviction, sentence, etc.). See also Part 39.

Under section 13 of the Administration of Justice Act 1960, a person found to be in contempt of court may appeal to the Supreme Court from a decision of the Court of Appeal on an appeal to the court under that section. See also Part 39.

Under article 12 of the Criminal Justice Act 2003 (Mandatory Life Sentence: Appeals in Transitional Cases) Order 2005, a party may appeal to the Supreme Court from a decision of the Court of Appeal on an appeal to the court under paragraph 14 of Schedule 22 to the Criminal Justice Act 2003 (appeal against minimum term review decision). See also Part 39.

Under article 15 of the Serious Organised Crime and Police Act 2005 (Appeals under Section 74) Order 2006, a party may appeal to the Supreme Court from a decision of the Court of Appeal on an appeal to the court under section 74 of the Serious Organised Crime and Police Act 2005 (appeal against sentence review decision). See also Part 39.

Under section 24 of the Serious Crime Act 2007, a party may appeal to the Supreme Court from a decision of the Court of Appeal on an appeal to that court under that section (appeal about a serious crime prevention order). See also Part 39.

Under section 36(3) of the Criminal Justice Act 1972, the Court of Appeal may refer to the Supreme Court a point of law referred by the Attorney General to the court. See also Part 41.

Under section 36(5) of the Criminal Justice Act 1988, a party may refer to the Supreme Court a sentencing decision referred by the Attorney General to the court. See also Part 41.

Under section 33(3) of the Criminal Appeal Act 1968, there is no appeal to the Supreme Court—

(a)   from a decision of the Court of Appeal on an appeal under section 14A(5A) of the Football Spectators Act 1989 (prosecutor's appeal against failure to make football banning order). See Part 39.

(b)   from a decision of the Court of Appeal on an appeal under section 159(1) of the Criminal Justice Act 1988 (appeal about reporting or public access restriction). See Part 40.

The rules in Part 36 (Appeal to the Court of Appeal: general rules) also apply where this Part applies.]

43.2.   Application for permission or reference

(1)   An appellant must—

(a)   apply orally to the Court of Appeal—

(i)   for permission to appeal or to refer a sentencing case, or

(ii)   to refer a point of law

immediately after the court gives the reasons for its decision; or

(b)   apply in writing and serve the application on the Registrar and every other party not more than—

     (i)   14 days after the court gives the reasons for its decision if that decision was on a sentencing reference to which [Part 41]¹ applies (Attorney General's reference of sentencing case), or

     (ii)   28 days after the court gives those reasons in any other case.

(2)   An application for permission to appeal or to refer a sentencing case must—

    (a)   identify the point of law of general public importance that the appellant wants the court to certify is involved in the decision; and

    (b)   give reasons why—

     (i)   that point of law ought to be considered by the Supreme Court, and

     (ii)   the court ought to give permission to appeal.

(3)   An application to refer a point of law must give reasons why that point ought to be considered by the Supreme Court.

(4)   An application must include or attach any application for the following, with reasons—

    (a)   an extension of time within which to make the application for permission or for a reference;

    (b)   bail pending appeal;

    (c)   permission to attend any hearing in the Supreme Court, if the appellant is in custody.

(5)   A written application must be in the form set out in the Practice Direction.

[Note. In some legislation, including the Criminal Appeal Act 1968, permission to appeal is described as 'leave to appeal'.

Under the provisions listed in the note to rule 43.1, except section 36(3) of the Criminal Justice Act 1972 (Attorney General's reference of point of law), an appellant needs permission to appeal or to refer a sentencing case. Under those provisions, the Court of Appeal must not give permission unless it first certifies that—

    (a)   a point of law of general public importance is involved in the decision, and

    (b)   it appears to the court that the point is one which the Supreme Court ought to consider.

If the Court of Appeal gives such a certificate but refuses permission, an appellant may apply for such permission to the Supreme Court.

Under section 36(3) of the Criminal Justice Act 1972 an appellant needs no such permission. The Court of Appeal may refer the point of law to the Supreme Court, or may refuse to do so.

For the power of the court or the Registrar to shorten or extend a time limit, see rule 36.3. The time limit in this rule—

(a) for applying for permission to appeal under section 33 of the Criminal Appeal Act 1968 (28 days) is prescribed by section 34 of that Act. That time limit may be extended but not shortened by the court. But it may be extended on an application by a prosecutor only after an application to which Part 27 applies (Retrial after acquittal).

(b) for applying for permission to refer a case under section 36(5) of the Criminal Justice Act 1988 (Attorney General's reference of sentencing decision: 14 days) is prescribed by paragraph 4 of Schedule 3 to that Act. That time limit may be neither extended nor shortened.

(c) for applying for permission to appeal under article 12 of the Criminal Justice Act 2003 (Mandatory Life Sentence: Appeals in Transitional Cases) Order 2005 (28 days) is prescribed by article 13 of that Order. That time limit may be extended but not shortened.

(d) for applying for permission to appeal under article 15 of the Serious Organised Crime and Police Act 2005 (Appeals under Section 74) Order 2006 (28 days) is prescribed by article 16 of that Order. That time limit may be extended but not shortened.

For the power of the Court of Appeal to grant bail pending appeal to the Supreme Court, see—

(a) section 36 of the Criminal Appeal Act 1968;

(b) article 18 of the Serious Organised Crime and Police Act 2005 (Appeals under Section 74) Order 2006.

For the right of an appellant in custody to attend a hearing in the Supreme Court, see—

(a) section 38 of the Criminal Appeal Act 1968;

(b) paragraph 9 of Schedule 3 to the Criminal Justice Act 1988;

(c) article 15 of the Criminal Justice Act 2003 (Mandatory Life Sentences: Appeals in Transitional Cases) Order 2005;

(d) article 20 of the Serious Organised Crime and Police Act 2005 (Appeals under Section 74) Order 2006.]

Amendment

1   Substituted by the Criminal Procedure (Amendment) Rules 2016, SI 2016/120, rr 2, 13.

43.3. Determination of detention pending appeal, etc.

On an application for permission to appeal, the Court of Appeal must—

    (a)   decide whether to order the detention of a defendant who would have been liable to be detained but for the decision of the court; and

    (b)   determine any application for—

        (i)   bail pending appeal,

        (ii)   permission to attend any hearing in the Supreme Court, or

        (iii)   a representation order.

[Note. For the liability of a defendant to be detained pending a prosecutor's appeal to the Supreme Court and afterwards, see—

    (a)   section 37 of the Criminal Appeal Act 1968;

    (b)   article 19 of the Serious Organised Crime and Police Act 2005 (Appeals under Section 74) Order 2006.

For the grant of legal aid for proceedings in the Supreme Court, see sections 14, 16 and 19 of the Legal Aid, Sentencing and Punishment of Offenders Act 2012.]

43.4. Bail pending appeal

Rules 39.8 (Application for bail pending appeal or retrial), 39.9 (Conditions of bail pending appeal or re-trial) and 39.10 (Forfeiture of a recognizance given as a condition of bail) apply.

PART 44
REQUEST TO THE EUROPEAN COURT FOR A PRELIMINARY RULING

44.1. When this Part applies

This Part applies where the court can request the Court of Justice of the European Union ('the European Court') to give a preliminary ruling, under Article 267 of the Treaty on the Functioning of the European Union.

[Note. Under Article 267, if a court of a Member State considers that a decision on the question is necessary to enable it to give judgment, it may request the European Court to give a preliminary ruling concerning—

    (a)   the interpretation of the Treaty on European Union, or of the Treaty on the Functioning of the European Union;

    (b)   the validity and interpretation of acts of the institutions, bodies, offices or agencies of the Union.]

44.2.   Preparation of request

(1)   The court may—

    (a)   make an order for the submission of a request—

        (i)   on application by a party, or

        (ii)   on its own initiative;

    (b)   give directions for the preparation of the terms of such a request.

(2)   The court must—

    (a)   include in such a request—

        (i)   the identity of the court making the request,

        (ii)   the parties' identities,

        (iii)   a statement of whether a party is in custody,

        (iv)   a succinct statement of the question on which the court seeks the ruling of the European Court,

        (v)   a succinct statement of any opinion on the answer that the court may have expressed in any judgment that it has delivered,

        (vi)   a summary of the nature and history of the proceedings, including the salient facts and an indication of whether those facts are proved, admitted or assumed,

        (vii)   the relevant rules of national law,

        (viii)   a summary of the relevant contentions of the parties,

        (ix)   an indication of the provisions of European Union law that the European Court is asked to interpret, and

        (x)   an explanation of why a ruling of the European Court is requested;

    (b)   express the request in terms that can be translated readily into other languages; and

    (c)   set out the request in a schedule to the order.

44.3.   Submission of request

(1)   The court officer must serve the order for the submission of the request on the Senior Master of the Queen's Bench Division of the High Court.

(2)   The Senior Master must—

    (a)   submit the request to the European Court; but

(b)   unless the court otherwise directs, postpone the submission of the request until—

    (i)   the time for any appeal against the order has expired, and

    (ii)   any appeal against the order has been determined.

Appendix C

A Guide to Commencing Proceedings in the Court of Appeal (Criminal Division)

CONTENTS

A. **Applications for Leave to Appeal Conviction, Sentence and Confiscation orders**
A1. Advice and Assistance
A2. Lodging Form NG and grounds of appeal
A3. Form NG and grounds of appeal
A4. Applications by fresh legal representatives
A5. Specific grounds of appeal
A6. Time Limits
A7. Transcripts and notes of evidence
A8. Perfection of grounds of appeal
A9. Respondent's Notice
A10. Referral by the Registrar
A11. Oral applications for leave to appeal
A12. Powers of the single Judge
A13. Bail pending appeal (CrimPR 39.8)
A14. Funding for grant of leave or reference to full Court
A15. Refusal by the single Judge
A16. Directions for loss of time
A17. Abandonment
A18. Case Management duties

B. **Interlocutory Appeals against rulings in Preparatory Hearings**

C. **Appeals by a Prosecutor against a "terminating" ruling**

D. **Other Appeals**
D1. Prosecution appeal against the making of a confiscation order or where the Court declines to make one (save on reconsideration of benefit)
D2. Prosecution and third party appeal against a determination, under s.10A Proceeds of Crime Act 2002, of the extent of the defendant's interest in property
D3. Appeal in relation to a restraint order

D4.   Appeal in relation to a receivership order
D5.   Appeal against an order of the Crown Court in the exercise of its jurisdiction to punish for contempt – usually a finding of contempt or sentence for contempt
D6.   Appeal against a minimum term set or reviewed by a High Court Judge
D7.   Attorney General's reference of an unduly lenient sentence
D8.   Attorney General's reference of a point of law on an acquittal
D9.   Appeal against a finding of unfitness to plead or a finding that the accused did the act or made the omission charged
D10.   Appeal against a verdict of not guilty by reason of insanity
D11.   Appeal against the order following a verdict of not guilty by reason of insanity or a finding of unfitness to plead
D12.   Appeal against review of sentence
D13.   Appeal against an order for trial by jury of sample counts
D14.   Appeal against an order relating to a trial to be conducted without a jury where there is a *danger* of jury tampering
D15.   Appeal against an order that a trial should continue without a jury or a new trial take place without a jury *after* jury tampering
D16.   Appeal against orders restricting or preventing reports or restricting public access
D17.   Appeal against a wasted costs order
D18.   Appeal relating to Serious Crime Prevention Orders
D19.   Appeal against the non-making of a football banning order

E.   Application for a Retrial for a Serious Offence
E1.   Application by a prosecutor to quash an acquittal and seek a retrial of aqualifying offence
E2.   Application by a prosecutor for a determination whether a foreign acquittal is a bar to a trial and if so, an order that it not be a bar
E3.   Application for restrictions on publication relating to an application under s.76
E4.   Representation orders

A.   APPLICATIONS FOR LEAVE TO APPEAL CONVICTION, SENTENCE AND CONFISCATION ORDERS

A1.   Advice and Assistance

A1-1   Provision for advice and assistance on appeal is included in the trial representation order issued by the Crown Court. Solicitors should not wait to be asked for advice by the defendant. Immediately following the conclusion of the case, the legal representatives should see the defendant and advocates should express orally a view as to the prospects of a successful appeal (whether against conviction or sentence or both). If there are reasonable grounds, grounds of appeal should be drafted, signed and sent to instructing solicitors as soon as possible, bearing in mind the time limits that apply to lodging an appeal (*see section A6. Time Limits*). Solicitors should immediately send a copy of the documents received from the advocate to the defendant.

A1-2   Prior to the lodging of the notice and grounds of appeal by service of Form NG, the Registrar has no power to grant a representation order. The Crown Court can only amend a representation order in favour of fresh legal representatives if advice on appeal has not been given by trial representatives and it is necessary and reasonable for another legal representative to be instructed. Where advice on appeal has been given by trial legal representatives, application for funding prior to the lodging of the notice and grounds of appeal may only be made to the Legal Aid Authority (LAA).

A1-3   Once the Form NG has been lodged, the Registrar is the relevant authority for decisions about whether an individual qualifies for representation for the purposes of criminal proceedings before the Court of Appeal Criminal Division (ss.16(1) & 19(1) Legal Aid, Sentencing and Punishment of Offenders Act 2012 and Reg.8 Criminal Legal Aid (Determinations by a Court and Choice of Representative) Regulations 2013).

A1-4   Where, in order to settle grounds of appeal, work of an exceptional nature is contemplated or where the expense will be great, legal representatives should not contact the LAA for funding but should submit a Form NG with provisional grounds of appeal and with a note to the Registrar requesting a representation order to cover the specific work considered necessary to enable final grounds of appeal to be settled. The Registrar will then consider whether it is appropriate to grant funding for this purpose.

A2.   Lodging Form NG and grounds of appeal

A2-1   In respect of applications lodged **before 1 October 2018**, where the advocate has advised an appeal and the defendant's instructions have been obtained, the solicitor should lodge Form NG and signed grounds of appeal at the **Crown Court** where the defendant appeared accompanied by such other forms as may be appropriate.

A2-2   Following a change in procedure, which comes into force **on the 1 October 2018**, Form NG, signed grounds of appeal and any such accompanying forms must be **lodged directly on the Registrar of Criminal Appeals** (CrimPR 39.2). A separate Form NG should be completed for each substantive application which is being made. Each application (conviction, sentence and confiscation order) has its own Form NG and must be drafted and lodged as a stand-alone application (CPD IX Appeal 39C).

A2-3   Electronic service at criminalappealoffice.applications@hmcts.x.gsi. gov.uk is encouraged, with large attachments being sent in clearly marked separate emails. Service will be accepted by post at the Criminal Appeal Office, Royal Courts of Justice, Strand, London, WC2A 2LL. Representatives must not lodge Form NG and grounds of appeal on to the Digital Case System (DCS), as this will not alert the Criminal Appeal Office ("CAO") and service will not be effected. However, should the grounds of appeal rely upon trial documents that are already uploaded to the DCS, advocates are encouraged to identify the location of the document on the DCS in their grounds of appeal, which can then be obtained by the CAO. If Form NG and grounds of appeal are lodged with the Crown Court on or after the 1 October 2018, service will not be effected and the Crown Court will send the documents back to the representatives.

A2-4   Direct Lodgment on the Registrar of Criminal Appeals applies to all applications to appeal conviction, sentence and confiscation falling within Part 39 of the CrimPR (*see Section D. Other Appeals for specific information on where to lodge applications in relation to other types of appeal*).

A2.5   It should be noted that Form NG and grounds of appeal are required to be served within the relevant time limit in all cases whether or not leave to appeal is required (e.g. where a trial Judge's certificate has been granted). However, on a reference by the Criminal Cases Review Commission (CCRC), if no Form NG and grounds are served within the required period, then the reference shall be treated as the appeal notice (CrimPR 39.5 (2)).

A3.   *Form NG and grounds of appeal*

A3-1   Grounds must be settled with sufficient particularity to enable the Registrar, and subsequently the Court, to identify clearly the matters relied upon. A mere formula such as "the conviction is unsafe" or "the sentence is in all the circumstances too severe" will be deemed ineffective.

A3-2   CrimPR 39.3 (1) sets out the information that must be contained in the appeal notice. The notice must:

(a)   Specify:

    (i)   the conviction, verdict or finding,

    (ii)   the sentence, or

    (iii)   the order, or the failure to make an order

    about which the appellant wants to appeal;

(b)   identify each ground of appeal on which the appellant relies (and see paragraph (2));

(c)   identify the transcript that the appellant thinks the Court will need, if the appellant wants to appeal against a conviction (*see section A7. Transcripts and notes of evidence*);

(d)   identify the relevant sentencing powers of the Crown Court, if sentence is inissue;

(e)   include or attach any application for the following, with reasons–

       (i)   permission to appeal, if the appellant needs the court's permission,

       (ii)   an extension of time within which to serve the appeal notice,

       (iii)   bail pending appeal,

       (iv)   a direction to attend in person a hearing that the appellant could attend by live link, if the appellant is in custody,

       (v)   the introduction of evidence, including hearsay evidence and evidence of bad character,

       (vi)   an order requiring a witness to attend court,

       (vii)   a direction for special measures for a witness,

       (viii)   a direction for special measures for the giving of evidence by the appellant;

(f)   identify any other document or thing that the appellant thinks the Court will need to decide the appeal.

A3-3   The grounds of appeal should set out the relevant facts and nature of the proceedings concisely in one all-encompassing document, not separate grounds of appeal and advice (CPD IX Appeal 39C). Pursuant to CrimPR 39.3(2) the grounds must:

(a)   include in no more than the first two pages a summary of the grounds that makes what then follows easy to understand;

(b)   in each ground of appeal identify the event or decision to which that ground relates;

(c)   in each ground of appeal summarise the facts relevant to that ground, but only to the extent necessary to make clear what is in issue;

(d)   concisely outline each argument in relation to each ground;

(e)   number each ground consecutively if there is more than one;

(f)   identify any relevant authority and-

       (i)   state the proposition of law that the authority demonstrates, and

       (ii)   identify the parts of the authority that support that proposition; and

(g)   where the Criminal Cases Review Commission refers a case to the court, explain how each ground of appeal relates (if it does) to the reasons for the reference.

A3-4   The intended readership of this document is the Court and not the lay or professional client. Its purpose is to enable the single Judge to grasp quickly the facts and issues in the case. In appropriate cases, draft grounds of appeal may be perfected before submission to the single Judge. A **separate** list of authorities must be provided which should contain the appellant's name and refer to the relevant paragraph numbers in each authority (CPD XII General Application D1) *(see section A8-5)*.

A3-5   Failure to comply with the requirements in CrimPR 39 and the CPD referred to above, will result in a direction from the Registrar that the defects be remedied prior to the case being allocated to a single Judge. Failure to do so may be brought to the attention of the single Judge and/or full Court and legal representatives may be personally required to explain the reasons for non-compliance.

A3-6   Advocates should not settle or sign grounds unless they consider that they are properly arguable. An advocate should not settle grounds they cannot support because they are "instructed" to do so by a defendant.

A4.   *Applications by fresh legal representatives*

A4-1   In all cases where fresh solicitors or fresh advocates are instructed, who did not act for the appellant at trial, it is necessary for the fresh solicitors or advocate to approach the solicitors and/or advocate who previously acted to ensure that the facts upon which the grounds of appeal are premised are correct, unless there are exceptional circumstances and good and compelling reasons not to do so. Such exceptional circumstances would likely be very rare (R v McCook [2014] EWCA Crim 734; [2016] 2 Cr App R 30). Where necessary, further steps should be taken to obtain objective and independent evidence to establish the factual basis for the appeal (R v Lee [2014] EWCA Crim 2928). The duty to make proper and diligent enquiries of previous representatives is not restricted to cases where criticism is being made of the trial representatives. It extends to all cases where there are fresh representatives acting (R v McGill & others [2017] EWCA Crim 1228).

A4-2   In cases where fresh representatives seek to adduce fresh evidence that was not adduced at trial, not only will the fresh representatives be required to comply with their duties pursuant to McCook; but the Registrar will usually also instigate the "waiver of privilege" procedure or require written reasons as to why the procedure should not be instigated (R v Singh [2017] EWCA Crim 466).

A4-3   Where a ground of appeal by fresh representatives criticises trial advocates and/or trial solicitors and in any other circumstance the Registrar considers necessary as set out above, the Registrar will instigate the waiver of privilege procedure. The appellant will be asked to waive privilege in respect of instructions to and advice at trial from legal representatives. If the appellant does waive privilege, the grounds of appeal are sent to the appropriate trial representative(s) and they are invited to respond. Any response will be sent to the appellant and his fresh legal representatives for comment. All of these documents will be sent to the single Judge when considering the application for leave. If the criticism is implicit, the Registrar may still instigate the procedure or he will refer the decision whether to instigate the procedure to a single Judge (R v JH [2014] EWCA Crim 2618). The single Judge may draw inferences from any failure to participate in the process. Waiver of privilege is a procedure that should be instigated by the Registrar and not by fresh legal representatives. However, if it is clear that the procedure will need to be instigated, the fresh representatives should lodge a signed waiver of privilege with the grounds of appeal (and any fresh evidence) but go no further.

A5.   Specific grounds of appeal

A5-1.   Applications to call fresh evidence

A5-1.1   Where grounds of appeal rely upon fresh evidence that was not adduced at trial, an application pursuant to s. 23 Criminal Appeals Act 1968 must be made. If the fresh evidence is provided by a witness, representatives should obtain a statement from the witness in the form prescribed by s9 of the Criminal Justice Act 1967. If the fresh evidence is documentary or real evidence, the representatives should obtain statements from all those involved formally exhibiting the evidence. A Form W should be lodged in respect of each witness dealing with the fresh evidence. The Form W should indicate whether there is an application for a witness order. The Registrar or single Judge may direct the issue of a witness order but only the Court hearing the appeal may give leave for a witness to be called and then formally receive the evidence under s23 of the Criminal Appeal Act 1968.

A5-1.2   A supporting witness statement (in s9 form), or an affidavit from the appellant's solicitor must accompany the fresh evidence and Form W(s), setting out why the evidence was not available at trial and how it has come to light (Gogana The Times 12/07/1999). This will implicitly require fresh representatives to comply with McCook (*see section A4. Applications by fresh legal representatives*).

A5-2.   Insufficient weight given to assistance to prosecution authorities

Where a ground of appeal against sentence is that the Judge has given insufficient weight to the assistance given to the prosecution authorities, the "text" which had been prepared for the sentencing Judge is obtained by the Registrar. Grounds of appeal should be drafted in an anodyne form with a note to the Registrar alerting him to the existence of a "text". The CAO will obtain the "text" and the single Judge will have seen it when considering leave as will the full Court before the appeal hearing and it need not be alluded to in open Court.

A5-3. Applications based on a change in law

A5-3.1 If an application to appeal which is based on a change in law is lodged within time, (*see A6. Time Limits*) the test to be applied by the Court of Appeal is whether the conviction is unsafe (R v Johnson & Ors [2016] EWCA Crim 1613).

A5-3.2 If an application which is based on a change in law is lodged outside the time limits, exceptional leave will be required. Exceptional leave will only be granted if the applicant would otherwise suffer "substantial injustice" due to the change in law. Grounds of appeal should therefore set out why the substantial injustice test is met (R v Johnson & Ors [2016] EWCA Crim 1613). For examples of how the Court of Appeal has applied these principles see: R v Uthayakumar [2014] EWCA Crim 123 and R v Ordu [2017] EWCA Crim 4.

A6. Time Limits

A6-1 Notice and grounds should be lodged within 28 days from the date of conviction, sentence, verdict, finding or decision that is being appealed (s. 18 Criminal Appeal Act 1968 and CrimPR 39.2(1)). On a reference by the CCRC, Form NG and grounds should be served on the Registrar not more than 28 days after the Registrar has served notice that the CCRC has referred a conviction or sentence (CrimPR 39.2 (2)).

A6-2 Where sentences were passed on different dates there may be two appeals against sentence. For example, there may be an appeal against a custodial term and an appeal against a confiscation order (R v Neal [1992] 2 Cr App R (S) 352).

A6-3 An application for an extension of the 28 day period in which to give notice of an application must always be supported by details of the delay and the reasons for it (R v Wilson [2016] EWCA Crim 65). Often a chronology will assist. It is not enough merely to tick the relevant box on the Form NG.

A6-4 For out of time applications based on a change in law see A5-3. above.

A6-5 Applications for an extension of time should be submitted when the application for leave to appeal against either conviction or sentence is made and not in advance. Notwithstanding the terms of s18 (3) Criminal Appeal Act 1968, it has long been the practice of the Registrar to require the extension of time application to be made at the time of service of the notice and grounds of appeal. This practice is now reflected in CrimPR 36.4 and 39.3(2)(h)(ii).

A7. Transcripts and notes of evidence

A7-1   In publicly funded conviction cases, transcripts of the summing up and proceedings up to and including verdict are obtained as a matter of course. There is an obligation under CrimPR 39.3(2)(c) for advocates to identify any further transcript which they consider the Court will need and to provide a note of dates and times to enable an order to be placed with the transcription company. This is particularly important where there have been early directions and/or a split summing-up. Whether or not any further transcript is required is a matter for the judgment of the Registrar or his staff. Transcripts of evidence are not usually ordered; it may be appropriate for the advocate to provide an agreed note of evidence.

A7-2   In sentence cases, transcripts of the prosecution opening of facts on a guilty plea and the Judge's observations on passing sentence are usually obtained. The Registrar will also obtain the relevant transcript in an application for leave to appeal against a confiscation order, an interlocutory appeal from a preparatory hearing or any other appeal providing the application has not been made by the prosecution.

A7-3   A transcript should only be requested if it is essential for the proper conduct of the appeal in light of the grounds. If the Registrar and the advocate are unable to agree the extent of the transcript to be obtained, the Registrar may refer that matter to a Judge.

A7-4   In certain circumstances the costs of unnecessary transcripts may be ordered to be paid by the appellant. Where a transcript is obtained otherwise than through the Registrar, the cost may be disallowed on taxation of public funding.

A7-5   If an appellant is paying privately for his legal representation, an order for transcripts should be placed directly with the transcription company and a copy provided to the Registrar upon receipt. If the Registrar has already obtained transcripts in a private case, the appellant's legal representatives will be required to pay the cost of the transcripts before they are released to them.

A8. Perfection of grounds of appeal

A8-1   The purpose of perfection is (a) to save valuable judicial time by enabling the Court to identify at once the relevant parts of the transcript and (b) to give the advocate the opportunity to reconsider the original grounds in the light of the transcript. Perfected grounds should consist of a fresh document which supersedes the original grounds of appeal and contains *inter alia* references by page number and letter (or paragraph number) to all relevant passages in the transcript.

A8-2   In conviction or confiscation appeals, the Registrar will almost certainly invite the advocate to perfect grounds to assist the single Judge or full Court. As a general rule, the advocate will not be invited to perfect the grounds of appeal in a sentence case. Where an advocate indicates a wish to perfect grounds of appeal against sentence, the Registrar will consider the request and will only invite perfection where he considers it necessary for the assistance of the single Judge or full Court.

A8-3   If perfection is appropriate, the advocate will be sent a copy of the transcript and asked to perfect the grounds, usually within 14 days. In the absence of any response from the advocate, the existing notice and grounds of appeal will be placed before the single Judge or the Court without further notice. If an advocate does not wish to perfect the grounds, a note to that effect will ensure that the case is not unnecessarily delayed.

A8-4   If, having considered the transcript, the advocate is of the opinion that there are no valid grounds, the reasons should be set out in a further advice and sent to his instructing solicitors. The Registrar should be informed that this has been done, but the advocate should not send the Registrar a copy of that advice. Solicitors should send a copy to the appellant and obtain instructions, at the same time explaining that if the appellant persists with his application the Court may consider whether to make a loss of time order.

A8-5   Advocates should identify any relevant authorities (CrimPR 39.3(2) (g)) and submit a separate list of authorities with the perfected grounds of appeal and include copies of any unreported authorities.

A9.   Respondent's Notice

A9-1   The Criminal Procedure Rules provide for the service of a Respondent's Notice. Pursuant to CrimPR 39.6(1) the Registrar may serve the appeal notice on any party directly affected by the appeal (usually the prosecution) and must do so in a CCRC case. That party may then serve a Respondent's Notice if it wishes to make representations and must do so if the Registrar so directs (CrimPR 39.6(2)(b)). If directed, the Respondent's Notice should be served within 14 days (CrimPR 39.6(4)(a)). However, unless the case is urgent (in which case the Registrar may impose a deadline shorter than 14 days), 21 days is normally allowed for service. The Respondent's Notice should be served on the Registrar and any other party on whom the Registrar served the appeal notice.

A9-2   The Respondent's Notice must be in the specified Form RN and should set out the grounds of opposition (CrimPR 39.6(5)) including the information set out in CrimPR 39.6(6).

A9-3   In practice, this procedure primarily applies prior to consideration of leave by the single Judge. However, a Respondent's Notice may be sought at any time in the proceedings including at the direction of the single Judge. The Attorney General and the Registrar, following consultation with representatives from the Crown Prosecution Service (CPS) and the Revenue and Customs Prosecution Office (RCPO), have agreed guidance on types of cases and/or issues where the Registrar should consider whether to serve an appeal notice and direct or invite a party to serve a Respondent's Notice before the consideration of leave by the single Judge.

Examples of when the Registrar might direct a Respondent's Notice include:

(i)   where the grounds concern matters which were the subject of public interest immunity (PII);

(ii)   allegations of jury irregularity;

(iii)   criticisms of the prosecution or the conduct of the Judge;

(iv)   complex frauds;

(v)   inconsistent verdicts;

(vi)   fresh evidence;

(vii)   where the grounds claim that the wrong statute, rule or regulation was applied.

The CPS will always be invited to lodge a Respondent's Notice in the following cases:

(i)   all *conviction and sentence* applications involving a fatality;

(ii)   all *conviction applications* involving rape, attempted rape or a serious sexual offence;

(iii)   all *conviction applications* where a CPS Complex Casework Unit dealt with the case;

(iv)   all *conviction applications* where the offence was perverting the course of justice, misconduct in public office and any conspiracy.

A9-4   In conviction cases where leave to appeal has been granted or where the application for leave has been referred to the full Court, the Crown is briefed to attend the hearing and required to submit a Respondent's Notice/ skeleton argument. In relation to sentence cases where leave has been granted, referred or an appellant is represented on a renewed application, the sentence protocol set out in CPD IX Appeal 39A Appeals against conviction and sentence – the provision of notice to the prosecution, will apply. In those cases, a Respondent's Notice/skeleton argument will have to be served when the Crown indicates a wish to attend a hearing or when the Registrar directs the Crown to attend. There is no need to serve a skeleton argument in addition to a Respondent's Notice.

A10. Referral by the Registrar

A10-1 Where leave to appeal is required, the Registrar, having obtained the necessary documents, will usually refer the application(s) to a single Judge for a decision (on the papers) under s. 31 Criminal Appeal Act 1968. The Registrar does have the power to refer an application for leave directly to the full Court, in which case he will usually grant the advocate a representation order for the hearing. Where an application is referred because an unlawful sentence has been passed or other procedural error identified, a representation order will ordinarily be granted unless the error is such that the Court could correct it on the papers, but advocates should be aware that the Court may make observations for the attention of the determining officer that a full fee should not be allowed on taxation. A representation order will not be granted where the presence of an advocate is not required, such as where there has been a technical error that the Court can correct without the need for oral argument. An applicant would not have the right to attend the hearing because the appeal is on a point of law only (s.22 Criminal Appeal Act 1968; R v Hyde and others [2016] EWCA Crim 1031; [2016] 1 WLR 4020).

A10-2 Leave to appeal is required in all cases except:

- Where the trial or sentencing Judge has certified that the case is fit for appeal;

- Where the appeal has been referred by the Criminal Cases Review Commission (CCRC);

- Where the appeal is under s13 Administration of Justice Act 1960 (contempt proceedings);

- Where there is no provision for the grant of leave by a Single Judge; for example an appeal against an order for trial without jury (*see Section D Other Appeals*).

A10-3 Where leave to appeal is not required, the Registrar will usually grant a representation order for the hearing of the appeal.

A11. Oral applications for leave to appeal

All applications for leave (together with any ancillary applications such as for bail, extension of time, or a representation order) are normally considered by a single Judge on the papers, unless it can be demonstrated that there are exceptional reasons why an oral hearing is required. An advocate or solicitors may request an oral hearing, but that request must be supported by written reasons stating why the case is exceptional and any reasons why that hearing should be expedited (expedition will be a matter for the Registrar). That application should be copied to the prosecution. The single Judge determining the substantive application will then decide whether an oral hearing should be arranged. An advocate may make an application for a representation order at the hearing itself. Oral applications for leave and bail are usually heard in Court but in chambers at 9.30am before the normal Court sittings. Advocates appear unrobed. If the advocate considers that an application may take longer than 20 minutes, the Registrar must be notified. If the single Judge declines to hear the application at an oral hearing, the application will then be considered on the papers by that Judge.

A12. Powers of the single Judge

The single Judge may grant the application for leave, refuse it or refer it to the full Court. In conviction cases and in sentence cases where appropriate, the single Judge may grant limited leave i.e. leave to argue some grounds but not others. Advocates must notify the Registrar within 14 days whether the grounds upon which leave has been refused are to be renewed before the full Court. If a representation order is granted, in a limited leave case, public funding will only cover grounds of appeal which the single Judge or the full Court say are arguable (R v Cox & Thomas [1999] 2 Cr App Rep 6 and R v Hyde and others [2016] EWCA Crim 1031; [2016] 1 WLR 4020). The single Judge may also grant, refuse or refer any ancillary application.

A13. Bail pending appeal (CrimPR 39.8)

A13-1 Bail may be granted (a) by a single Judge or the full Court or (b) by a trial or sentencing Judge who has certified the case fit for appeal. In the latter case, bail can only be granted within 28 days of the conviction or sentence which is the subject of the appeal and may not be granted if an application for bail has already been made to the Court of Appeal (CPD III Custody and bail 14H.5).

A13-2 An application to the Court of Appeal for bail pending appeal must be supported by a completed Form B which must be served on the Registrar and the prosecution. The Court must not decide such an application without giving the prosecution the opportunity to make representations.

A13-3 An application for bail will not be considered by a single Judge or the Court until notice of application for leave to appeal conviction or sentence or notice of appeal has first been given. In practice, Judges will also require the relevant transcripts to be available so they may consider the merits of the substantive application at the same time as the bail application.

A13-4   Where bail is granted pending appeal, the Court may attach any condition that must be met before the party is released, and may direct how such a condition must be met. The Registrar must serve a certificate recording any such condition on the party, the party's custodian and any other person directly affected by the condition (CrimPR 39.9). A condition of residence is always attached.

A14.   Funding for grant of leave or reference to full Court

A14-1   Where the single Judge grants leave or refers an application to the Court, it is usual to grant a representation order for the preparation and presentation of the appeal. This is usually limited to the services of an advocate only. The advocate who settled grounds of appeal will usually be the assigned advocate. If the applicant is a litigant in person, an advocate may be assigned by the Registrar. In such cases the Registrar will provide a brief but does not act as an appellant's solicitor. The Registrar may assign one advocate to represent more than one appellant if appropriate. If it is considered that a representation order for two advocates and/or solicitors is required, the advocate should notify the Registrar and provide written justification in accordance with Criminal Legal Aid (Determinations by a Court and Choice of Representative) Regulations 2013 (S.I. 2013/614).

A14-2   If solicitors are assigned, it should be noted that by virtue of Regulation 12 of the Criminal Legal Aid (Determinations by a Court and Choice of Representative) Regulations 2013, SI 2013/614, a representation order can only be issued to a solicitor if they hold a Standard Crime Contract with the LAA. A solicitor not holding such a franchise may apply to the LAA for an individual case contract (ICC) by virtue of which the solicitor is employed on behalf of the LAA to represent an appellant in a given case.

A14-3   In some circumstances, the Registrar may refer an application to the full Court. This may be because there is a novel point of law, there is fresh evidence to be considered pursuant to s.23 of the Criminal Appeal Act 1968 or because in a sentence case, the sentence passed is very short. A representation order for an advocate is usually granted. The advocate for the prosecution usually attends a Registrar's referral.

A15.   Refusal by the Single Judge

A15-1   Where the single Judge refuses leave to appeal, the Registrar sends a notification of the refusal, including any observations which the Judge may have made, to the appellant, who is informed that he may require the application to be considered by the Court by serving a renewal notice (Form SJ-Renewal) upon the Registrar within 14 days from the date on which the notice of refusal was served on him.

A15-2   A refused application which is not renewed within 14 days lapses. An appellant may apply for an extension of time in which to renew his application for leave (CrimPR 36.3 – 36.5 and s.31 Criminal Appeal Act 1968). The Registrar will normally refer such an application to the Court to be considered at the same time as the renewed application for leave to appeal. An application for an extension of time in which to renew must be supported by cogent reasons.

A15-3   If it is intended that an advocate should represent the appellant at the hearing of the renewed application for leave to appeal, whether privately instructed or on a pro bono basis, such intention must be communicated to the CAO in writing as soon as that decision has been made. Whilst a representation order is not granted by the Registrar in respect of a renewed application for leave, the advocate may apply at the hearing to the Court for a representation order to cover that appearance and any further work done in preparation of the renewal retrospectively. In practice, this is only granted where the application for leave is successful.

A16.   Directions for loss of time

A16-1   S.29 Criminal Appeal Act 1968 empowers the Court to direct that time spent in custody as an appellant shall not count as part of the term of any sentence to which the appellant is for the time being subject. The Court will do so where it considers that an application is wholly without merit. Such an order may not be made where leave to appeal or a trial Judge's certificate has been granted, on a reference by the CCRC or where an appeal has been abandoned. An appeal is not built into the trial process but must be justified on properly arguable grounds (R v Fortean [2009] EWCA Crim 437; [2009] Crim LR 798).

A16-2   The only means the Court has of discouraging unmeritorious applications which waste precious time and resources is by using the powers in the Criminal Appeal Act 1968 and the Prosecution of Offences Act 1985. In every case where the Court is presented with an unmeritorious application, consideration should be given to exercising these powers.

A16-3   The mere fact that an advocate has advised that there are grounds of appeal will not be a sufficient answer to the question as to whether or not an application has indeed been brought which was wholly without merit (R v Gray and Others [2014] EWCA Crim 2372; [2015] 1 Cr App Rep (S) 197).

A16-4   The Form SJ, on which the single Judge records his decisions, and the reverse of which is used by appellants to indicate their wish to renew, includes:

- a box for the single Judge to initial in order to indicate that that the full Court should consider loss of time or a costs order if the application is renewed; and

- a box for the applicant to give reasons why such an order should not be made, whether or not an indication has been given by a single Judge.

A16-5 Where the single Judge has not indicated that the full Court should consider making a loss of time order because the applicant is not in custody, the single Judge also has the option of considering whether to make any directions in respect of costs, which could include the prosecution costs (usually in providing a Respondent's Notice). The Practice Direction in relation to costs should be followed.

A17. Abandonment

A17-1 An appeal or application may be abandoned at any time before the hearing without leave by completing and lodging Form A. An oral instruction or letter indicating a wish to abandon is insufficient.

A17-2 At the hearing, an application or appeal can only be abandoned with the permission of the Court (CrimPR 36.13(2)(b)). An appeal or application which is abandoned is treated as being a final determination of the full Court (CrimPR 36.13(4)(c)).

A17-3 A notice of abandonment cannot be withdrawn nor can it be conditional. A person who wants to reinstate an application or appeal after abandonment must apply in writing to the Registrar with reasons (CrimPR 36.13(5)). The Court has power to allow reinstatement only where the purported abandonment can be treated as a nullity and the applicant must provide the Court with the relevant information to determine the application (R v Medway (1976) 62 Cr App R 85 and R v Zabotka [2016] EWCA Crim 1771).

A17-4 An application to treat the abandonment as a nullity is heard by the full Court. If the Court does agree to treat the abandonment as a nullity, the status of the application is restored as if there had been no interruption.

A18. Case Management Duties

A18-1 CrimPR 36.2 gives the Court and parties the same powers and duties of case management as in Part 3 of the Rules. In accordance with those duties, for each application received, the Registrar nominates a case progression officer, (the 'responsible officer'). There is also a duty on the parties to actively assist the Court to progress cases. Close contact between the advocate and solicitors and the responsible officer is encouraged in order to facilitate the efficient preparation and listing of appeals, especially in complex cases and those involving witnesses.

A18-2 Powers under the Criminal Appeal Act 1968 exercisable by the single Judge and the Registrar are contained in s.31 Criminal Appeal Act 1968 (as amended by s.87 Courts Act 2003, s.331 & Sched.32 Criminal Justice Act 2003 and Sched.8 Criminal Justice and Immigration Act 2008). These powers include the power to make procedural directions for the efficient and effective preparation of an application or appeal and the power to make an order under s.23(1)(a) Criminal Appeal Act 1968 for the production of evidence etc. necessary for the determination of the case.

A18-3 Where the Registrar refuses an application by an appellant to exercise any of the Registrar's case management powers under s.31 Criminal Appeal Act 1968 in the appellant's favour, the appellant is entitled to have the application determined by a single Judge (s. 31A (4) of the Act). There is no provision for any appeal against a procedural direction given by a single Judge and thus such decisions are final.

B. INTERLOCUTORY APPEALS AGAINST RULINGS IN PREPARATORY HEARINGS

Appeal against a ruling pursuant to s.9 of the Criminal Justice Act 1987 or a decision pursuant to s.35 of the Criminal Procedure and Investigations Act 1996 (Part 37 CrimPR)

B1 Where a Judge has ordered a preparatory hearing, they may make a ruling as to the admissibility of evidence and any other question of law relating to the case (s.9(3)(b) & (c) CJA 1987 and s.31(3)(a) &(b) CPIA 1996). Given the co-extensive powers of case management outside the preparatory hearing regime, Courts should now be very cautious about directing a preparatory hearing (barring terrorist cases) (R v L & L [2018] EWCA Crim 69; R v BM [2018] EWCA Crim 560).

B2 Pursuant to s.9(11) CJA 1987 and s.35(1) CPIA 1996 the defence or the prosecution may appeal to the CACD (and ultimately to the Supreme Court) against such a ruling, but only with the leave of the trial Judge, single Judge or the full Court. As to the scope of a Judge's powers in relation to a preparatory hearing and thus the extent of appeal rights, see the decision of the House of Lords in H [2007] UKHL 7 on appeal from [2006] EWCA Crim 1975; R v VGA [2010] EWCA Crim 2742.

B3 If the trial date is imminent and the application is urgent, the Registrar should be notified so that he may consider referring the application directly to the full Court.

B4   If an application for leave to appeal is made to the trial Judge, it should be made orally immediately after the ruling, or within two business days by serving a notice of an application on the appropriate officer of the Crown Court and all parties directly affected (CrimPR 37.4). Whether leave is granted by the trial Judge or not or no such application is made to the trial Judge, notice of an appeal or application for leave to appeal **(Form NG (Prep))** is to be served on the Registrar, the Crown Court and the parties within five business days of the ruling or the trial Judge's decision whether to grant leave (CrimPR 37.2).

B5   The notice and grounds of appeal having been served on the other parties, grounds of opposition should be served in a Respondent's Notice **(Form RN (Prep))** within five business days of service of the appeal notice (CrimPR 37.5).

B6   Defence representatives are usually covered by the Crown Court representation order if one is in force (Paragraph 2(2), Schedule 3, Access to Justice Act 1999).

B7   If the relevant time limits are not complied with, the Court has power to grant an extension of time. Where a single Judge refuses leave to appeal or an extension of time within which to serve a notice, the application may be renewed for determination by the full Court by serving the notice of renewal, appropriately completed, upon the Registrar within five business days of the refusal being served (CrimPR 37.7).

C.   APPEALS BY A PROSECUTOR AGAINST A "TERMINATING" RULING

S.58 Criminal Justice Act 2003 (Part 38 CrimPR)

C1   S.58 Criminal Justice Act 2003 provides the prosecution with a right of appeal in relation to a "terminating" ruling: a ruling where the prosecution agree to the defendant's acquittal if the appeal is not successful (Y [2008] EWCA Crim 10). This is wide enough to encompass a case-management decision (C [2007] EWCA Crim 2532).

C2   There is no right of appeal in respect of a ruling that the jury be discharged or a ruling in respect of which there is a right of appeal to the Court of Appeal by virtue of another enactment (s.57(2) CJA 2003). The prosecution should therefore consider whether there is a right of appeal under s.9 CJA 1987 or s.35 CPIA 1996.

C3   The prosecution must inform the Court that it intends to appeal or request an adjournment to consider whether to appeal (s.58(4) CJA 2003), which will be until the next business day (CrimPR 38.2(2)). The Judge has discretion to adjourn for longer if there is a real reason for doing so (H [2008] EWCA Crim 483). The prosecution can ask the trial Judge to grant leave to appeal immediately after the ruling or after the granted adjournment to consider the same (CrimPR 38.5). Leave should be granted only where the Judge considers there is a real prospect of success and not to speed up the hearing of the appeal (JG [2006] EWCA Crim 3276). If the prosecution do not ask the trial judge for leave to appeal, the notice and application to appeal **(Form NG (Pros))** must be served on the Crown Court, Registrar and every defendant affected by the ruling the next business day if the trial Judge expedites the appeal or five business days after telling the Judge of the intent to appeal if the Judge does not expedite the same (CrimPR 38.3). The prosecution must give the undertaking (as to the defendant's acquittal if the appeal is abandoned or leave to appeal is not obtained) at the time when it informs the Court of its intention to appeal. The failure to give it then is fatal to an application to the Court of Appeal for leave (ss.58(8) CJA 2003) (LSA [2008] EWCA Crim 1034; NT [2010] EWCA Crim 711; B [2014] EWCA Crim 2078).

C4   Whether or not leave is granted, the trial Judge must decide if the appeal is to be expedited and if so, adjourn the case. If he decides that the appeal should not be expedited then he can adjourn the case or discharge the jury (s.59 CJA 2003).

C5   The notice and grounds of appeal having been served on the other parties, grounds of opposition should be served in a Respondent's Notice **(Form RN (Prep))**. The Respondent's Notice must be served the next business day if the trial judge expedites the appeal or within five business days of service of the appeal notice if the appeal is not expedited (CrimPR 37.5).

C.6   Defence representatives are usually covered by the Crown Court representation order if one is in force (such proceedings being considered incidental within Paragraph 5(3) of Schedule 3 to the Legal Aid, Sentencing and Punishment of Offenders Act 2012).

C7   Expedition does not impose time limits on the Registrar or Court of Appeal. However, if leave has not been granted by the trial Judge, the application may be referred to the full Court by the Registrar to ensure that the matter is dealt with quickly.

C8   The Registrar endeavours to list prosecution appeals where a jury has not been discharged as quickly as possible. He is unlikely to be able to list an appeal in less than a week from the ruling because it is necessary for the prosecution to obtain transcripts, papers to be copied and the Judges to read their papers. It is of great assistance if it is anticipated that there is to be an appeal against a ruling where the jury has not been discharged that a phone call is made to the Registrar or CAO General Office (020 7947 6011) notifying the office even before the appeal notice is sent, so that preliminary views can be taken as to the constitution which may be able to hear the appeal. The listing of an urgent appeal invariably means that other cases have to be removed from the list.

D. OTHER APPEALS

D1. *Prosecution appeal against the making of a confiscation order or where the Court declines to make one (save on reconsideration of benefit)*

- S.31(1) & (2) Proceeds of Crime Act 2002

- Part 42 CrimPR

- Proceedings are commenced by serving a **Form PoCA 1** on the defendant and the Crown Court within 28 days of the decision appealed against (Article 3(2)(a) Proceeds of Crime Act (Appeals under Part 2) Order 2003)

- A Respondent's Notice **Form PoCA 2** is to be served on the Registrar of Criminal Appeals and the appellant not later than 14 days after receiving **Form PoCA 1**

- An undischarged Crown Court representation order will cover advice and assistance on the merits of opposing the appeal and drafting the Respondent's Notice, otherwise an application for a representation order can be made to the Registrar. In any event where an application for a representation order is made on Form **PoCA 2,** the Registrar will consider a representation order for the hearing

- Leave to appeal can be granted by a single Judge or the full Court

D2. *Prosecution and third party appeal against a determination, under S.10A Proceeds of Crime Act 2002, of the extent of the defendant's interest in property*

- S.31(4) & (5) Proceeds of Crime Act 2002

- Part 42 CrimPR

- Proceedings are commenced by serving a **Form PoCa 1** on the defendant and the Crown Court within 28 days of the decision appealed against

- A Respondent's Notice **Form PoCA 2** is to be served on the Registrar of Criminal Appeals and the appellant not later than 14 days after receiving **Form PoCA 1**

- An undischarged Crown Court representation order will cover advice and assistance on the merits of opposing the appeal and drafting the

Respondent's Notice, otherwise an application for a representation order can be made to the Registrar. In any event where an application for a representation order is made on **Form PoCA 2,** the Registrar will consider a representation order for the hearing

- Leave to appeal can be granted by a single Judge or the full Court

D3. *Appeal in relation to a restraint order*

- S.43 Proceeds of Crime Act 2002

- Part 42 CrimPR

- The prosecution or an accredited financial investigator can appeal a refusal to make a restraint order. A person who applied for an order or who is affected by the order can apply to the Crown Court to vary or discharge the order and then appeal that decision to the Court of Appeal

- Proceedings are commenced by serving a **Form PoCA 3** on the Crown Court within 28 days of the decision being appealed. **Form PoCA 3** must then be served on any respondent, any person who holds realisable property to which the appeal relates, or is affected by the appeal, not later than seven days after the form is lodged at the Crown Court. The documents which are to be served with **Form PoCA3** are set out in CrimPR 42.15

- A Respondent's Notice **Form PoCA 4** is to be served on the Registrar of Criminal Appeals not later than 14 days after the respondent is notified that the appellant has leave to appeal or notified that the application for leave and the appeal are to be heard together. **Form PoCA 4** is then to be served on the appellant and any other respondent as soon as is practicable and not later than seven days after it was served on the Registrar

- Criminal Defence Service Regulations do not apply to these proceedings and thus no representation orders will be granted by the Registrar or the Court

- Leave to appeal can be granted by a single Judge or full Court

- An application for a restraint order can be made as soon as a criminal investigation has begun. The proposed defendant may not have been charged (s.40 Proceeds of Crime Act 2002)

D4. *Appeal in relation to a receivership order*

- S.65 Proceeds of Crime Act 2002

- Part 42 CrimPR

- The appointment, non-appointment or powers of a receiver can be appealed, as can an order giving a direction to a receiver and the variation or discharge of a receivership order. An appeal can be brought by the person who applied for the order, a person who is affected by the order or the receiver

- Proceedings are commenced by serving a **Form PoCA 3** on the Crown Court within 28 days of the decision being appealed

- **Form PoCA 3** must then be served on any respondent and any person who holds realizable property to which the appeal relates, or is affected by the appeal, not later than seven days after the form is lodged at the Crown Court

- A Respondent's Notice **Form PoCA 4** to be served on the Registrar of Criminal Appeals not later than 14 days after the respondent is notified that the appellant has leave to appeal or is notified that the application for leave and the appeal are to be heard together. **Form PoCA 4** is then to be served on the appellant and any other respondent as soon as is practicable and not later than seven days after it was served on the Registrar

- Criminal Defence Service Regulations do not apply to these proceedings and thus no representation orders will be granted by the Registrar or the Court

- Leave to appeal can be granted by a single Judge or full Court

D5.   *Appeal against an order of the Crown Court in the exercise of its jurisdiction to punish for contempt – usually a finding of contempt or sentence for contempt*

- S.13 Administration of Justice Act 1960

- Part 39 CrimPR

- Anyone dealt with by the Crown Court for contempt may appeal

- Proceedings are commenced by lodging a **Form NG** at the Crown Court (if the notice and grounds are lodged before 1 October 2018) or directly on the Registrar of Criminal Appeals (if the notice and grounds are lodged on or after 1 October 2018) not more than 28 days after the order to be appealed (*see section A2. Lodging Form NG and grounds of appeal*)

- The Registrar may direct a Respondent's Notice **Form RN** or the prosecution may serve one if they wish to make representations to the Court

- An undischarged Crown Court representation order will cover advice and assistance on appeal. The Registrar will consider a representation order for the hearing (s.19 Legal Aid, Sentencing and Punishment of Offenders Act 2012; Reg.8 Criminal Legal Aid (Determinations by Court and Choice of Representative) Regulations 2013 [SI 2013/614])

- No leave to appeal is required. The appeal is as of right (s. 13 Administration of Justice Act 1960)

- Appeals occur most frequently when an appellant wishes to appeal a sentence for failing to appear at the Crown Court as the failing to appear is dealt with as if it were contempt

D6.   Appeal against a minimum term set or reviewed by a High Court Judge

- Para. 14 of Schedule 22 Criminal Justice Act 2003

- Part 39 CrimPR

- A defendant with a mandatory life sentence imposed before 18 December 2003 who has had his minimum term set or reviewed by a High Court Judge can appeal

- Proceedings are commenced by service of **Form NG (MT)** on the Registrar not more than 28 days after the decision

- The Registrar may direct a Respondent's Notice **Form RN** or the prosecution may serve one if they wish to make representations to the Court

- An application for a representation order can be made to the Registrar (s.19 Legal Aid, Sentencing and Punishment of Offenders Act 2012; Reg.8 Criminal Legal Aid (Determinations by Court and Choice of Representative) Regulations 2013 [SI 2013/614])

- Leave to appeal is required and can be granted by the full Court or a single Judge (Part 2 Para.8 Criminal Justice Act 2003 (Mandatory Life Sentences: Appeals in Transitional Cases Order 2003) [S.I. 2005/2798])

D7.   Attorney General's reference of an unduly lenient sentence

- S.36 Criminal Justice Act 1988

- Part 41 CrimPR

- The Attorney General can refer sentences only in relation to specific offences or sentences (ss.35 & 36 Criminal Justice Act 1988 and Criminal Justice Act 1988 (Reviews of Sentencing) Order 2006)

- Although CrimPR 41.3(1) implies there is a specific form to commence proceedings, in practice a standard letter with supporting documents is sent to the Registrar of Criminal Appeals by the Attorney General's Office no more than 28 days after sentence

- If the defendant wishes to make representations to the Court he must serve a Respondent's Notice within 14 days of the Registrar serving the application upon him. Again, there is no specific form available

- Representation orders are granted by the Registrar to respond to an Attorney General's reference

- The leave of the Court of Appeal is required

D8. *Attorney General's reference of a point of law on an acquittal*

- S.36 Criminal Justice Act 1972

- Part 41 Crim PR

- The Attorney General can refer a point of law to the Court of Appeal for their opinion on the acquittal on indictment of the defendant

- Although CrimPR 41.3(1) implies there is a specific form to commence proceedings, there is no such form and CrimPR 70.3 sets out what should be included in the reference. All references which identify the defendant should be excluded

- There is no time limit

- If the defendant wishes to make representations to the Court he must serve a Respondent's Notice within 28 days of the Registrar serving the application upon him. Again there is no specific form available

- Representation orders are granted by the Registrar to respond to an Attorney General's reference

- Leave is not required

D9. *Appeal against a finding of unfitness to plead or a finding that the accused did the act or made the omission charged*

- S.15 Criminal Appeal Act 1968

- Part 39 CrimPR

- The accused can appeal (by the person appointed to represent the accused) against a finding of unfitness to plead (but not fitness to plead) and that he did the act or made the omission charged. The appeal does not lie until both findings have been made

- Proceedings are commenced by the service of **Form NG** on the Crown Court (if the application is lodged prior to the 1 October 2018) or directly on the Registrar of Criminal Appeals (if the application is lodged on or after the 1 October 2018) not more than 28 days after the finding made which the accused wishes to appeal (*see section A2. Lodging of Form NG and grounds of appeal*)

- The prosecution should serve a Respondent's Notice **Form RN** if directed by the Registrar or if they wish to make representations to the court

- The costs of the person appointed to put the case on appeal are paid from central funds, but the mechanism will depend on the outcome of the appeal proceedings, thus the issue should be considered only at the conclusion of proceedings. Where an appeal is allowed, the Court may make a defendant's costs order under s16(4)(a)(iii) of the Prosecution of Offences Act 1985, which will include legal costs (s16A(3)(c)). Where leave to appeal is not granted or the appeal is not successful, the costs of the person appointed to put the case on appeal are covered by Part IIIA of the regulations made under s19(3)(d) of the 1985 Act (Antoine [1999] 2 Cr. App.R.225)

- Leave to appeal may be granted by the Crown Court Judge, a single Judge or the full Court

D10.   *Appeal against a verdict of not guilty by reason of insanity*

- S.12 Criminal Appeal Act 1968

- Part 39 CrimPR

- The defendant can appeal a verdict of not guilty by reason of insanity

- Proceedings are commenced by the service of **Form NG** on the Crown Court (if the application is lodged prior to the 1 October 2018) or directly on the Registrar of Criminal Appeals (if the application is lodged on or after 1 October 2018) not more than 28 days after the verdict (*see section A2. Lodging of Form NG and grounds of appeal*)

- The prosecution should serve a Respondent's Notice **Form RN** if directed by the Registrar or if they wish to make representations to the court

- S.16(4) Prosecution of Offences Act 1985 provides that where the Court of Appeal **allows an appeal** then the court may make a defendant's costs order. If the appeal is not allowed costs from central funds should be available on the same basis as was allowed in Antoine (above) in the absence of any statutory provision

- Leave to appeal may be granted by the Crown Court Judge, a single Judge or the full Court

D11.   *Appeal against the order following a verdict of not guilty by reason of insanity or a finding of unfitness to plead*

- S.16A Criminal Appeal Act 1968

- Part 39 CrimPR

- An accused who, as a result of a verdict of not guilty by reason of insanity or a finding of fitness to plead has a hospital order, interim hospital order or supervision order made against him may appeal against the order

- Proceedings are commenced by the service of **Form NG** on the Crown Court (if the application is lodged prior to the 1 October 2018) or directly on the Registrar of Criminal Appeals (if the application is lodged on or after 1 October 2018) not more than 28 days after the verdict (*see section A". Lodging Form NG and grounds of appeal*)

- The prosecution should serve a Respondent's Notice **Form RN** if directed by the Registrar or if they wish to make representations to the court

- S.16(4) Prosecution of Offences Act 1985 provides that where the Court of Appeal **allows an appeal** then the court may make a defendant's costs order. If the appeal is not allowed costs from central funds should be available on the same basis as was allowed in Antoine (above) in the absence of any statutory provision

- Leave to appeal may be granted by the Crown Court Judge, a single Judge or the full Court

D12.   *Appeal against review of sentence*

- S.74(8) Serious Organised Crime and Police Act 2005

- Part 39 Crim PR

- A defendant or specified prosecutor may appeal

- Proceedings are commenced by serving a **Form NG (RD)** on the Crown Court (if the application is lodged prior to 1 October 2018) or directly on the Registrar of Criminal Appeals (if the application is lodged on or after 1 October 2018) not more than 28 days after the review (*see section A2. Lodging Form NG and grounds of appeal*)

- A Respondent's Notice **Form RN** should be served if directed by the Registrar or if the respondent wishes to make representations to the Court

- An application for a representation order can be made to the Registrar (Legal Aid, Sentencing and Punishment of Offenders Act 2012 s.19; Reg .9 Criminal Legal Aid (General) Regulations 2013)

- Leave to appeal can be granted by the single Judge or full Court (Serious Organised Crime and Police Act 2005 (Appeals under s.74) Order 2006/21)

D13.   *Appeal against an order for trial by jury of sample counts*

- S.18 Domestic Violence, Crime and Victims Act 2004

- Part 37 Crim PR

- The defendant and the prosecution can appeal the determination of an application to make the order

- An application for the jury to try some counts as sample counts and the Judge to try the remainder if the jury convict, must be determined at a preparatory hearing and s.18 confers rights of interlocutory appeal. A **Form NG (Prep)** must be served on the Crown Court, the Registrar and any party directly affected not more than five business days after the order or the Crown Court Judge granting or refusing leave (*For applications to the Crown Court Judge see Part B above*)

- A Respondent's Notice **Form RN (Prep)** should be served if the Court directs or the prosecution (or any party affected) wants to make representations to the Court

- Defence representatives are usually covered by the Crown Court representation order if one is in force, the proceedings being considered incidental within Paragraph 5(3) of Schedule 3 to Legal Aid, Sentencing and Punishment of Offenders Act 2012

- The Crown Court Judge, single Judge or full Court can grant leave

D14. Appeal against an order relating to a trial to be conducted without a jury where there is a danger of jury tampering

- S.45(5) and (9) Criminal Justice Act 2003 amending s.9(11) Criminal Justice Act 1987 and s.35(1) Criminal Procedure and Investigations Act 1994

- Part 37 CrimPR

- The prosecution can appeal the refusal to make an order; the defence can appeal the making of an order

- A **Form NG (Prep)** must be served on the Crown Court, the Registrar and any party directly affected not more than five business days after the order or the Crown Court Judge granting or refusing leave (*For applications to the Crown Court Judge see Part B above*)

- A Respondent's Notice **Form RN (Prep)** should be served if the Court directs or the Crown (or any party affected) wants to make representations to the Court

- Defence representatives are usually covered by the Crown Court representation order if one is in force, the proceedings being considered incidental within Paragraph 5(3) of Schedule 3 to Legal Aid, Sentencing and Punishment of Offenders Act 2012

- The Crown Court Judge, single Judge or full Court can grant leave

D15.   Appeal against an order that a trial should continue without a jury or a new trial take place without a jury after jury tampering

- S.47 Criminal Justice Act 2003

- Part 37 CrimPR (relating to appeals against an order made in a preparatory hearing notwithstanding there will have been no preparatory hearing)

- Both the prosecution and defence can appeal a decision that the trial should continue without a jury or a new trial should take place without a jury

- A **Form NG (Prep)** must be served on the Crown Court, the Registrar and any party directly affected not more than five business days after the order or the Crown Court Judge granting or refusing leave (*For applications to the Crown Court Judge see Part B above*)

- A Respondent's Notice **Form RN (Prep)** should be served if the Court directs or the Crown (or any party affected) wants to make representations to the Court

- Defence representatives are usually covered by the Crown Court representation order if one is in force, the proceedings being considered incidental within Paragraph 5(3) of Schedule 3 to Legal Aid, Sentencing and Punishment of Offenders Act 2012

- The Crown Court Judge, single Judge or full Court can grant leave

D16.   Appeal against orders restricting or preventing reports or restricting public access

- S.159 Criminal Justice Act 1988

- Part 40 CrimPR

- A person aggrieved may appeal

- Applications against orders restricting reporting shall be made within 10 business days after the date on which the order was made by lodging **Form NG (159)** on the Registrar, the Crown Court, the prosecutor and defendant and any other affected person. Applications against orders to restrict public access must be made the next business day after the order was made. If advance notice of an order restricting public access is given, then advance notice of an intention to appeal may be made not more than five business days after the advance notice is displayed

- A person on whom an appeal notice is served should serve a Respondent's Notice **Form RN (159)** if he wishes to make representations to the Court or the Court so directs within three business days

- The Court may make such order as to costs as it thinks fit (s.159(5)(c) Criminal Justice Act 1988), but not out of central funds (Holden and others v. CPS No.2 [1994] 1 AC 22)

- A single Judge or the full Court can grant leave (s.31(2B) Criminal Appeal Act 1968)

- Applications for leave to appeal and appeals in relation to reporting restrictions may be heard in private (CrimPR 36.6(1)). Applications for leave to appeal and appeals relating to restricting public access may be decided without a hearing but the decision must be announced at a hearing in public (Crim PR 36.6(3)). In either case, if the hearing relates to public interest immunity, it must be in private unless the Court otherwise directs (Crim PR 36.6(2))

D17. Appeal against a wasted costs order

- Regulation 3C Costs in Criminal Cases (General) Regulations 1986

- A legal or other representative against whom a wasted costs order has been made in the Crown Court

- There is no specific form. Notice of appeal should be served on any interested party within 21 days of the order being made.

- Any interested party can make representations orally or in writing

- Leave to appeal is not required (s. 19 A Prosecution of Offences Act 1985)

D18. Appeal relating to Serious Crime Prevention Orders

- S.24 Serious Crime Act 2007

- Part 39 CrimPR

- A person subject to the order, an applicant authority or anyone given the opportunity to make representations at the Crown Court about the making, variation or non-variation of an order

- Proceedings are commenced by the service of **Form NG (SCPO)** on the Crown Court (if the application is lodged prior to 1 October 2018) or directly on the Registrar of Criminal Appeals (if the application is lodged on or after 1 October 2018) not more than 28 days after the order (*see section A2. Lodging Form NG and grounds of appeal*)

- A Respondent's Notice **Form RN** should be served if directed by the Registrar or if the respondent wishes to make representations to the Court. Proceedings before the Crown Court or the Court of Appeal relating to serious crime prevention orders and arising by virtue of ss.19, 20, 21 or 24 of the Serious Crime Act 2007 are criminal proceedings for the purposes of Legal Aid, Sentencing and Punishment of Offenders

Act 2012 s.19; Reg.9(s) Criminal Legal Aid (General) Regulations 2013. Accordingly, the Registrar may grant a representation order to a person subject to the order. A person who made representations at the Crown Court can apply to the LAA for a representation order. The Court has discretion to order costs as it thinks fit (Part 3 Orders as to costs Serious Crime Act 2007 (Appeals under s.24) Order 2008/1863)

- Leave can be granted by the Crown Court Judge, full Court or single Judge (Art.9 Serious Crime Act 2007 (Appeals under s.24) Order 2008/1863)

D19. *Appeal against the failure to make a football banning order*

- S.14A(5A) Football Spectators Act 1989
- Part 39 CrimPR
- The CACD has no power to deal with these. An appeal lies to the Civil Division (R v Boggild [2011] EWCA Crim 1928)

E. APPLICATION FOR A RETRIAL FOR A SERIOUS OFFENCE

E1. *Application by a prosecutor to quash an acquittal and seek a retrial of a qualifying offence*

(S.76(1) Criminal Justice Act 2003 and Part 27 CrimPR)

E1-1 There must be new and compelling evidence and it must be in the interests of justice for the acquitted person to be re-tried (ss.78 and 79 Criminal Justice Act 2003 and Dunlop [2006] EWCA Crim 1354; Sanjuliano [2007] EWCA Crim 3130). Evidence was "new" if it had not been adduced at trial and for the purposes of s.78(2) evidence was "adduced" if it had been put forward in evidence (R v Henry [2014] EWCA Crim. 1816; [2015] 2 Cr.App.R. 1).

E1-2 Proceedings can begin in one of two ways:

(1) By serving notice of the application under s.76 on the Registrar of Criminal Appeals and the acquitted person within two days of the decision having been made (s.80 Criminal Justice Act 2003). This notice charges the acquitted person with the offence. It requires the personal written consent of the Director of Public Prosecutions (DPP) (s.76(3)).

If the acquitted person is not in custody the prosecution can ask the Crown Court to issue:

    i)   A summons for the acquitted person to appear before the Court of Appeal for the hearing of the application

    ii)   A warrant for his arrest (s.89(3))

Once arrested on the warrant the acquitted person must be brought before the Crown Court within 48 hours (s.89(6)).

(2)   An acquitted person may be charged with the offence <u>before</u> an application under s76 has been made. This may be after an arrest in an investigation authorised by the DPP (s 85(2)) or where no authorisation has been given, after arrest under a warrant issued by a justice of the peace (s87(1) Criminal Justice Act 2003). Having been charged, the acquitted person must be brought before the Crown Court to consider bail within 24 hours (s.88(2) Criminal Justice Act 2003). He can then be remanded in custody or on bail for 42 days whilst an application under s.76 is prepared (s.88(6)) unless extended by s.88(8) Criminal Justice Act 2003). Once a notice of application under s.76 has been made, stating that the acquitted person has previously been charged with the offence, the acquitted person must be brought before the Crown Court to consider bail within 48 hours of the notice being given to the Registrar, if the acquitted person is already in custody under s.88 (above) (s.89(2)).

E1-3   Thus in either case, bail is dealt with largely by the Crown Court. The Court of Appeal only considers bail on the adjournment of the hearing of the application under s.76 (s.90 (1) Criminal Justice Act 2003).

E1-4   The notice **(Form NG (ACQ))** should where practicable be accompanied by the witness statements which are relied on as the new and compelling evidence, the original witness statements, unused statements, indictment, paper exhibits from the original trial, any relevant transcripts from the original trial and any other documents relied on (CrimPR 27.2(2)).

E1-5   An acquitted person who wants to oppose a s.76 application must serve a response **(Form RN (ACQ))** not more than 28 days after receiving the notice (CrimPR 27.3(2)).

E2.   *Application by a prosecutor for a determination whether a foreign acquittal is a bar to a trial and if so, an order that it not be a bar*

(S.76(2) Criminal Justice Act 2003 and Part 27 CrimPR)

E2-1   The prosecution can apply, with the personal written consent of the DPP (s.76(3) Criminal Justice Act 2003) for a determination whether an acquittal outside the UK is a bar to the acquitted person being tried in England

and Wales and if it is found to be so, an order that the acquittal not be a bar. Proceedings can begin in the same way as for an application under s.76(1).

E3.   Application for restrictions on publication relating to an application under s.76

(S.82 Criminal Justice Act 2003 and Part 27 CrimPR)

E3-1   An application can be made by the DPP for reporting restrictions. This can be made after a notice of an application for a re-trial has been made and may also be made by the Court of its own motion (s.82(5) Criminal Justice Act 2003). An application can also be made by the DPP for reporting restrictions **before** a notice of an application for a retrial if an investigation has been commenced (s.82(6) Criminal Justice Act 2003). The application for reporting restrictions must be served on the Registrar **(Form REP (ACQ))** and (usually) the acquitted person (CrimPR 27.8(1)).

E3-2   A party who wants to vary or revoke an order for restrictions on publication under s.82(7) may apply to the Court of Appeal in writing at any time after the order was made (CrimPR 27.9(1)).

E4.   Representation orders

E4-1   The Registrar will grant a representation order to the acquitted person for solicitors and counsel to respond to any of the above applications.

Appendix D

Sample pleadings

1 SAMPLE GROUNDS OF APPEAL AGAINST CONVICTION AND APPLICATION TO EXTEND THE TIME LIMITS

The following is a sample that has been drafted in order to indicate a possible approach to a straightforward application for leave to appeal against conviction and an application for extension of the time limit within which to give notice of application for leave to appeal. It is not intended as a rigid blueprint.

IN THE COURT OF APPEAL

CRIMINAL DIVISION

REGINA

-v-

NED KELLY

GROUNDS OF APPEAL AGAINST CONVICTION AND APPLICATION FOR EXTENSION OF TIME WITHIN WHICH TO APPLY LEAVE TO APPEAL

Introduction

1.   The Applicant appeals against his conviction for possessing an offensive weapon. He does so on the grounds of a material misdirection at his trial, whereby the Judge failed to tell the jury what, in law, they would have to find proved to be sure the petrol bomb was an 'offensive weapon'. Had the jury been directed that it was for the prosecution to make them sure that the bomb was made to injure a person, they may well have doubted whether the prosecution had proved its case.

2.   The Applicant also apples for an extension of time within which to apply for leave, given these *Grounds* are submitted approximately 18 months after conviction. That application is dealt with as a discrete topic at the end of these *Grounds*.

Facts

3.   The allegations concerned an incident that took place on 11 August 2011. Police in the London Borough of Tower Hamlets were patrolling the local area in a police carrier as violent disturbances took place across London. At around 1:20 am, the carrier was travelling along Mile End Road, E1 the location of the rear entrance to Stepney Police Station. Officers saw four to six males standing near to the rear gates of the police station. On seeing the carrier, the males ran and entered a parked Ford Escort car. The Applicant, who had been part of that group, did not enter the car but ran off. It later transpired that the car belonged to him.

4.   The carrier attempted to stop the car but was unable to do so. One of the officers chased and caught up with the Applicant. He stopped, turned towards the officer and raised his hands above his head. He was detained. An officer found a pair of gloves on the route that the Applicant had run. While speaking to the Applicant it was noted that he smelt of petrol.

5.   A search of the area around the rear of the police station revealed four petrol bombs. The Applicant was arrested for possession of an offensive weapon. He was taken back to the police stationed and interviewed. In interview, the Applicant denied the offence saying that he had been walking towards his girlfriend's house when he had been confronted by a group of young men wearing gloves and masks. He denied that it was his vehicle that the men had fled into and that he had ever seen the petrol bombs before.

6.   Further enquiries by the police demonstrated that much of what the Applicant had said in interview was untrue. At trial, he accepted that he had travelled to the police station in his car. He claimed that he had been kidnapped and taken there by drug dealers to whom he owed money. Once at the scene he had been forced to assist in making petrol bombs by pouring petrol into beer bottles. He had no involvement with the bombs thereafter and had just been standing alongside the group when the police carrier had turned the corner.

The trial

7.   The Applicant stood trial before His Honour Judge Jones at Inner London Crown Court in February 2012 charged with the following two counts:

    (1)   Count 1. Possessing petrol bombs with intent to destroy or damage property, contrary to section 3(a) of the Criminal Damage Act 1971.

(2)   Count 2. Possessing an offensive weapon, the petrol bombs, contrary to section 1 of the Prevention of Crime Act 1953.

8.   The two counts were in the alternative. In opening the case Prosecution Counsel said in terms:[1]

> 'You will see there are two counts on the indictment and these counts are in the alternative ... If [count 1] is proved ... then you don't need to consider count 2.'

9.   In summing up the Judge:

(1)   Made clear the two counts were in the alternative.[2]

(2)   Directed the jury that petrol bombs were offensive weapons and 'no-one has suggested" otherwise, given "there is no lawful or peaceful reason to put petrol in a bottle with a paper wick that anyone can think of. It is designed specifically for use as a weapon, as a missile, to cause fire and damage'.[3]

(3)   Explored the issues the jury would need to consider on count 1, including 'did he share the intention in count 1 to destroy or damage property, whether the police station or some other building or a car or whatever, by the use of those items?'[4]

10.   After lengthy deliberations and following a majority direction, the jury acquitted the Applicant of count 1, but convicted him of count 2 by a majority of 10 to 2 on 20 February 2012.

Events after trial

11.   After the Applicant was convicted and imprisoned he and his family sought fresh advice. After some delay those now acting for the Applicant were supplied with the papers in the case and have settled these *Grounds*. The history of the new representation is dealt with in more detail in the final section below, seeking an extension of the normal leave period.

12.   Pursuant to the Court's guidance in *R v McCook* [2014] EWCA Crim 734, those now representing the Applicant, who did not act at trial, have sent these *Grounds* in draft form to the trial advocate; his reply is attached to this document. In essence he accepts that it would have been preferable had he raised the point taken in these *Grounds* with the trial judge before the summing up. The Applicant is grateful for that concession and would note that the judge and prosecuting advocate fell into what is submitted to be the same error.

---

1   Transcript 1, 5B then 6B.
2   Transcript 2, 6B and 27D.
3   Transcript 2, 6E to H.
4   Transcript 2, 9A.

315

Appendix D   *Sample pleadings*

Submissions

13.   Section 1 of the Prevention of Crime Act 1953 [as amended], insofar as relevant to this appeal, states:

   '(1)   Any person who without lawful authority or reasonable excuse, the proof whereof shall lie on him, has with him in any public place any offensive weapon shall be guilty of an offence ...

   ...

   (4)   In this section ... "offensive weapon" means any article made or adapted for use for causing injury to the person, or intended by the person having it with him for such use by him or by some other person.'

14.   In *R v Simpson* (1984) 78 Cr App R 115, Lord Lane CJ identified three categories of offensive weapon: those made for use for causing injury to the person (offensive per se), those adapted for such a purpose, and those not so made or adapted, but carried with the intention of causing injury to the person. In the first two categories, the prosecution do not have to prove that the defendant had the weapon with him for the purpose of inflicting injury. Once a jury are sure that the weapon is offensive per se, the defendant will only be acquitted if he establishes lawful authority or reasonable excuse.

15.   The jury at the Applicant's trial were told that petrol bombs were offensive weapons and 'no-one has suggested' otherwise, given 'there is no lawful or peaceful reason to put petrol in a bottle with a paper wick that anyone can think of. It is designed specifically for use as a weapon, as a missile, to cause fire and damage'.[5]

16.   It is submitted this is wrong. An incendiary device can be made either to injure people or damage property. Indeed, it was the prosecution case that the latter was probably what was intended here; see the nature of count 1 and the summing up in respect of that count:

   'did he share the intention in count 1 to destroy or damage property, whether the police station or some other building or a car or whatever, by the use of those items?'[6]

17.   There may be many cases in which the circumstances of the possession of a petrol bomb may provide an irresistible basis for an inference that it was made with the intent of injuring a person or persons. However, on the facts of this case there was an alternative possibility, that the Applicant was in possession of the bomb with the intention of causing damage to property; indeed that alternative was the main thrust of the prosecution case.

---

5   Transcript 2, 6E to H.
6   Transcript 2, 9A.

18. It follows that had the issue been left to the jury they may have entertained at the very least a doubt, and consequently the conviction for count 2 is unsafe and this appeal should be allowed.

Application for an extension of leave period

19. The Solicitor who now acts for the Applicant has made a witness statement, attached to these *Grounds*, setting out the history of the passage of time between the Applicant's conviction and these *Grounds* being lodged. In essence the time was taken up as follows:

   (1) Trial Counsel advised that there were no grounds of appeal; given the concession now made by Counsel, it is submitted that that advice may not have been correct.

   (2) Thereafter the Applicant and his family made numerous efforts to seek fresh advice. Those efforts were handicapped both by their lack of wealth and the fact that, perhaps unsurprisingly, they did not spot the technical legal point now pursued.

   (3) Some months later they made contact with the Solicitor now acting who agreed to consider whether there were grounds for an appeal. There was then a very considerable delay while the trial papers were obtained from the previous solicitors. Those papers were 'chased' on numerous and regular occasions.

   (4) Once the papers were located and passed on, Counsel was instructed and she advised that a transcript of the summing up was required. The Legal Aid Authority then refused the application for funding and that refusal had to be appealed to the area Committee.

   (5) Once the transcript was finally obtained and supplied to Counsel along with all the trial papers, these *Grounds* were drafted and lodged within three weeks.

Conclusion

20. In conclusion, it is submitted that this Applicant has always protested his innocence and he and his family have done all that was practically possible to get fresh advice. Once new lawyers were in place it is submitted that they acted properly and efficiently in getting these *Grounds* in a fit state to be lodged. For all these reasons it is submitted that the Court should allow the extension now sought.

[Signed by the advocate drafting]

Quality Street Chambers

25 September 2014

2   SAMPLE GROUNDS OF APPEAL AGAINST SENTENCE

This is a sample that has been drafted in order to indicate a possible approach to a straightforward application for leave to appeal against sentence. It is not intended as a rigid blueprint.

IN THE COURT OF APPEAL

CRIMINAL DIVISION

REGINA

-v-

KARON JOSEPH

GROUNDS OF APPEAL AGAINST SENTENCE

Introduction

1.   The Applicant applies for leave to appeal against her sentence of seven years' imprisonment, passed by HHJ Jolly at Acton Crown Court on 13 February 2014. In summary the grounds advanced are:

   (1)   The Judge was wrong to reject the basis of plea without at least warning that he was minded to do so. Such a warning would have allowed the Applicant's advocate to make submissions and inform the Judge of unused material of which he was unaware.

   (2)   The Judge was wrong to only allow a reduction of 12.5 per cent for the Applicant's guilty plea at the pleas and case management hearing.

Facts

2.   The Applicant was arrested on 23 September 2013 after police officers entered and searched the address where she lived. They found a knotted carrier bag under the Applicant's bed that contained some 25 wraps of crack cocaine. Each wrap was made from cling film, with a total weight of 120 grams. They also found electronic scales with two pans that a scientist was later to say had 'very probably' been used to make crack cocaine from the powered form of the drug, 14 rolls of cling film [all in the kitchen] and three mobile phones in the sitting room that rang on numerous occasions during the search. A police officer attempted to answer these calls but when he did so the calls were immediately terminated. These facts were all evident from the prosecution papers that were supplied to the Judge.

3.   The unused material contained the following material [as attached to these *Grounds*] that was not served on the Court and consequently was not known to the Judge:

(1)   Various documents that suggested at least three other people lived in the same house, including Martin Jones and Ken Owen.

(2)   Jones had a number of previous convictions for supplying cannabis and heroin, and a recent conviction for possession of a small amount of cocaine.

(3)   Owen had two previous convictions for possessing cocaine and cannabis and seven for offences of violence, mainly of a low level but he had served a six-year sentence for wounding with intent some eight years before the time of the search.

4.   The Applicant did not speak at all when the house was being searched or when she was arrested on suspicion of possession with intent to supply the crack cocaine. She was later interviewed under caution and answered 'no comment' to all the questions asked of her. She had one previous conviction for assault police some five years previously for which she had received a community order. She was aged 27 at the time of sentence and worked part time as a carer.

5.   In preparing the case her solicitor had taken a number of statements from her mother, father and elder sister who between them suggested that she had little money and would often borrow small sums of money from them or allow them to buy her drinks on social occasions.

6.   The Applicant was committed to the Crown Court. At a preliminary hearing no plea was entered despite HHJ Dour QC reminding her and her advocate that under the authority of *Caley*, maximum credit for any guilty plea could only be guaranteed by a plea indicated or entered at that hearing.

7.   At the PCMH the Applicant pleaded guilty to the single count she faced, that of possessing cocaine with intent to supply. She did so on the basis of a written basis of plea [copy attached] that included the passage:

'The defendant was not a drug dealer in the sense that she did not sell to drug users or anybody else, but she admits by her plea that she possessed the drugs intending to supply them; another person had given her the drugs to look after. While she does not claim to have been acting under duress, she did feel obliged to help out another who lived in the same house from time to time, so she put the drugs under her bed until that other person would ask for them back.'

8.   The Prosecution opened the facts of the case to HHJ Jolly, but made clear they 'could not gainsay' the basis of plea and did not seek a *Newton* hearing. The mitigation advanced on behalf of the Applicant included:

(1)   Reliance on the basis of plea and the submission that this placed the Applicant in the category of 'lesser role' in the sentencing guidelines. Given the Prosecution's stance and the very heavy list that HHJ Jolly was dealing with, no further time was taken up rehearsing the items of unused material or familial evidence, as set out above, such as supported the basis.

(2)   A submission that the Applicant, as a woman of almost good character, could be forgiven for being too scared of the inevitable custodial sentence that would follow to plead at the preliminary hearing, and that therefore the Court should grant her maximum, or close to maximum, credit for her timely plea at the PCMH.

9.   In passing sentence HHJ Jolly said:

(1)   He did not believe a word of the basis of plea. The Defendant was a grown woman. It was all too easy for any major drug dealer to claim, when caught red handed, that they were only minding the drugs for no profit. Yet here was a defendant arrested in her own house, surrounded by all the accoutrements of a busy commercial drug dealer. She had not said a word about any lesser role either upon arrest or in her interviews under caution. Therefore he would take her role to be a 'leading role' under the sentencing guidelines. Given that the drugs were clearly being packaged and prepared for sale to street level users [which was not in dispute] this was a category 3 case. He therefore adopted a starting point of eight years six months.

(2)   *Caley* makes clear the sentencing judge is not deprived of all flexibility; this was a defendant who had chosen to stay silent at interview, had not indicated a plea at the preliminary hearing despite being specifically warned, and now entered a guilty plea when confronted with overwhelming evidence of guilt; the drugs, the wrappings, the scales, the pans and the 'dealer phones'. As such while he would of course make a reduction for the guilty plea, it would be a moderate one.

10.   The judge then took the above starting point, eight years six months, deducted six months for the defendant's lack of relevant previous convictions and deducted one year (thus an eighth or 12.5 per cent) for the guilty plea. The Judge consequently passed a sentence of seven years imprisonment.

Submissions

11.   It is submitted the Judge was wrong to disregard the basis of plea without at least warning the Applicant that he was minded to do so, see *R v Smith (Patrick)* (1988) 87 Cr App R 393 and *R v Dudley* [2012] 2 Cr

App R (S) 15. Similarly, paragraph B10, *Criminal Practice Directions (Sentencing)* [2013] 1 WLR 3164 states in terms that, 'A Judge is not entitled to reject a defendant's basis of plea absent a Newton hearing unless it is determined by the court that it is manifestly false'. It is submitted that the basis advanced was not manifestly false and, in any event, if the Judge were of that belief he was still obliged to warn the Applicant of that view.

12. This was not merely a technical failing. The unused and defence material, as set out above, would have allowed submissions to be made that:

   (1) There was an obvious better candidate for the person with the senior position in the drugs supply from that house, Martin Jones.

   (2) Another person who was a perfectly sensible candidate for playing a role in the supply of drugs, also linked to the house was Ken Owen. His history of violence provided a perfectly credible explanation for why the Applicant might not have been keen to set out the history of her limited involvement with the drugs either on arrest or in interview.

   (3) The evidence from the Applicant's family would have gone beyond merely providing other possible candidates for the main drug dealing, and would have been positive evidence that she was not engaged in what is obviously a highly lucrative trade.

13. It is therefore submitted that the Judge was wrong not to warn of his view of the facts. Had he done he may well have been persuaded that he should accept the Applicant's basis of plea was the proper basis for sentence.

14. As such, it is submitted, the proper starting point in the Applicant's case, from the sentencing guidelines, for a defendant with a lesser role in category 3, one of three years' custody.

15. This Court will be very familiar with the case of *Caley* [2013] Cr App R (S) 47 and the Sentencing Guidelines Council guidelines on credit for guilty pleas. To summarise the relevant parts for the purposes of this appeal [with paragraph numbers from *Caley*]:

   (1) Whilst the sentencing judge does have flexibility as to the first reasonable time for a guilty plea to be indicated or entered, the criminal justice system should aim to be consistent between defendants, thus allowing those who act for them to advise properly [9].

   (2) The Court specifically rejected using the police interview as the first opportunity [12]

   (3) The reduction for a plea at the PCMH will be about a quarter [19]

    (4)   The Courts need to be very slow and cautious before concluding a case is overwhelming and withholding the normal reduction. Even in a truly overwhelming case where the sentencing court was entitled to reduce the credit, it would still not go below 20 per cent for a plea at the first opportunity [23 and 24].

16.   Applying the above to the facts of the instant application, it is submitted:

    (1)   The Judge was quite entitled to reject the defence application for full, 33 per cent, credit as there had been no plea at the preliminary hearing.

    (2)   The Judge was wrong to attach significance to the Applicant remaining silent in interview and at the scene, given the views of this Court in *Caley*.

    (3)   This was not an overwhelming case. Although it was obvious that the house was being used as a centre for drug dealing, the existence of other candidates who were identified as users of the house, including a man who had been convicted of serious offences of violence and the Applicant's very limited criminal history may have lead some defendants in her position to seek to advance the defence of duress. As such the Applicant should have received the usual 25 per cent reduction. If this Court accepts that argument, the final sentence should have been in the region of 23 months [in other words three years as above, reduced by 25 per cent] plus any allowance such as the Judge made for the lack of any relevant convictions.

    (4)   Even if the case were overwhelming, it is submitted the reduction the Judge allowed, of 12.5 per cent, was simply insufficient for a plea at the PCMH.

17.   For all these reason it is submitted this Applicant should be granted leave and her sentence should be very significantly reduced.

Anthony Advocate

Criminal Solicitors

Date

3   DRAFT STATEMENT OF FACTS AND STATEMENT OF ALLEGED VIOLATION AND LEGAL ARGUMENTS FOR AN APPLICATION TO THE EUROPEAN COURT OF HUMAN RIGHTS

An application to the European Court of Human Rights must be made using the Court's own application form. However, the substance of the application will be contained in the statement of facts and the statement of alleged violation(s) and relevant legal arguments that will accompany the form itself. This is a sample that is intended to indicate a possible approach to both drafting exercises. It is not intended to be a blueprint.

Statement of the facts

1. On 10 September 2010, Alfred Jones was the victim of various offences. He gave police an account of being parked outside his home waiting for his friend Ralph to join him when he was kidnapped and placed into a van. Thereafter he was driven around, assaulted, robbed and demands were made to his friends via his own mobile phone to bring large amounts of cash to a meeting place. His car was also stolen. He was able to escape some hours later. He supposedly identified the Applicant Davies as the man who first approached him as part of the kidnap and identified a blue Suzuki van as the vehicle used in the kidnap, false imprisonment and blackmail. There were a series of links between the Applicant Dawes and that van.

2. The purported identification of Davies was, at its highest, qualified. In essence, Mr Jones stated at the identification procedure that he could not be sure ['Out of all of them number 3 gave me an inkling … Can't be 100 per cent sure but I'd say number 3', number 3 being the position in the video line up at which the Applicant Davies was shown] but by stages ended up claiming in a later witness statement that he was sure of his identification of Davies as the man who had first approached him.

3. There were various alleged links between the Applicant Dawes and a blue Suzuki van. After describing the van used by his abductors in terms no more than, at best, consistent with the blue Suzuki van ['a Rascal … a little Nissan van … a little blue thing … that royal kind of blue … a transit'], six months later he was shown photographs of that van and said, 'This is the type of van I was kidnapped in … I can say that this is exactly the van that it was'.

4. In the course of the kidnap Mr Jones was asked to tell the kidnappers where his cocaine was to be found and the abductors clearly assumed that his friends would have ready access to large amounts of cash. Peter Huseyin, a friend of Jones who became a prosecution witness, first became aware of these events when the friend Ralph drove up and said that 'someone's tried to rob me and Alf outside his flat. I saw some guys near Alf's car but I don't know where he is'. Huseyin then drove for a few minutes to the area of Jones' flat. Ralph did not assist the police and was not a witness. Neither Ralph nor Huseyin called the police. Jones' girlfriend eventually called the police and the call was logged as being received at 00:20.

5. In addition to the identifying evidence from Jones, the prosecution relied on phone calls between the three defendants' mobile phones, and all three phones being cell sited in the same general area where the offences were taking place. It is noted in passing that the Applicant Davies was acquitted of counts 2 and 3 [false imprisonment and blackmail] and the

co-defendant Phipps acquitted of all counts. Thus the jury did not regard the cell site alone evidence as sufficient proof of guilt on any count.

6.   Counts 4 and 5 on the trial indictment alleged that the Applicant Dawes and the co-defendant Phipps had committed an aggravated burglary on 24 September. That allegation was based on phone evidence, the use of the car stolen from Jones in the course of counts 1 to 3, and the possession of a blackberry mobile phone, stolen in the aggravated burglary, by Phipps shortly afterwards. Both men were acquitted.

7.   Count 6 alleged a robbery of a lorry delivering cigarettes on 24 November 2010. A camera in that lorry showed that the Suzuki van to which Dawes had the links was used by the robbers and a photograph from the same source was said to be him; he was found guilty of that count.

8.   The trial was fixed for 7 June 2012. In the days before trial Mr Jones notified the police that he would not attend Court to give evidence. He alleged that on Monday 30 May his mother received a call on her landline number asking to speak to him. He then received a phone call on his mobile phone. According to Mr. Jones' statement 'It was from a private number on my mobile phone number ending 138. A male voice said, "I would advise you not to go to trial. There are a lot of people upset, they are on standby waiting for the word". I did not recognise this voice. It sounded black. I hung up the phone. Straightaway the phone rang back with private number. I answered the call but did not say anything. I did not listen to the phone and hung up. The phone rang again and my girlfriend Simone answered the call. They told her the same things and said they were in ********. She told them not to ring again and hung up the phone. During the first phone call the person told me details about the case such as what I said in my statement and details about the identity parade. I do not know if I want to go to court now. I am scared for my family. I am worried that they know details about the case.'

9.   Mr Jones was visited by Detective Constable Stewart who offered him various forms of witness protection and told him he might be witness summonsed; he replied that in that case he would not say anything in Court and would not give his evidence.

10.   The prosecution did not seek a summons or warrant but applied to read Mr Jones' evidence under section 116 of the Criminal Justice Act 2003.

11.   The application was opposed and the arguments advanced encompassed the conditional or mixed nature of the identifying claims made by the witness. Further, as regards the potential for the defendants to have been responsible for the threats, it was known that at the time that the Appellant Davies was in custody and in solitary confinement and the Appellant Dawes, being under 21, was in a Young Offenders Institution, separate from both his co-defendants.

12.   In addition, there was submitted to be another candidate for having made the threats; Darren Davies was a cousin of both Applicants. He was, at

the time leading up to the trial, wanted as a suspect with regard to all the counts on the indictment and was indeed named as another offender on count 6 of the trial indictment. He was arrested a few days prior to trial and found to have the trial committal bundle stored on his laptop, with the statements by Alfred Jones highlighted. He was charged, but at a later stage the Prosecution dropped all charges against him.

13. The trial Judge ruled that the evidence could be adduced. His decision was based on his finding that the Appellants had played some part in the threats being made. The terms of that finding were:

'(1) On basis of material available to me at the moment, I conclude as a matter of fact, so that I am sure about it, that Mr. Jones was put in a state of extreme fear by these defendants or by somebody associated with them and with their knowledge and/ or approval. In other words, these defendants are associated with those threats. I find that as a fact to the criminal standard.

(2) I have found as a fact it is through deliberate actions attributable to these defendants or with their approval that Mr. Jones is absent.'

14. The Judge also accepted that Mr Jones' evidence was 'sole or decisive' in one sense, though there was supporting evidence in the phone evidence. This ruling also, in effect, admitted the partial identifications, as it considered that aspect and made reference to section 78 of the Police and Criminal Evidence Act 1984. The Judge also referred to both *Horncastle* and *Al-Khawaja*.

15. In terms of whether the evidence was reliable, the Judge did not deal with the later recognition of the van, but dealt with the identification of the Appellant Davies; he held that the stages of the move from the uncertain terms of the identification procedure to the later witness statements were all documented and provided a 'clear line of reasoning' for his doing so, concluding that in his judgment, 'the evidence of Mr Jones is reliable in the senses that I have described. It is documented, it is reasoned, it can be tested and it can be fully commented upon'.

16. The trial proceeded. The defendants all gave evidence and proffered various reasons for their phone contact and the presence of their phones in or around the general area of the kidnap. In summary, Dawes spoke of being in the area driving around selling cannabis. Davies testified that he had left his phone at the home of his cousin Darren Davies and it was being returned to him. The co-defendant Phipps spoke of being in the area and calling Dawes to try to buy some cannabis from him.

17. The Judge summed up and gave warnings as to the difficulties faced by the defence through the absence of the witness. He also gave a traditional Turnbull direction, to warn the jury of the dangers of identification evidence, namely that an honest witness can nonetheless be mistaken. In dealing with Mr Jones' 'identification' of the blue Suzuki van, the Judge

again warned the jury of the disadvantage the defence said they faced, but went on to suggest that the other links between the Appellant Dawes and the van could support the identification [whereas, it is submitted they were the distinct next link in the evidential chain, which only became relevant once the jury accepted that first identification]:

> 'The question for you, I would suggest, is that the van, that particular blue van, linked to the crimes? I have reminded you, I think though, on Mr Jones' evidence he gives a general description of the van for you to consider. He is then shown photographs and I have reminded you about those and what he has said about it, and how the defence say they have been disadvantaged by him not having him here to question him. But you also have, have you not, other evidence, if you accept it, which links Mr. Dawes to that particular van, where police observations of him in the street going to it are on two occasions at least.'

18.   After their retirement the jury posed a question about the identification of the van by Alfred Jones, namely:

> 'In reference to admission 5, do the defence say that Alfred Stevens positively identified the Suzuki van with the registration X493LBJ? We feel there is a contradiction between paragraph 5 of the admissions and Mr Dunn's [defence Counsel at trial for Dawes] closing statement regarding the positive identification of the particular van.'

19.   The Judge answered the question, pointing out that the admissions merely gave the date, 18 March 2011, when Alfred Jones 'wrote a statement concerning the Suzuki Supercarry panel van X493LBJ'. He added a reminder of the disadvantage that the defendant faced given the inability to question Mr Jones about that identification.

20.   Amongst the varied verdicts, the jury acquitted of a number of counts that were founded on phone use and cell site evidence placing phones connected to the three defendants in the area of the false imprisonment, namely counts 2 and 3 against the Appellant Davies, and counts 1 to 3 against the defendant Phipps.

21.   All the convictions that are the subject of these appeals were by way of majority verdicts.

22.   The Applicant's appealed against their convictions. Both were given leave to appeal against their convictions on the basis of the trial Judge's admission of Alfred Stephen's evidence. In summary, their grounds of appeal submitted:

(1)   There was no evidential basis such as allowed for the conclusion reached by the trial Judge that the Defendants were behind threats made to the complainant Alfred Jones such as prevented him from attending to give evidence at trial.

(2) Further, it is submitted that the combined effect of *Horncastle* in the Supreme Court and *Al-Khawaja and Tahery* in the Grand Chamber of the European Court of Human Rights was such that in the absence of an individual defendant threatening a witness away from trial, 'sole or decisive' evidence should not be admitted as hearsay unless there is exceptional and compelling support such as to suggest it is truthful and accurate.

23. The Applicants were granted leave to appeal. The Court of Appeal heard their case on 7 September 2012. The Court dismissed their appeal, finding:

(1) The trial Judge should have required the prosecution to make attempts to get Mr Jones to come to court, but that failing was not fatal to the conviction.

(2) The trial Judge's finding that the Applicants could be blamed for the fear of Mr Jones was impeccable. The Court did not identify what, if any, evidence could possibly be the basis for such a finding.

(3) The Court held that the evidence was admissible under the test expounded in *R v Riat* [see below].

24. On the same day, the Applicants applied to the Court of Appeal for the following question to be certified as a point of law of general public importance [thus allowing the Applicants to apply for permission to appeal to the UK Supreme Court]:

'Should the sole or decisive evidence of an absent witness be admitted as hearsay if it is not demonstrably reliable?'

25. Later that day the Court of Appeal indicated, by way of phone calls between Lady Justice Thorne's clerk and defence Counsel's clerks that the Court would not certify the question.

26. In the light of the refusal to certify, there was no further avenue of appeal open to the Applicant's in the domestic Courts.

Statement of alleged violation(s) of the convention and relevant arguments

The law

RELEVANT STATUTORY PROVISIONS

1. Section 116 of the *Criminal Justice Act* 2003 states as follows:

'116. Cases where a witness is unavailable

(1) In criminal proceedings a statement not made in oral evidence in the proceedings is admissible as evidence of any matter stated if–

(a)   oral evidence given in the proceedings by the person who made the statement would be admissible as evidence of that matter,

(b)   the person who made the statement (the relevant person) is identified to the court's satisfaction, and

(c)   any of the five conditions mentioned in subsection (2) is satisfied.

(2)   The conditions are–

(a)   that the relevant person is dead;

(b)   that the relevant person is unfit to be a witness because of his bodily or mental condition;

(c)   that the relevant person is outside the United Kingdom and it is not reasonably practicable to secure his attendance;

(d)   that the relevant person cannot be found although such steps as it is reasonably practicable to take to find him have been taken;

(e)   that through fear the relevant person does not give (or does not continue to give) oral evidence in the proceedings, either at all or in connection with the subject matter of the statement, and the court gives leave for the statement to be given in evidence.

(3)   For the purposes of subsection (2)(e) "fear" is to be widely construed and (for example) includes fear of the death or injury of another person or of financial loss.

(4)   Leave may be given under subsection (2)(e) only if the court considers that the statement ought to be admitted in the interests of justice, having regard–

(a)   to the statement's contents,

(b)   to any risk that its admission or exclusion will result in unfairness to any party to the proceedings (and in particular to how difficult it will be to challenge the statement if the relevant person does not give oral evidence),

(c)   in appropriate cases, to the fact that a direction under section 19 of the Youth Justice and Criminal Evidence Act 1999 (special measures for the giving of evidence by fearful witnesses etc) could be made in relation to the relevant person, and

(d)   to any other relevant circumstances.

(5)   A condition set out in any paragraph of subsection (2) which is in fact satisfied is to be treated as not satisfied if it is shown that the circumstances described in that paragraph are caused–

(a)   by the person in support of whose case it is sought to give the statement in evidence, or

(b)   by a person acting on his behalf,

in order to prevent the relevant person giving oral evidence in the proceedings (whether at all or in connection with the subject matter of the statement).'

RELEVANT ARTICLE OF THE CONVENTION

1.   Article 6 states:

'(1)   In the determination of his civil rights and obligations or of any criminal charge against him, everyone is entitled to a fair and public hearing within a reasonable time by an independent and impartial tribunal established by law. Judgment shall be pronounced publicly but the press and public may be excluded from all or part of the trial in the interest of morals, public order or national security in a democratic society, where the interests of juveniles or the protection of the private lives of the parties so require, or to the extent strictly necessary in the opinion of the court in special circumstances where publicity would prejudice the interests of justice.

(2)   Everyone charged with a criminal offence shall be presumed innocent until proved guilty according to law.

(3)   Everyone charged with a criminal offence has the following minimum rights:

(a)   to be informed promptly, in a language which he understands and in detail, of the nature and cause of the accusation against him;

(b)   to have adequate time and facilities for the preparation of his defence;

(c)   to defend himself in person or through legal assistance of his own choosing or, if he has not sufficient means to pay for legal assistance, to be given it free when the interests of justice so require;

(d)   to examine or have examined witnesses against him and to obtain the attendance and examination of witnesses on his behalf under the same conditions as witnesses against him;

(e)   to have the free assistance of an interpreter if he cannot understand or speak the language used in court.'

Case law

1.   A series of cases in the European Court of Human Rights considered the meaning of the Article 6(3)(d) right to 'examine or have examined witnesses against him'. In *Luca v Italy* (2003) 36 EHRR 46 at paragraph 40, the Court stated as follows:

'If the defendant has been given an adequate and proper opportunity to challenge the depositions, either when made or at a later stage, their admission in evidence will not in itself contravene Article 6.1 and 3(d). The corollary of that, however, is that where the conviction is both solely or to a decisive degree based on depositions that had been made by a person whom the accused has had no opportunity to examine or to have examined, whether during the investigation or at the trial, the rights of the defence are restricted to an extent that is incompatible with the guarantees provided by Article 6.'

2. This line of authority was ultimately considered by the Supreme Court in *R v Horncastle* [2010] 1 Cr App R 17. The Court rejected the 'sole or decisive' test, Lord Phillips holding at paragraph 108:

    'In these circumstances I have decided that it would not be right for this court to hold that the sole or decisive test should have been applied rather than the provisions of the 2003 Act, interpreted in accordance with their natural meaning.'

3. The Court declined to follow the earlier ECHR section judgment in *Al-Khawaja and Tahery*, in the following terms [paragraph 11]:

    'There will, however, be rare occasions where this court has concerns as to whether a decision of the Strasbourg Court sufficiently appreciates or accommodates particular aspects of our domestic process. In such circumstances it is open to this court to decline to follow the Strasbourg decision, giving reasons for adopting this course. This is likely to give the Strasbourg Court the opportunity to reconsider the particular aspect of the decision that is in issue, so that there takes place what may prove to be a valuable dialogue between this court and the Strasbourg Court. This is such a case.'

4. That reconsideration duly occurred when the Grand Chamber gave judgment in the UK government's appeal, *Al-Khawaja and Tahery* [2012] 54 EHRR 53. In essence, the Grand Chamber reaffirmed the 'sole or decisive' rule but modified the rigidity with which it should be applied. Thus at paragraph 147:

    'The Court therefore concludes that, where a hearsay statement is the sole or decisive evidence against a defendant, its admission as evidence will not automatically result in a breach of Article 6 § 1. At the same time where a conviction is based solely or decisively on the evidence of absent witnesses, the Court must subject the proceedings to the most searching scrutiny'

5. Neither of the absent witnesses in *Al-Khwaja and Tahery* had been kept from court by the acts of the accused, but in discussing that situation the Grand Chamber stated [at paragraph 123]:

    'When a witness's fear is attributable to the defendant or those acting on his behalf, it is appropriate to allow the evidence of that witness to be introduced at trial without the need for the witness to give live evidence or be examined by the defendant or his representatives – even if such evidence was the sole or decisive evidence against the defendant. To allow the defendant to benefit from the fear he has engendered in witnesses would be incompatible with the rights of victims and witnesses. No court could be expected to allow the integrity of its proceedings to be subverted in this way. Consequently, a defendant who has acted in this manner must be taken to have waived his rights to question such witnesses under art. 6(3)(d). The same conclusion must apply when the threats or actions which lead to the witness being afraid to testify come from those who act on behalf of the defendant or with his knowledge and approval.'

6. In applying the modified test as to when 'sole or decisive' hearsay might be admitted, the Grand Chamber discussed the facts of the two cases. In *Al-Khawaja* the Court allowed the UK's appeal, finding that it 'would be difficult to conceive of stronger corroborative evidence' [paragraph 156] for the accuracy and truthfulness of the absent witness. In contrast, in *Tahery* the finding of a violation was upheld; in that case the victim had been stabbed but was unable to say which of the various men in the vicinity had stabbed him. The only witness who claimed that Tahery was the stabber made a statement to police within two days, then refused to attend court through a fear of being seen as an informer, which fear could not be shown to be brought about by Tahery. The Grand Chamber spoke of his evidence in these terms: 'Even though the testimony may have been coherent and convincing on its face it cannot be said to belong to the category of evidence that can be described as "demonstrably reliable"' [paragraph 160].

7. In *R v Ibrahim* [2012] EWCA Crim 837, the Court of Appeal considered the differing conclusions of *Horncastle* and the Grand Chamber judgment and suggested [at paragraph 89]:

    'This difference may be more one of form than substance, however. Thus, the Court of Appeal talked of a conviction being based "solely or to a decisive degree on hearsay evidence admitted under the CJA" and the Supreme Court talked of the hearsay evidence being "critical evidence". That may not be very different from the Grand Chamber's concept of "sole or decisive". Next, the Court of Appeal and the Supreme Court both emphasise that when the untested hearsay evidence is "critical", the question of whether the trial is fair will depend on three principal factors. First, the English courts accept that there has to be good reason to admit the untested hearsay evidence. To decide this under English law there must be compliance with the statutory code. The Grand Chamber necessarily puts this requirement on a more general basis, but it emphasised the need for "justification". Secondly, and we think most importantly, all three courts stipulate that there must be an enquiry as to whether that evidence can be shown to be reliable. Thirdly, all three courts are concerned with the extent to which there are "counterbalancing measures" and if so whether they have been properly applied in deciding whether to admit the "critical" untested hearsay evidence or to allow the case to proceed. In the case of England and Wales those "counterbalancing measures" must include all the statutory safeguards in the "code", as well as a proper application of common law safeguards, such as proper directions in the summing up. The Grand Chamber emphasised the same thing at paragraph 144 and particularly in its "general conclusion on the sole or decisive rule" at paragraph 147'

8.   In the subsequent case of *R v Riat* [2012] EWCA Crim 1509, the Court of Appeal considered a number of appeals in the light of the Supreme Court judgment in *Horncastle*, the Grand Chamber decision in *Al-Khawaja and Tahery*, and the Court of Appeal's judgment in *Ibrahim*. At paragraphs 4–6 and 17, the Court explained that if *Horncastle*, *Al-Khawaja* and *Ibrahim* had been understood to suggest that evidence that was central or sole and decisive should only be admitted if it was clearly or manifestly reliable, that is to say accurate, then that was a misunderstanding. In fact, the position is that evidence can be admitted either if it is manifestly reliable or if any possible unreliability is such as can be tested by the jury.

Submissions: alleged violations of Article 6 of the Convention

1.   The Grand Chamber in *Al Khawaja and Tahery* constructed a delicate accommodation so as to guard the rights of those within signatory states and yet to concede a degree of sovereignty to national courts as to the manner in which such rights are protected. It is submitted, with regret, that the decision in this case show that the English Court of Appeal has disregarded that delicate balance and that the current state of law now propounded by the UK Court of Appeal permits flagrant breaches of the right to a fair trial. It is further submitted that the response of the UK perhaps, with respect, confirms the fears of honourable dissenting Judges in the Grand Chamber decision, that:

> 'The sole or decisive rule that has been followed so far was intended to protect human rights against the "fruit of the poisonous tree" … The adoption of the counterbalancing approach means that a rule that was intended to safeguard human rights is replaced with the uncertainties of counterbalancing.'

2.   It is submitted that the Applicants rights under Article 6(3)(d) to 'examine witnesses against him' were violated at their trial. The witness Jones was central to the cases against both men. Without his account the prosecution could not have even begun their case. The evidence adduced was such as to identify the Applicant Davies and to identify the vehicle

closely associated with the Applicant Dawes. It is submitted to be telling that the other counts that were not supported by such identifications, both against these Applicants and against their co-defendant at trial, led to acquittals.

3. In the Grand Chamber of *Al-Khawaja and Tahery* this honourable Court adopted the modified test of not absolutely barring 'sole or decisive' hearsay evidence, but subjecting such evidence to 'the most searching scrutiny'. That level of scrutiny was illustrated in the outcome of those cases, whereby the 'demonstrably reliable' evidence against the Applicant Al-Khawaja led to the UK's appeal being allowed, whereas the lack of such evidence led to the decision in *Tahery* being unchanged. To apply a similar test, the evidence of the absent witness in the Applicants' case, his identification of the Applicant Davies was a flawed example of a form of evidence, identification evidence, that is considered dangerous even when given by a 'live' witness. In the Applicant Dawes's case, a bland statement describing a very common type of van in the most general terms was then followed much later by an assertion that the vehicle linked to the Applicant was the very same van.

4. In addition to the obvious weaknesses and potential for error in the nature of the evidence the missing witness gave, there was what could be seen as a 'drugs' background, in that his friends declined to call the police and the demands made of Mr Jones were, according to him, for cash and cocaine. Without expecting this honourable Court to make any finding adverse to that absent witness, that background of possible criminal activity by the complainant and his associates is such as to make his account even more in need of the most careful testing under cross examination.

5. If there were any evidential basis for the trial Judge's finding that the Applicants were both responsible for the absent witness being placed in fear, then it is accepted that this case would be outside the judgment in *Al-Kahwaja and Tahery*. It is submitted that there was simply no evidence of the Applicants being those responsible. It is submitted to be telling that neither the trial Judge nor the Court of Appeal even purported to identify any evidence such as could justify such a finding. Whilst this Court will very often defer to the facts found by the trial tribunal, if the Court is to guarantee rights that are practical and effective, it must be prepared not to allow a national court to shield its breaches of Convention rights by completely indefensible findings of fact.

6. The decision of the Court of Appeal in *Ibrahim* had the potential to resolve the dispute between this Court and the UK domestic courts by an accommodation that seemed to allow for the use of sole or decisive hearsay only it was manifestly reliable. The later judgment in *Riat* specifically 'explained away' that approach such that no such limit is now in place in the English law.

7.   This Court will notice that the 'valuable dialogue' that Lord Phillips spoke of in the Supreme Court judgment in *Horncastle* has not taken place. This is because the English Court of Appeal has refused to certify a point of law of public important, thus cutting off the possibility of a further appeal within the English system, as section 33(2) of the Criminal Appeal Act 1968 states, inter alia, that an 'appeal lies only with the leave of the Court of Appeal or the Supreme Court; and leave shall not be granted unless it is certified by the Court of Appeal that a point of law of general public importance is involved in the decision'.

8.   The Applicants therefore submit that they have suffered a violation of their right to a fair trial in that the trial judge's admitted sole or decisive evidence that they had no chance to challenge.

Appendix E

Court of Appeal Bill of Costs

COURT OF APPEAL (CRIMINAL DIVISION)
BILL OF COSTS
FOR TAXATION BY REGISTRAR

If you require a version of this form to use with a screen reader (such as JAWS), or if you have a question about the form, please contact the Cost Office.

CRIMINAL APPEAL REFERENCE NO: ....

Regina v	Representation Order granted by lower Court
Messrs	Representation Order granted by Court of Appeal dated
of	
	Prosecution costs against Appellant
Ref	
V.A.T. No	Appellant/Prosecution costs from central funds

PLEASE READ NOTES ON PAGE 4 IMMEDIATELY

Solicitors should send with the Bill of Costs:- (a) The Brief and any instructions to and advice from Counsel: (b) The file of correspondence and record of attendances: (c) Details of all Disbursements and Accounts where appropriate.

DO NOT ENCLOSE COPY STATEMENTS OR EXHIBITS

In Representation Order cases no item in this Bill should relate to work undertaken prior to the date of conviction or sentence in the Crown Court, or prior to the date from which a Representation Order was granted in the Court of Appeal.

THIS BILL MUST BE COMPLETED IN BLACK INK OR BE TYPEWRITTEN FOR PHOTOGRAPHIC PURPOSES

1. PREPARATION OF APPLICATION FOR LEAVE TO APPEAL AND/OR APPEAL – PREPARATION AND CONSIDERATION OF DOCUMENTS.

Documents/Prepared considered (state nature and specify)	Status of Fee Earner ie Sen Sol, Sol Sen L Ex, Sen Clk, L Ex, or Art Clk	Date Work Undertaken	Time Taken Hrs Mins	Claimed £ p	Allowed £ p
			C.F.	£	

The Criminal Defence Services (Funding) Order 2001.

336

2.   PREPARATION OF APPLICATION FOR LEAVE TO APPEAL AND/OR APPEAL –
ATTENDANCES

PERSON INTERVIEWED [State name and whether client (c) or witness (w) and if alibi, factual, expert etc] and reasons for interview	Status of Fee Earner ie Sen Sol, Sol Sen L Ex, Sen Clk, L Ex, or Art Clk	Date Work Undertaken	Time Taken Hrs Mins	Claimed £ p	Allowed £ p
Brought forward from page 1				£	
The necessity for an interview with the client, in the prison or other place must depend upon the difficulty of the case.					
Travelling time to be shown separately.					
Show location of interviews.					
CONFERENCES [State purpose, Conferences held at Court should not be included here].					
LETTERS/EMAILS (Routine)					
TELEPHONE CALLS (Routine)					
NOTE Petty disbursements such as telephone charges, postage, etc form part of the overheads and should NOT be claimed.					
Totals carried forward to Summary on page 3				£	

State below any unusual features of the case or any particular problems that were experienced in preparation which contributed materially to weight or difficulty.

Court of Appeal Bill of Costs

3. CONDUCT OF APPLICATION FOR LEAVE TO APPEAL AND/OR APPEAL AT COURT – ATTENDANCES

PURPOSE [Specify as appn for bail, hearing etc. conferences at Court are normally included in the daily fee unless they represent material progress: please specify]	Status of Fee Earner ie Sen Sol, Sol Sen L Ex, Sen Clk, L Ex, or Art Clk	Date Work Undertaken	Time Taken Hrs Mins	Claimed £ p	Allowed £ p
	Totals carried down to Summary below:			£ 0.00	

		CLAIMED £ p	ALLOWED £ p

SUMMARY

B/f from page 2 – PREPARATION OF APPLICATION FOR LEAVE TO APPEAL AND/OR APPEAL   £

B/d from above   CONDUCT OF APPLICATION FOR LEAVE TO APPEAL AND/OR APPEAL AT COURT   £0.00

DISBURSEMENTS LIABLE TO V.A.T. [please specify]

(a) Travelling expenses [identified by reference to parts 1 and 3]
    Miles @

     TOTAL for V.A.T. purposes   £

     V.A.T.   £

DISBURSEMENTS NOT LIABLE TO V.A.T. [eg agency work]
Please specify and include vouchers

     TOTAL CLAIMED AND ALLOWED   £

Determining Officer: DATE:

COURT OF APPEAL – CRIMINAL DIVISION

IMPORTANT – PLEASE READ IMMEDIATELY

1. Where work of an exceptional nature is contemplated, or where the expenses will be heavy eg in travelling a long distance for a conference, it will be wise to consult the Registrar beforehand as to whether the work or the expense is likely to be regarded as reasonable.

   IF IN ANY DOUBT, DO PLEASE CHECK FIRST.

2. Appeals against Sentence: It is very rare that the Court grants Representation Order to solicitors – it is normally confined to Counsel only.

3. Appeals against Conviction: Although Representation Order to Solicitors is granted more frequently than in appeals against Sentence, it is still only granted in a small minority of cases: see note 2 above.

4. If Representation Order is granted to solicitors to cover attendance at the appeal hearing, consideration should be given to the instruction of solicitor agents if the cost of travel will be heavy.

5. Typing and Photocopying: these items are not normally allowed on taxation – if copies of Committal documents, transcripts etc are considered necessary, you should consult the Registrar before undertaking any expense.

6. A claim must be submitted within 3 months of the conclusion of the proceedings to which the Representation Order relates (Para 11, Schedule 1). No claim can be considered after this unless an extension of time is granted (Para 23, Schedule 1).

7. Reminders: Where

   (a) there are special circumstances, which should be drawn to the attention of the appropriate authority, the solicitor must specify them;

   (b) the solicitor claims that paragraph 4 of schedule 2, part 1 (ie enhanced rates) should be applied in relation to an item of work, he must give full particulars in support of the claim (Para 11, Schedule 1).

Appendix F

New Client Appeal Enquiry Form

GT STEWART SOLICITORS
APPEAL ENQUIRY FORM

Contact Details

Full Name:	Date of Birth:
Address/Prison:	Gender:
	Mobile:
Prison No:	Landline:
National Insurance no:	Email:
Family member or friend who can we discuss your case with:	
Name:	Contact number/email:
How did you hear about us?	Inside Time Internet Recommended by: _____ Other (specify): _____

Conviction Details

	Charge	Plea	Sentence	Type
1.		Guilty / Not guilty		Consecutive / Concurrent
2.		Guilty / Not guilty		Consecutive / Concurrent
3.		Guilty / Not guilty		Consecutive / Concurrent

Court and Legal Team Details

Trial Court:	Type: Youth / Magistrates / Crown Court
Your Solicitors:	Date of Trial:
Contact name:	Date of Sentence:
Tel number:	Advocate / Barrister:
Address:	Advocate / Barrister's Chambers:

About Your Case:

Names of other parties to the case

Name of complainant(s): ....

Nameofco-defendant(s):..

The facts of the case

Please answer the questions below, explaining who, what, why, when, where and how

Please briefly explain what the prosecution said happened:

....
....
....
....
....
....
....
....
....
....
....

Please briefly explain what you say happened:

....
....
....
....
....
....
....
....
....
....
....

New Client Appeal Enquiry Form

Previous Advice on Appeal

Please answer the questions below. Once you have answered these, if there is anything else you would like to add about these questions, please use the space at the bottom of the page.

1. Did you receive advice on appeal from your trial solicitor or barrister?   Yes / No

2. Was this positive or negative advice?   Positive / Negative

3. Have you received advice on appeal from any other solicitor or barrister?   Yes / No

4. Was this within the last six months?   Yes / No

4. Was this advice positive or negative?   Positive / Negative

5. Did you apply to the Court of Appeal?   Yes / No

6. Did you have legal representation for this application?   Yes / No

7. Did the single judge at the Court of Appeal grant or refuse your application?

Grant / Refuse / Waiting

8. If your application was refused, did you renew to the full Court of Appeal?   Yes / No

9. Have the full Court of Appeal rejected your application?   Yes / No / Waiting

10. Have you submitted an application to the CCRC?   Yes / No

11. If yes, when?   ....

12. Has a lawyer helped you with the application to the CCRC?   Yes / No

13. If yes, who: ....

14. Have you received a decision from the CCRC?   Yes / No

15. Was the decision of the CCRC positive or negative?   Positive / Negative

Additional information: ....

....

....

....

....

....

....

....

If you have any paperwork relating to any of the questions stated above (for example, a copy of the advice on appeal from your trial legal representatives), please provide copies of these to us.

Reasons For Appeal

What do you want to appeal against?   Conviction / Sentence / Both

Appeals Against Conviction:

Tell us why you want to appeal – tick all that apply and describe why in the spaces provided

1. New evidence ☐

....
....
....

Please note that new evidence must be something that was not available at your trial. For example, if a witness was available at trial but your trial team decided not to call the person for tactical reasons, this does not count as new evidence.

2. Mistake by the Judge at trial ☐

....
....
....

3. Perverse verdict ☐

....
....
....

4. Unfair trial ☐

....
....
....

5. Incompetence by your legal representative ☐

....
....
....

6. Any other reason your conviction is unsafe ☐

....
....
....

New Client Appeal Enquiry Form

<u>Appeals Against Sentence:</u>

In order to appeal against a sentence, you must be able to show that your sentence is 'manifestly excessive'.
When sentencing, a judge will consider 'aggravating' factors which can make a sentence longer and 'mitigating' factors which can make a sentence shorter.
An example of an aggravating factor may be if the victim was vulnerable.
An example of a mitigating factor may be if you suffer from mental health issues.
The judge will use these factors and the circumstances of the offence to decide on which category of sentence should be given.

Please answer the following questions:

1. Do you know what category of offence the judge used to sentence you?

....
....
....

2. What did the prosecution say were aggravating factors?

....
....
....

3. What did your defence advocate / barrister say were mitigating factors?

....
....
....

4. What did the judge say were aggravating factors?

....
....
....

5. What did the judge say were mitigating factors?

....
....
....

New Client Appeal Enquiry Form

6. Are there any other mitigating factors which were not considered, or which the judge did not give enough weight to?

....
....
....

7. Were any mental health assessments carried out?

....
....
....

Legal Aid Eligibility

If you are in prison, what is your prison income?	£_____ per week
If you are not in prison, do you receive benefits?	Yes / No
If yes, what benefits do you receive?	
If you have a partner, what are their contact details?	
Do you have any savings or valuable property?	Yes / No
If yes, approximately how much are they worth?	£_____
Have you signed another CRM1 and CRM2 with another solicitor in the past six months?	Yes / No
If yes, please explain why they are no longer providing you with advice and assistance	

Please return to us in the stamped addressed envelope provided:

1. **This form**

2. **Completed CRM 1+ 2**

3. **Signed client authority**

Please note that we will be unable to assess your case unless you have completed every section of the CRM1 and CRM2 form and the client authority.

Index

All references are to paragraph numbers

A

Absolute discharge 14.16
Abuse of process 2.14
  unfair conviction 3.16
Acquittal agreement
  prosecution appeals against rulings
    under s 58 CJA 13.5, 13.7–8
Acquittals
  prosecution's rights of appeal
    13.2
Acts of Parliament 2.1
Address
  correspondence 1.26
  Court of Appeal judges 1.17
Admissibility 5.5
  applications to ECtHR 11.19
Adverse publicity
  appeals founded on 3.46
Advice and assistance
  application for CCRC referral 9.17
  funding *see* Funding
  unfair convictions 3.28
Advocacy 7.1–3, 7.38–39
Advocate (formerly Bar *Pro Bono* Unit)
  8.56
Advocates
  advice from 8.40
  claims for work done in Court of
    Appeal 8.17
  expectations of 7.39
  fees 8.40
Advocates Graduated Fee Scheme
  (AGFS) 8.7
Aggravated trespass 10.5
Alibi evidence 3.58
'Alleged violations'
  section of form for applications to
    ECtHR 11.14
Allowing appeal 3.61
Alternative verdicts
  leaving to jury 3.35
Anti-social behaviour orders 4.11

Appeals
  against conviction 3.1
    adverse publicity 3.46
    appeal following guilty plea 3.29
    categories not closed 3.60
    changes in law 3.59
    citation of authorities 6.25
    court's powers *see* Court's powers
    defective summing up *see* Defective
      summing up
    errors of defence lawyers 3.52–58
    fresh evidence 3.47–51
    grounds
      allegations of jury misconduct
        3.40–43
      jury selection 3.39
      possible jury bias 3.44–45
    meaning of 'unsafe' *see* Unsafe
      convictions
    trial rulings 3.30–31
  against sentence 1.13, 1.19, 4.1–5,
    5.5
    citation of authorities 6.26
    confiscation orders *see* Confiscation
      orders
    disparity in sentence 4.35
    failure to credit time spent on
      qualifying curfew 4.39
    grounds for 4.4, 4.19–20, 6.22
      assistance provided to police
        6.23
      court to consider whether total
        sentence is wrong 4.25
      failure to follow guidelines
        4.26–31
      manifestly excessive 4.21–24
    indictment/cases sent from
      Magistrates' Court 4.6–7
    'sentence' 4.8–9
      anti-social behaviour orders
        4.11
      costs 4.10

Appeals – *contd*
  against sentence – *contd*
    indictment/cases sent from
      Magistrates' Court – *contd*
      'sentence' – *contd*
        financial reporting orders 4.14
        fixed by law, appeals 4.15
        making/varying of sexual
          offences prevention orders
          4.12
        more than one 4.17–18
        parents/guardians, appeals 4.16
        restraining orders 4.13
    post-sentence developments
      4.33–34
    principles 4.4, 4.19–39
    procedural unfairness 4.32
    prosecution's rights of appeal 13.2
    unlawful sentences and slip rule
      4.36–38
  defendants suffering from mental
    disorder 14.1–5
  findings of unfitness to plead/
    accused made act or omission
    charged 14.6–11
  insanity
    order made under s.5 of Criminal
      Procedure (Insanity) Act
      1964 14.16–19
    verdict of not guilty by reason of
      14.12–15
  dismissal 7.40–44
  interlocutory rulings 12.1–3
    exceptions to 12.2
    procedure 12.3
  leave to appeal *see* Leave to appeal
  pre-1995 regime 1.11
  removal of automatic right of 1.10
  Supreme Court 10.1–22, 13.40
  test for 1.10
  under s.35 of Criminal Procedures and
    Investigations Act 1996 12.12–17
    procedure 12.16
    reporting restrictions 12.17
    scope 12.14–15
    terrorism cases 12.13
Appellant/applicant
  absconding 7.21
  attendance at Supreme Court 10.20
  costs 7.48–50

Appellant/applicant – *contd*
  death of 7.22–23
  insanity or disability of 7.17
  personal representative of 7.22
  presence at hearing 7.17, 7.19–23
  widow/widower of 7.22
Appellate Committee of the House of
  Lords 10.1
Arrest records 5.13
Asset recovery
  confiscation orders/other orders
    4.40–43
Assisted suicide 10.5
Assize Courts 1.2
Attorney-General's References 13.20
  court's approach to 13.28–30
  discount for double jeopardy 13.32–35
  full hearings 13.26–27
  funding for respondent's
    representation 13.25
  grounds for appeal 13.21
  notification of appeal and reply
    13.23–24
  permission for 13.26
  procedure 13.22
  types of sentence subject to 13.20
Authorities 7.14–15
Automatic right of appeal
  removal of 1.10

B

Bad character
  evidence of 6.31
Bad legal advice
  abandonment of application for leave
    to appeal a nullity 6.73
Bail 1.20, 10.19
  applications for 6.36–40
  re-trial 3.75
Bar *Pro Bono* Unit 8.56
Bias
  jury 3.44–45
Bristol University
  innocence project 8.52

C

Capacity
  applicant for appeal 6.17
Case file 5.12
Case law 1.14

Case management 1.21
Case preparation 1.22, 7.1–3
Case summary 7.7–9
 consideration of 7.8
Casework 1.23, 1.28
CCTV 5.13
Centre for Criminal Appeals 8.55
Certification of fitness to appeal 14.5
Changes in law 3.59, 6.32–35
Character witness 5.5
Children
 evidence from 7.26
 financial eligibility 8.31
Chronology 5.14
Circuit judges 1.16
Citation of authorities 6.24–27
 justification for 6.26
Civil partner
 financial eligibility 8.28
Claims
 work done in Court of Appeal 8.13–19
Comments
 judge 3.32–33
Common law
 interpreting in accordance with
  ECHR 2.7
Communication
 applications to ECtHR 11.21
 with Court 1.26–28
 with parties 1.22
Compensation
 applications to ECtHR 11.31
Competence
 trial lawyers 3.56
Complex fraud trials
 appeals against rulings made at
  preparatory hearing in 12.4–11
 circumstances in which ruling may
  be appealed 12.6–9
 procedure 12.10
 reporting restrictions 12.11
Composition 1.18–19
Computer hard drives 5.13
Confiscation orders
 appeals against 4.5
 appeals made by consent 4.47–48
 extension of time to appeal against
  4.49–50
 fresh evidence 4.46
 grounds of appeal 4.44

Confiscation orders – *contd*
 appeals against – *contd*
  powers of court 4.51
  principles relating to 4.44–50
  rights of appeal 4.40–43
  prosecution 4.52–53
  slip rule 4.45
  'sentence' in relation to offence 4.8
Consent
 appeals against confiscation orders
  4.47–48
Contemporaneous notes 5.13
Contempt of court 10.5
Convention rights
 violations of 11.14
Conviction
 appeals against 3.1–83, 6.20
  citation of authorities 6.25
 circumstances in which re-trial may be
  ordered 3.67
 date of 6.8
 fresh evidence received after 3.47–51
 obligations of prosecution after 10.5
 quashing 3.51
 safeness of 1.10
 substitution 3.62, 3.64–66
 'unsafe' 3.2–28
Correspondence 1.26–28
Costs 7.46
 appealing 4.10
 applications to ECtHR 11.32
 from central funds 7.48
 law relating to 7.47
 renewal of application for leave to
  appeal 6.67
 Supreme Court 10.21
 third parties 7.55
 unnecessary or improper expenses
  7.50
 wasted costs orders 7.51–54
 unsuccessful appellant/applicant 7.49
Costs Judge
 appeal to 8.18
Court bundle 7.5
Court of Appeal
 applications at conclusion of case
  7.40–56
 cases referred by Criminal Cases
  Review Commission (CCRC)
  9.1–33

Court of Appeal – *contd*
  claiming fees for work done
    advocate's claims 8.17
    all claims 8.13
    appealing the assessment 8.18
    disbursements 8.16
    other costs orders 8.19
    solicitor's claims 8.14
      enhanced hourly rates 8.15
  communicating with 1.26–28
  composition 1.18–19
  consolidation of powers 1.8
  costs 7.46–47
  current statutory regime 1.12–13
  development of 1.2
  framework for 1.9
  function of 1.1
  governance of 1.9
  hearings
    appeals with leave 7.32–35
    appellant
      absconded 7.21
      death of 7.22–23
      representation of prosecution 7.24
    listing 7.16
    preparation 7.1–4
      authorities 7.14–15
      considering Court bundle 7.5–10
      new grounds of appeal 7.13
      skeleton arguments 7.11–12
    presence of appellant/applicant
      hearings with leave 7.17
      renewed applications for leave
        7.19–20
    public immunity applications 7.30
    public right to attend 7.25–26
    renewed applications for leave
      7.36–37
    reporting restrictions 7.27–29
    suggestions for advocacy 7.38–39
    televised 7.31
  history of 1.2
  investigations by CCRC at direction of
    9.30–32
  jurisdiction 1.12
  legislation establishing 1.3–4
  location 1.24
  permanent judges 1.16
  reconstitution of 1.7
  reforms of 1.7, 1.10

Court of Appeal – *contd*
  representation order *see* Court of
    Appeal representation order
  sittings 1.25
  type of law interpreted and applied
    by 2.1
Court of Appeal representation order
  representation under 8.4
    actual representation replaces advice
      and assistance 8.5
    pro bono assistance 8.6
  work under
    advice covered 8.8–10
    funding rules 8.7
    single judge
      effect of refusal by 8.11
      post-refusal advice 8.12
Court's powers 3.61–63
  re-sentencing 3.80
  re-trial order 3.62
    bail 3.75
    circumstances 3.67–68
    court listing of legal argument 3.74
    court's power to amend indictment
      3.76
    defendant arraigned on new
      indictment 3.72
    time scale 3.72–73
    legal aid 3.79
    limitations on court 3.77
    procedure for making 3.69–71
    procedure once order made
      3.72–79
    taking effect of sentence following
      3.78
  venire do novo 3.82–83, 14.10
  substituting a conviction 3.64–3.66
Courts Martial
  appeals from 1.1
CPS Appeals Unit 6.57
Crime scene
  on private property 5.29
  visiting and recording 5.29
Criminal Appeals Office 1.22, 6.62, 7.5,
  7.7, 7.14
Criminal Appeals Review Commission
  1.10
Criminal Bills Assessment Manual
  (CBAM) 8.3
  disbursements 8.39

Criminal Cases Review Commission
(CCRC) 3.1, 3.42, 4.17, 5.3, 5.33,
7.23, 9.1–2
application for referral 9.10–25
definition of 'new argument' 9.12
'exceptional circumstances' 9.14–15
making application 9.16–18
assistance 9.17
guidance 9.16
time limits 9.13
when to apply 9.11–13
who may apply 9.10
applications 5.32, 8.40
previous 5.13
special considerations 8.41–45
cases
referral by Court of Appeal 9.1–33
transcripts 8.40
criticisms 9.33
disclosure by 9.28
establishment of 9.3
investigations by 5.31–33
appointment of investigating officer
9.28
decision-making process 9.21–22
direction of Court of Appeal
9.30–32
final decision 9.24
likely timeframe for decision 9.25
overview of investigatory powers
9.28–29
provisional statement of reasons
9.23
requesting 9.19–20
observations 9.33
powers
deployment 5.31
investigations 9.28–29
referral to Court of Appeal 9.4–6
referral to Court of Appeal 8.52
application 9.10–25
challenging refusal 9.26
discretion 9.9
powers 9.4–6
procedure following 9.27
test 9.7–8
role 9.3
Criminal Justice Act 2003
prosecution appeals against rulings
under s.58 13.3–6

Criminal Justice Act 2003 – *contd*
prosecution appeals against rulings
under s.58 – *contd*
acquittal agreement 13.7–8
valid 13.5
appeal to Supreme Court 13.40
notice of intention to appeal 13.5
procedure 13.9–12
Attorney-General's References
see Attorney-General's
References
hearing 13.16–19
respondent's notice 13.13–15
responding to appellant's case
13.36–39
when appeal may be brought 13.5–6
Criminal law 2.12
Criminal legal aid contracts 6.44
Criminal liability 2.15
Criminal offences
creation of 2.15
Criminal Practice Direction 1.14
provisions on skeleton arguments
7.11
Criminal procedure 2.12
Criminal Procedure (Insanity) Act 1964
appeals against order made under s.5
of 14.16–19
Criminal Procedure Rules (CPR) 1.14
Criminal Procedures and Investigations
Act 1996
appeals under s.35 12.12–17
procedure 12.16
reporting restrictions 12.17
scope 12.14–15
terrorism cases 12.13
Criticism
previous lawyers 6.30
cautious approach 3.57
Crown Court
appeals from 1.1, 4.6
Crown Court Bench Book 3.37
Crown Court representation order
advice and assistance under 8.2
work under
advice covered 8.8–10
funding rules 8.7
single judge
effect of refusal by 8.11
post-refusal advice 8.12

Crown Prosecution Service (CPS) 5.13,
5.19, 6.38

D

Data Protection Act 2018
Subject Access Requests (SARs)
5.21–25
Death of party
Supreme Court 10.22
Decision-making
CCRC investigation 9.21–25
Declaration of incompatibility
with ECHR 10.17
Defective summing up
getting law wrong 3.36
judge commenting on evidence
3.32–33
leaving alternative verdicts to jury 3.36
significance of 'specimen directions'
3.37–38
summing up on difference basis to that
advanced at trial 3.34
Defence investigations 5.1–5
conduct of 5.11
ethics of 5.7–9
funding 5.10
material already in hands of defence,
establishing 5.12–16
planning 5.11
seeking additional material from
prosecution 5.17–20
seeking new material 5.21–30
techniques of 5.10–29
who may carry out 5.6
Defence lawyers
errors of 3.52–58
police station attendance notes 5.13
Defendant
assistance to 6.31
right to seek second opinion 6.7
Delay
leave to appeal 6.11
Deportation 4.8
Directions
investigations by CCRC 9.31–32
Directives 2.12, 2.14
Director of Public Prosecutions (DPP)
10.5
Disability
appellant/applicant 7.17

Disbursements
claiming for work done in Court of
Appeal 8.16
funding extension 8.22, 8.39
LAA recouping 8.26
payment before case concluding 8.22
receipts or vouchers 8.13
Disclosure 5.18, 5.27
common law duty for 5.17
Criminal Cases Review Commission
(CCRC) 9.28
failure of 3.8
non-voluntary 5.20
serious failures by prosecution in duty
of 9.31
statutory duty of 5.17
third party material 6.46–48
Discretion
following previous decisions 2.6
Dismissal 3.61, 7.40–44
Disparity in sentence 4.35
Disposable capital
financial eligibility 8.30
Disposable income
financial eligibility 8.29
Documents
application to ECtHR 11.11
defence investigations 5.13
inclusion in court bundle 7.6
significance to Supreme Court 10.16
Double jeopardy
discount 13.32–35
Doubt
as to guilt 3.5–8
Driving offences 10.5
Due diligence
contacting trial lawyers (*McCook*) 6.13

E

Easter sittings 1.25
eForm
CRM5 8.39
Electronic files 5.14
Enhancement
hourly rates for solicitors 8.15
Error
defence lawyers 3.52–58
giving rise to doubt as to guilt 3.5–8
Ethics
defence investigations 5.7–9

European Convention on Human Rights
(ECHR) 2.1
declaration of incompatibility with 10.17
interpreting legislation to give effect
to 2.7
European Court of Human Rights
(ECtHR) 2.11, 7.42
applications to 7.45, 11.1–32
acknowledgement of 11.15
admissibility 11.19
allocation to judge or judges 11.17
communication 11.21
composition of Chamber 11.20
consequences of successful outcome
compensation 11.31
costs 11.32
judgment 11.30
criteria for 11.5
drafting 11.10–16
exhaustion of domestic remedies
11.6–7
final determination 11.24
form for 11.12
'alleged violations' section of
11.14
'friendly settlement' 11.26–27
hearings before determining case
11.23
inadmissibility 11.18
information required for 11.10
legal aid 11.29
progress of 11.17–24
delay 11.16
referral to Grand Chamber 11.25
representation 11.28
right of reply 11.22
standing 11.9
statement of facts for 11.13
supply of documents for 11.11
time limits for lodging 11.8
decisions of 2.1
judgments of 2.7–11
taking account of 2.8–9
language of 11.14
power of 11.4
reference to 11.3
renewing application for leave to
appeal when taking case to 6.68
role of 11.1
scope 11.2

European Union
Directives 2.12, 2.14
growing impact of 2.2
law 2.1, 2.12–15
Evidence *see also* Fresh evidence
appeals against conviction 6.21
children 7.26
hearings 7.33
minors 7.26
non-accordance with 1.5
obtained by non-lawyers 5.6
obtaining 5.2–3, 5.7
vulnerable adults 7.26
'Exceptional circumstances'
CCRC referral to Court of Appeal
9.14–15
Expedited hearing 6.41
Expenses
unnecessary or improper 7.50–54
Expert evidence 8.44
Expert opinion 8.40
Expert reports 5.13
Extradition 10.5

F

Failure of disclosure 3.8
Fair trial
denial of regarded as unsafe conviction
3.17
right to 3.17
Fees
advocates 8.40
claiming for work done in Court of
Appeal 8.13–19
Filming
crime scene 5.29
Final determination
applications to ECtHR 11.24
Final Statement of Reasons
CCRC investigation 9.24
Financial reporting orders 4.14
Form A 14.5
Form B 6.38
Form CRM1/CRM2
completing 8.35
further advice 8.48
Form EX107 8.40
Form NG 6.19, 6.33, 6.35, 6.44, 9.27,
14.5
Form RN 6.57

Form SJ 6.60, 6.63, 6.67
Form W 6.31, 6.47
Fraud trials
  appeals against rulings made at
      preparatory hearing in complex or
      lengthy trials 12.4–11
  circumstances in which ruling may
      be appealed 12.6–9
  procedure 12.10
  reporting restrictions 12.11
Freedom of Information Act 2000
  requests for material under 5.26–27
Fresh evidence
  confiscation orders 4.46
  giving rise to doubt as to guilt
      3.9–12
  leave to appeal, grounds 6.31
    appeals against conviction 6.21
  received after conviction 3.47–51
'Friendly settlement'
  applications to ECtHR 11.26–27
Funding
  alternative sources of 8.49–50
    Advocate (formerly Bar *Pro Bono*
        Unit) 8.56
    Centre for Criminal Appeals 8.55
    innocence projects 8.51–8.54
  applications for 6.44–45
  Court of Appeal representation
      order *see* Court of Appeal
      representation order
  Crown Court representation order
      see Crown Court representation
      order
  Standard Criminal Contract *see*
      Funding under SCC
  types 8.1–4
Funding under SCC
  advice and assistance
    authorised providers 8.23
    bars 8.24–25
    claiming for work done under
        scheme 8.46–47
    further advice 8.48
    justification 8.38
    sufficient benefits test (merits)
        8.32–34
    types provided 8.20
  applications
    appeals against refusals 8.40

Funding under SCC – *contd*
  applications – *contd*
    completing CRM1/CRM2 8.35
    further advice 8.48
    postal 8.37
    specific 8.40
  CCRC applications, special
      considerations 8.41–45
  extension applications 8.33, 8.39
  filtering requests 8.36
  financial eligibility
    children 8.31
    deemed eligibility 8.27
    disposal capital 8.30
    disposal income 8.29
    Means Regulations 8.26
    partner 8.28
    sufficient benefits test (merits)
        8.32–34
  outward travel 8.37
  using the SCC
    advantages 8.21
    disadvantages 8.22

G

Gogana statements 6.31
Good faith
  decisions made by trial lawyers in 3.55
Grand Chamber
  ECtHR, referral to 11.25
Grounds
  in relation to jury 3.39–45
Grounds of appeal
  leave to appeal
    appeal against sentence 6.22
      assistance provided to police
          6.23
    appeals against conviction
        (evidence) 6.21
    change in law
      application for extension of time
          6.33–34
      other documents lodged in
          support of application 6.35
    citation of authorities 6.24–27
    direct lodgement 6.50–52
    form and content of grounds
        6.18–20
    fresh and amended grounds
        procedure 6.14

Grounds of appeal – *contd*
  leave to appeal – *contd*
    fresh evidence 6.31
      appeals against conviction 6.21
    new arguments 6.28
      criticism of previous lawyers
        6.30
      failure to object to things said in
        summing up 6.29
    perfecting grounds 6.53–55
    purpose of grounds 6.18
    who may draft grounds 6.17
  new, leave to advance 7.13
  sentence, against 4.4, 4.19–20, 6.22
    assistance provided to police 6.23
    confiscation orders 4.44
    court to consider whether total
      sentence is wrong 4.25
    failure to follow guidelines
      4.26–31
    manifestly excessive 4.21–24
Guardians
  appeals by 4.16
Guidance notes 1.14
Guide to Commencing Proceedings
  in the Court of Appeal (Criminal
  Division) 1.14
Guilt
  doubt as to 3.5–8
  evidence of 3.15
Guilty plea
  appeal following 3.29

H

Hearings
  before determining case for application
    to ECtHR 11.23
  Court of Appeal
    appeals with leave 7.32–35
    appellant
      absconded 7.21
      death of 7.22–23
      representation of prosecution
        7.24
    listing 7.16
    preparation 7.1–4
      authorities 7.14–15
      considering Court bundle 7.5–10
      new grounds of appeal 7.13
      skeleton arguments 7.11–12

Hearings – *contd*
  preparation – *contd*
    presence of appellant/applicant
      hearings with leave 7.17
      renewed applications for leave
        7.19–20
    public immunity applications
      7.30
    public right to attend 7.25–26
    renewed applications for leave
      7.36–37
    reporting restrictions 7.27–29
    suggestions for advocacy 7.38–39
    televised hearings7.31
  evidence 7.33
  expedited 6.41
  interventionist approach 7.32
  leave to appeal 6.3, 6.76
    expedited hearing, request for 6.41
    oral leaving hearing, request for
      6.49
    procedure 7.32–35
    renewal of application 6.64,
      7.36–37
  listing 7.16
  preparing for 1.28, 7.1–57
  presence of appellant/applicant
    7.17–18
  private 7.25–26
  procedure 7.32–37
  prosecution appeals against rulings
    under s.58 CJA 13.16–19
    Attorney-General's References
      13.26–27
  prosecution representation at 7.24
  public right to attend 7.25–26
  renewed applications for leave 7.19–
    24, 7.36–39
  reporting restrictions 7.27–29
  Supreme Court 10.13, 10.18
  televised 7.31
  witnesses 7.34
Hearsay evidence 6.31
High court judges 1.16
Hilary sittings 1.25
Hospital direction 4.8
Hospital orders 4.3, 4.8, 4.34, 14.16
Hourly rates
  solicitors, enhancement 8.15
Human trafficking 2.14

I

Improper expenses 7.50–54
Inadmissibility
  applications to ECtHR 11.18
Independent Costs Assessor (ICA) 8.39
Index
  appeal issues 5.14
Indictment
  appeal against sentence *see* Appeals
  court's power to amend for re-trial 3.76
Information
  application to ECtHR 11.10
Information Commissioner 5.26
Innocence projects 8.51–54
Insanity
  appeals against verdict of not guilty by
    reason of 14.12–15
  appellant/applicant 7.17
'Interests of justice' considerations 4.29
Interim hospital orders 4.8, 14.19
Interlocutory rulings
  appeals against 12.1–3, 13.5
    exceptions 12.2
International conventions 2.14
International law 2.1, 12–15
  composition of 2.13
  growing impact of 2.2
Interventionist approach
  hearings 7.32
Interviews
  conduct of 5.30
  demeanour of investigator 5.30
  location of 5.30
  note-taking 5.30
  pauses in 5.30
  potential witnesses 5.30
  preparation for 5.30
  use of open-ended questions 5.30
Investigating officer
  appointment by CCRC 9.28
Investigations *see* Criminal Cases
  Review Commission (CCRC);
  Defence investigations; Journalistic
  investigations
Investigatory bodies
  cooperating with 5.31–36

J

Job applications
  disclosure of spent convictions in 10.5

Journalistic investigations 5.34–35
  caution required over 5.35
  risks and benefits of 5.36
Judges 1.15–20
  comments by 3.32–33
  conduct 3.33
  Crown Court 1.16
  form of address 1.17
  High Court judges 1.16
  permanent judges 1.16
  single judge 1.20
    decision of 6.59–62
    work under Crown Court/Court
      of Appeal representation
      orders
    effect of refusal 8.11
    post-refusal advice 8.12
  trying certain counts alone 12.26–
    28
Judge's clerk 1.28
Judgment 7.35
  applications to ECtHR 11.30
Judicial Committee of the House of
  Lords 2.3
Judicial Committee of the Privy Council
  2.3
Juries
  allegations of misconduct 3.40–43
  bias 3.44–45
  deliberations, irregularity in 9.31
  discharge of 13.5
  dispensing with where tampering has
    taken place 12.20–25
  failure to properly direct 3.36–37
  grounds in relation to 3.39–45
  leaving alternative verdicts to 3.35
  role of 1.2
  selection giving rise to appeal 3.39
  tampering *see* Jury tampering
Jurisdiction 1.12
Jury impact test
  new evidence 3.9–12
Jury tampering
  appeals where tampering taken place
    12.20–25
  risk of 1.18–19
    appeals 12.18–19
    procedure 12.19
  termination of trial 12.21
  test for 12.20, 12.22

L

Language
ECtHR 11.14
Leave to appeal 1.4, 6.1–4
abandoning application 6.70–71
hearing 6.76
judgment 6.77
making application for
reinstatement 6.74
miscellaneous appeals 6.78
nullity 6.72
bad legal advice 6.73
skeleton arguments 6.75
advice on appeal
defendant's right to seek second
opinion 6.7
due diligence (*McCook*) 6.13
fresh and amended grounds
procedure 6.14
obtaining transcripts for purpose of
6.12
time limits, extensions and need for
expedition 6.8–11
trial lawyers
contacting (*McCook*) 6.13
duty 6.5–6
bail applications 6.36–40
consideration for 6.10
decision of single judge 6.59–62
delay 6.11
disclosure of third party material
6.46–48
expedited hearing, request for 6.41
funding applications 6.44–45
grounds of appeal
appeal against sentence 6.22
assistance provided to police 6.23
appeals against conviction
(evidence) 6.21
change in law
application for extension of time
6.33–34
other documents lodged in
support of application 6.35
citation of authorities 6.24–27
direct lodgement 6.50–52
form and content 6.18–20
fresh and amended, procedure 6.14
fresh evidence 6.31
appeals against conviction 6.21

Leave to appeal – *contd*
grounds of appeal – *contd*
new arguments 6.28
criticism of previous lawyers 6.30
failure to object to things said in
summing up 6.29
perfecting 6.53–55
purpose of 6.18
who may draft 6.17
hearings 6.3, 6.76
expedited hearing, request for 6.41
oral leaving hearing, request for
6.49
procedure 7.32–35
renewal of application 6.64, 7.36–39
oral leaving hearing, request for 6.49
procedural rules 6.4
renewal of application 1.19, 6.63–65,
7.19–24
hearings 6.64, 7.36–39
renewal of other applications 6.69
risk of loss of time and costs
6.66–67
taking case to ECtHR 6.68
responses from trial lawyers and
respondent 6.56–58
successful, applications for
representation order following
7.56
Supreme Court 10.9–13
applications to 7.40–44
consideration of 10.13
funding for 10.11
lodging of additional papers 10.12
test for 10.4
time limit 10.10
timetable following grant of 10.17
types of cases 10.4–8
terminology 6.4
time extension for 6.9
time limit for 6.8
transcripts, requests for 6.42–43
trial judge's certificate, applying for
6.15–16
Legal aid *see also* Funding
applications to ECtHR 11.29
re-trial 3.79
Legal Aid Agency (LAA) 8.20, 8.35
funding extension 8.39
further advice justification 8.38

Legal Aid Agency (LAA) – *contd*
  Means Regulations enforcement 8.26
  ongoing checks 8.22
  sufficient benefits test 8.34
Legal interpretation 8.43
Lengthy fraud trials
  appeals against rulings made at
    preparatory hearing in 12.4–11
  circumstances in which ruling may be
    appealed 12.6–9
  procedure 12.10
  reporting restrictions 12.11
Life sentence 4.3, 4.15
Limitation direction 4.8
Listing
  hearings 7.16
Litigation Graduated Fee Scheme
  (LGFS) 8.7
Location
  interviews 5.30
Lord Chancellor 1.15
Lord Chief Justice 1.14, 2.10
  appointment 1.15
Lord/Lady Justices of Appeal 1.16
Loss of time order 6.66–67
Lurking doubt 3.23–24

M

Magistrates' Court
  appeal against sentence *see* Appeals
Manifestly excessive
  sentence 4.21–24
Measurements
  crime scene 5.29
Medical evidence 5.5
Mental disorders
  appeals in relation to defendants
    suffering from 14.1–2
  appeal process 14.5
  findings of unfitness to plead/
    accused made act or omission
    charged 14.6–11
  funding 14.4
  insanity
    order made under s.5 of Criminal
      Procedure (Insanity) Act
      1964 14.16–19
    verdict of not guilty by reason of
      14.12–15
  procedures 14.1

Mental disorders – *contd*
  appeals in relation to defendants
    suffering from – *contd*
    who may appeal 14.3
Michaelmas sittings 1.25
Minors
  evidence from 7.26
Miscarriages of justice 1.6, 5.1
  journalistic investigations into 5.34
  role of Criminal Cases Review
    Commission (CCRC) in 9.3
Misconduct
  allegations of jury 3.40–43
Misjoinder 3.22
Multiple counts 12.26

N

'New argument' 6.28–30
  definition for application to CCRC for
    referral 9.12
New evidence *see* Fresh evidence
New indictment
  arraignment 3.72
  time scale 3.72–73
New material
  attempts to obtain 5.19
  conducting interviews with potential
    witnesses 5.30
  entitlement to 5.23
  information required for 5.24
  purposes of 5.22
  records collection generally 5.28
  requests under Freedom of
    Information Act 2000 5.26–27
  Subject Access Requests (SARs)
    5.19
    Data Protection Act 2018 5.21–25
  visiting and recording crime scene and
    other significant locations 5.29
News media reports 5.13
'No case to answer' 13.3
Northern Ireland
  right to legal aid in criminal cases
    10.5
Note-taking
  interviews 5.30
Nullity 3.83
  abandoning application for leave to
    appeal 6.72
  bad legal advice 6.73

O

Offences
  appeals against sentence under s.10 of CAA 1968 4.8
Offender Assessment System (OASys) reports 5.13
Older cases 5.15
Open-ended questions
  interviews 5.30
Opinion
  expert 8.40
Oral hearings 1.20
Oral leave hearing
  request for 6.49
Orders
  types appealed *see* Appeals
Outward travel
  funding application 8.37

P

Parents
  appeals by 4.16
Parole Board 10.5
Parties
  communication with 1.22
Partner
  financial eligibility 8.28
Pauses
  interviews 5.30
Per incuriam 2.5–6
Perfecting
  grounds for appeal 6.53–55
Personal information 5.21–22
Personal representative
  appellant/applicant 7.22
Photography
  crime scene 5.29
Point of law
  certifying 7.40–44
Point of law of public importance 10.9
Police
  assistance provided to, ground of appeal 6.23
  files 5.18
  officers 5.3
    investigations on behalf of CCRC 9.28
  statements 5.13
Post-sentence developments 4.33–34

Postal applications
  funding for advice and assistance 8.37
Pre-trial detention records 5.13
Preliminary view 7.2
Preparatory hearings 12.28
  appeals against rulings made in complex or lengthy fraud cases 12.4–11
Prerogative of mercy 9.3
Previous decisions
  departure from 2.2
  discretion in following 2.6
  effects of not following 2.6
  exceptions to following 2.4–5
  per incuriam 2.5–6
Prison/prisoner records 5.13
Private
  hearings in 7.25–26
Private property
  crime scene 5.29
Privilege
  waiver 3.53, 6.30
Pro bono assistance 8.1–56
Probation files 5.13
Procedural irregularities 3.19–22
  approach of courts towards 3.21
  misjoinder 3.22
Procedural rules and guidance 1.14
Procedural unfairness 4.32
Prosecuting counsel 6.57
Prosecution 5.3
  appeals against rulings under s.58 CJA 13.3–6
    acquittal agreement 13.7–8
    valid 13.5
  appeal to Supreme Court 13.40
  notice of intention to appeal 13.5
  procedure 13.9–12
    Attorney-General's References *see* Attorney-General's References
  hearing 13.16–19
  respondent's notice 13.13–15
  responding to appellant's case 13.36–39
  when appeal may be brought 13.5–6
  appeals, responding to 13.1–40
  obligations after conviction 10.5
  representation at hearing 7.24

Prosecution – *contd*
  rights of appeal 13.2
    confiscation cases 4.52–53
  seeking additional material from
    5.17–20
  serious failures in duty of disclosure
    by 9.31
Prosecution opening facts
  transcripts 6.42
Provisional statement of reasons
  CCRC investigation 9.23
Public
  right to attend hearings 7.25–26
Public bodies
  definition by CCRC 9.28
Public interest
  disclosure 5.27
Public Interest Immunity 7.25
  hearings regarding 7.30
Publicly funded appeals advice *see*
  Funding
Puisne judges 1.16

Q
Qualifying curfew
  failure to credit time spent on 4.39
Quashing conviction 3.62
Question of law 1.5
Questioning
  witnesses 5.9

R
Re-sentencing 3.62, 3.80–81
Re-trial order 3.62
  bail 3.75
  circumstances 3.67–68
  court listing of legal argument 3.74
  court's power to amend indictment
    3.76
  defendant arraigned on new indictment
    3.72
    time scale 3.72–73
  legal aid 3.79
  limitations on court 3.77
  procedure for making order for
    3.69–71
  procedure once order made 3.72–79
  taking effect of sentence following
    3.78
  venire do novo 3.82–83, 14.10

Receivership orders
  appeals against 4.43
Recording
  crime scene 5.29
Recordings
  transcribed statements 5.13
Records collection 5.27
Registrar of Criminal Appeals 1.21–23
Registrar of the Supreme Court 10.2
Reporting restrictions 7.27–29, 12.11,
  12.17
  statutory provisions on 7.27–28
Representation
  applications to ECtHR 11.28
Representation orders
  applications for 6.44–45, 7.56
  Attorney General's References 13.25
  Court of Appeal *see* Court of Appeal
    representation order
  Crown Court *see* Crown Court
    representation order
Representatives
  wasted costs orders against 7.51–54
Respondent
  responses from 6.56–58
Respondent's notice
  prosecution appeals against rulings
    under s.59 CJA 13.13–15
Restraining orders 4.13
Restraint orders
  appeals against 4.43
Right of reply
  applications to ECtHR 11.22
Right to fair trial 3.17
Royal Court of Justice, Strand 1.24
Rulings
  appeals against 13.2

S
Sample counts 12.26–27
Second opinion
  defendant's right to seek 6.7
Sentence
  appeals against *see* Appeals
Sentencing
  following re-trial 3.78
Sentencing guidelines
  application in flexible manner 4.28
  departure from 13.28–29
  failure to follow 4.26–31

Sentencing guidelines – *contd*
  'interests of justice' considerations 4.29
  interpretation, Court of Appeal's role
    4.30
Sentencing remarks
  transcripts 6.42
Sessions Courts 1.2
Setting aside
  reasons for 1.5
Sexual behaviour
  evidence of complainant's previous 6.31
Sexual offences prevention orders
    4.12
Single judges 1.20
  decision of 6.59–62
  work under Crown Court/Court of
    Appeal representation orders
    effect of refusal 8.11
    post-refusal advice 8.12
Skeleton arguments 6.75, 7.11–12
Slip rule
  confiscation orders and 4.45
  unlawful sentences and 4.36–38
  use 6.1
Solicitors
  claims for work done in Court of
    Appeal 8.14
    enhanced hourly rates 8.15
  working files 5.13
Solicitor's Code of Conduct 5.8
Specimen directions
  significance of 3.37–38
Spent convictions
  disclosure of in job applications 10.5
Spouse
  financial eligibility 8.28
Standard Crime Contract (SCC)
  advice and assistance under 8.3
    funding *see* Funding under SCC
Standing
  ECtHR 11.9
Stare decisis doctrine 2.3–6
Statement of fact
  application to ECtHR 11.13
Statements
  defence witness 5.13
  police 5.13
  witness 5.13, 5.30
Statutes
  requirement to apply 2.2

Statutory Instruments 2.1
  interpreting in accordance with
    ECHR 2.7
Subject Access Requests (SARs) 5.19
  Data Protection Act 2018 5.21–25
Substitution
  conviction 3.62, 3.64–66
Success
  chance of 6.6
Successful applicant/appellant
  costs 7.48
Successful outcome
  applications to ECtHR 11.30–32
Sufficient benefits test (merits)
  advice and assistance under
    SCC 8.32–34
Summing up
  appeal against ruling under
    s.58 CJA 13.5
  defective 3.32–38
  different basis to that advanced at trial
    3.34
  failure to object to things said in 6.29
  transcripts 6.42
Superior Courts
  decisions of 2.1
Supervision orders 14.16, 14.19
Supreme Court 2.3, 7.42
  appeals to 10.1–22, 13.40
    funding 10.11
  attendance of appellant 10.20
  bail 10.19
  costs 10.21
  death of party 10.22
  drafting case for 10.15
  establishment of 10.1
  form and content of documents 10.16
  hearings 10.18
    types 10.13
  justification for consideration by 10.8
  leave to appeal 10.9–13
    applications 7.40–44
      consideration of 10.13
    funding for 10.11
    lodging of additional papers 10.12
    test for 10.4
    time limit 10.10
    timetable following grant of 10.17
    types of cases 10.4–8
  limitations on 10.6

Supreme Court – *contd*
    lodging of additional papers 10.12
    point of law of public importance
        10.9
    preparing case for 10.14–17
    procedure 10.2
    reasons for appeals from Court of
        Appeal 10.7
    role of 10.2
    scope of 10.5
    terminology 10.3
Suspects 5.2

T

Telephone advice
    funding 8.37
Televised hearings 7.31
'Terminating' ruling
    right to appeal 13.3
Terminology
    Supreme Court 10.3
Terrorist offences 10.5
Third parties
    costs against 7.55
Third party material
    disclosure 6.46–48
Time estimate for case 7.10
Time extension
    leave to appeal 6.9
        application for extension 6.33–34
Time limits
    appeal against confiscation orders
        4.49–50
    application to CCRC for referral to
        Court of Appeal 9.13
    leave to appeal 6.8
        Supreme Court 10.10
    lodging application to ECtHR 11.8
Time served
    risk of loss of 6.66–67
Transcribed statements
    recordings 5.13
Transcripts 8.40
    requests for 6.42–43
Travel time 8.40
Trial
    exhibits/material 5.13
    termination of 12.21
    transcript *see* Trial transcript
Trial judge's certificate 6.15–16

Trial lawyers
    cautious approach to criticism of 3.57
    competence 3.56
    contacting (*McCook*) 6.13
    decisions made in good faith 3.55
    duty to advise on appeal 6.5–6
    responses from 6.56–58
Trial notes 3.54
Trial rulings
    challenging 3.30–31
Trial transcript 5.13, 5.16
    obtaining 6.12
Trinity sittings 1.25

U

Undue leniency 13.29
'Unfair'
    'unsafe' compared 3.13–18
Unfair conviction
    abuse of process may be 3.16
Unfair trial 3.5
Unfairness
    courts approaching issue of 3.27
Unfitness to plead
    appeals against findings of 14.6–11
    court has no power to order retrial
        14.10
Unfitness to stand trial
    defendant in custody 14.5
Unlawful sentences
    slip rule and 4.36–38
Unnecessary expenses 7.50–54
Unreasonableness 1.5
Unsafe convictions
    concluding comments on 'unsafe' as
        flexible test 3.25–28
    error/new evidence giving rise to doubt
        as to guilt 3.5–8
    jury impact test 3.9–3.12
    lurking doubt 3.23–24
    meaning of 'unsafe' 3.2–3
    procedural irregularities 3.19–22
    'unfair' trial 3.13–18
        breaches of Art.6 ECHR 3.18
    wrongful conviction 3.4, 3.28
Unsuccessful appellant/applicant
    costs 7.49
Unused material 5.13
Urgency
    granting of bail 6.39

V

Venire do novo order 3.82–83, 14.10
Verdict
  proper and reasonable 3.6
Vice President of the Criminal Division
  1.14, 2.10
  appointment 1.15
Visits
  crime scene 5.29
Vulnerable adults
  evidence from 7.26

W

Waiver
  privilege 3.53, 6.30

Wasted costs orders 7.51–54
Witness statements 6.31, 6.35
Witnesses
  assistance to 6.31
  hearings 7.34
  interviewing potential 5.30
  power to order attendance of 6.31
  questioning 5.9
  statements 5.13, 5.30
Writ of *venire de novo* 14.10
Written directions 6.35
Wrongful conviction
  unsafe conviction may be considered
  3.4

DOUGHTY STREET CHAMBERS

ClSC doughty street chambers

Criminal Appeals

Since its foundation in 1990, Doughty Street Chambers and its barristers have taken as their guiding principle the use of the law for the advancement of the protection of human rights and civil liberties. It is now amongst the very largest and most wide-ranging civil liberties practices in the world, providing specialist advice, advocacy and training in the UK and around the world. Their practice areas include crime and criminal appeals, international crime (such as war crimes), fraud and financial services regulation, extradition, prisoners' rights, actions against the police, immigration, media law, professional regulation, children's rights, social welfare and housing, clinical negligence and more.

The Criminal Team is the largest practice group at Doughty Street Chambers. Its members have long-standing experience of defending in many of the most serious and complex criminal trials, appeals and extradition cases to come before the UK Supreme Court, Privy Council, Court of Appeal and High Court, as well as their daily work in the Crown and Magistrates' Courts. Abroad they appear in the courts of Northern Ireland, Hong Kong, Singapore, the Caribbean, South America, the International Criminal Court and the European Court of Human Rights.

The Appeals Unit at Doughty Street Chambers spans all this criminal work, and is widely regarded as home to several of the best appellate lawyers in the UK. A wrongful conviction or sentence at any level can have a devastating impact on an appellant and his family, and the appeal specialists at Doughty Street Chambers advise across the full range of cases, from the relatively minor, challenging decisions of Magistrates, right up to drafting submissions to the Criminal Cases Review Commission, appeals in cases of homicide and terrorism, and appearing at all levels up to the Supreme Court and the European Court of Human Rights. Their work includes appeals on sentencing (including whole life tariffs and indeterminate sentences), jury irregularities, psychiatric issues (e.g. automatism, loss of control and provocation), sexual offences prevention orders, deficient trial representation, fraud and confiscation appeals, appeals by way of Case Stated and Judicial Review.

Doughty Street Chambers also offers its solicitor clients use of a Criminal Appeals Advice Line, which provides free preliminary advice and guidance for those considering potential appeals and CCRC matters. More information on this, and the criminal appeals and other barristers at Doughty Street Chambers, can be found at www.doughtystreet.co.uk or by e-mailing crime@ doughtystreet.co.uk.